D0205896

*Nutrition and Economic Development in
the Eighteenth-Century Habsburg Monarchy*

JOHN KOMLOS

Nutrition and Economic Development in the Eighteenth-Century Habsburg Monarchy

An Anthropometric History

PRINCETON UNIVERSITY PRESS

PRINCETON, NEW JERSEY

Published by Princeton University Press, 41 William Street,
Princeton, New Jersey 08540
In the United Kingdom: Princeton University Press, Oxford

Library of Congress Cataloging-in-Publication Data

Komlos, John, 1944–
Nutrition and economic development in the eighteenth-century Habsburg
monarchy : an anthropometric history / John Komlos.
p. cm.   Bibliography: p.   Includes index.
ISBN 0-691-04257-8 (alk. paper)
1. Industry and state—Austria—History—18th century. 2. Austria—
Industries—History—18th century. 3. Nutrition—Austria—History—
18th century. 4. Demographic transition—Austria—History—
20th century. 5. Population—Austria—History—18th century.
6. Austria—Economic policy—18th century.
I. Title.
HD3616.A92K66 1989   338.9436—dc19   89-30637

Publication of this book has been aided by the
Whitney Darrow Fund of Princeton University Press

This book has been composed in Linotron Galliard

Clothbound editions of Princeton University Press books
are printed on acid-free paper, and binding materials are
chosen for strength and durability. Paperbacks, although satisfactory
for personal collections, are not usually suitable for library rebinding

Printed in the United States of America by Princeton University Press,
Princeton, New Jersey

Designed by Laury A. Egan

To the staff and fellows
of the Carolina Population Center
of the University of North Carolina
at Chapel Hill

CONTENTS

CONTENTS

LIST OF FIGURES

LIST OF TABLES

PREFACE

A LARGE-SCALE research project, requiring the extraction of nearly two hundred thousand often difficult-to-read records from archival sources, cannot be undertaken without an enormous amount of financial and moral support. I was fortunate enough to receive such support, although by no means continuously throughout the writing of the manuscript. I obtained two small grants from the American Philosophic Society and the National Research Council at the very beginning of the project. Grants from the American Council of Learned Societies enabled me to overcome difficulties at junctures of my intellectual career when their absence could easily have meant the end of the research. The financial aid of the National Science Foundation was essential to the successful completion of the project. I am grateful to Mr. Warren Thompson of the N.S.F. for his enthusiastic support. Yet one needs more than money to be able to write at ease; one also needs the proper moral support. I am indebted to Liliane and to Frieda for making the atmosphere of our private life conducive to creative thinking. I am indebted furthermore to the late Professor Edward März for inviting me to the University of Vienna, thereby bringing me closer to the archives, and to Professors Gerhard Botz, Herbert Matis, and Erich Streißler for supporting my stay in Vienna and for making it one of the truly pleasant years of my life. Without them, I fear that the project might very well not have come to fruition. Professor Roman Sandgruber, then of the Department of Economics and Social History of the University of Vienna, and now of the University of Linz, and Dr. Helmut Selinger, librarian of the Department of Economics, helped me in a number of ways too numerous to mention. Maria Botz and Dr. Ernö Deák, the latter of the Austrian Academy of Sciences, were kind enough to help me to arrange the details of my private life, aid that is always welcomed in a foreign environment.

In 1984 I was fortunate to receive a postdoctoral fellowship at the Carolina Population Center of the University of North Carolina at

Chapel Hill, supported by the NICHD National Research Service Award no. 2 T32HD07168. This fellowship provided me with two years to work on the manuscript without the usual pressures of academic life. I am grateful to the staff of the Center for the many invaluable ways in which they made my task easier. J. Richard Udry and Boone Turchi were instrumental in providing me with the prerequisites for intensive research. The warm welcome extended to me in North Carolina included invitations to lecture at North Carolina State and at Duke University, made possible through the efforts of Richard Sylla and Roy Weintraub, respectively. Once I was invited to join the faculty of the University of Pittsburgh, the friendly support of my colleagues made the completion of the manuscript an easy task.

Most of all, I am indebted to Professor Robert Fogel of the University of Chicago for awakening in me an interest in anthropometric history, and to Professor James Tanner of the Institute of Child Health, University of London, who has devoted a lifetime to understanding the process of human growth, for sustaining and supporting this interest. In addition to Robert Fogel and Scott Eddie, who were kind enough to scrutinize the whole manuscript, many colleagues and friends generously commented on various chapters as they went through revision. These include Rudolph Blitz, Rondo Cameron, A. W. Coats, Peter Coclanis, Stefano Fenoaltea, Roderick Floud, Robert Gallman, Jack Goldstone, David Good, Eric L. Jones, Paul Mageli, William McNeill, Paul Riggs, Peter Salamon, Roman Sandgruber, Richard Steckel, Gunter Steinmann, James Tanner, and Peter Temin. Roderick Floud and Annabel Gregory of the University of London kindly provided me with a version of the QBE computer program that was very useful in the statistical analysis. The preliminary results of Chapter 2 were presented at seminars at the universities of Chicago, Harvard, Vanderbilt, Northwestern, Pittsburgh, Nebraska, Washington (St. Louis), Pennsylvania, Salzburg, Linz, Vienna, Knox College, the 1984 Cliometrics conference at Miami University of Ohio, the Institute for Advanced Studies in Vienna, the Historical Institute of the Hungarian Academy of Sciences in Budapest, the Carolina Population Center of the University of North Carolina at Chapel Hill, and the Triangle Economic History Workshop. Parts of Chapter 2 appeared in *The American Historical Review* (Dec. 1985) and in *Annals of Human Biology* (January/February 1986). An earlier version of Chapters 3 and 6 appeared in the *Journal of European Economic History* (1987). The results of Chapter 6 were presented at seminars at Stanford, Berkeley, Pennsylvania, MIT, Pittsburgh, and the Carolina Population Center of the University of North Carolina. Paul Mageli, Peter Waugh, Asha Narang, and Nona Valeriano Schlegel devoted many hours to retrieving information from dusty manuscripts that had not seen daylight for two hundred years. I appreciate the generous help of the staff of the Viennese Kriegsarchiv—in particular, that of Dr. Tepperberg and Dr. Eggert. Markus Hein and Erich Foltyn helped diligently with the data processing. Computations were done at the EDV Zentrum of the Vienna School of Economics. I would especially like to thank Professor Herbert Matis, Chairman of its Department of Economic and Social History, for his support of the computational aspects of the project. My gratitude to them all.

Nutrition and Economic Development in
the Eighteenth-Century Habsburg Monarchy

"One cannot repress the thought that perhaps the whole industrial revolution of the last two hundred years has been nothing else but a vast secular boom, largely induced by the unparalleled rise in population." SIR JOHN R. HICKS, *Value and Capital: An Inquiry into Some Fundamental Principles of Economic Theory*

INTRODUCTION

THIS STUDY explores the importance of nutrition to the industrial revolution, with particular emphasis on its role in the eighteenth-century Habsburg Monarchy. For the first time, biological, demographic, and economic processes are integrated into a theory of the industrial revolution applicable not only to East-Central Europe, but to the European experience in general.

In my previous work on the Habsburg Monarchy I explored the salient features of its economic development in the nineteenth century.[1] I sought to understand the dynamics of growth, ascertain the importance of institutional change, and look for spurts great and small—in short, to determine what were some of the strategic factors promoting or inhibiting the growth of this economy. I felt compelled to attempt to identify the beginning of the process of industrialization, hoping that by doing so I would come closer to realizing what made the European economies evolve as they did in the nineteenth century. What troubled me most, although I probably could not have articulated my unease in these terms, was the absence of any accepted conceptual framework applicable to the process of industrialization which might have helped to organize the thoughts of a beginning student of the problem. In other words, there was no consensus on a model of the industrial revolution. While the take-off thesis had been widely discredited, it was not replaced by another model.[2] In some ways, it even continued to be attractive, and perhaps a vague hope persisted among some historians that parts of it at least could somehow be resurrected.

Walt W. Rostow had fused the stage theory of the German historical school with the theory of discontinuous industrialization fashionable

---

[1] John Komlos, *The Habsburg Monarchy as a Customs Union: Economic Development in Austria-Hungary in the Nineteenth Century* (Princeton: Princeton University Press, 1983).

[2] Walt W. Rostow, ed., *The Economics of Take-Off into Sustained Growth* (London: Macmillan, 1963).

after the Second World War.[3] Rostow emphasized the importance of the "two or three decades when the economy and society . . . transform themselves in such ways that economic growth is, subsequently, more or less automatic."[4] He referred to this turning point as the "take-off." The industrial revolution, in his model, begins with a discontinuity after a set of preconditions have been achieved. Most importantly, Rostow argued—without much evidential warrant—that the take-off came about through a rise in capital accumulation from 5 to 10 percent of national product.[5] However, he was not able to specify convincingly either why the rate of accumulation would suddenly double or why an economy would grow automatically after the take-off phase.

Among the first to show skepticism of this theoretical framework was Douglass North.[6] Subsequent efforts to measure the saving rate in England and elsewhere during the alleged take-off could not confirm Rostow's hypothesis. The rate of saving increased slowly and not discontinuously, and did not double in a matter of decades. A recent estimate for England has it increasing from 5.7 percent in 1760 to 7.9 percent in 1801.[7] Not until the 1820s, by the end of the so-called take-off phase, did the value of this parameter double.

Indeed, it was somewhat naive to imagine that an eighteenth-century society would have suddenly increased its rate of saving so dramatically. What could have motivated individuals to do so voluntarily? Had the real rates of return increased, the inducement to save might have become greater, but it is difficult to imagine a rise in the interest rate of sufficient magnitude to cause a doubling in the rate of saving. Furthermore, the increased ability to save implies that incomes would have been rising faster than the desire to consume. If this had been brought about by an acceleration in incomes, then it would have meant that the industrial revolution was already under way. In that case the increased rate of saving would have been a consequence of growth and not its cause, as

[3] The example of post-war economic growth must have influenced the thinking of this school of development economists, including Alexander Gerschenkron.

[4] Walt W. Rostow, "The Take-off into Self-Sustained Economic Growth," *Economic Journal* 66 (1956): 25–48.

[5] Walt W. Rostow, *The Stages of Economic Growth: A Non-Communist Manifesto* (Cambridge, England: Cambridge University Press, 1960), p. 41.

[6] In a note of criticism, he stated that "it is doubtful whether the diverse paths by which economies may expand and/or industrialize can be encompassed into any framework of universal applicability, at least in the present stage of knowledge." Douglass C. North, "A Note on Professor Rostow's 'Take-off' into Self-Sustained Economic Growth," *Manchester School of Economic and Social Studies* 26 (1958): 68–75.

[7] N.F.R. Crafts, "British Economic Growth, 1700–1831: A Review of the Evidence," *Economic History Review*, 2d ser., 36 (1983): 177–199.

the above figures for England actually suggest.[8] On the other hand, a sudden rise in the saving rate is not likely to have been brought about by a fall in consumption, because individuals usually do not decrease their consumption dramatically through an exogenous change in taste in favor of accumulation.

Governments could have increased the rate of taxation in order to undertake investments, but this remained only a theoretical possibility given the difficulties eighteenth-century governments generally faced when they attempted to increase taxes. This, in fact, was a contributing factor to the outbreak of both the American and the French revolutions. Of course, in a command economy, as has been demonstrated in the twentieth century, the rate of saving can be increased dramatically through fiat, by forcibly minimizing consumption, but that is hardly an applicable model for prior centuries. Because of the above considerations, the sudden-increased-saving-rate theory of the industrial revolution is not plausible theoretically and is also contradicted by the empirical evidence.[9] While Rostow's theory was quite misleading, it did have the beneficial consequence of giving rise to a large number of quantitative studies on industrialization.[10]

Alexander Gerschenkron was another prominent advocate of the discontinuity school of industrialization. Gerschenkron used the notion of a great spurt, not much of an improvement over Rostow's model, to analyze the industrialization process.[11] He postulated that the intensity

[8] This notion is advanced in N.F.R. Crafts, *British Economic Growth during the Industrial Revolution* (Oxford: Clarendon Press, 1985), p. 74.

[9] Decades before Rostow's theory, Schumpeter had rejected the notion that rapid industrialization could be brought about by the accumulation of capital. Joseph Schumpeter, *The Theory of Economic Development* (Cambridge, MA: Harvard University Press, 1934), p. 67.

[10] Even including one on the role of railroads in the process of American economic growth. Robert W. Fogel, *Railroads and American Economic Growth: Essays in Econometric History* (Baltimore: The Johns Hopkins University Press, 1964).

[11] Alexander Gerschenkron, *Economic Backwardness in Historical Perspective: A Book of Essays* (Cambridge, MA: Harvard University Press, 1962), p. 353; idem, *Europe in the Russian Mirror: Four Lectures in Economic History* (London: Cambridge University Press, 1970). Gerschenkron's framework differed in significant ways from Rostow's typology. The former continued to analyze the industrial sector, while the latter generally focused on the whole economy. Moreover, Gerschenkron did not accept fully the notion of necessary prerequisites of industrial development and suggested that governments, as well as financial institutions, could provide substitutes for the prerequisites of growth. (He nonetheless suggested that the emancipation of the peasantry in 1861 was a prerequisite of Russia's "great spurt.") Rostow, in addition, stressed the importance of a few branches of industry, which he called leading sectors, in the take-off, and emphasized the propagation of growth impulses emanating from these sectors to the whole economy. As Gerschen-

of the "great spurt" depended on the relative backwardness of the economy in question. "The speed of industrial growth in the early stages of industrialization was intimately associated . . . with the degree of backwardness of the countries concerned."[12] In Russia, argued Gerschenkron, the "great spurt of modern industrialization came in the middle of the 1880s," when "the railroad building of the state assumed unprecedented proportions."[13] This, however, was a quite misleading view of the process of industrialization. The boom of the 1880s was just another upswing of the European business cycle; it was not confined to Russia. Moreover, the performance of Russian industry in the 1880s and 1890s turns out not to have been as spectacular as Gerschenkron imagined. This information was, in fact, available to him through the work of Raymond Goldsmith, but he apparently chose to disregard it.[14]

Subsequent work tended also to cast doubt on the notion of an intense, discontinuous period of economic activity in Tsarist Russia. "The rate of industrial growth from the mid-80s to 1913 was not much higher than from 1860 to 1913, if at all."[15] Industrial production did perhaps grow at a slightly faster rate in the 1890s than during other upswings of the business cycle, but small differences—one percent, at most—in the rate of growth can hardly be considered a great spurt. Gerschenkron also failed to duly acknowledge the importance of industrial growth for the decades prior to the alleged great spurt; the Russian economy had, in fact, been growing quite rapidly relative to the experience of other European economies.[16]

There is plenty of evidence that many branches of the Russian industry did well throughout the nineteenth century. Pig iron production, for instance, in the 1840s was growing faster than in Germany and France. In the 1850s it still grew at a respectable rate of 2.7 percent per annum. The same can be said of cotton textile production. In the 1830s

kron himself admitted, his ideas were not as easily quantifiable as were Rostow's, and consequently they were not as easily refutable. Idem, *Economic Backwardness*, p. 43.

[12] Alexander Gerschenkron, "The Discipline and I," *Journal of Economic History* 27 (1967): 443–459.

[13] Gerschenkron, *Economic Backwardness*, pp. 16, 19.

[14] Raymond Goldsmith, "The Economic Growth of Tsarist Russia, 1860–1913," *Economic Development and Cultural Change* 9 (1961): 441–476.

[15] Gregory Grossman, "The Industrialisation of Russia and the Soviet Union," in Carlo Cipolla, ed., *The Fontana Economic History of Europe* (London: William Collins and Sons, 1973), vol. 4, *The Emergence of Industrial Societies*, pp. 486–531.

[16] According to the most recent calculation, the Russian economy grew at a rate of 3.4 percent per annum between 1885 and 1900, and 3.1 percent per annum between 1900 and 1913. Paul Gregory, *Russian National Income, 1885–1913* (New York: Cambridge University Press, 1982), p. 133.

raw cotton imports expanded at a rate of 13 percent, in the 1840s at 12 percent, and in the 1850s at 9 percent per annum.[17] These were rapid growth rates even in international comparisons. In fact, Russia's industrial sector in the 1870s and 1880s, that is, prior to Gerschenkron's alleged great spurt, outperformed the industrial sectors of Germany, France, Austria, Italy, Sweden, and the United Kingdom.[18] In the 1850s the length of railway lines, as in Germany, nearly doubled, and in the 1860s quintupled.[19] Hence, there is considerable evidence of economic growth throughout the nineteenth century, and the expansion of the 1890s was by no means preceded by a period of secular stagnation. Thus Gerschenkron's was a spurt that never was, and to the extent that Russia in the 1890s did perhaps experience slightly above-average growth rates, such an experience was due to a periodic upswing of the business cycle and nothing more.

Gerschenkron's theoretical construct does not fit the other nineteenth-century economies either. German industry, for instance, managed to catch up to Great Britain's not through a great spurt, but because it was able to sustain a relatively higher growth rate for an extended period of time.[20] The United States, too, had its great industrial expansion after the end of the Napoleonic Wars, as did many European economies, including Austria and France, without a true spurt of economic activity.[21] As Gerschenkron himself noted, Italy's experience with industrialization was unusual in that the intensity of the big spurt was not commensurate with its backwardness. Yet he rationalized the failure of the Italian example to fit his model by casually suggesting that the weak spurt was due to the "ill-advised economic policy of the

---

[17] John Komlos, "Economic Growth under the Romanovs and the Bolsheviks," *Rivista di storia economica*, 2d ser., 2 (1985): 194–201.

[18] Even in the 1860s it grew faster than the industrial sectors of France and Italy and as fast as that of the United Kingdom.

[19] Brian R. Mitchell, *European Historical Statistics, 1750–1970* (New York: Columbia University Press, 1975), pp. 355, 391, 428, 584.

[20] The annual growth rate of the German industrial sector was:

1850–60	2.9%	1880–1890	4.3%
1860–70	4.0%	1890–1900	4.4%
1870–80	3.3%	1900–1910	3.4%

Walther Hoffmann, *Das Wachstum der deutschen Wirtschaft seit der Mitte des 19. Jahrhunderts* (Berlin: Springer, 1965), p. 393; Charles P. Kindleberger, "Germany's Overtaking of England, 1806–1914," *Weltwirtschaftliches Archiv* 3 (1975): 253–281, 477–504.

[21] Komlos, *Habsburg Monarchy as a Customs Union*, Chapter 3; Richard Roehl, "French Industrialization: A Reconsideration," *Explorations in Economic History* 12 (1976): 230–281.

government."[22] At one point Gerschenkron's dogmatism went so far as to insist that "industrialization either comes as a big spurt or does not come at all."[23]

If that were the case, then not many of the European countries would have industrialized. How did they then become industrial nations? Given these fundamental conceptual difficulties, his framework did not prove more useful in organizing my thoughts either on the industrial revolution of the eighteenth century or on the process of industrialization which followed it.[24]

Hence, in my earlier work I approached the topic of Austro-Hungarian industrialization without a firm theoretical foundation. I attempted to identify spurts or take-offs, but instead found business cycles which, of course, evinced upswings that could easily be mistaken for spurts, but which on closer examination were not found to vary greatly relative to other cycles of the century. Moreover, I did not find the degree of back-

[22] Gerschenkron, *Economic Backwardness*, p. 362.

[23] Ibid., p. 34. Years later he modified his point of view by suggesting that "some industrialization can take place in advance of the great spurt. . . . [but] the discontinuity of the great spurt provides the basis for a sustained rate of industrial growth and for a reduction of the country's degree of economic backwardness." Alexander Gerschenkron, *An Economic Spurt That Failed* (Princeton: Princeton University Press, 1977), p. 52. This assertion, however, overlooks the fact that sustained growth had been the European experience throughout the nineteenth century with or without great spurts. It also disregards the possibility that while an industrial spurt might reduce a country's degree of economic backwardness *vis-à-vis* some countries, it need not do so relative to all countries.

[24] Gerschenkron also erred in supposing that a relationship existed between the degree of backwardness, on the one hand, and the intensity of the big spurt, the size of plants utilized during the spurt, and the degree of dominance of the production of investment goods during the spurt, on the other. The point Gerschenkron overlooked was that the underlying character of the industrial advance of the late nineteenth century was fundamentally different from that of a century earlier. The sectors experiencing major innovations during the so-called second industrial revolution were the heavy industries, whereas those experiencing fundamental technical change in the eighteenth century were the consumer goods industries. Hence, regardless of how backward or how advanced an economy was in the late nineteenth century, if it participated in this advance, it was bound to do so in these sectors. The United States was not a backward economy in the late nineteenth century, yet its growth was quite intense: GNP increased by 42 percent in the 1890s, and industrial production by 69 percent. U.S. Department of Commerce, *Historical Statistics of the United States: Colonial Times to 1970* (Washington, DC: U.S. Bureau of the Census, 1975), Vol. 1, p. 224; Vol. 2, p. 667. Moreover, heavy industries were also quite important in the American industrialization drive of the late nineteenth century: the number of electric motors increased in the 1890s from 15,000 to 494,000, and the number of all power-driven machines in use practically doubled to reach 11 million by 1899. The decade also witnessed a trebling of steel output. Thus it was the nature of the economic possibilities that determined the outlines of late-nineteenth-century industrialization rather than the degree of backwardness of the economies in question.

wardness of this economy to have been an important determinant of its performance. Instead, I found that the economy grew cyclically from the 1820s on, but with a relatively even upward trend. In none of its business cycles was industrial performance exceptional.[25] Yet by the twentieth century Austria had gradually become a truly industrialized country.[26]

I sought some explanation for my finding in Simon Kuznets's notion of the beginning of modern economic growth. According to Kuznets, modern economic growth occurs if increases in output per capita are "sustained over a period long enough to reflect more than a cyclical expansion." He added that it is important to consider not only the growth of output, but also of population and of productivity, because a sustained increase in product per capita "does not appear to have characterized the pre-modern past."[27] In some sense, the Austrian experience fit into this theoretical construction simply because the 1820s had

[25] Gerschenkron argued in this regard that "it is precisely Austria's failure to have had a great spurt of industrialization, the sluggishness of its growth, . . . that make me believe that, in the last years of the nineteenth century, Austria was ready for a great spurt of industrialization, . . ." which, he adds, was finally aborted. Gerschenkron, *An Economic Spurt That Failed*, p. 54.

[26] David F. Good, *The Economic Rise of the Habsburg Empire, 1750–1914* (Berkeley: University of California Press, 1984).

[27] Simon Kuznets, *Six Lectures on Economic Growth* (New York: Free Press, 1959), p. 13; idem, *Modern Economic Growth: Rate, Structure, and Spread* (New Haven: Yale University Press, 1966), p. 20. Other theories have been posited, primarily variations on the stage theories of growth. Lloyd Reynolds, for instance, considers that a "turning point" is important as a signal of the beginning of industrialization. He defined this as the period that separates extensive from intensive growth, that is, "a period characterized by a sustained rise in per capita output." Lloyd Reynolds, "The Spread of Economic Growth to the Third World: 1850–1980," *Journal of Economic Literature* 21 (1983): 941–980. This idea is essentially the same as Kuznets's concept of modern economic growth, and therefore suffers from the same difficulties. Episodes of intensive growth are not unique to the modern era: they have occurred throughout the history of Western civilization.

W. Arthur Lewis tried a slightly different approach. He defined the turning point as the time when the labor surplus is exhausted. W. Arthur Lewis, "Economic Development with Unlimited Supplies of Labour," *Manchester School of Economic and Social Studies* 22 (1954): 139–191. This concept is also problematical because in England the labor surplus might have vanished before the industrial revolution, at least during prosperous times. Referring to the late seventeenth century, Gregory King mentioned a large group of cottagers and paupers (in the same category) who did not increase the National Income. However, this only means that their earnings did not cover their maintenance, not that they were unemployed. He put the number of vagrants at only 0.5 percent of the population. Phyllis Deane, *The First Industrial Revolution* (Cambridge, England: Cambridge University Press, 1965), p. 8. Seasonal underemployment did exist, and continued to persist in many parts of Europe well into the twentieth century. François Crouzet, *The Victorian Economy* (New York: Columbia University Press, 1982), p. 140.

been preceded by a quarter century of stagnation. This tended to magnify its importance relative to the previous decades. I had also explored industrial growth in Austria in the late eighteenth century and acknowledged its dynamic character.[28] Yet these early advances did not quite fit Kuznets's, definition of modern economic growth, because progress was interrupted by the Napoleonic wars. According to Kuznets, the economic advance had to be "long enough to reflect more than a cyclical expansion." I was, in any case, predisposed to reject the seemingly heretical notion that modern economic growth in Austria began at about the same time as in Great Britain.

I opted for the 1820s as the beginning of modern economic growth in Austria, but shortly after completing the manuscript I began to explore the nature of industrialization in the late eighteenth century. I hoped that the theory of protoindustrialization, expounded by Franklin Mendels, would be helpful.[29] Protoindustrialization, a variant of the stage theories of economic development, is predicated on the hypothesis that the industrial revolution was preceded by the growth of rural handicrafts, organized on a traditional basis. This first phase of the process of industrialization led to the industrial revolution, argued Mendels, because it fostered the accumulation of human and physical capital, and because it provided economic opportunities that encouraged family formation. As rural handicrafts expanded, rising marginal costs of subcontracting due to rising transportation costs and the increased difficulties of controlling the quality of the final product eventuallly induced entrepreneurs to concentrate production in factories.[30] Thus, with the gains in productivity of the factories came the beginning of the industrial revolution.

In some ways this framework fits the European experience, because industrial production in many regions, including some areas in the Habsburg lands, was decentralized through subcontracting. The advantages of this mode of industrial organization were partly technological: the machines used in the production process fit into the peasant cot-

[28] In fact, Hermann Freudenberger had personally urged me to place a greater emphasis on developments of that period.

[29] Franklin F. Mendels, "Proto-Industrialization: The First Phase of the Industrialization Process," *Journal of Economic History* 32 (1972): 241–261; Pierre Deyon and Franklin F. Mendels, "Proto-industrialization: Theory and Reality," *Eighth International Conference on Economic History* (Budapest: Akadémiai Kiadó, 1982); Rudolph Braun, *Industrialisierung und Volksleben: Die Veränderung der Lebensformen in einem Industriegebiet vor 1800* (Zürich: E. Rentsch, 1960).

[30] This is essentially the model expounded in David S. Landes, *The Unbound Prometheus: Technological Change and Industrial Development in Western Europe from 1750 to the Present* (Cambridge, England: Cambridge University Press, 1969), pp. 41–59.

tages. In addition, such firms were saving capital because, instead of building new plants, they were turning the living rooms of the peasants into workshops. Moreover, the labor used had low opportunity cost, since the peasantry first recruited into the protoindustrial sector were underemployed or seasonally unemployed in the agricultural sector. Therefore it was reasonable that entrepreneurs initially organized the textile industry on such a decentralized basis. Rural industries also saved lives, in the sense that the mortality rate in towns above a certain threshold size was much higher than in rural areas.[31] If the peasants could have entered the industrial sector only in towns, the toll in lives would have been appreciably higher.[32]

While the notion of protoindustrialization is useful in describing this phase of economic development, it did not contribute to my understanding of the dynamics of the process. Why did protoindustrialization accelerate in Bohemia, Moravia, and Lower Austria during the second half of the eighteenth century? After all, rural industries had been growing for at least half a millennium prior to the industrial revolution, not only in this region but in many other regions of Europe, without bringing about an industrial revolution.[33] Why did protoindustrialization lead to the industrial revolution in the eighteenth century and not earlier? In what sense is protoindustrialization the first phase of the industrial revolution if it could proceed for centuries without achieving a breakthrough? Although protoindustrialization is an important concept in itself, it cannot be considered a theory of the industrial revolution: it lacks an internal dynamic.

Another important shortcoming of the theory is that it underestimates the contribution of urban industries to economic development. Silk production, for instance, was generally an urban, not a rural, phenomenon. The large royal manufactories were not organized on the basis of subcontracting. In short, one should not overlook the significant contributions that urban craftsmen, in and out of guilds, had made to the process of industrialization, not only immediately before the industrial revolution, but for hundreds of years prior to it as well. Their activity fostered the accumulation of capital, skill, and organizational know-how just as the protoindustrial sector did. As a consequence, protoindustrial forms of production were generally in a symbiotic relation-

[31] Michael W. Flinn, *The European Demographic System, 1500–1820* (Baltimore: The Johns Hopkins University Press, 1981), p. 22.

[32] Personal communication from Professor Jack Goldstone of Northwestern University.

[33] D. C. Coleman, "Proto-Industrialization: A Concept Too Many," *Economic History Review*, 2d ser., 36 (1983): 435–448.

ship not only with the agricultural surroundings, which the advocates of the theory stress, but with urban systems as well. Rural producers depended on the town as a source of demand, or as finishers of the intermediate products they produced. In the Habsburg Monarchy the towns of Reichenberg, Brünn, Prague, and Vienna were important industrial centers. Industrial organization in the second half of the eighteenth century can best be characterized as a mix of workshop, household, and factory production, in both rural and urban settings. There is no a priori reason why one should stress the importance of one kind of firm over another.

Another weakness of the protoindustrialization model is that it places undue emphasis on the organization of the textile sector. The iron and glass industries, which in some regions contributed significantly to the industrial revolution, were organized on quite different principles, because of the nature of their technologies. In these sectors decentralized subcontracting was not important, and, as in mining, large-scale units of production were often the rule even in the Middle Ages.

By ascribing so much importance to the contribution of rural artisans to the process of industrialization, the theory of protoindustrialization commits an error of misplaced emphasis similar to that of those economic historians who have stressed the importance of the manufactories. These early proto-factories, although not yet extensively mechanized, were nonetheless centralized firms; many specialized in finishing or bleaching textiles. In the German-speaking world, historians have often pointed to the manufactories as the most important aspect of economic development during the half century prior to the industrial revolution; they even referred to the period as the period of manufactories.[34] Giving names to periods might have heuristic value, but it imparts no information in itself; it might even mislead by pretending to be an explanation. Yet it is no more justified to label the eighteenth century the era of manufactories than it is to call it the era of protoindustrialization.

After the completion of my book I also became disillusioned with Kuznets's definition of modern economic growth, because he was mistaken in thinking that sustained population growth and increases in output per capita were unique to the modern epoch.[35] During numerous

[34] Gustav Otruba, "Österreichs Industrie und Arbeiterschaft im Übergang von der Manufaktur zur Fabrikaturepoche (1790–1848)," *Österreich in Geschichte und Literatur* 15 (1971): 569–604.

[35] Does his definition mean that an economy in which per capita product grows but population does not is not experiencing modern economic growth? That would mean that

other times in the past, including the Middle Ages and the sixteenth century, per capita output expanded for a very long time. One need only think of the harnessing of the power of the wind and water, innovations in iron smelting such as the water-powered bellows and iron hammers, the great technological advances of the mining sector that made possible ever deeper penetration of the earth's crust, and the atmospheric steam engine to be in awe of the transformations of the means of production preceding the industrial revolution.[36] The urban expansion of the high Middle Ages must have been impossible at per capita output levels of the prior centuries. Thus each expansion of European civilization led to human and physical capital accumulation of unprecedented levels. Carlo Cipolla expressed this sentiment by stating "that the average *per capita* consumption of energy in Western Europe must have been much higher during the thirteenth century than during the seventh or that the average Roman of the first century A.D. must have controlled much more energy . . . than any early Neolithic cultivator in Jarmo in the fifth millennium B.C."[37] From this long-term perspective the upswing of the eighteenth century loses much of its significance.

To be sure, Kuznets noted several other distinguishing features of modern economic growth in addition to the ones mentioned above. He pointed out that urbanization was an important factor in modern economic growth, without acknowledging the fact that urbanization had been going on for a thousand years before the modern epoch.[38] The shift away from agricultural and toward industrial production is another aspect of the modern epoch emphasized by Kuznets, but this shift was also one that began much earlier. On the eve of the industrial revolution, only about 40 percent of England's national product originated in agriculture.[39] If one considers that at the beginning of the Middle Ages this share must have been close to 90 percent, then one can gain an idea of the immensity of the sectoral shifts that preceded the modern era. Another factor mentioned by Kuznets was the "extended application of

---

many European nations, whose populations are stagnating at this time, are no longer experiencing modern economic growth.

[36] Carlo Cipolla, *Before the Industrial Revolution: European Society and Economy, 1000–1700*, 2d ed. (New York: Norton and Co., 1980), p. 168.

[37] Carlo Cipolla, *The Economic History of World Population* (1962; reprint, Baltimore: Penguin Books, 1970), p. 50.

[38] On the eve of the industrial revolution, England's population was about 20 percent urban. Paul M. Hohenberg and Lynn Hollen Lees, *The Making of Urban Europe, 1000–1950* (Cambridge, MA: Harvard University Press, 1985).

[39] Phyllis Deane and W. A. Coale, *British Economic Growth* (Cambridge, England: Cambridge University Press, 1962), p. 142. Less than half of the labor force was employed in agriculture. Crafts, *British Economic Growth during the Industrial Revolution*, p. 2.

science to problems of economic production."[40] Yet the great innovations of the eighteenth century were not predicated on scientific knowledge; rather, they were "largely independent of basic science."[41]

Thus, I ultimately became dissatisfied with Kuznets's framework, because the expansion of the eighteenth and nineteenth centuries no longer appeared to me to be a unique experience in the history of mankind. I adopted the view that it was an upswing of economic activity similar to the upswings of the twelfth and sixteenth centuries. Admittedly, the nineteenth and twentieth centuries did witness rates of per capita growth that were perhaps not achieved earlier, but that distinction Kuznets failed to emphasize. Another reason I became somewhat uncomfortable with my previous position was that distinguishing between the growth of the second half of the eighteenth century and that of the 1820s on the basis of the happenstance of the intervening wars, and their impact on the economy, appeared in retrospect to have been a rigid application of Kuznets's framework. Thus, having discarded all of the available theories of the industrial revolution, including Kuznets's, I essentially resigned myself to giving up.

Then the appearance of four publications in 1981 dramatically changed my views on this entire problem. The first was Eric Jones's *The European Miracle*,[42] in which he argued persuasively that the fundamental feature of the economic history of Europe was the persistence of growth. Jones resurrected and gave potency to arguments advanced by an earlier generation of economic historians, that the industrial revolution was an outgrowth of processes begun centuries earlier.[43] In Jones's view, it does not make sense to look for a beginning, because there was none, unless one would like to think of the Neolithic agricultural revolution as a beginning of sorts. Indeed, European growth can be characterized by a continuity of economic processes, and instead of looking for spurts one should seek to understand why growth was occasionally interrupted. Jones's argument was broader and more general than those of his predecessors, but it lacked a plausible mechanism capable of explaining the intermittent nature of growth. How did continuous processes give rise to cyclical growth?

[40] Kuznets, *Modern Economic Growth*, p. 9.

[41] Douglass North, *Structure and Change in Economic History* (New York: Norton, 1981), p. 162.

[42] Cambridge, England: Cambridge University Press, 1981.

[43] John U. Nef, "Consequences of an Early Energy Crisis," *Scientific American* 237 (November 1977): 140–151; idem, "The Progress of Technology and the Growth of Large Scale Industry in Great Britain, 1540–1640," *Economic History Review*, 1st ser., 5 (1934): 3–24.

Douglass North's *Structure and Change in Economic History*, which *North* appeared the same year, also stressed the evolutionary nature of economic development. North emphasized the importance of institutional change in lowering transaction costs and in clarifying and ensuring property rights, thereby bringing social and private returns closer to one another. His work reinforced Jones's by stressing the evolutionary nature of those changes that brought about the European transformation.

Rondo Cameron had observed earlier the cyclical nature of European aggregate economic activity, and had also made a connection between population growth and the growth in per capita product during the accelerating phase of each of the cyclical advances.[44] In other words, he made an attempt to integrate population dynamics into the framework of European economic cycles, something that the above two authors did not stress. Unfortunately Cameron's view made little impression on the profession when it was first published.[45] Yet, upon rereading this somewhat obscure publication, it became clear that these were the very elements that were lacking in Jones's and North's framework. These three ideas became influential in the formation of my model of the industrial revolution, because they tended to support the notion that it can be thought of as a cyclical upswing of economic activity, i.e., one of the many phases of expansion in the economic history of Europe. It followed from this reasoning that its roots must be sought in the distant past. To be sure, the eighteenth-century expansion, to which I continue to refer as the industrial revolution, differed in one fundamental way from previous expansions: it was not followed by a severe downturn in economic activity.

Another publication of 1981 furthered my understanding of this aspect of the eighteenth-century expansion. This was Anthony Wrigley and Roger Schofield's *The Population History of England, 1541–1871: A Reconstruction*.[46] The finding in their book that proved to be the most important for my purposes was that in the late eighteenth century England's Malthusian demographic system was superseded by one in which population growth was no longer food controlled. Here was the distinguishing feature of European economic growth of the nineteenth century: its population, in contrast to those of prior centuries, was not subject to frequent, severe subsistence and mortality crises. Famines had

W+S
'81

---

[44] Rondo Cameron, "The Logistics of European Economic Growth: A Note on Historical Periodization," *Journal of European Economic History* 2 (1973): 145–148.

[45] Recently the cyclical nature of pre-industrial economic development has been emphasized again in Myron P. Gutmann, *Toward the Modern Economy: Early Industry in Europe, 1500–1800* (New York: Alfred A. Knopf, 1988).

[46] Cambridge, MA: Harvard University Press, 1981.

been endemic as late as the seventeenth century, even in an advanced country such as England. In 1623, for instance, thousands starved to death in Cumberland, Westmoreland, Yorkshire, and Lancashire.[47] In 1649, too, the poor of the northern counties were "famished," and many were reported to "have died in the highways for the want of bread."[48] It is true that chronic malnutrition persisted in plaguing a large segment of the European populations well into the nineteenth century, but major subsistence and mortality crises disappeared. The last mortality crisis in England in which the crude death rate exceeded the crude birth rate was in the 1740s.[49] Hence these pre-industrial subsistence crises could have been the factor that Jones sought to identify, events that interrupted population growth sufficiently to occasionally force Europe to deviate from its steady-state growth path. Through Cameron's cycles, Wrigley and Schofield's finding could be integrated into Jones's and North's framework.

The fourth important publication of 1981 was Ester Boserup's *Population and Technological Change: A Study of Long-Term Trends*.[50] She argued forcefully that the effect of population growth need not be capital-diluting in the long run, and provided evidence that the Malthusian view of the world should be supplemented by one in which population growth can have positive economic consequences. This argument was important insofar as it enabled me to think of the industrial revolution as a Boserupian episode, given Wrigley and Schofield's evidence cited above.

The jigsaw puzzle was now almost complete, perhaps it was actually complete, but in my mind the various pieces still did not quite coalesce into a complete model of economic growth. The catalyst came from an unexpected source. In the late 1960s French scholars had begun to explore the history of human stature.[51] Soon reaching American shores,[52] the results of this line of analysis appeared already in the late 1970s, but were first brought to my attention in 1982 by Professor Robert Fogel of the University of Chicago.[53] I became interested in anthropometric

[47] Andrew Appleby, *Famine in Tudor and Stuart England* (Stanford: Stanford University Press, 1978), pp. 1, 95.

[48] Joan Thirsk and J. P. Cooper, *Seventeenth-Century Economic Documents* (Oxford: Clarendon Press, 1972), p. 51.

[49] Wrigley and Schofield, *Population History*.

[50] Chicago: University of Chicago Press, 1981.

[51] Jean-Paul Aron, Paul Dumont, and Emmanuel Le Roy Ladurie, *Anthropologie du conscrit français* (Paris: Mouton, 1972).

[52] Through the intermediation of Peter Laslett, according to Professor James Tanner of the University of London.

[53] Robert W. Fogel, Stanley Engerman, James Trussell, Roderick Floud, Clayne L.

history the following year out of sheer curiosity, and not because I anticipated a breakthrough in the problem that had been my major concern for the prior decade.

The examination of the time profile of human stature of the Austro-Hungarian population soon indicated that there was an impending Malthusian crisis on the eve of the industrial revolution. This finding enabled me to synthesize the work of the above-mentioned scholars into the "Austrian" model of the industrial revolution. If human beings actually shrank physically as a consequence of a nutritional crisis brought about by population growth in the eighteenth century, when the European economies were already much more advanced than previously, then it is eminently plausible that prior population expansions had had similar, perhaps even more profound, biological consequences. In retrospect, it is clear that the difficulties encountered by the European societies in the late eighteenth century were evident in the work of such historians as Wilhelm Abel, who emphasized the increase in food prices and the concomitant rise in poverty of the time; his work, however, did not present the idea of an impending Malthusian crisis as vividly as does the anthropometric evidence.[54]

In previous centuries, the collapses of the population played a crucial role in occasionally interrupting that persistent advance of the European economies noted by Jones. With the discovery that nutritional status provides an important link connecting economic, demographic, and biological processes, a new conceptualization of the industrial revolution emerged.

The model is explained fully in Chapter 6, and its mathematical version appears in Appendix C. The computer simulations were done in collaboration with Marc Artzrouni, then of the Carolina Population Center, of the University of North Carolina at Chapel Hill, and now of the Department of Mathematics of Loyola University of New Orleans. With only a few equations, the model can replicate the salient features of population growth from the ancient world to the industrial revolution. The conceptualization of the model resolves the apparent paradox between the continuity of economic and demographic processes over the millennia and the great discontinuity in output, population growth, and per capita output of the eighteenth century. The industrial revolu-

Pope, and Larry T. Wimmer, "The Economics of Mortality in North America, 1650–1910: A Description of a Research Project," *Historical Methods* 11 (1978): 75–108.

[54] Wilhelm Abel, *Agrarkrisen und Agrarkonjunktur; Eine Geschichte der Land- und Ernährungswirtschaft Mitteleuropas seit dem hohen Mittelalter* (1935; reprint, Hamburg and Berlin: Paul Parey, 1966); idem, *Massenarmut und Hungerkrisen im vorindustriellen Europa* (Hamburg and Berlin: Paul Parey, 1974).

tion in this view becomes another cyclical advance similar to the ones the European populations experienced in the twelfth, thirteenth, and sixteenth centuries. It differed from the previous ones in that the Malthusian ceilings were for the first time lifted, and, at least in Europe, it seems permanently so. The society, the economy, and the political institutions finally became strong enough to overcome the Malthusian menace. During each of the prior advances society accumulated capital, knowledge, and skills. Population grew, but as it did, its nutritional status declined. A Malthusian crisis would ensue, because production could not keep pace with population growth. Yet the unceasing process of accumulation, or Jones's technological drift, meant that future generations could benefit from prior achievements even if they themselves were not successful in avoiding a Malthusian crisis. Subsequent generations were in a better position to escape from the Malthusian trap because they had at their disposal a larger stock of human and physical capital. Thus the cycle of population growth, capital accumulation, and economic expansion, followed by nutritional crisis, population collapse or stagnation, and economic contraction, repeated itself over the millennia until eventually the production and import of nutrients could proceed quickly enough to prevent the degree of malnutrition experienced earlier. With the food constraint lifted, population growth could continue, breaking the cycle of population expansions and collapses of an earlier era.

Here was the mechanism that helped to clarify the nature of nineteenth-century growth which has been called self-sustaining in the sense that it was continuous. In other words, there was no repetition of the collapses of the Dark Ages and of the fourteenth century, or of the slowdown of the seventeenth century. This aspect of nineteenth-century development can be understood only in the context of its demographic history. The European population managed to grow, and that made economic growth appear self-sustaining. Labor, after all, is an important element in a classical production function, and, in contrast to capital, it tends to reproduce itself. Why have scholars concentrated to such an extent on capital accumulation? The growth of the labor force was just as crucial an element in the growth of output as was the growth of the capital stock. Providing that the food constraint was no longer binding, the continued reproduction of the labor force implies self-sustained growth even if the rate of capital accumulation did not increase. If, in addition, an increase in population densities had positive externalities in a Boserupian sense, then the absence of Malthusian limits would imply self-sustained growth even on a per capita basis. A denser population led to economies of scale in education and to the expansion of scientific

18

knowledge, with subsequent repercussions on technological change. Hence the advances in the science-based technologies were only one part of the many-faceted transformation brought about by the industrial revolution.

In this model, population growth becomes a necessary, but not a sufficient, condition for the industrial revolution. An adequate nutritional base and a developed economy were also needed before the industrial revolution could become a reality. Thus the difference between the population expansions of the sixteenth and eighteenth centuries was that during the former period neither the nutritional base nor the level of development was sufficient to enable the population to escape permanently from the Malthusian trap. Hence, the industrial revolution becomes another episode of population expansion, but one with a difference: during this episode the Malthusian constraints melted away.

Focusing on the nutritional link shows that the industrial revolution can be integrated into the pre-industrial epoch, yet at the same time might signal a profound break with the pre-industrial demographic regime. Biological man is thereby placed in the center of the economic and demographic processes leading to the industrial revolution, i.e., the escape from the Malthusian trap.

The outline of the book is as follows. In Chapter 1, I explore the relationship between nutrition, human stature, and economic and demographic processes, as well as the well-being of a society. Since human stature is a robust proxy for the nutritional status of a population, it becomes a quantitative indicator of its food consumption, providing that the claims on calorie intake such as the incidence of disease or of work intensity remain unchanged. Because the demand for food depends on real income, the human stature of a population depends, *inter alia*, on the level of per capita income of a society. In this chapter, I also delve deeper into the role of nutrition in determining the rates of fertility and mortality of a population, and suggest that changes in human stature can be related to changes in vital rates. In Chapter 2, I examine the temporal profile of human stature in the eighteenth-century Habsburg Monarchy and conclude that a Malthusian crisis was threatening this society. Chapter 3 is devoted to an exposition of the government's response to this nutritional crisis through institutional change and how its policy opened the way for the beginning of the industrial revolution in Austria. In Chapter 4, I summarize my findings and outline the "Austrian" model of the industrial revolution. In Chapter 5 I argue that the model is useful for understanding the English industrial revolution as well. The English experience in the eighteenth century resembles the Austrian pattern, with the modification that institutional change in Austria played a much more important role than it did in England in bringing about the expansion of the market during the second half of the century. In Chapter 6 the model is extended to encompass pre-industrial economic growth in general by suggesting that the earlier population cycles culminated in the industrial and demographic revolutions of the eighteenth century. Hence the Austrian model of the industrial revolution is actually a European model; it was baptized as such because the data on which it is based were obtained in Austria and because the model was first formulated with the Austrian experience in mind.[55]

[55] It is not meant as a reference to the Austrian school of political economy.

THE "AUSTRIAN" MODEL

CHAPTER 1

THE THEORY OF
ANTHROPOMETRIC
HISTORY

Economic historians have recently begun to analyze the ways in which economic, demographic, and biological processes interacted in the eighteenth and nineteenth centuries. The history of human stature plays a role in this research program because nutritional status until adulthood is a determining factor of the degree to which the height of an individual, and of a population, reaches its genetic potential.[1] At the

[1] Roderick Floud and Kenneth Wachter, "Poverty and Physical Stature: Evidence on the Standard of Living of London Boys, 1770–1870," *Social Science History* 6 (1982): 422–452; Robert W. Fogel, "Nutrition and the Decline in Mortality since 1700: Some Preliminary Findings," in Stanley L. Engerman and Robert Gallman, eds., *Long Term Factors in American Economic Growth*, National Bureau of Economic Research, Studies in Income and Wealth, vol. 51 (Chicago: University of Chicago Press, 1987), pp. 439–555; Robert W. Fogel, Stanley L. Engerman, Roderick Floud, Gerald Friedman, Robert A. Margo, Kenneth Sokoloff, Richard H. Steckel, T. James Trussell, Georgia Villaflor, and Kenneth W. Wachter, "Secular Changes in American and British Stature and Nutrition," *Journal of Interdisciplinary History* 14 (1983): 445–481; Robert W. Fogel, Stanley L. Engerman, and James Trussell, "Exploring the Uses of Data on Height: The Analysis of Long-Term Trends in Nutrition, Labor Welfare, and Labor Productivity," *Social Science History* 6 (1982): 401–421; Gerald C. Friedman, "The Heights of Slaves in Trinidad," *Social Science History* 6 (1982): 428–515; Robert Margo and Richard H. Steckel, "The Height of American Slaves: New Evidence on Slave Nutrition and Health," *Social Science History* 6 (1982): 516–538; Robert Margo and Richard H. Steckel, "Heights of Native Born Northern Whites during the Antebellum Period," *Journal of Economic History* 43 (1983): 167–174; Lars G. Sandberg and Richard H. Steckel, "Soldier, Soldier, What Made You Grow So Tall? A Study of Height, Health, and Nutrition in Sweden, 1720–1881," *Economy and History* 23 (1980): 91–105; Kenneth Sokoloff and Georgia C. Vil-

conceptual level, nutritional status is a measure of the intake of nutrients minus the claims of basal metabolism, of energy expenditure, and of disease encounters. The higher the nutritional status, the more calories and protein remain available for growth.

Because nutrition influences both fertility and mortality, and because human stature can be used as a proxy for nutritional status, changes in the stature of a population have a powerful explanatory value for demographic trends. In addition, since food consumption in these centuries was an important component of total expenditure,[2] changes in stature can be interpreted as reflecting changes in economic conditions and in the well-being of populations. The mean stature of a population is therefore an important variable, one with implications for both economic and demographic processes, and its longitudinal and cross-sectional analysis affords insights that have hitherto eluded the historian.

The relationship between human height and nutrition did not escape nineteenth-century social observers,[3] who, for instance, pointed to the small stature of the English working class as a sign of its miserable material condition.[4] In the twentieth century the study of human stature

---

laflor, "The Early Achievement of Modern Stature in America," *Social Science History* 6 (1982): 453–481; Richard H. Steckel, "Height and Per Capita Income," *Historical Methods* 16 (1983): 1–7; Richard H. Steckel, "Slave Height Profiles from Coastwise Manifests," *Explorations in Economic History* 16 (1979): 363–380; Lars G. Sandberg and Richard H. Steckel, "Heights and Economic History: The Swedish Case," *Annals of Human Biology* 14 (1987): 101–110; Roderick Floud, "The Heights of Europeans since 1750: A New Source for European Economic History," National Bureau of Economic Research, Working Paper No. 1318, 1984; idem, "Wirtschaftliche und soziale Einflüsse auf die Körpergrössen von Europäern seit 1750," *Jahrbuch für Wirtschaftsgeschichte* (1985): 93–118; José Miguel Martinez Carrion, "Estatura, Nutricion y Nivel de Vida en Murcia, 1860–1930," *Revista de Historia Económica* 4 (1986): 67–99; A. Theodore Steegman, Jr., "18th Century British Military Stature: Growth Cessation, Selective Recruiting, Secular Trends, Nutrition at Birth, Cold and Occupation," *Human Biology* 57 (1985): 77–95; Antonio Gómez Mendoza and Vincente Pérez Moreda, "Estatura y nivel de vida en la Espana del primer tercio del siglo XX," *Moneda y Credito* 174 (1985): 29–64; John Komlos, "The Height and Weight of West Point Cadets: Dietary Change in Antebellum America," *Journal of Economic History* 47 (1987): 897–927.

[2] As much as 80 percent of income was often spent on food. Carlo Cipolla, *Before the Industrial Revolution: European Society and Economy, 1000–1700*, 2d ed. (New York: Norton and Co., 1980), p. 30.

[3] An 1829 publication, for instance, stated that "human height becomes greater and growth takes place more rapidly, other things being equal, in proportion as the country is richer . . . nourishment better. . . ." L. R. Villermé, "Mémoire sur la taille de l'homme en France," *Annales d'hygiène publique* 1 (1829): 551–559.

[4] Roderick Floud, Kenneth Wachter, and Annabel Gregory, "The Physical State of the British Working Class, 1860–1914: Evidence from Army Recruits," National Bureau of Economic Research, Working Paper No. 1661, 1985; James Trussell and Kenneth Wachter, "Estimating the Covariates of Historical Heights," National Bureau of Economic Re-

remained the purview of physicians, physical anthropologists, and biologists.[5] Not until the late 1960s, and then more seriously in the 1970s, did French, British, and American social and economic historians begin to show an interest in anthropometric history.[6]

The French historian Emmanuel Le Roy Ladurie revived this line of reasoning in 1969 by showing that the height of French recruits born in the late 1840s depended on their education and wealth. Illiterates averaged 164.3 cm, while those able to read and write were 1.2 cm taller. Presumably literate men were wealthier, and spent more time at education and less at work than did illiterates. A more sedentary life meant that more of their caloric intake was available for growth.[7] Thus in nineteenth-century France stature correlated positively with such socioeconomic variables as wealth and literacy.[8]

Exploration of the American evidence by Robert Fogel and several collaborators soon unearthed some equally intriguing patterns. By the early eighteenth century the height of the colonial population was already well above European norms; this implied that the nutritional en-

---

search, Working Paper No. 1455, 1984; Friedrich Engels, *The Condition of the Working Class in England* (Stanford: Stanford University Press, 1968), p. 226. At age 18 boys employed in factories were 6.5 inches shorter than those who were not. Thomas Edward Jordan, *Victorian Childhood: Themes and Variations* (Albany, NY: State University of New York Press, 1987), p. 4.

[5] For an extensive treatment of this subject see James M. Tanner, *A History of the Study of Human Growth* (Cambridge, England: Cambridge University Press, 1981).

[6] To be more precise, the stature of army recruits was also studied earlier, but more from a military than from a socioeconomic point of view. Joseph Ruwet, *Soldats des régiments nationaux au XVIIIᵉ siècle* (Brussels: Palais des Académies, 1962); André Corvisier, *L'armée française de la fin du XVIIᵉ siècle au ministère de Choiseul. Le Soldat* (Paris: Presses Universitaires de France, 1964).

[7] Emmanuel Le Roy Ladurie, *Le territoire de l'historien* (Paris: Gallimard, 1973), pp. 112–114; E. Le Roy Ladurie, N. Bernageau, and Y. Pasquet, "Le conscrit et l'ordinateur. Perspectives de recherches sur les archives militaires du XIXᵉ siècle français," *Studi Storici* 10 (1969): 260–308; E. Le Roy Ladurie and N. Bernageau, "Étude sur un Contingent Militaire (1868). Mobilité géographique, délinquance et stature, mises en rapport avec d'autres aspects de la situation des conscrits," *Annales de démographie historique* (1971): 311–337; Jean-Paul Aron, Paul Dumont, and Emmanuel Le Roy Ladurie, *Anthropologie du conscrit français* (Paris: Mouton, 1972). Moreover, those able to avoid military service by paying for replacements were one cm taller than those who actually became soldiers. Only 9.5 percent of those literate men wealthy enough to buy replacements were shorter than 159 cm, and 27.6 percent were taller than 170 cm. Yet, of those who did not buy replacements and were illiterate, 22.1 percent were shorter than 159 cm and only 14.6 percent were taller than 170 cm.

[8] A similar pattern has been found for late-nineteenth-century Paris. Stature and the rate of rejection from military service varied systematically with occupation and district of residence. Lenard R. Berlanstein, *The Working People of Paris, 1871–1914* (Baltimore: The Johns Hopkins University Press, 1984), pp. 55, 72.

vironment of the New World must have been especially favorable.[9] Although slaves appear to have been neglected as children, even they benefited from the abundance of food in America, since as adults their height was close to that of the white population.[10] In fact, Americans were so well nourished that not until the middle of the twentieth century did the height of Europeans approach American standards.[11] In contrast to America, the nutritional status of the poor boys of London was truly miserable at the end of the eighteenth century. They were shorter than practically all modern populations, with the possible exception of such groups as the Lume of New Guinea.[12] Using stature as a proxy for nutritional status, these studies paved the way for further exploration of demographic and economic trends in the eighteenth and nineteenth centuries, for which data relevant to these issues are extremely scarce.

Height as a Measure of Nutritional Status

The use of human stature as a proxy for nutritional status is justified by modern medical research, which has established beyond doubt that the net cumulative nutritional intake of a population over its growing years has a major influence on its average height, with maternal nutrition also playing a role.[13] "Environmental factors," such as those summarized by socioeconomic status, "are far more important than genetic factors in accounting for most of the observed differences in body size within and among countries," with the exception of the Far East. Hence, "most nutritionists regard both height-for-age . . . and weight-for-age . . . as significant indicators of malnutrition."[14]

[9] Robert W. Fogel, Stanley L. Engerman, James Trussell, Roderick Floud, Clayne L. Pope, and Larry T. Wimmer, "The Economics of Mortality in North America, 1650–1910: A Description of a Research Project," *Historical Methods* 11 (1978): 75–108; Stanley L. Engerman, "The Height of U.S. Slaves," *Local Population Studies* 16 (1976): 45–50.

[10] Richard H. Steckel, "A Peculiar Population: The Nutrition, Health and Mortality of American Slaves from Childhood to Maturity," *Journal of Economic History* 46 (1986): 721–742.

[11] Roderick Floud, "Two Cultures? British and American Heights in the Nineteenth Century," unpublished manuscript, Department of History, University of London, 1985.

[12] Floud and Wachter, "Poverty and Physical Stature," p. 444.

[13] Animal experiments suggest that intergenerational transfer of malnutrition is significant. Fogel, Engerman, and Trussell, "Uses of Data on Height," pp. 405, 406, 417.

[14] Reynaldo Martorell, "Genetics, Environment, and Growth: Issues in the Assessment of Nutritional Status," in Antonio Velazques and Hector Bourges, eds., *Genetic Factors in Nutrition* (New York: Academic Press, 1984), as cited in John Mellor and Bruce Johnston, "The World Food Equation: Interrelations among Development, Employment, and

Height measures cumulative net nutrition: the food consumed over the growing years minus such claims on the nutrients as disease and physical exertion. Therefore, the height of a birth cohort is influenced by the nutritional and other environmental circumstances of the successive two decades, but food intake during the neonatal period and the adolescent growth spurt is particularly important. If prolonged and moderate malnutrition occurs during the formative years, the individual will continue to grow beyond the age at which a well-fed individual ceases to grow. Moreover, if temporarily malnourished individuals resume an adequate diet, their bodies will attempt to compensate for the prior slowdown in growth through "catch-up" growth.[15] Severe or prolonged malnutrition, however, may so alter the adolescent growth-spurt pattern that permanent stunting results. Nutritional status can therefore be measured not only by the age-by-height profile but also by the age at which the growth spurt is reached, the size of the greatest annual growth increment during adolescence, and the age at which growth ceases.[16] While height is a cumulative measure of food intake, weight standardized for height is an indicator of contemporaneous nutritional status.[17] Additionally, the birth weight of babies is an indicator of the mother's nutritional status.[18]

Food Consumption," *Journal of Economic Literature* 22 (1984): 531–574; Reynaldo Martorell, C. Yarborough, R. G. Klein, and A. Leichtig, "Malnutrition, Body Size, and Skeletal Maturation: Interrelationships and Implications for Catch-Up Growth," *Human Biology* 51 (1979): 371–389; Lawrence Greene and Francis Johnston, eds., *Social and Biological Predictors of Nutritional Status, Physical Growth, and Neurological Development* (New York: Academic Press, 1980); Edwin Driver and Aloo Driver, "Social Class and Height and Weight in Metropolitan Madras," *Social Biology* 30 (1983): 189–204. Stunting "is the result of environmental factors because it is reversible under favorable conditions." World Health Organization, *Energy and Protein Requirements. Report of a Joint FAO/WHO/UNO Expert Consultation* (Geneva: World Health Organization, 1985), p. 21.

[15] James M. Tanner, "Growth as a Target-Seeking Function: Catch-up and Catch-down Growth in Man," in Frank Falkner and James M. Tanner, eds., *Human Growth: A Comprehensive Treatise*, 2d ed. (New York and London: Plenum Press, 1986), Vol. 1, pp. 167–179.

[16] James M. Tanner, *Foetus into Man: Physical Growth from Conception to Maturity* (Cambridge, MA: Harvard University Press, 1978).

[17] The Body-Mass Index (weight/height^2, with weight measured in kilograms and height in meters) is another useful measure of nutritional status. Robert W. Fogel, "Biomedical Approaches to the Estimation and Interpretation of Secular Trends in Equity, Morbidity, Mortality, and Labor Productivity in Europe, 1750–1980," unpublished manuscript, Graduate School of Business Administration, University of Chicago, 1987.

[18] W. Peter Ward and Patricia C. Ward, "Infant Birth Weight and Nutrition in Industrializing Montreal," *American Historical Review* 89 (1984): 324–345. Birth weight in Vienna correlated highly with the cost of living index. W. Peter Ward, "Weight at Birth

Although the stature of a population is indicative of its food consumption as well as of its disease environment, some caveats are in order. The consumption of adulterated or contaminated food might detract from nutritional status. In addition, the composition of the food consumed is also of some consequence, because the mix of calorie and protein intake matters for growth. In a low-calorie diet the proteins will not be used for growth, but will be converted into energy for basal metabolism. The question is complicated by the fact that protein is made up of many amino acids, and it is the combination of amino acids, not only their quantity, that is important to growth and the body's well-being.[19] Animal proteins are especially important, because they have a better balance of amino acids than the proteins found in grains. If the amino acids are not available in the right proportion malnutrition might result, particularly among children, even if the quantity of protein exceeds the minimum requirement.[20] This implies that there is no one-to-one correspondence between stature and the quantity or value of food consumed; the combination of the food intake is also a factor to consider.

The terminal height an individual reaches in a given population is, of course, influenced by genetic factors as well as by the quantity of food consumed. This consideration, however, does not affect studies of human height as long as the genetic composition of the population is not altered through large-scale in- or out-migration. For this reason historical studies frequently focus on the changes in the terminal height attained by a given population over time, because such changes are not influenced by genetic factors.[21]

---

in Vienna, Austria, 1865–1930," *Annals of Human Biology* 14 (1987): 495–506; Richard H. Steckel, "Birth Weights and Infant Mortality among American Slaves," *Explorations in Economic History* 23 (1986): 173–198.

[19] ". . . a diet may be deficient in quantity or quality of protein." Moreover, at any level of protein intake the addition of calories to the diet enhances protein synthesis and reduces amino acid oxidation. World Health Organization, *Energy and Protein Requirements*, pp. 54, 58.

[20] Martha W. Williams, "Infant Nutrition and Economic Growth in Western Europe from the Middle Ages to the Modern Period," unpublished Ph.D. dissertation, Department of Economics, Northwestern University, 1988, Chapter 2; F. W. Clements, "Some Effects of Different Diets," in S. V. Boyden, ed., *The Impact of Civilisation on the Biology of Man* (Toronto: University of Toronto Press, 1970), pp. 109–141.

[21] During the course of thousands of years the genetic composition of a population might, indeed, change. In a low nutritional environment, for instance, the individuals with a higher probability of surviving in the very long run would be those who had lower nutritional requirements, i.e., who were shorter. The early Norse settlers of Greenland were thought to have become quite stunted in the Middle Ages. H. H. Lamb, *The Changing Climate* (London: Methuen, 1966), p. 188, as cited by Reid A. Bryson and Thomas

The Relationship between Human Stature and the Economy

In order to explore the relationship between human stature and the economy, consider that the demand for food F is a function of real income Y, the price index of a typical basket of food products P_F relative to all other prices P_{AOG} (where AOG = All Other Goods), and tastes T (assumed constant). Let P_F/P_{AOG} be designated by Z. Then

$$F_t = (f_1, f_2, \ldots, f_n) = k(Y_t, Z_t, T), \qquad (1.1)$$

where f_i is the quantity of the ith foodstuff. The vector F_t is determined by utility maximization. The ith foodstuff has a caloric content c_i, protein content r_i, and price P_i per unit. The total caloric intake C is given by:

$$C = j(f_1, f_2, \ldots, f_n) = j(F_t) = f_1 c_1 + f_2 c_2 + \ldots + f_n c_n \qquad (1.2a)$$

and, similarly, the total protein intake R is given by:

$$R = b(f_1, f_2, \ldots, f_n) = b(F_t) = f_1 r_1 + f_2 r_2 + \ldots + f_n r_n. \qquad (1.2b)$$

Following the consensus among biologists, the terminal height of a population H must be between the genetically determined minimum H_{min} and the maximum H_{max}. The effect of nutrition on adult stature is constrained within these bounds. H_{min} should be considered the height that would be attained if the human organism were just barely kept alive and H_{max} the maximum height attainable without a budget constraint. The degree to which H exceeds H_{min} is determined by the intake of calories C and of protein R above the requirements of basal metabolism, the work effort, and the nutrients claimed by diseases. Let all of these claims on the nutrients be designated by W. Then

$$H = H_{min} + \int_{t=-1}^{t=25} [h(C_t, R_t, W_t, t)] \, dt \leq H_{max}, \qquad (1.3)$$

where h is the instantaneous growth rate and t designates age. The integral is from -1 to 25 in order to signify, on the one hand, that intrauterine nutrition also influences nutritional status, and, on the other hand, that physical growth usually does not continue beyond the mid-twenties. From equations 1.1, 1.2a, 1.2b, and 1.3 follows:

Murray, *Climates of Hunger: Mankind and the World's Changing Weather* (Madison: The University of Wisconsin Press, 1977), p. 71. However, the notion of the drastic decline of the height of the Norse settlers has been challenged on the basis of a new interpretation of the archeological evidence. Knud J. Krogh, *Viking Greenland* (Copenhagen: The National Museum, 1967), p. 51.

$$H = H_{min} + \int_{t=-1}^{t=25} \left[g(\Upsilon_t, Z_t, T, W_t, t) \right] dt \leq H_{max}, \quad (1.4)$$

where g is a composite function.[22] Note that $\partial g / \partial \Upsilon > 0$ and $\partial g / \partial Z < 0$. Thus the mean height of a population depends on its real income and some other variables such as Z, T, and W. To the extent that Z, T, and W remain constant, there should be a positive correlation between Υ and H. Indeed this correlation has been amply documented for twentieth-century populations,[23] even in a socialist economy.[24] However once H reaches H_{max}, additional nutrient intake does not lead to further growth, and the correlation between H and Υ ceases to hold true.

By considering the change in stature over time ΔH, H_{min} drops out of consideration.[25] Let the integral in eq. 1.4 be designated by Φ. Then, in the absence of significant in- or out-migration which might affect H_{min} and h, the change in the mean height of a population becomes:

$$\Delta H = H_2 - H_1 = (H_{min} + \Phi_2) - (H_{min} + \Phi_1) = \Phi_2 - \Phi_1. \quad (1.5)$$

One should note, however, that the relationship between food consumption and real income in eq. 1.1 is in terms of monetary units. Yet in eq. 1.3 the relationship between height and food consumption is specified in terms of another attribute of the food consumed, namely its caloric and protein content. Because the price of calories and of proteins varies depending on the food through which they are consumed, the

---

[22] $g(\Upsilon, Z, T, W, t) = h(C(F(\Upsilon, Z, T)), R(F(\Upsilon, Z, T)), W, t)$. Note that the simplifying assumption is made that there is no interaction between genetic attributes and the function g. However, it is probable that at any given time the marginal propensity to grow in response to a change in nutritional intake is not equal across all members of the society. To the extent that g varies with genetics, it does matter who in the society experiences the change in income. The analysis should be acceptable nonetheless as a first approximation as long as the change in income is randomly distributed with respect to the marginal propensity of the population to grow.

[23] Steckel, "Height and Per Capita Income"; Henk Jan Brinkman, J. W. Drukker, and Brigitte Slot, "Height and Income: A New Method for the Estimation of Historical National Income Series," *Explorations in Economic History* 25 (1988): 227–264. In Glasgow there was a positive correlation between children's height and living space, itself a function of income. T. Christopher Smout, *A Century of the Scottish People, 1830–1950* (London: Collins, 1986), p. 126.

[24] János Nemeskéri, Attila Juhász, and Balázs Szabady, "Az 1973. évi sorköteles fiatalok testi fejlettsége," *Demográfia* 20 (1977): 208–281; idem, *A 18 Éves Sorköteles Fiatalok Fejlettsége Biologiai, Egészségi Állapota*, A Központi Statisztikai Hivatal Népességtudományi Kutató Intézetének és a Magyar Tudományos Akadémia Demográfiai Bizottságának Közleményei, No. 53, 1983, p. 81.

[25] As long as the time period analyzed is not extended to thousands of years, because then H_{min} could change, and as long as heterosis, or hybrid vigor, remains insignificant.

relationship between H and Υ in eq. 1.4 cannot hold monotonically unless the vectors of ratios $(c_1/P_1, c_2/P_2, \ldots, c_n/P_n)$ and $(r_1/P_1, r_2/P_2, \ldots, r_n/P_n)$ are both constant. In other words, if the relative price of calories, or of proteins, changes, then H ceases to be a simple function of real income even with Z, T, and W remaining constant. For each value of Υ there would not be a corresponding unique value of H. Hence the correlation between food consumption and real income should not be expected to have been perfect.[26]

Another factor which complicates this relationship is that human stature is a function of both calorie and protein consumption. It is the mix of caloric and protein intake which affects the body's ability to grow. In addition, price and income elasticities of demand for food, or certain food products, may vary among societies at any moment in time and within a society over time. Thus, increases in income do not always bring about equivalent increases in nutritional status. Such food items as coffee and tea may have had a high income elasticity of demand when they were introduced into the diet in prior centuries, but they did not contribute to nutritional status. Sugar provides calories but no protein. Other foods, such as potatoes, may provide calories and appease hunger, but do not by themselves provide sufficient protein for growth. Consuming alcoholic beverages may become inimical to growth, although if pure water is not readily available, wine might actually be a life-saving staple.

Furthermore, one should not disregard the cultural context of food consumption. Habits may develop that prevent the attainment of a level of nutritional status commensurate with actual real income. For instance, the consumption of white bread or of polished rice, instead of whole-wheat bread or unpolished rice, might increase with income, but might detract from the body's well-being. Insofar as cultural habits change gradually over time, significant lags could develop between income and nutritional status.

Improvements in medical technology, by protecting the body from diseases, can raise nutritional status sufficiently to have an effect on terminal height. Exposure to disease can also change through urbanization, internal migration, or improvements in the amenities of urban life. Moreover, in a nonmarket economy, P_{AOG} in eq. 1.1 may be undefined. Consequently, the structure of food consumption may change discontinuously once P_{AOG} becomes finite through market integration. Com-

[26] Meat consumption, for instance, does correlate positively with income per capita, but there are some outliers. In countries in which low population densities enable a large animal stock to be maintained, meat consumption might be higher than anticipated on the basis of per capita income.

mercialization and economic development might also lead to the introduction of new products, which could be perceived as substitutes for some food items. This in turn may lead to shifts in the demand for food as well as to changes in the elasticities of the demand for food independent of any changes in income per capita.

Finally, one should note that income distribution is a significant determinant of the mean height of a population because human growth is probably not a linear function of nutritional status.[27] Although this relationship has not been investigated, the marginal product of nutrients is likely to depend on the initial level of nutrition.[28] Another aspect of this question is the fact that as income increases, "consumers will spend a decreasing fraction of their food budget on pure nourishment," and spend a larger fraction on satisfying their palates.[29] Thus, if a certain amount of purchasing power were to be taken away from a high-income family, its child's nutrient consumption might decline only slightly. In contrast, increasing the income of a low-income family by the same amount might increase the nutrient consumption of its children sufficiently to make a considerable difference in their stature. Thus the mean height of a population might increase with a more equal distribution of income even if the average income were to remain unchanged.

These caveats indicate clearly that the analysis of changes in the stature of a population cannot be reduced to a mechanical exercise, particularly at this stage of the research program. There is not a one-to-one correspondence between income and nutritional status, and one must carefully analyze economic changes before assessing their interaction with the biological aspects of human growth. Each episodic change in the height of a population should be investigated in detail by determining which of the variables in eq. 1.4 was most likely to have caused it.

Height and Demographic Processes

The present section develops the notion that nutritional status is an important determinant of demographic rates (Figure 1.1). Because a rise in nutritional status raises birth rates and lowers death rates while at the same time increasing the mean stature of a population, one should ex-

[27] Steckel, "Height and Per Capita Income."

[28] An increase of 400 calories in the diet of an individual may double the amount of protein available for growth, if protein had been previously converted into calories to meet the body's metabolic needs. Yet a decrease of 400 calories in the diet of a child with adequate nutritional intake might have no appreciable effect at all on his stature.

[29] Eugen Silberberg, "Nutrition and the Demand for Tastes," *Journal of Political Economy* 93 (1985): 881–900.

Figure 1.1. The Effect of Nutrition on Population Growth in a Non-Contraceptive Pre-industrial Population

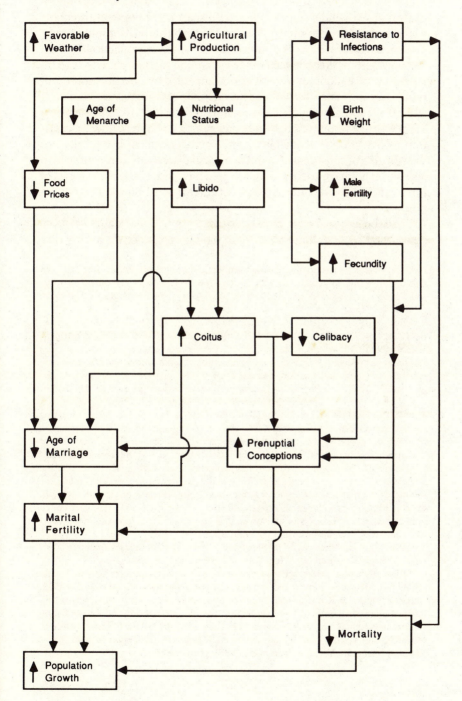

pect a positive correlation to exist between changes in the rate of population growth and changes in the mean stature in a non-contraceptive, pre-industrial population. In order to establish this relationship it is important to explore the role of nutrition in human reproduction.

An important link between nutrition and population growth is fertility.[30] European famines were often accompanied by a decline in conceptions because malnourished women ovulate less frequently or not at all.[31] If the initial weight of a woman is sufficiently low, a loss of even 15 percent of body weight suffices to induce amenorrhea, i.e., a cessation of ovulation.[32] Many eighteenth-century women, living "close to the margins of subsistence"[33] and in a harsh disease environment, which also laid claim to nutrients, might indeed have lacked the critical level of body fat needed for uninterrupted maintenance of reproductive function.

That the age at menarche is sensitive to nutritional status has been established beyond doubt by modern biological research.[34] In America,

[30] The increase in fertility in the early twentieth century in northeastern Italy has been linked to the elimination of dietary deficiencies. Massimo Livi-Bacci, "Fertility, Nutrition, and Pellagra: Italy during the Vital Revolution," *Journal of Interdisciplinary History* 16 (1986): 431–454.

[31] Emmanuel Le Roy Ladurie, "L'aménorrhee de famine (XVIIᵉ–XXᵉ siècles)," *Annales E.S.C.* 24 (1969): 1589–1601; Rose E. Frisch, "Population, Food Intake and Fertility," *Science* 199 (1978): 22–30; idem, "Nutrition, Fatness and Fertility: The Effect of Food Intake on Reproductive Ability," in W. Henry Mosley, ed., *Nutrition and Human Reproduction* (New York and London: Plenum Press, 1978), pp. 91–122; Ansley J. Coale, "History of the Human Population," *Scientific American* 231 (September 1974): 40–51.

[32] Rose E. Frisch, "Population, Nutrition and Fecundity," in Jacques Dupâquier, ed., *Malthus Past and Present* (London: Academic Press, 1983). James Trussell has argued that the statistical evidence presented by Frisch and her colleagues is insufficient to establish a relationship between body weight and female reproductive ability. He did not claim to "invalidate [the] hypothesis, but [to] establish clearly that more careful testing is needed." James Trussell, "Menarche and Fatness: Reexamination of the Critical Body Composition Hypothesis," *Science* 200 (June 1978): 1506–1509. In her response Frisch disputes the validity of the criticism and argues that the weight of evidence is on her side. Rose E. Frisch, "Reply to James Trussell," *Science* 200 (June 1978): 1509–1513. She cites her 24 publications exploring this issue and asserts that Trussell's critique "contains many incorrect statements, both historical and statistical. . . ."

[33] Peter Mathias, "Preface," in R. Max Hartwell, ed., *The Causes of the Industrial Revolution in England* (London and New York: Methuen, 1967), p. vii.

[34] Physical exertion delays menarche insofar as it lays claim to nutrients. Rose E. Frisch, "Body Fat, Menarche, Fitness and Fertility," *Human Reproduction* 2 (1987): 521–533; Theodor Feigelman, Rose E. Frisch, Maureen MacBurney, Isaac Schiff, and Douglas Wilmore, "Sexual Maturation in Third and Fourth Decades, after Nutritional Rehabilitation by Enteral Feeding," *Journal of Pediatrics* 111 (1987): 620–623; Rose E. Frisch, "Fatness, Menarche and Fertility," in Sharon Golub, ed., *Menarche: The Transition from Girl to Woman* (Lexington, MA: Heath and Co., 1983), pp. 5–20.

for instance, well-nourished girls experience menarche two years earlier than undernourished ones. The age at menarche has declined by about three years during the course of the last century, primarily because of improvements in nutritional status. In the middle of the nineteenth century the average age at menarche in Europe was about 16, but it is about 13 in the developed countries of today. The age at menarche has been found to vary negatively with socioeconomic status: middle- and upper-class girls experience menarche earlier than do lower-class girls.[35]

Despite the acceptance of the notion that the age at menarche depends on nutritional status, some demographers have nonetheless argued that this does not necessarily mean that nutrition affected fertility and hence population growth. In pre-industrial societies births generally took place in marriage, and the time elapsed between the age at menarche and the age at marriage was on the order of nine years.[36] Consequently, the two variables must have been unrelated, and even if menarche itself was sensitive to nutrition, marital fertility could not have been. According to one demographer, "Age at menarche signals the beginning of potential childbearing, but actual reproduction starts at marriage. The mean age at marriage is almost always higher than the mean age of menarche. . . . In populations where the mean age at marriage is near 20 or higher, one can hardly expect a fertility effect from nutritional variations in age of menarche."[37] Consequently, even if improvements in nutrition would have induced a fall in the age at menarche in historical populations, because marriage was so delayed, the age at first birth would not have been affected by the rise in nutritional status.

However, this line of reasoning has now been shown to be incorrect.[38] A strong positive correlation has been found between the age at

---

[35] Frisch, "Population, Food Intake and Fertility," p. 24.

[36] John Hajnal, "European Marriage Patterns in Perspective," in David V. Glass and David E. C. Eversley, eds., *Population in History: Essays in Historical Demography* (London: E. Arnold, 1965); E. Anthony Wrigley and Roger S. Schofield, "English Population History from Family Reconstitution: Summary Results, 1600–1799," *Population Studies* 37 (1983): 157–184.

[37] John Bongaarts, "Does Malnutrition Affect Fecundity? A Summary of the Evidence," *Science* 208 (1980): 564–569. This position was recently reiterated: "With marriage so late, . . . [the] age of menarche . . . would have had little effect on fertility. . . . Only in populations in which marriage is closely tied to menarche is it conceivable that nutrition could significantly influence overall fertility through a fall in age at menarche." Jane Menken, James Trussell, and Susan Cotts Watkins, "The Nutrition Fertility Link: An Evaluation of the Evidence," *Journal of Interdisciplinary History* 11 (1981): 425–441; Susan Cotts Watkins and Etienne van de Walle, "Nutrition, Mortality, and Population Size: Malthus's Court of Last Resort," *Journal of Interdisciplinary History* 14 (1983): 205–226.

[38] John Komlos, "The Age at Menarche in Vienna: The Relationship between Nutrition and Fertility," *Historical Methods* 22 (1989), forthcoming.

menarche and the age at first birth among lower-class Viennese women born in the late nineteenth century, even though the two events were separated from one another by seven years. The lower the age at which the women reached menarche, the younger they were at their first pregnancy. Because a rise in nutritional status would lower the age at which the girls reach menarche, it would also lower the age at first birth and therefore affect the population growth rate in a non-contraceptive society.

Judged by the rise in prenuptial pregnancies throughout eighteenth-century Europe,[39] which subsequently often led to marriage, one might suppose that conceptions determined the age at marriage in pre-industrial societies at least as much as the other way around.[40] If the age at first conception were an increasing function of the age at menarche, as the Viennese evidence indicates, then the secular rise in prenuptial pregnancies, the decline in the age of first marriage, and the rise in illegitimate births could all have been nutrition-related, rather than exogenous developments.[41]

The mean menarcheal age was 15.5 in Oslo in the 1860s.[42] If one allows up to two years of postmenarcheal subfecundity,[43] then many women must have been unable to conceive until age 18. Since postmen-

---

[39] E. Anthony Wrigley and Roger S. Schofield, *The Population History of England, 1541–1871: A Reconstruction* (Cambridge, MA: Harvard University Press, 1981), p. 254; Michael W. Flinn, *The European Demographic System, 1500–1820* (Baltimore: The Johns Hopkins University Press, 1981), p. 26.

[40] Wrigley and Schofield, "English Population History."

[41] Peter Laslett, "Age at Menarche in Europe since the Eighteenth Century," *Journal of Interdisciplinary History* 2 (1971): 221–236; James M. Tanner, "Trend towards Earlier Menarche in London, Oslo, Copenhagen, The Netherlands, and Hungary," *Nature* (London) 243 (1973): 95–96; Edward Shorter, "L'âge des premières règles en France, 1750–1950," *Annales E.S.C.* 36 (1981): 495–511; G. Wyshak and Rose E. Frisch, "Evidence for a Secular Trend in Age of Menarche," *New England Journal of Medicine* 306 (1982): 1033–1035.

[42] However, about 20 percent of the girls reached menarche at 17 or above. J. E. Brudevoll, K. Liestol, and L. Walloe, "Menarcheal Age in Oslo during the Last 140 Years," *Annals of Human Biology* 6 (1979): 407–416; A. Ducros and P. Pasquet, "Evolution de l'âge d'apparition des premières règles (ménarche) en France," *Biométrie Humaine* 13 (1978): 35–43; E. Manniche, "Age at Menarche: Nicolai Edvard Ravn's Data on 3385 Women in Mid-19th Century Denmark," *Annals of Human Biology* 10 (1983): 79–82. In nineteenth-century Germany the age at menarche was about 16. Arthur E. Imhof, "Unsere Lebensuhr- Phasenverschiebungen im Verlaufe der Neuzeit," in Peter Borscheid and Hans J. Teuteberg, eds., *Ehe, Liebe, Tod. Zum Wandel der Familie, der Geschlechts- und Generationsbeziehungen in der Neuzeit* (Münster: F. Coppenrath, 1983), pp. 170–198.

[43] Rose E. Frisch, "Demographic Implications of the Biological Determinants of Female Fecundity," *Social Biology* 22 (1975): 17–22.

archeal sterility itself is also sensitive to nutrition, better nutrition could have led to shorter intervals of sterility among adolescents and thereby to a larger number of prenuptial pregnancies even with the frequency of intercourse unchanged. This could have contributed to a fall in the age at first marriage, because the decision to marry must often have been linked to conception. Thus the entry of some women into the marriage market might have depended on the age at which they reached menarche. Such a relationship exists today "even when the gap between menarche and marriage is a decade," for social as well as biological reasons.[44] The decline in age at menarche could thus have had an effect on age at marriage.

Recent research has shown that the age at menarche also influences fecundity by affecting the number of ovulatory cycles long after the onset of menses.[45] This is important because it means that nutritional experience early in life can affect the frequency of ovulation, and therefore the probability of conception throughout the reproductive span.

Another factor that contributes to the rise of the marriage rate is a fall in food prices. Ronald Lee found that the effect of wheat prices on nuptiality was strongly negative in England from the sixteenth to the nineteenth centuries: "41 percent of the short-run timing of marriages could be associated with variation in scarcity or plenty. . . . a doubling of wheat prices in one year led to a permanent loss . . . of 22 percent of the normal annual number of marriages."[46] In France, too, conceptions

[44] "Pubertal hormones lead to early development of secondary sexual characteristics which are attractive to males, providing early opportunity for intercourse"; and because "peers provide encouragement for early intercourse to the woman with early menarche." In addition, "increased release of sex hormones leads to increased libido, and consequently to early intercourse. Those women with early puberty are more fecund than women with later puberty, leading to earlier births for a given exposure to the risk of pregnancy." J. Richard Udry and R. L. Cliquet, "A Cross-Cultural Examination of the Relationship between Ages at Menarche, Marriage, and First Birth," *Demography* 19 (1982): 53–63.

[45] In one study girls who reached menarche prior to age 12 experienced ovulatory menstrual cycles 50 percent of the time within one year after menarche, while girls who reached it above age 13 did not experience ovulatory menstrual cycles 50 percent of the time until 4.5 years after menarche. The former group, weighing 6 kilograms more than the latter group, was experiencing 100 percent ovulatory cycles 5.5 years after reaching menarche, whereas the latter group was even then still experiencing only 50 percent ovulatory cycles. Dan Apter and Vihko Reijo, "Early Menarche, a Risk Factor for Breast Cancer, Indicates Early Onset of Ovulatory Cycles," *Journal of Clinical Endocrinology and Metabolism* 57 (1983): 82–86. Another study found that girls experienced ovulation only 45 percent of the time even 3 or 4 years after menarche. M. G. Metcalf, D. S. Skidmore, G. F. Lowry, and J. A. Mackenzie, "Incidence of Ovulation in the Years after the Menarche," *Journal of Endocrinology* 97 (1983): 213–219.

[46] As quoted in Roger S. Schofield, "The Impact of Scarcity and Plenty on Population Change in England, 1541–1871," *Journal of Interdisciplinary History* 14 (1983): 265–291;

were low when the price of wheat was high. Favorable economic conditions also meant that the number of beggars fell. This must have affected the rate of celibacy, because beggars were not generally considered suitable mates.[47] In sum, lower food prices induced more people to marry and at younger ages.

The fertility rate is also influenced by male physiology. "Good nutrition certainly plays a helpful role in the continuous production of sperm cells. A diet well balanced in proteins, fats, carbohydrates, vitamins, and minerals is essential" not only to sperm count but also to its volume and quality.[48] Moreover, there are nutritional thresholds below which sexual desire diminishes greatly, or even ceases.[49] Hence a change in nutritional circumstances could influence the sex drive, and therefore influence the rate of intercourse, prenuptial pregnancies, and the desire to marry[50] (Figure 1.1).

In addition to influencing the birth rate and the marriage rate, nutritional status also affects the death rate, because nutritional status tends to influence the body's ability to fight many diseases.[51] Childhood nu-

---

Jean Meuvret, "Les crises de subsistances et la démographie de la France d'Ancien Régime," *Population* 4 (1946): 643–650.

[47] Peter Lindert and Jeffrey Williamson, "Reinterpreting Britain's Social Tables, 1688–1913," *Explorations in Economic History* 20 (1983): 94–109.

[48] Vitamins E, A, and C are also important. Richard D. Amelar, Lawrence Dubin, and Patrick C. Walsh, *Male Infertility* (Philadelphia: W. B. Saunders and Co., 1977), p. 82; Ancel Keys *et al.*, *The Biology of Human Starvation* (Minneapolis: The University of Minnesota Press, 1950), Vol 1, p. 762; Harvey H. Feder, "Essentials of Steroid Structure, Nomenclature, Reactions, Biosynthesis, and Measurements," in Norman T. Adler, ed., *Neuroendocrinology of Reproduction, Physiology and Behavior* (New York and London: Plenum Press, 1981), pp. 19–64.

[49] Roger S. Schofield suggests that there was a relationship between sexual activity and nutrition in "Impact of Scarcity and Plenty," p. 283; Herbert Moller, "Voice Change in Human Biological Development," *Journal of Interdisciplinary History* 16 (1985): 239–253.

[50] The relationship between nutrition and sexual activity has been extensively studied in animal populations. The results indicate that there is a relationship between sexual activity and nutrition, but that their interaction is by no means simple. "For instance, prenatally [nutritionally] stressed animals showed a significant reduction in the cumulative percent ejaculating. . . ." Reuben W. Rhees and Donovan E. Fleming, "Effect of Malnutrition, Maternal Stress, or ACTH Injections during Pregnancy on Sexual Behavior of Male Offspring," *Physiology and Behavior* 27 (1981): 879–882. In another experiment, however, rats subjected to levels of undernutrition that caused them to weigh 20 percent below normal showed no effects on onset of puberty. Stefan Hansen, Knut Larsson, Sven Carlsson, and Patrick Sourander, "The Development of Sexual Behavior in the Rat: Role of Preadult Nutrition and Environmental Conditions," *Developmental Psychobiology* 11 (1978): 51–61.

[51] Thomas McKeown and R. G. Record, "Reasons for the Decline in Mortality in England and Wales during the Nineteenth Century," *Population Studies* 16 (1962): 94–122.

trition affects health well into adulthood.[52] Experiments in contemporary underdeveloped societies "provide evidence that nutrition and mortality are linked in populations in which malnourishment is chronic."[53] There is widespread agreement that "the links between undernutrition and infection among the poor of today's third world are socially and demographically significant." At least nine major fatal diseases are sensitive to nutrition, and another seven are somewhat sensitive,[54] partly because there is a relationship between protein intake and antibody production.[55] The duration and severity of the disease encounters are also affected.

Infant mortality is particularly responsive to nutrition.[56] Diarrhea and

In the nineteenth century mortality among the poor was "dramatically higher" than among the upper classes.

[52] George Clarke et al., "Poor Growth prior to Early Childhood: Decreased Health and Life-Span in the Adult," *American Journal of Physical Anthropology* 70 (1986): 145–160.

[53] Nevin Scrimshaw, "The Value of Contemporary Food and Nutrition Studies for Historians," *Journal of Interdisciplinary History* 14 (1983): 529–534; Watkins and van de Walle, "Nutrition, Mortality," pp. 205–226. However, nutrition alone does not account for the incidence of various diseases at any moment in time, or for the differential trend of the various diseases over time. A. J. Mercer, "Relative Trends in Mortality from Related Respiratory and Airborne Infectious Diseases," *Population Studies* (1986): 129–145; Ann Carmichael, "Infection, Hidden Hunger, and History," *Journal of Interdisciplinary History* 14 (1983): 245–265; Carl Mosk, "Nutrition and Fertility: A Review Essay," *Historical Methods* 14 (1981): 43–46.

[54] Some of the major diseases sensitive to nutrition include measles, diarrhea, tuberculosis, respiratory infections, intestinal parasites, cholera, and leprosy; diseases somewhat sensitive include typhus, diphtheria, influenza, and worm infections. Bellagio Conferees, "The Relationship of Nutrition, Disease, and Social Conditions: A Graphical Presentation," *Journal of Interdisciplinary History* 14 (1983): 503–506; John Post, "Climatic Variability and the European Mortality Wave of the Early 1740's," *Journal of Interdisciplinary History* 15 (1984): 1–30; Carl E. Taylor, "Synergy among Mass Infections, Famines, and Poverty," *Journal of Interdisciplinary History* 14 (1983): 483–501.

[55] Keys et al., *Biology*, Vol. 1, pp. 1003–1005. Proteins are important for the production of antibodies since antibodies are themselves proteins and consequently "must ultimately be derived from dietary protein." Of course the relationship between antibody production and protein intake is complex. In addition, the body temperature of malnourished men is below normal, which might be favorable for the penetration of infectious organisms into the blood.

[56] The relationship between nutritional status and child mortality was especially dramatic, and illustrates the importance of looking not only at famines but also at hidden hunger. "Perinatal mortality was reduced most when the diet of mothers was supplemented particularly with iron and folic acid." Carl E. Taylor, "Synergy," p. 486. According to at least one contemporary estimate, "Malnutrition was a factor in the deaths of at least 10 million children." Alan Berg, *Malnourished People: A Policy View* (Washington, DC: Publications Department, The World Bank, 1981), p. 2, as cited by Gretel Pelto and Pertti Pelto, "Diet and Delocalization: Dietary Changes since 1750," *Journal of Interdisciplinary*

pneumonia within the first two years of life, a major killer in pre-industrial societies, has been linked to protein-calorie malnutrition.[57] Maternal nutrition is also important, since it affects the child's birth weight, which in turn correlates negatively with infant mortality. Poorly nourished women may produce less breast milk and less nutritious milk than well-nourished women. In addition, during a subsistence crisis people are more likely to consume contaminated food. Children are quite vulnerable even prior to birth; even today malnutrition accounts for a large percentage of premature births.[58]

Yet Ronald Lee found the relationship between grain prices and the crude death rate to have been weak in England between the sixteenth and the nineteenth centuries: "only 16 percent of the short-run variation in mortality was associated with price changes. . . . Except when prices were extremely high, the net . . . effect over five years was essentially zero."[59] This result, however, does not do irreparable harm to the notion that nutrition and mortality were related. During the seventeenth century, the relationship must have been much stronger than appears from the above statement. Of the 17 major peaks in wheat prices between the middle of the sixteenth and the middle of the eighteenth century only two (in 1697 and 1713) were not followed either by a mortality crisis or by a substantial decline in the number of conceptions.[60] Increases in grain prices have also been linked to higher death rates in London among middle and older age groups. The death rate from epidemics, for example, was strongly influenced by increases in the price of grain.[61]

Recently, Robert Fogel has shown that Lee's work is misleading, because wheat prices do not correlate perfectly with food prices and be-

---

History 14 (1983): 507–528. Field studies in India demonstrated the importance of nutrition to perinatal mortality. Fogel, "Nutrition and the Decline in Mortality since 1700."

[57] Stephen J. Kunitz, "Speculations on the European Mortality Decline," *Economic History Review* 36 (1983): 349–364.

[58] Maurice Aymard, "Toward the History of Nutrition: Some Methodological Remarks," in Robert Forster and Orest Ranum, eds., *Food and Drink in History* (Baltimore: The Johns Hopkins University Press, 1979), pp. 1–16.

[59] Cited in Schofield, "Impact of Scarcity and Plenty."

[60] Wrigley and Schofield define a crisis as either a 10 percent increase in the crude death rate or a 10 percent reduction in the crude birth rate. W. G. Hoskins, "Harvest Fluctuations and English Economic History, 1480–1619," in W. E. Minchinton, ed., *Essays in Agrarian History* (The British Agricultural Society; Newton Abbot, England: David and Charks, 1968), vol. 1, pp. 93–116; idem, "Harvest Fluctuations and English Economic History, 1620–1759," *Agricultural History Review* 16 (1968): 15–31; Leslie Clarkson, *Death, Disease and Famine in Pre-Industrial England* (New York: St. Martin's Press, 1976); Wrigley and Schofield, *Population History*.

[61] Patrick R. Galloway, "Annual Variations in Deaths by Age, Deaths by Cause, Prices, and Weather in London, 1670 to 1830," *Population Studies* 39 (1985): 487–505.

cause the price of wheat is not a perfect proxy for the quantity of output. The price elasticity of demand for wheat plays an important role in translating fluctuations in output into fluctuations in price.[62] Fogel calculates that the standard deviation of wheat prices was about four times as high as that of wheat output, and asserts furthermore that "with a highly inelastic demand for grains, even a weak relationship between mortality and wheat prices . . . would be consistent with the [notion] . . . that mortality rose even when the declines in the supply of food were quite small." He concludes that Lee's "finding does not eliminate *chronic* malnutrition as a significant component of pre-industrial mortality rates."[63]

The fact that the life expectancy of British peers and Italian jesuits was not well above average for pre-industrial societies tends to cast doubt on the nutrition-mortality link.[64] One explanation for this anomaly is that the nutritional intake of the European upper classes has been overestimated, if not for adults, then at least for infants. Evidence presented in the next chapter points in this direction, since the stature of the sons of the lower nobility increased between 1735 and 1755, implying that they had not reached their genetic maximum in the 1730s.[65] If the upper-class children were fed by ordinary servants and received the same diet early in life as the rest of the population, then their nutritional status in their youth might not have been much better than the average.[66] Their abundant consumption as adults would not have compensated fully for their earlier experience and would not have necessarily increased their life expectancy at birth beyond that of the population at large.

The correspondence between Maria Theresia and her daughter, Marie Antoinette, gives an indication that the biological advantage of the upper classes has been idealized. The frequent mention of diarrhea, upset stomachs, vomiting, fainting, fever, bouts with colds, and the flu shows that they did not always consume a balanced diet and that the food they consumed was probably not always pure. They also kept religious fast days, thereby voluntarily reducing their nutritional intake. In addition,

---

[62] Moreover, in a pre-industrial setting, the existence of a self-sufficient peasantry, not linked to commercial agriculture, implies that the supply of marketed output might change dramatically in response to even a small change in total product.

[63] Fogel, "Nutrition and the Decline in Mortality since 1700," pp. 484, 495.

[64] Massimo Livi-Bacci, "The Nutrition-Mortality Link in Past Times: A Comment," *Journal of Interdisciplinary History* 14 (1983): 293–298.

[65] John Komlos, "Patterns of Children's Growth in East-Central Europe in the Eighteenth Century," *Annals of Human Biology* 13 (1986): 33–48. It is by no means clear whether any population today has reached its genetic potential.

[66] Clarke *et al.*, "Poor Growth."

they were often bled, even during pregnancy, and were given purgatives which must have been inimical to their health.[67]

Moreover, custom and the lack of knowledge of nutrition might also have deterred the nobility from consuming a balanced diet, and excessive consumption of alcoholic beverages might have been unhealthy.[68] Thus evidence on the life expectancy of British peers need not be viewed as contradicting the notion that the crude death rate was nutrition-sensitive. After all, the life expectancy of peers increased faster than that of the population at large during the second half of the eighteenth century, and that could have been nutrition-related.[69]

I have argued in this section that nutritional status is an important component of those factors whose interaction affects biological processes and ultimately the rate of growth of a population.[70] Because human stature is a proxy for nutritional status, changes in height should correlate positively with changes in the rate of population growth. This notion is in keeping with "extensive clinical and epidemiological studies . . . that height at given ages, weight at given ages, and weight-for-height . . . are effective predictors of the risk of morbidity and mortality."[71]

The link between biological and demographic processes provides support for the notion already espoused by a previous generation of scholars that "the slow growth of the human population before the eighteenth century was due mainly to lack of food, and the rapid increase from that time resulted largely from improved nutrition."[72] The

[67] Paul Christoph, *Maria Theresia und Marie Antoinette: Ihr geheimer Briefwechsel* (Vienna: Cesam Verlag, 1952), pp. 22, 36, 46, 77, 88, 89, 126, 135, 148, 171, 179, 193, 197, 212, 227, 234, 268, 282, 309, 313.

[68] Fogel, "Nutrition and the Decline in Mortality since 1700." An increase in income among the Japanese had the tendency to increase the consumption of polished rice, nutritionally inferior to unpolished rice. Susan Hanley, "A High Standard of Living in Nineteenth-Century Japan: Fact or Fantasy?" *Journal of Economic History* 43 (1983): 183–192.

[69] Thomas H. Hollingsworth, "The Demography of the British Peerage," Supplement to *Population Studies* 18 (1964–65): 1–108.

[70] In the nineteenth century mortality among the lower classes was much higher than among the upper or middle classes. Benjamin Ward Richardson, *The Health of Nations: A Review of the Works of Edwin Chadwick, with a Biographical Dissertation* (London: Longmans, Green and Co., 1887), Vol. 2, p. 99; Lemuel Shattuck, *Report of the Sanitary Commission of Massachusetts* (1850; reprint, Cambridge, MA: Harvard University Press, 1948).

[71] Fogel, "Biomedical Approaches."

[72] Thomas McKeown, "Food, Infection, and Population," *Journal of Interdisciplinary History* 14 (1983): 227–247; idem, *The Modern Rise of Population* (New York: Academic Press, 1976). Of course the relationship between nutrition and population growth in preindustrial societies could have differed greatly from that in the contemporary third world, because changes in medical technology have altered the incidence of infections, and be-

contention that the availability of food was a crucial component of pre-industrial economic development will be developed further in the chapters that follow.

Height and the Standard of Living

Insofar as height may be used as a proxy for the nutritional status of a population, and food consumption correlates with real income per family, the analysis of the secular trend in stature may well provide a new perspective on the relationship between the standard of living and the industrial revolution. Food consumption in the eighteenth century was clearly a large, though by the nineteenth century perhaps a slowly declining, share of the populations' total consumption bundle. Prior to the nineteenth century typically close to three-fourths of personal income was spent on alimentation.[73] Consequently, in such an economy nutritional status can be considered as a fairly good, and perhaps the best available, indicator of the material well-being of a population.[74] Until recently efforts to measure the variations in food consumption systematically have been limited to the exploration of food inventories in probate records, food allowances in institutions such as hospitals, workhouses, and the military, and food purchases of prison authorities, abbeys, or noble households.[75] Given the paucity of data having any bearing on the well-being of pre-industrial populations, a new source that promises to illuminate changes in the standard of living should be welcomed.

The relationship between industrialization and the standard of living

---

cause the variance in the availability of nutrients must have diminished even in those societies in which the average food intake remains precariously near minimum requirements.

[73] Fernand Braudel, *Civilization and Capitalism 15th–18th Century* (New York: Harper and Row, 1981), vol. 1, *The Structures of Everyday Life: The Limits of the Possible*, p. 138. In some societies approximately half of the daily expenditures was used to purchase grain. In 1600, 78 percent of a bricklayer's family income was spent on food. In 1800, the share was 73 percent. Wilhelm Abel, *Agrarkrisen und Agrarkonjunktur: Eine Geschichte der Land- und Ernährungswirtschaft Mitteleuropas seit dem hohen Mittelalter* (1935; reprint, Hamburg and Berlin: Paul Parey, 1966), p. 241. Between the thirteenth and nineteenth centuries, according to Joan Thirsk, 80 percent of household expenditures was on food. "The Horticultural Revolution: A Cautionary Note on Prices," *Journal of Interdisciplinary History* 14 (1983): 299–302; Cipolla, *Before the Industrial Revolution*, p. 30.

[74] Roderick Floud, "Measuring the Transformation of the European Economies: Income, Health, and Welfare," unpublished manuscript, Department of History, University of London, 1984.

[75] Sarah McMahon, "Provisions Laid Up for the Family: Toward a History of Diet in New England, 1650–1850," *Historical Methods* 14 (1981): 4–21; Fogel, "Biomedical Approaches," p. 8.

has been a controversial issue ever since contemporaries argued about the problem. The debate has been particularly heated in regard to the British experience: the "optimists" have argued forcefully that the industrial revolution caused a rise in real income and an increase in well-being; the "pessimists," however, while conceding the long-run benefits of industrialization, have argued with equal fervor that at least for one or two generations it lowered workers' living standards.[76] So conceived, the controversy is difficult to resolve,[77] not only because of the shortage of vital economic indicators but also because of the fact that the psychological disamenities accompanying industrialization cannot easily be weighed against the greater income earned in the industrial sector compared with that which would have been obtained in its absence or diminution.[78] A recent effort to address this issue uses infant mortality as a proxy measure of disamenities associated with urban life.[79] Even if, for the sake of simplicity, one were to disregard the psychological component of this question, there are at least two distinct problems to be re-

[76] A weak pessimist might be one who argues that living standards stagnated during the first half of the nineteenth century. Joel Mokyr, "Is There Still Life in the Pessimist Case? Consumption during the Industrial Revolution, 1790–1850," *Journal of Economic History* 48 (1988): 69–92. For a negative view of the effect of the industrial revolution on the standard of living in Britain, see, for instance, J. L. Hammond, "The Industrial Revolution and Discontent," *Economic History Review*, 1st ser., 2 (1930): 215–228; for a positive view, see R. M. Hartwell, "The Rising Standard of Living in England, 1800–1850," *Economic History Review*, 2d ser., 13 (1961): 397–416; for a discussion on the subject, see E. J. Hobsbawm and R. M. Hartwell, "The Standard of Living during the Industrial Revolution: A Discussion," *Economic History Review*, 2d ser., 16 (1963–64): 119–146. For a good, recent summary of the debate, see John Rule, *The Labouring Classes in Early Industrial England, 1750–1850* (London and New York: Longman, 1986).

[77] Gertrude Himmelfarb, *The Idea of Poverty* (New York: Knopf, 1983), p. 136.

[78] P.R.G. Layard and A. A. Walters, *Microeconomic Theory* (New York: McGraw-Hill, 1975), p. 146; Alan S. Milward and S. B. Saul, *The Economic Development of Continental Europe, 1780–1870* (London: George Allen & Unwin, 1973), p. 21. For a recent controversy over various indexes of well-being, see Michael W. Flinn, "English Workers' Living Standards during the Industrial Revolution: A Comment," *Economic History Review* 37 (1984): 88–92; Peter Lindert and Jeffrey Williamson, "English Workers' Living Standards during the Industrial Revolution: A New Look," *Economic History Review*, 2nd ser., 36 (1983): 1–25; N.F.R. Crafts, "English Workers' Real Wages during the Industrial Revolution: Some Remaining Problems," *Journal of Economic History* 45 (1985): 139–144; L. D. Schwarz, "The Standard of Living in the Long Run: London, 1700–1860," *Economic History Review*, 2d ser., 38 (1985): 24–41.

[79] Jeffrey G. Williamson, "Was the Industrial Revolution Worth It? Disamenities and Death in 19th Century British Towns," *Explorations in Economic History* 19 (1982): 221–245; idem, "Urban Disamenities, Dark Satanic Mills, and the British Standard of Living Debate," *Journal of Economic History* 44 (1981): 75–84. The weakness in Williamson's approach lies in the assumption that the marginal worker was fully compensated for the greater incidence of infant mortality in cities than in rural areas.

solved: "What actually happened to the standard of living, and what might have happened in the absence of industrialization."[80]

The pessimistic view grew out of an intellectual tradition dating back to Malthus and Ricardo, and was reinforced by the young Engels's indictment of the English middle class in a tract that transmitted to future generations the idea of the misery of one segment of the population.[81] An important aspect of Engels's argument was that "the poverty of the proletariat was quantitatively different from the poverty of the old poor—the preindustrial poor were less impoverished, less hardworking, less miserable."[82] This view was later adopted by Marx and his followers, who, in the words of an eminent historian, "saw the pauperization of the workers as the baptismal act of capitalism."[83]

The German historian Wilhelm Abel pointed out that this view is untenable because it ignores the prevalence of pre-industrial rural pov-

[80] G. N. von Tunzelmann, "The Standard of Living Debate and Optimal Economic Growth," in Joel Mokyr, ed., *The Economics of the Industrial Revolution* (Totowa, NJ: Rowman & Allanheld, 1985), pp. 207–226.

[81] See W. O. Henderson and W. H. Chaloner's introduction to Friedrich Engels, *The Condition of the Working Class in England*, trans. W. O. Henderson and W. H. Chaloner (New York: Oxford University Press, 1958).

[82] Himmelfarb, *Idea of Poverty*, p. 285. Engels's eyewitness account of the misery of a segment of British workers should not be considered as either fully accurate, or as representative of the whole working population (Engels, *Condition of the Working Class*, p. xxv). He documented the suffering of the very poor and attributed their plight to the rise of the factory system only because he was not cognizant of their condition prior to the onset of the industrial revolution (pp. xxx–4). Pre-industrial children, he thought, "grew up in idyllic simplicity." Weavers "earned enough to live on" and "enjoyed a comfortable and peaceful existence" (pp. 9, 11). As he made clear, the culprit was "the expansion of trade . . . [that] led to severe competition which had an adverse effect on the standard of living of the workers" (p. 9). "Industry alone," he asserted time and again, "has been responsible for . . . their wretched conditions" (p. 64). "Every new machine brings with it unemployment, want and suffering" (p. 156). True, Engels admitted that one segment of the workers was better off than the ones whose conditions he documented, but he did not attempt to write about their lives; nor did he think about the income distribution of the workers (pp. 90–92). Consequently, his analysis is not to be taken as a reflection of conditions of a cross section of the labor force; however, Marx accepted it as such and incorporated it into his immiseration doctrine. Engels did mention several times that industrialization increased wages (pp. 24, 29), but he must have meant nominal instead of real wages (p. 91), for he insisted that the pre-industrial artisan's "standard of life was much better than that of the factory worker of today [1845]" (p. 10). He also accepted the notion that urban workers were better off than the rural proletariat, whose lot had deteriorated even more since the beginning of the industrial revolution (p. 295). Does it not follow from this that the living standards of factory workers would have declined to the level of rural laborers had industrialization not proceeded as it did?

[83] Emmanuel Le Roy Ladurie, *The Territory of the Historian* (Chicago: The University of Chicago Press, 1979), p. 13.

erty.[84] Abel devoted a monograph to describing the process of immiseration, which, with long-run fluctuations, stretched into the nineteenth century.[85] Consequently, the poverty of the working class in England and elsewhere should be viewed in a comparative perspective rather than analyzed in isolation. T. S. Ashton put it this way: "Some writers have compared the semi-skilled operatives in the new factories with the small farmers and craftsmen of an earlier generation. If comparison is to be made at all, it must be with the squatters of the countryside and the paupers of the towns, from whose ragged ranks the factory workers were largely drawn."[86] What, in other words, would have happened to the landless segment of the population and their descendants in the nineteenth century without industrialization? Bruno Hildebrand, for instance, argued that the poverty of the working class in Germany during the first half of the nineteenth century was due to the low level of industrialization.[87] Emmanuel Le Roy Ladurie suggests that immiseration in Europe "seems to have been above all the distinctive mark of a blocked society, one incapable of raising productivity and hence the living standards of the lower classes."[88]

To be convinced of the intensity of rural poverty prior to the spread of industrialization one might consider the case of Bohemia during the subsistence crisis of 1771.[89] An eyewitness description of it is appalling. Sickness and hunger were prevalent, malnutrition was endemic, and the quality of clothing was poor. Children started strenuous work early in life. Peasants were uprooted, since they had to look for work in areas where the harvest came early. The people were dirty. Adults were sleeping on straw, and children were lying naked near the fire. People were eating grass and bread made of weeds and flour dust. Some peasants worked as long as factory workers did, spinning and weaving flax day and night.[90] This description is, of course, no more representative of the

---

[84] Abel, *Agrarkrisen*, p. 241.

[85] Wilhelm Abel, *Massenarmut und Hungerkrisen im vorindustriellen Europa* (Hamburg and Berlin: Paul Parey, 1974), p. 14.

[86] T. S. Ashton, *An Economic History of England. The 18th Century* (1955; reprint, London: Methuen & Co, 1972), p. 234.

[87] He cited the case of Oberhessen and the unindustrialized areas of Prussia. Bruno Hildebrand, *Die Nationalökonomie der Gegenwart und Zukunft* (Jena: G. Fischer, 1922), as cited by Abel, *Agrarkrisen*, p. 227.

[88] Le Roy Ladurie, *Territory of the Historian*, p. 13.

[89] The bad harvests of 1771/72 brought about disastrous death rates in Sweden as well; E. F. Heckscher, "Swedish Population Trends before the Industrial Revolution," *Economic History Review*, 2d ser., 2 (1950): 266–277; P.G.M. Dickson, *Finance and Government under Maria Theresia, 1740–1780* (Oxford: Clarendon Press, 1987), p. 14.

[90] Franz Mayer, "Die volkswirtschaftliche Zustände Böhmens um den Jahren 1770," *Mittheilungen des Vereins für Geschichte der Deutschen in Böhmen* (1876): 125–149. The observer pointed out the inadequate nourishment in Prachiner County by stating that the

condition of the rural population than the sketches we have from Engels's pen are representative of the condition of the industrial worker. Yet it does put the situation of the nineteenth-century working class in a different light: their pre-industrial counterparts often did not fare any better if the harvest failed or if their land allotments shrank due to frequent subdivisions.[91]

Scholars have concluded from the rise in cereal prices in the second half of the eighteenth century that the European standard of living must have fallen.[92] "We see how great a slice had been taken out of wages, and how much the purchasing power of the classes lowest in the social scale had dwindled. It was a process of impoverishment, against which they stood helpless."[93] This makes sense. It is difficult to imagine that the majority of the population would have been able to protect itself against such violent and unanticipated price increases. In France prices rose by "65 percent in the last two decades of the *ancien régime* as opposed to a 22 percent rise in wages."[94] Contemporaries, too, noted that wages did not keep pace with prices.[95] Yet even with that, the case for a deteriorating standard of living is not proven. Calculations of real wages are, even for England, notoriously controversial. According to one suggestion, during the century after 1750 they either remained the same or increased by 150 percent.[96]

For the Austrian case, even such rough estimates are not available.

---

people were short, p. 131. One might also consider the pre-industrial children of Tyrol who journeyed at an early age to Germany in search of work. Otto Uhlig, *Die Schwabenkinder aus Tirol und Vorarlberg* (Innsbruck: Universitätsverlag Wagner, 1978). I am indebted to Professor Roman Sandgruber for bringing this citation to my attention.

[91] Heckscher, "Swedish Population Trends," p. 277.

[92] There is a high correlation among the price movements in different parts of Europe. Schwarz, "Standard of Living in the Long Run," p. 35.

[93] B. H. Slicher van Bath, *The Agrarian History of Western Europe, A.D. 500–1850*, trans. Olive Ordish (London: Edward Arnold, 1963), p. 226; Hans J. Teuteberg and Günter Wiegelmann, *Der Wandel der Nahrungsgewohnheiten unter dem Einfluss der Industrialisierung* (Göttingen: Vandenhoeck und Ruprecht, 1972), p. 64.

[94] Olwen H. Hufton, "Social Conflict and the Grain Supply in Eighteenth-Century France," *Journal of Interdisciplinary History* 14 (1983): 303–331; idem, *The Poor of Eighteenth Century France, 1750–1789* (Oxford: Clarendon Press, 1974), p. 16. The American experience has been less controversial. A recent regional study has argued, for instance, that real hourly wages stagnated during the first two decades of the nineteenth century, but then increased by two-thirds by 1860. Donald Adams, "The Standard of Living during American Industrialization: Evidence from the Brandywine Region, 1800–1860," *Journal of Economic History* 42 (1982): 903–917.

[95] Abel, *Agrarkrisen*, p. 188. In Italy, too, living conditions of the rural population are said to have worsened at the end of the eighteenth century. Livi-Bacci, "Fertility, Nutrition, and Pellagra."

[96] G. N. von Tunzelmann, "Trends in Real Wages, 1750–1850, Revisited," *Economic History Review*, 2d ser., 32 (1979): 33–49.

Data on the price of grain are inconclusive because wage data are less reliable and scarcer than price data and because daily wages cannot be accurately converted into annual income. In addition, wage data are typically limited to a few occupations.[97] They are also suspect because according to many records they often remained constant over decades, in some occupations for a century, in spite of great volatility in commodity prices.[98] Did length of the workday, intensity of effort, and incidence of under- or unemployment or compensations in kind vary sufficiently to offset the fluctuations in real wages obtained by deflating the nominal wage series with the price of grain? There was, furthermore, considerable geographic variation in prices and rents, since some regions maintained their isolation from the world market into the nineteenth century.[99] Furthermore, annual harvest data are available only for the latter third of the nineteenth century, and consequently earlier grain output can be estimated for only a limited number of years.[100]

Thus the problems associated with the construction of real wage series on either the regional or the national level seem insurmountable despite recent noteworthy efforts.[101] This difficulty is in part caused by the poor quality or absence of data, the ambiguity of weights attached to the various component series, and the many assumptions that must be made to overcome the limitations of the evidence. How well different segments of the population fared during these changing economic circumstances is, of course, another complicating factor. This is particularly true because a large share of the population in the eastern half of the Habsburg Monarchy, as in many other parts of Europe, was isolated from market forces reflected in cereal prices at the beginning of our period. Since this segment of the peasantry produced for its own consumption, fluctuations in grain prices did not affect them. East European peasants engaged in subsistence agriculture did not benefit from high agricultural prices because they had little or no surplus grain to offer for sale even in the eighteenth century. Nor did they benefit from

[97] "We should remind ourselves," notes Joan Thirsk, "of the crude measures used to establish the standard of living index." Thirsk, "Horticultural Revolution," pp. 299–302.

[98] Alfred Přibram, *Materialien zur Geschichte der Preise und Löhne in Österreich* (Vienna: Ueberreuters, 1938).

[99] On the estate of Teschen in Bohemia, for instance, the price of wheat did not rise permanently until 1800; Arthur Salz, *Geschichte der Böhmischen Industrie in der Neuzeit* (München and Leipzig: Duncker und Humblot, 1913), p. 539.

[100] Roman Sandgruber, *Österreichische Agrarstatistik 1750–1918* (Vienna: Verlag für Geschichte und Politik, 1978); Gyula Benda, *Statisztikai adatok a Magyar mezőgazdaság történetéhez, 1767–1867* (Budapest: Központi Statisztikai Hivatal, 1973).

[101] Jeffrey Williamson, *Did British Capitalism Breed Inequality?* (Boston: Allen & Unwin, 1985).

low prices because they had no money with which they might have bought food to supplement their regular diet. The real income of this class of peasant was, therefore, determined essentially by the size of the land under its control, weather conditions, and family size. Had the peasants received a money wage for the work they rendered to the lord, one would expect that it would have risen as the price of cereals rose. Instead of money, the peasants received the use of land for the work they provided. The land allotment was fixed either by custom or long-term contract, and was legally not allowed to fluctuate countercyclically with cereal prices. Hence the subsistence peasant's standard of living did not depend on the price of grain. For these reasons the use of real-wage indexes as indicators of the well-being of European societies in the eighteenth century is fraught with uncertainties.

Consequently, an examination of the evidence of the cycling of human stature is bound to enhance our knowledge of the dynamics of economic and population growth in a period when reliable statistics on these variables were not collected. Because there is no one-to-one-correspondence between stature and real income in eq. 1.4, one must allow for the possibility that the biological well-being of a population might diverge from conventional measures of well-being such as per capita aggregate output.[102] Height is a measure of the biological well-being of the human organism in the sense that it correlates positively with life expectancy and fecundity and negatively with morbidity. It is also an indicator of the general level of public health. The biological standard of living is a component of the standard of living as conventionally conceived, but is only one dimension of it. Hence one need not insist that the biological standard of living always correlate perfectly with real wages, the index most often used as a proxy for the standard of living.

Although anthropometric indexes are not perfect proxies for the material well-being of a population it is important that this line of research continue. Conventional approaches to the standard-of-living debate using real-wage indexes have not achieved any consensus on the major issue: the initial effect of economic development on the welfare of the labor force.[103] Because of the persistence of the debate, an independent line of inquiry should be welcomed.[104]

The purpose of this chapter has been to provide the main outlines of

[102] Komlos, "Height and Weight of West Point Cadets."

[103] A recent article refers to this debate as having become "confused . . . arcane . . . of ever greater statistical complexity." Floud and Wachter, "Poverty and Physical Stature," p. 422.

[104] Lindert and Williamson, "English Workers' Living Standards"; Mokyr, "Is There Still Life in the Pessimist Case?"

the theory of anthropometric history: how human stature (or nutritional status) is related to population growth, to real income and hence to the well-being of a society. Because human stature is related not only to real income but also to the relative price of food, its fluctuations enable one to gain new insights into economic processes. This is particularly valuable for that segment of the peasantry that was not integrated into the market, because conventional price indexes do not relate to them. Moreover, human stature is also related to vital demographic rates, and its cross-sectional and longitudinal analysis should provide information on demographic processes at a time when direct evidence on these variables is scarce. Finally, human stature is indicative of the health of a population, and of the prevalence of certain diseases.

We therefore turn to the history of human stature in eighteenth-century East-Central Europe in the hope of gaining a better understanding of economic development in general, of the industrial and demographic revolutions in particular, and at the same time perhaps even of expanding our knowledge of the effect of economic change on a society's well-being. These are questions that have hitherto posed a formidable puzzle for the empirical historian. The opportunities opened through the exploration of anthropometric evidence are extremely useful, because during the eighteenth century, when industrialization once again accelerated, data were recorded on the height of soldiers at a time when other statistics were either not collected or were of poor quality. The nutritional status of the population, and, more importantly, changes in its level of nourishment can be inferred from data on the height of the soldiers.

Data and Method

Data have been collected on the height of military recruits born in five provinces of the Habsburg Monarchy: Galicia, Moravia, Bohemia, Lower Austria, and Hungary.[105] The records list the birth date, height, year of measurement, birth place, and occupation of the recruits. This part of the sample consists of about 150,000 records. Bohemia is divided into two regions in order to explore the possibly diverging nutritional experience of those born in the four mountainous counties in the

[105] Hungarian data exclude men born in Croatia and Transylvania. Moravian data do not include Silesian soldiers. Kriegsarchiv, Vienna, Musterlisten and Standestabellen, 1770–1819, thereafter Grundbücher, 1820–1867. Data for the late nineteenth century are in Stellungslisten 1867–1913, Kriegsarchiv, Vienna, and in Hadtörténeti Levéltár, Budapest, "Kiegészitő parancsnokságok és bevonulási központok, állitási lajstromok," 1867–1945.

northern part of the province (Bunzlau, Leitmeritz, Bidschow, and Königgratz). These counties were agriculturally less productive than the rest of the province,[106] and their inhabitants were therefore the first to seek employment outside of the agricultural sector. The two groups will be referred to as the four counties and the twelve counties of Bohemia. The Hungarian population, too, is analyzed at the county level. Urban-born recruits are distinguished from those born in rural areas.[107]

The sample is clearly biased by the imposition of the minimum height requirement for recruits. Hence the left tail of the population's height distribution is underrepresented and the sample mean $\bar{x}$ is an unreliable measure of central tendency. The problem is complicated by changes in the minimum height requirement over time (Appendix A). The extent of truncation can, however, be estimated by assuming that the underlying height distribution of the population was normal.[108] The divergence of the sample distribution from normality can be attributed to the bias caused by the minimum height requirement for recruits, and the sample average $\bar{x}$ can be corrected. Because observations in the left tail of the sample distribution are missing, we can imagine increasing the size of the sample N by N' until the sample distribution resembles a normal one. (N' is the estimate of the number of men rejected by the recruiting officer because of their stunted growth.) $N'/(N+N')$ is the shortfall in the sample distribution. With the use of regression analysis, the sample distribution can be corrected by comparing it to a known normal distribution. From the divergence of the two distributions the shortfall can be calculated, and $\hat{x}$, an estimate of the underlying population's mean height, can be obtained.[109] This procedure, known as the

[106] In 1793 the average per capita output of wheat and rye was four Lower Austrian metzen. In contrast, in the four industrial counties it was only about three metzen.

[107] Urban-born West European immigrants to the United States during the late eighteenth century were 2.5 cm shorter than their rural-born counterparts. The heights of native-born urban residents diverged about as much from those of rural residents during the American Revolutionary War; this was not true at the mid-eighteenth century, perhaps because of the low level of urbanization at the time. The divergence between urban and rural heights surfaced once again during the Civil War. Sokoloff and Villaflor, "Early Achievement of Modern Stature," pp. 463, 466, 471; Margo and Steckel, "Heights of Native Born Northern Whites," p. 169.

[108] Quetelet first noticed that the height distribution of a population was normal. Austria, *Militär-Statistisches Jahrbuch für das Jahr 1871* (Vienna: k. k. Hof- und Staatsdruckerei, 1873), vol. 1, p. 48. Yet there are examples of height distributions that deviate slightly from normality. J. L. Boldsen and D. Kronberg, "The Distribution of Stature among Danish Conscripts in 1852–56," *Annals of Human Biology* 11 (1984): 555–565.

[109] "The Quantile Bend estimator corrects the raw distribution of heights for the apparent undercount of short persons by matching the upper part of the distribution, . . . to an appropriate normal distribution of heights." Floud and Wachter, "Poverty and Physical

quantile bend estimate (QBE), was undertaken by decades, in each age category, and also by skill level for cells in which there were at least 150 observations.[110] However, with experience it became clear that actually many more observations were needed to obtain stable estimates of the population height, $\hat{x}$, from the sample height distributions. Generally, the larger the sample size was, the more robust was the estimate of the mean height of the population, because then outliers posed less of a threat to accuracy. The larger the sample, the smaller is the likelihood that the addition of a small number of observations would significantly change $\hat{x}$. Because the estimating procedure can still be somewhat unstable, it is quite important that one corroborate the results of the QBE estimates by other means.

Confidence in the QBE estimates can be increased in a number of ways. The sample frequency distributions should themselves be inspected visually (Appendix B). If the frequency distributions shift in the same direction as do the values of $\hat{x}$ obtained from the QBE program, then the two results support one another. Another reason one should examine the distributions is that one can identify those sample cells that are obviously not normal and for which the QBE program is likely to produce biased results.

In addition, one can consider the trend in the proportion of very tall recruits in that part of the sample unaffected by changes in the minimum height requirement. Because in the Habsburg army the truncation point was always to the left of 63 Austrian inches (165.8 cm),[111] the composition of recruits above this height was not changed by lowering the minimum height requirement to 62 or 61 Austrian inches. Define Θ as the number of soldiers above 175 cm divided by the number of soldiers above 165.8 cm. Θ is then the proportion of very tall recruits in the part of the sample that was not affected by changes in the truncation point. It has the advantage of being quite sensitive to slight shifts in the sample height distribution.

Yet another measure worth exploring is the mean of the part of the

Stature," p. 434. The method is described in detail by Kenneth W. Wachter and James Trussell, "Estimating Historical Heights," *Journal of the American Statistical Association* 77 (1982): 279–293; Kenneth W. Wachter, "Graphical Estimation of Military Heights," *Historical Methods* 14 (1981): 279–303; Trussell and Wachter, "Covariates of Historical Heights."

[110] I am grateful to Professor Roderick Floud and Annabel Gregory of the University of London for providing me with a copy of the QBE computer program to estimate and correct this source of bias.

[111] One Austrian inch was 2.63 cm. The original data, given in Austrian inches, have been converted into cm. The frequency distributions, however, have been kept in the original units in order not to mask possible tendencies toward heaping.

sample above 165.8 cm ($\bar{x}'$). This again is the part of the sample that is not affected by changes in the minimum height requirement; therefore the trend in the mean of this part of the sample should move in the same direction as the true population mean and should therefore correlate with the other indexes mentioned above. Although $\bar{x}'$ is not a useful indicator of the population's mean height, computer simulations have shown that it is an unbiased indicator of the changes in the mean height.[112] This approach is inappropriate, and should be bypassed for samples for which this critical criterion does not hold. Only if $\bar{x}$, $\hat{x}$, $\bar{x}'$, and Θ evince similar trends can one be reassured that the results are not due to some statistical artifact, but truly reflect secular changes in nutritional status.

Because the minimum height requirement changed frequently and was never rigidly enforced, and because the details of the recruitment procedure were never clearly defined, it is reassuring that non-truncated data do exist on the stature of children born in the Habsburg Monarchy.[113] A sample of about 25,000 records was collected on children and adolescents. If the results of these two kinds of samples corroborate one another one gains more confidence in the estimated trends for human stature in East-Central Europe.

The eighteenth-century Habsburg army consisted partly of volunteers and partly of draftees, but the draft procedure depended on local authorities and consequently remains somewhat obscure. Thus eighteenth-century soldiers are not perfectly representative of the male population at large. This is less of a problem for soldiers drafted after 1827, when selection was mandated to take place by lot. Therefore a comparison of the eighteenth-century data with that of the early-nineteenth-century samples should indicate if there were major biases in the earlier sample.[114] Such an analysis can be done only on Hungarian data, because these alone were extant for the birth cohorts of the early 1800s, the first to be recruited under the 1827 law. This comparison indicates

---

[112] I appreciate the help of Joe Salemi and Phil Sidel of the Social Science Computer Research Institute of the University of Pittsburgh for undertaking this exercise.

[113] Vienna, Austria, Kriegsarchiv: Standestabellen, Erziehungshäuser, Musterlisten, Faszikel 3925, 3926, 3927; Josephinisches Waisenhaus, Faszikel 3922; Theresianische Militärakademie, Faszikel 434.

[114] Austria, *Militär-Statistisches Jahrbuch für das Jahr 1871*, vol. 1, p. 48. Universal conscription was introduced in 1868, and thereafter data exist for the whole population of males between the ages of 19 and 21, even for those who were not accepted into the military. These data show that there was not much difference between the height of the soldiers and that of the population. The height of Lower Austrian draftees of 1870 deviated only 0.7 cm from the height of the whole population measured.

that the change in recruiting practices does not appear to have made a substantial difference in the stature estimates (Tables 2.1 and B.1). Therefore the recruiting procedure appears not to have had a significant impact on the estimated height of the population.

If a bias does exist for the eighteenth-century sample, then it is in a downward direction, insofar as the soldiers must have been drawn from the lower half of the income distribution. Throughout the eighteenth century recruits came overwhelmingly from the landless and unmarried segment of the rural population.[115] Thus the cycling of stature in our sample until the nineteenth century reflects changes in the nutritional circumstances of the landless peasantry and the poorer elements among the town dwellers. Because these men were more vulnerable to economic changes than those higher up on the income or wealth distribution, they probably experienced larger fluctuations in nutritional intake than the population at large, with the exception of the sick, the old, and the paupers. As long as one keeps these attributes of the sample in mind, one's understanding of the impact of economic processes on the nutritional status of the population will not be hindered. With these preliminary observations, the exploration of the anthropometric history of the Habsburg Monarchy can begin.

[115] Officers are not part of the sample because their height was seldom recorded.

CHAPTER 2

HUMAN STATURE IN
EAST-CENTRAL EUROPE:
THE EIGHTEENTH CENTURY

IF, AS HAS BEEN demonstrated in the previous chapter, human stature is indicative of a population's nutritional status, then analyzing its pattern cross-sectionally and longitudinally affords the researcher a fresh insight into the dynamics of economic development—in particular, the ways in which economic, demographic, and biological processes intertwined in this period. The argument is now advanced that the cycles in human height in East-Central Europe were intricately related to demographic developments, the process of industrialization, institutional change, commercialization, and the effect of weather conditions on agricultural production. (Unless otherwise noted, all references to stature at a particular time are to the stature of the cohorts born at that time.)

Height of Adult Soldiers

At the beginning of the century human stature was generally increasing in East-Central Europe; it reached an apex among the peasantry in the 1740s, and then declined for several decades. Although the downward trend was successfully halted, thereby averting a full-blown nutritional crisis, perhaps a century and a half elapsed before the stature of the population once again reached its eighteenth-century maximum.[1]

The evidence begins with recruits born in the 1730s. Thereafter nu-

---

[1] In Hungary, for instance, 21- and 22-year-old men are estimated to have been about 167 cm tall in the 1740s, a height they did not reach again until the beginning of the twentieth century (Table B.1, Appendix B).

55

tritional status must have been increasing, because the birth cohorts of the 1740s tended to be taller than the ones of the previous decade.[2] Both $\bar{x}$ and $\bar{x}'$, the mean of the sample after observations below 165.8 cm, the minimum height requirement at the time, were discarded, increased consistently[3] (Table 2.1 and Figure 2.1). The sample sizes for the 1730s birth cohort are not large enough to enable one to calculate $\hat{x}$ for all of the provinces, but for Moravian and Hungarian recruits $\hat{x}$ did increase considerably (Table 2.1 and Figure 2.2). The upward trend is confirmed by the shift to the right of the frequency distributions in the 1740s relative to the previous decade[4] (Figure B.1, Appendix B). With the truncation point held constant (at 165.8 cm), the share of tall recruits in the sample, Θ, also tended to increase in the 1740s in most cases (Table 2.2). Disaggregated on an annual basis, the upward trend in $\bar{x}'$ is most evident among the Hungarian soldiers, who are the most numerous in the sample (Figure 2.3). Finally, the results of regression analysis on that part of the sample above the minimum height requirement of 165.8 cm are also consistent with the above finding[5] (Table B.2). Additional evidence will be presented below that this pattern is not confined to the military sample: the stature of youth was also increasing at the time.

Hence, various indicators corroborate the notion that nutritional status was generally improving in the 1740s, although with different intensities in the various regions of the Monarchy. The height of the population ($\hat{x}$) in some provinces is estimated to have increased by as much as 2.5 cm (Table 2.1). While increases in stature of such magnitude within a decade are unusual, they are within the biologically feasible range.[6] However, because the height estimates $\hat{x}$ calculated by the QBE program are subject to a certain amount of error, the magnitude of the

[2] The same pattern is obtained if the sample is divided into skilled and unskilled recruits (Tables B.3 and B.4).

[3] While $\bar{x}$, of course, is a biased estimate of the population's mean height, if the minimum height requirement remains unchanged, as it did in these decades, then $\partial\bar{x}/\partial t$ nonetheless should have the same sign as the trend in the true height of the population.

[4] With the possible exception of the frequency distribution of the recruits born in the 12 counties of Bohemia (Figure B.1).

[5] The intercept of the regression is clearly biased upward because the sample has been censored. The estimated time trend, however, is unaffected by restricting the sample to recruits taller than 165.8 cm. The coefficient of the time trend does not reflect accurately the true change in average height of the population from decade to decade, only its direction.

[6] Italian heights, for instance, increased as much in the 1920s as did the height of recruits in several European states in the 1950s or 1960s. Roderick Floud, "Wirtschaftliche und soziale Einflüsse auf die Körpergrössen von Europäern seit 1750," *Jahrbuch für Wirtschaftsgeschichte* (1985): 93–118.

Table 2.1 Height of Adult[a] Soldiers by Year and Place of Birth, 1730-1859

Place of Birth

Decade of Birth	Moravia				Bohemia				Hungary				Galicia				Lower Austria			
	N	x̄	x̂	x̄'	N	x̄	x̂	x̄'	N	x̄	x̂	x̄'	N	x̄	x̂	x̄'	N	x̄	x̂	x̄'
1730	433	169.9	166.4	170.7	332	170.5	165.4	171.0	746	170.3	167.2	171.3					66	170.1		170.6
1740	1283	172.0	168.8	172.4	1095	170.8	165.5	171.3	2620	171.4	169.8	172.1	150	172.0	170.8	172.0	199	170.8	169.1	170.9
1750	2724	170.7	166.0	171.2	2149	169.7	164.3	170.5	9044	170.7	166.3	171.5	812	171.5	168.8	171.8	544	169.8	164.6	170.9
1760	1752	170.2	166.8	171.3	2244	168.7	164.6	170.3	6589	170.3	166.5	171.1	903	170.6	166.0	171.6	782	167.9	165.6	171.1
1770	1032	167.3	163.0	170.5	3203	167.4	162.6	170.4	3780	167.8	164.1	170.1	1552	168.6	163.5	170.8	809	166.7	161.8	170.2
1780	2011	167.5	163.1	170.0	2983	166.6	161.7	170.1	5841	167.9	163.9	170.6	1334	168.2	163.3	170.0	1126	166.6	163.6	169.6
1790	612	167.9	164.6	171.4	1197	166.9	161.1	170.2	8760	167.2	163.0	170.6	543	169.0	b	170.9	1588	165.9	161.2	169.7
1800	38	165.8							428	166.6	164.7	169.9								
1810	171	165.5			215	165.7			375	166.6	165.5	170.1	242	164.3		169.2				
1820	70	166.7			630	165.1		170.7	269	166.6		170.4	708	165.5		169.6	162	166.1		
1830									113	166.8		170.5	109	165.2		168.9				
1840					374	166.6														
1850	177	166.0	165.2														345	167.2	162.9	

Source: Kriegsarchiv, Vienna, Austria, Musterlisten, Standestabellen, and Grundbücher.
a Between the ages of 23 and 45; the sample is decomposed into skilled and unskilled recruits in Tables B.3 and B.4.
b An outlier generated by the unusual sample distribution (see Figure B.1).
N = Number of observations in the sample.
x̄ = Raw mean of the sample.
x̂ = Estimated height of the population using the QBE procedure (see text).
x̄' = Mean of the sample after observations below 165.8 cm, the minimum height requirement, was eliminated.

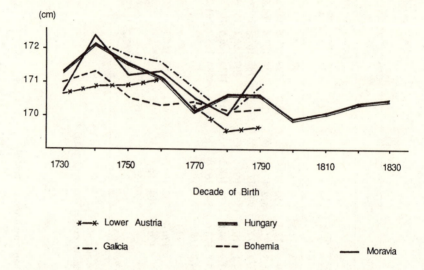

Figure 2.1. Estimated Trend of Adult Height ($\bar{x}'$) by Place and Decade of Birth (Restricted Sample), 1730–1839

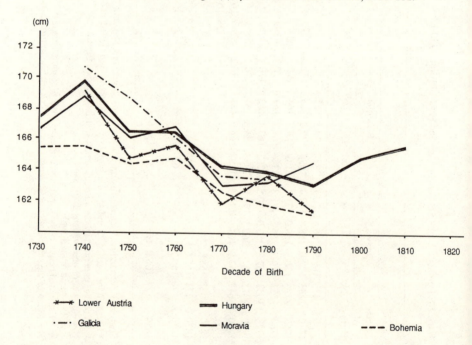

Figure 2.2. Estimated Adult Height ($\hat{x}$) by Place and Decade of Birth, 1730–1819

Table 2.2 The Share of Adult[a] Recruits in the Restricted[b] Sample Taller Than 175 cm Truncation Point Held Constant

Decade of Birth	Place of Birth					
	Galicia	Bohemia (4 counties)	Bohemia (12 counties)	Hungary	Lower Austria	Moravia
1730		12.8	13.7	13.4	8.2	11.2
1740	12.9	17.2	12.9	18.4	9.4	21.6
1750	14.5	7.7	13.3	14.7	12.7	12.6
1760	15.0	6.6	13.9	12.4	12.5	13.0
1770	12.2	6.1	13.0	9.2	10.2	12.4
1780	8.6	5.7	9.0	10.1	5.7	8.3
1790	9.0	4.4	19.3	11.0	5.7	16.7
1800				5.8		
1810				5.5		
1820				10.5		
1830				9.8		

Source: See Table 2.1

[a] Between the ages of 23 and 45.

[b] The shares are calculated in the part of the sample above 165.8 cm.

change from one decade to another is not emphasized in this study. Rather, the trend in stature is seen as being of more consequence.[7]

The increase in human stature seems to have been a quite widespread phenomenon. It was by no means confined to East-Central Europe, but is evident among contemporary French,[8] Swedish,[9] and American[10] sol-

[7] Due to the uncertainties associated with censored military samples the trend can be taken seriously only if the various indicators are consistent with one another, and if the *x̄*s are not fluctuating erratically from one estimate to another.

[8] The stature of French soldiers increased between 1716 and 1740 by about 4 cm. André Corvisier, *L'armée française de la fin du XVIIᵉ siècle au ministère de Choiseul. Le Soldat* (Paris: Presses Universitaires de France, 1964), vol. 2, p. 643. Although the author thought that the increase in stature must have been caused by a selection bias, he presented no evidence that the minimum height requirement was actually increased during this time.

[9] This pattern refers to calculations adjusted for shortfall; Lars G. Sandberg and Richard H. Steckel, "Heights and Economic History: The Swedish Case," *Annals of Human Biology* 14 (1987): 101–110; idem, "Overpopulation and Malnutrition Rediscovered: Hard Times in 19th Century Sweden," *Explorations in Economic History* 25 (1988): 1–19; idem, "Soldier, Soldier, What Made You Grow So Tall? A Study of Height, Health, and Nutrition in Sweden, 1720–1881," *Economy and History* 23 (1980): 91–105.

[10] Robert W. Fogel, "Physical Growth as a Measure of the Economic Well-Being of Populations: The Eighteenth and Nineteenth Centuries," in Frank Falkner and James M.

Figure 2.3. Estimated Trend of Adult Height ($\bar{x}'$) by Place and Year of Birth (Restricted Sample), 1734–1797

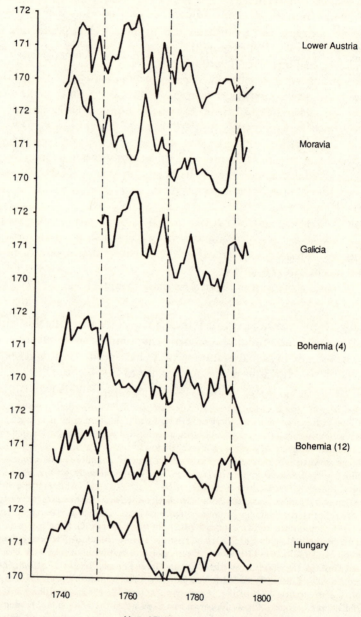

Year of Birth

diers as well. The Swedish population, for instance, is estimated to have become 1.4 cm taller between the 1720s and the 1740s. By the 1720s the height of the British colonists in North America was well above the stature of the European populations from which they originated.[11] This implies that their nutritional status must have been increasing substantially during the preceding decades.

The rise in nutritional status could have been brought about by an increase in food intake, by a decline in the claims on the nutrients due to a fall in the incidence of disease encounters, or to a combination of both factors (see equation 1.3). An amelioration in the disease environment is not likely to have been the major cause of the rise in nutritional status, because there is no evidence of a concerted effort to improve public health during the first half of the century.[12] Moreover, the trend in stature soon reversed, and it is improbable that the epidemiological environment would have improved only for a brief interval. In contrast, there is plenty of direct and indirect evidence to support the notion that both real income and food consumption were increasing in the Habsburg Monarchy as well as in other parts of Europe, because weather conditions, and hence harvests, were generally favorable during the early part of the century.

Sweden, for instance, enjoyed mild winters between 1721 and 1735.[13] In England warm weather was typical for the first four decades of the eighteenth century.[14] "The 'miserable seventeenth-century reality' [in France] was not entirely over until after 1730."[15] As a consequence of the favorable climate, harvests were good and grain prices were low throughout Europe.[16] In both England and France, the price of wheat

---

Tanner, eds., *Human Growth: a Comprehensive Treatise*, 2d ed. (New York and London: Plenum Press, 1986), vol. 3, pp. 263–282.

[11] A. Theodore Steegmann, Jr., and P. A. Haseley, "Stature Variation in the British American Colonies: French and Indian War Records, 1755–1763," *American Journal of Physical Anthropology* 75 (1988): 413–421.

[12] James C. Riley, *The Eighteenth-Century Campaign to Avoid Disease* (London: The Macmillan Press Ltd., 1987).

[13] Gustaf Utterström, "Climatic Fluctuations and Population Problems in Early Modern History," *Scandinavian Economic History Review* 3 (1955): 3–47.

[14] Gordon Manley, "Central England Temperatures: Monthly Means 1659 to 1973," *Quarterly Journal of the Royal Meteorological Society* 100 (1974): 389–405. The average temperature between 1700 and 1740 was 9.4 percent higher than between 1670 and 1699.

[15] Emmanuel Le Roy Ladurie, *The Territory of the Historian* (Chicago: The University of Chicago Press, 1979), p. 9; idem, *Times of Feast, Times of Famine: A History of Climate since the Year 1000* (Garden City, NY: Doubleday, 1971); Christian Desplat, "The Climate of Eighteenth-Century Béarn," *French History* 1 (1987): 27–48.

[16] Eric L. Jones, ed., *Agriculture and Economic Growth in England* (London: Methuen,

decreased by about thirty percent in the 1730s relative to the 1720s.[17] Favorable weather conditions raised agricultural productivity; that meant, in effect, that both per capita real income and per capita food intake increased.

For the American colonies there is direct evidence that the consumption of meat was increasing at this time.[18] In England per capita food intake in 1740 is estimated to have been about 50 percent greater than mid-seventeenth-century levels.[19] Menus of English institutions, too, indicate a rise in nutrient intake. In the case of the Habsburg Monarchy the hypothesis of a rise in per capita food consumption cannot be confirmed directly, as the first census of agriculture was not taken until 1789.[20] Yet information on the price of food and on the purchasing power of wages leads to the conclusion that food consumption must have been increasing there as well. In Vienna, the price of food relative to wages reached the lowest point of the century in the 1720s and 1730s (Table 2.3).

In sum, the absence of any anecdotal evidence that the disease environment was improving in Europe and America, only to deteriorate by mid-century, leads one to suppose that the cycling in human height was not likely to have been caused by epidemiological changes. In contrast, there is considerable evidence from wide-ranging sources that per capita food production rose. Food prices were low, real wages were high, the climate was favorable to agricultural production, and many contempo-

---

1967); Herman Freudenberger and Gaylord Cummins, "Health, Work, and Leisure before the Industrial Revolution," *Explorations in Economic History* 13 (1976): 1–12.

[17] An index of the price of consumables declined by 14 percent in the 1730s and by another 2 percent in the 1740s relative to the 1720s. Brian R. Mitchell and Phyllis Deane, *Abstract of British Historical Statistics* (Cambridge, England: Cambridge University Press, 1971), p. 486; James C. Riley, *The Seven Years War and the Old Regime in France: The Economic and Financial Toll* (Princeton: Princeton University Press, 1986), p. 10.

[18] Sarah McMahon, "Provisions Laid Up for the Family: Toward a History of Diet in New England, 1650–1850," *Historical Methods* 14 (1981): 4–21; probate records also show a considerable increase in the stock of amenities in American households, beginning in the second decade of the eighteenth century. Lois G. Carr and Lorena S. Walsh, "Inventories and the Analysis of Wealth and Consumption Patterns in St. Mary's County, Maryland, 1658–1777," *Historical Methods* 13 (1980): 81–104; Gloria L. Main and Jackson T. Main, "Economic Growth and the Standard of Living in Southern New England, 1640–1774," *Journal of Economic History* 48 (1988): 27–46.

[19] R. V. Jackson, "Growth and Deceleration in English Agriculture, 1660–1790," *Economic History Review*, 2d. ser., 38 (1985): 333–352; Carole Shammas, "The Eighteenth-Century English Diet and Economic Change," *Explorations in Economic History* 21 (1984): 254–269.

[20] Indeed, if information were available on agricultural production for the period, then studying the height of the population as a proxy for real income would be superfluous.

Table 2.3 Purchasing Power of a Day's Wages in Kilograms
of Bread in Vienna, 1700-1800

Decade	Bread (kg)	Decade	Bread (kg)
1700	4.4	1750	4.6
1710	3.8	1760	4.2
1720	4.9	1770	3.8
1730	5.3	1780	3.5
1740	4.0	1790	4.1

Source: Roman Sandgruber, <u>Die Anfänge der Konsum-
gesellschaft, Konsumgüterverbrauch, Lebensstandard und
Alltagskultur in Österreich im 18. und 19. Jahrhundert</u>
(Vienna: Verlag für Geschichte und Politik, 1982), p. 115.

rary reports indicated favorable harvests, particularly in the 1730s and
1740s. Thus the rise in nutritional status was most likely to have been
caused by a rise in food consumption. The disease environment must
have remained harsh but unchanging, and the increase in stature was
probably caused not by a fall in the claims on nutrients consumed but
by a rise in the intake of the nutrients themselves.

Because nutrition affects demographic events through a multitude of
interrelated ways (Figure 1.1), the rise in nutritional status resulted in
an acceleration in population growth[21] (Table 2.4). This was the beginning of the eighteenth-century demographic upswing characteristic of
most of Europe.[22] Although one cannot confirm directly that in the
Habsburg Monarchy the demographic revolution also started in the
1730s, because the first population census was not implemented until
1754, there is indirect evidence that there, too, population was growing
by mid-century.

[21] Nevin Scrimshaw, "The Value of Contemporary Food and Nutrition Studies for Historians," *Journal of Interdisciplinary History* 14 (1983): 529–534; Thomas McKeown, *The
Modern Rise of Population* (New York: Academic Press, 1976).

[22] The acceleration in the growth of the English population in the 1730s is explored in
detail in Chapter 5. See also E. Anthony Wrigley and Roger S. Schofield, *The Population
History of England, 1541–1871: A Reconstruction* (Cambridge, MA: Harvard University
Press, 1981); Colin McEvedy and Richard Jones, *Atlas of World Population History* (New
York: Penguin Books, 1978); Michael Anderson, *Population Change in North-Western Eu-
rope, 1750–1850* (London: Macmillan Education Ltd., 1988); for the similar pattern in
the Low Countries see Myron P. Gutmann, *Toward the Modern Economy: Early Industry in
Europe, 1500–1800* (New York: Alfred A. Knopf, 1988), pp. 135–141; for Russia see
Arcadius Kahan, *The Plow, the Hammer, and the Knout: An Economic History of Eighteenth-
Century Russia* (Chicago: The University of Chicago Press, 1985), p. 16.

Table 2.4 Population of the World, 1700-1800 (millions)

Year	Europe	Asia	Africa	America	World	Growth Rates (percent) Europe	Asia	Africa	America	World
1700	120	415	61	13	610					
1750	140	495		16	720	0.3	0.4		0.4	0.3
1800	180	625	70	24	900	0.5	0.5	0.1	0.8	0.4

Source: Colin McEvedy and Richard Jones, Atlas of World Population History (New York: Penguin Books, 1978).

According to the 1754 census, about a third of the population was under the age of sixteen[23] (Table 2.5). If the population had been stable, such a distribution could not have been obtained.[24] Model life tables indicate that only if the crude death rate had been about 44–50 would population have been stable.[25] This, however, is much higher than the actual rate, which was in the low 30s.[26] Given this level of mortality, and given the age structure of 1754, population growth rate was probably increasing and already reached 0.5 percent per annum.[27] The censuses taken thereafter confirm the notion that growth tended to accelerate and in some places even reached an annual rate of one percent (Table 2.6). In spite of the subsistence crisis of 1771/72, the population of the Czech lands rose from about 3 to 4.5 million, and that of the Austrian lands from 3.9 to 4.3 million, between 1754 and 1789.[28]

The change in age structure of the population in Bohemia and Mo-

[23] Note that newborns under one year of age might not have been counted. P.G.M. Dickson, *Finance and Government under Maria Theresia, 1740–1780* (Oxford: Clarendon Press, 1987), vol. 1, p. 443. In that case another 2–3 percent would have to be added to the share of the population under age 15 in order to compare these statistics with model life tables.

[24] Provided, that is, that the high share of children in the population was not caused by an unusual event, such as a sudden rise in mortality limited to the adult population.

[25] Ansley J. Coale and Paul Demeny, *Regional Model Life Tables and Stable Populations* (Princeton: Princeton University Press, 1966), pp. 122, 244, 464, 680. All four regional model life tables are consistent in this regard (mortality levels 1 or 2).

[26] Dickson, *Finance and Government*, vol. 1, p. 442.

[27] Coale and Demeny, *Regional Model Life Tables*, p. 470. This inference is drawn from Model East, mortality level 5. However, the other life tables have identical implications.

[28] Dickson, *Finance and Government*, vol. 1, pp. 33, 438. While there is some short-run variation in the census results, there can be no doubt that population growth was considerable during the second half of the century.

Table 2.5   Age Distribution of the Habsburg Population
Selected Provinces, 1754 - 1762 (percent)

	Age				
	1-15	15-20	20-40	40-50	50+
1754					
Bohemia	33.6	10.4	32.0	12.0	12.0
Moravia	35.8	10.4	33.1	10.3	10.4
Lower Austria	33.4	10.7	33.0	10.9	12.0
1762					
Bohemia	34.0	11.0	29.0	14.0	12.0
Moravia	36.3	10.3	30.9	11.8	10.6
Lower Austria	33.6	10.3	33.0	11.5	11.6

Sources: Henryk Großmann, Die Anfänge und
geschichtliche Entwicklung d. amtl. Statistik in
Österreich," Statistische Monatschrift (1916): 356; Alfred
Gürtler, Die Volkszählungen Maria Theresias und Josef II,
1753-1790 (Innsbruck: Wagner, 1909).

ravia between 1754 and 1762 is also consistent with the notion that
population growth accelerated, because the share of children in the population rose (Table 2.5). The English population underwent a similar
change in age structure as its growth rate increased (Table 2.7).

The above considerations pertain to the western half of the Monarchy.[29] In Hungary, the first full count of the population was not undertaken until 1787. Although historical demographers agree that its

[29] The above pattern is supported by statistics from the city of Vienna, with a population of 175,000 at mid-eighteenth century. Its population swelled to 231,000 by 1800
through in-migration. The crude death rate exceeded the crude birth rate in every decade,
but the difference was declining during the first half of the century and then increasing
again. The number of excess deaths declined from 2200 persons per annum in the 1710s
to a minimum of 58 persons per annum in the 1750s. This corroborates the notion that
the first half of the century was favorable to reproduction. For the first time in the century,
during the 1730s, the crude birth rate exceeded the crude death rate three times. The
hypothesis of an acceleration of population growth in the 1750s is also confirmed. There
were six consecutive years in the 1750s when the crude birth rate exceeded the crude death
rate. There were a few more such episodes in the 1760s, followed by a long hiatus. By
1800 the number of deaths exceeded the number of births by 4400 persons per annum.
G. A. Schimmer, "Die Bewegung der Bevölkerung in Wien seit dem Jahre 1710," Statistische Monatschrift 1 (1875): 119–133. According to Professor Roman Sandgruber of the
University of Linz this source has some statistical flaws, but they do not affect these
trends.

THE "AUSTRIAN" MODEL

Table 2.6 Population of the Habsburg Monarchy, Selected
Provinces, 1754-1827 (millions)

Year	Bohemia	Moravia	Lower Austria	Hungary[a]	Galicia[b]
1754	1.97	0.87	0.93		
1762	2.14	0.83	0.78		
1768	2.16				
1771	2.49				
1772	2.31				
1775	2.37	1.15			
1780	2.56	1.14			2.7
1784			0.99		3.1
1787				6.1[c]	
1789		1.26	1.27		
1790	2.87				
1800	3.04				
1804				6.9[c]	
1810	3.09				
1820	3.38				
1827	3.74				

Sources: Vincenz Göhlert, "Die Ergebnisse der in Österreich im vorigen Jahrhundert ausgeführten Volkszählungen im Vergleiche mit jenen der neueren Zeit," Sitzungsberichte der phil-hist. Klasse der kaiserlichen Akademie der Wissenschaften 14 (1855): 52-73; Henryk Großmann, "Die Anfänge und geschichtliche Entwicklung der amtl. Statistik in Österreich," Statistische Monatschrift (1916); Gusztáv Thirring, "Die Bevölkerung Ungarns zur Zeit Josephs II," Journal de la Société Hongroise de Statistique 2-3 (1938):160-181; idem, Az 1804. évi Népösszeirás (Budapest: Hornyánszky Viktor, 1936).

a Without Transylvania.
b Without Bukowina.
c Without the nobility; in 1787 there were about 0.4 million nobles.

population grew throughout the eighteenth century, estimates of its growth rate vary.[30] The important point is that Hungary, like the other lands of the Habsburg Monarchy, participated in the eighteenth-century demographic upswing characteristic of most of Europe.[31]

Population growth during the first half of the century evidently

[30] Zoltán Kováts, "A XVIII Századi Népességfejlödés Kérdéséhez," Agrártörténelmi Szemle 77 (1969): 218–225; Heimold Helczmanovski, "Austria-Hungary," in W. R. Lee, ed., European Demography and Economic Growth (New York: St. Martin's Press, 1979), pp.

Table 2.7 Age Distribution of the English Population,
1751 - 1766

	Age			
	0-14	15-24	25-54	60+
1751	32.9	17.5	41.4	8.2
1766	33.8	17.6	39.9	8.8

Source: Anthony Wrigley and Roger Schofield, The
Population History of England, 1541-1871: A
Reconstruction (Cambridge, MA: Harvard University
Press, 1981), p. 529.

meant that the birth cohorts of the 1750s began to encounter Malthusian limits. This can be inferred from the fact that, in contrast to developments of the 1740s, the stature of recruits evinced a downward trend
beginning with the 1750s (Figure 2.1). The decline in all indicators ($\bar{x}$,
$\hat{x}$, $\bar{x}'$, and Θ) is consistent[32] (Tables 2.1 and 2.2). In the 1750s $\hat{x}$ falls in
all of the samples and $\bar{x}'$ falls similarly, with but one exception[33] (Fig-
ures 2.1–2.3). The frequency distributions, too, shift visibly to the left[34]

27–78. According to one estimate Hungarian population (including Croatia and Transylvania) rose from about 6.2 million to 8.6 million between 1754 and 1787. Of this
increase, about 400,000 was due to immigration. Dickson, *Finance and Government*, vol.
1, p. 35. Even during the difficult times of the Napoleonic Wars the Hungarian population grew at a rate of 0.7 percent per annum (Table 2.6). In contrast, population growth
in Bohemia decelerated at the turn of the century. Between 1770 and 1814 the Viennese
population experienced excess deaths, as the declining living standards began to have an
effect on vital rates.

[31] Annual population growth between 1750 and 1800 in the Scandinavian countries
was as follows: Denmark, 0.3; Norway, 0.7; Sweden, 0.6; Finland, 1.3. E. F. Heckscher,
"Swedish Population Trends before the Industrial Revolution," *Economic History Review*,
2d ser., 2 (1950): 266–277.

[32] Declines in stature of several centimeters within a generation are not unique. The
stature of the male population in the United States declined by 3.5 cm within two decades
after 1830. Between the 1960s and the 1980s Brazilian recruits shrank 8 cm. Robert W.
Fogel, "Nutrition and the Decline in Mortality since 1700: Some Preliminary Findings,"
in Stanley L. Engerman and Robert Gallman, eds., *Long Term Factors in American Economic Growth*, National Bureau of Economic Research, Studies in Income and Wealth,
vol. 51 (Chicago: University of Chicago Press, 1987), pp. 439–555; *Latin American Regional Reports, Brazil*, February 12, 1987, p. 5. I am indebted to my colleague Reid An-
drews for bringing the latter source to my attention.

[33] The anomaly occurs in the Lower Austrian sample.

[34] The only way the decline in height after the 1740s could be an artifact of the sampling

(Figure B.1). Regression analysis carried out on that part of the sample above the minimum height requirement (165.8 cm) confirms the hypothesis of a decline in stature (Table B.2). Because of the consistent pattern among the various measures, the evidence is overwhelming that the diminution in stature was widespread. With some short-term variation it persisted through the 1760s and 1770s, but had stabilized by the end of the century. The few minor exceptions to this trend might be due to sampling error, uneven geographic coverage, or local variations in harvest conditions.[35]

Sample sizes are not large enough for meaningful analysis of short-run fluctuations of height, except for Hungarian recruits. Their height reached an apex in 1747 and, not unexpectedly, reached a nadir during the 1770s, when harvest failures were widespread; it then reversed and rose until the start of the French wars, only to fall again (Figure 2.3). Although these cycles correlate well with anecdotal accounts of agricultural conditions, their close analysis is outside the purview of this study.[36] Instead, I concentrate on the incontrovertible long-run trend: during the course of the second half of the eighteenth century, that part of the Habsburg population at risk of entering the military became stunted in its physical growth. Its nutritional status reached a nadir perhaps in the 1770s or 1780s, but had stabilized by the end of the century at the latest.

The decline in stature can be attributed to a decline in the caloric and

---

procedure is if, prior to the 1750s, the truncation point due to the minimum height requirement was to the right of the true population mean. Then the program estimating $\hat{x}$ would be upwardly biased in the 1740s. However, then $\bar{x}'$ would not decrease in the 1750s, as it does in most of the samples. Hence this notion is not very plausible.

[35] The QBE program is not accurate if the sampling distribution is not close to normal, as is the case, for instance, for Galician recruits in the 1790s (Table B.1).

[36] Two problems with the design of the sampling procedure render the analysis of short-run fluctuations difficult with relatively small samples. The first is the failure to restrict the sample to those recruits for whom information on the date of entering the military was available. (These data are available in the *Standestabellen*, but not in the *Musterlisten*, which are much easier to work with than the former records.) In retrospect, having this information would have been useful because during wartime recruiting the draft procedure and the minimum height requirement might have varied in the short run. Secondly, it would have been desirable to note down the grenadiers within the infantry regiments. The assumption was made early in the research project that the number of grenadiers per regular infantry within a regiment was essentially a constant, and therefore would not affect the analysis. Although this was true on average, in some cases, particularly with small sample sizes, it might not hold; variations in the grenadier-infantry ratio in the sample could conceivably cause slight shifts in the frequency distributions, because grenadiers were systematically selected from among the taller recruits. This would not have been a problem had the sample been restricted to the *Standestabellen*, because the selection of the grenadiers occurred at a later stage of the recruiting process.

protein intake of the population.[37] The rapid population growth and diminishing returns to labor in agriculture meant that the nutrients available on a per capita basis must have fallen,[38] because foreign trade in agricultural products was minimal. Total factor productivity in agriculture was increasing but by no means fast enough to keep pace with population growth and to avert a Malthusian crisis by itself.[39] It is suggestive in this regard that the cumulative decline in $\bar{x}$ between the 1740s and the 1790s was greatest in the four densely-populated counties of Bohemia[40] (Table B.7), where there was very little room for expansion of agricultural production.[41] Indeed, one would expect population pressure to be most severe in this region, where the average size of land holdings was no more than two or three hectares of plowland per family.[42]

In principle, the fall in nutritional status might have been caused not by a fall in the nutrient intake itself, but by a rise in the claims on the nutrients, that is, by an increase in work effort or in the incidence of childhood diseases. However, no evidence exists to support this possibility. Because the recruits were primarily landless and came from rural areas, they were not likely to have worked more in the 1770s or 1780s than they had in the previous decades. Indeed, it might be more plausible to suppose that opportunities declined in agriculture, the sector in which the recruits were most likely to have worked during their growing years, and that their work effort could therefore conceivably even

[37] ". . . a decrease in body size might be an advantageous adaptation to shortage in food supply." World Health Organization, *Energy and Protein Requirements. Report of a Joint FAO/WHO/UNO Expert Consultation* (Geneva: World Health Organization, 1985), p. 21.

[38] ". . . population growth was beginning to lead to a faster increase of the poorer classes." Dickson, *Finance and Government*, vol. 1, p. 14.

[39] Grain output per acre in Bohemia began to increase only in the nineteenth century. Frantisek Lom, "Die Arbeitsproduktivität in der Geschichte der Tschechoslowakischen Landwirtschaft," *Zeitschrift für Agrargeschichte und Agrarsoziologie* 19 (1971): 1–25; Herbert Matis, "Die Rolle der Landwirtschaft im Merkantilsystem-Produktionsstruktur und gesellschaftliche Verhältnisse im Agrarbereich," in Herbert Matis, ed., *Von der Glückseligkeit des Staates: Staat, Wirtschaft und Gesellschaft in Österreich im Zeitalter des aufgeklärten Absolutismus* (Berlin: Duncker und Humblot, 1981), p. 273.

[40] The cumulative decline in stature ($\bar{x}$) of the unskilled recruits was 5.1 cm and of the skilled recruits 4.6 cm, compared with 3 cm for Galician recruits and about 4 cm for the recruits born in the other provinces (Table B.7). Although $\bar{x}$ is a biased indicator of trend with a changing minimum height requirement, to the extent that the requirement was enforced equally in the various regions $\bar{x}$ should be an unbiased indicator of relative trends.

[41] Dickson, *Finance and Government*, vol. 1, p. 47.

[42] G. N. Schnabel, *Statistische Darstellung von Böhmen* (Prague: n.p., 1826).

have fallen. The sample contains virtually no persons who had worked in a factory and whose work intensity might have risen on this account.[43] Moreover, evidence is provided below that the nutritional status of children, who attended school and did not work, also fell. Consequently, the diminution in their nutritional status is unlikely to have been caused by a rise in calorie requirements related to their employment.

The hypothesis of a decline in nutrient intake is also supported by evidence, presented later in this chapter, that the growth increments of those soldiers who entered the military prior to attaining their final heights were smaller at the end of the century than they had been earlier. This, too, is not likely to have been caused by an increase in work effort, because the energy requirements of army life probably remained unchanged. For all of these reasons it appears implausible that the decline in nutritional status would have been caused by an increase in the energy expenditure of the population.

The disease explanation of the fall in nutritional status is equally unlikely, because there is no evidence at all of a marked increase in the incidence of infections.[44] On the contrary, there might actually have been some improvements in public health toward the end of the century, but these apparently did not counterbalance the decline in food consumption among the lower classes.[45] Hence nutritional status decreased even though the claims on nutrient intake due to the disease environment might have fallen after mid-century. Moreover, the trends in the height of the upper and lower classes diverged after the 1750s: while the nutritional status of the former continued to rise, the opposite was the case among the latter group.[46] Since changes in the epidemiological environment would probably have affected the whole society, the fall in nutritional status among the lower classes is not likely to have been caused by changes in the incidence of diseases.

[43] This is the case because there were few factories in the monarchy in the eighteenth century, and factory employees were generally exempt from military duty.

[44] James C. Riley, "Insects and the European Mortality Decline," *American Historical Review* 91 (1986): 833–858.

[45] Steps were taken during the second half of the century to diminish the incidence of diseases. These included better street drainage, better sewage disposal, street paving, elimination of moats, and the draining of marshes. The actual effects of these changes are unknown, but contemporaries were persuaded that they improved public health. Riley, *Eighteenth-Century Campaign*, p. 9.

[46] See the section on children's stature below. The nutritional status of upper-class German youth also rose in the 1770s. John Komlos, "Height and Social Status in Germany in the Eighteenth Century," *Journal of Interdisciplinary History* (1990), forthcoming.

Therefore, while there is no reason to think that the claims on the nutrient intake of this sample of recruits increased, there is considerable corroborating evidence that food consumption declined. In Vienna, for instance, real wages were about halved between the 1730s and the 1790s.[47] The rise in grain and meat prices was dramatic. Severe food scarcities arose as a result of the inclement weather and poor harvests of the early 1770s. In Bohemia thousands starved, as the Malthusian mechanism of positive checks once again exerted itself on a nutritionally weakened population.[48] Nature began to "audit her accounts with a red pencil."[49]

In addition, there is plenty of independent evidence of the disappearance of meat from the diet of the lower classes, or at least its great diminution, by the turn of the nineteenth century.[50] One can quantify probable per capita meat consumption, since some data on the animal stock do exist, but from these estimates it is impossible to construct a decadal index, since in the short run the rate of slaughter and animal weight could have varied and because the livestock census is not reliable enough for such an exercise. Yet the fact that per capita meat consumption in

[47] Dickson, *Finance and Government*, vol. 1, p. 131.

[48] Positive checks were misery and want, which would, through hunger and mortality, keep population in homeostatic equilibrium with the available resource base. As the nutritional level deteriorates, the body's ability to withstand attacks from microorganisms is weakened, thereby raising the level of mortality, other things being equal. Thomas R. Malthus, *An Essay on the Principle of Population* (1798; reprint, New York: Norton, 1976), p. 24; Dickson, *Finance and Government*, vol. 1, p. 33.

[49] The extremely cold winters of 1771 and 1772 were followed by poor harvests in Sweden as well; Gustaf Utterström, "Some Population Problems in Pre-industrial Sweden," *Scandinavian Economic History Review* 2 (1954): 103–165; John Komlos, "The End of the Old Regime in Rural Austria," *Journal of European Economic History* 14 (1985): 515–520. According to one estimate, 32,000 people died in 4 months in the mountains. Joseph Schreyer, *Kommerz, Fabriken und Manufakturen des Königreichs Böhmen, theils wie sie schon sind, theils wie sie es werden könnten* (Prague and Leipzig: Schönfeldisch Meiznerischen Buchhandlung, 1790), vol. 1, p. 18.

[50] Johann H. von Thünen theorized that during the initial phase of economic development the meat consumption of the poorer segments of the population would decline. Wilhelm Abel, *Agrarkrisen und Agrarkonjunktur: Eine Geschichte der Land- und Ernährungswirtschaft Mitteleuropas seit dem hohen Mittelalter* (1935; reprint, Hamburg and Berlin: Paul Parey, 1966), pp. 238–239. The income elasticity of demand for meat was about twice as high as for cereals in late-eighteenth-century England. Shammas, "English Diet," p. 259. For the decline in animal husbandry in Styria see Joseph Liechtenstern, *Allgemeine Uebersicht des Herzogthums Steiermark* (Vienna: n.p., 1799), p. 50. In Hungary contemporary reports indicate that population growth brought about the break-up of pasture land. This led to a fall in the stock of cattle. Ferenc Eckhart, *A bécsi udvar gazdasági politikája Magyarországon Mária Terézia korában* (Budapest: Budavári Tudományos Társaság, 1922), p. 36.

Austria declined substantially—perhaps by as much as a half—between 1750 and 1850 cannot be doubted. By the early nineteenth century weekly meat consumption per capita in Austria was not more than 0.7 pounds.[51] In Vienna, Linz, and Graz, meat consumption reached a nadir in 1850.[52]

The decline in meat consumption was general throughout Europe.[53] Although England was much more developed than the Habsburg Monarchy, its population growth during the second half of the century also outpaced the ability of the agricultural sector to maintain the population's nutritional status.[54] Because of the fall in real wages (Table 2.8), British per capita food intake is estimated to have declined by about 20 percent.[55] By the end of the century ". . . the levels of meat consumption

Table 2.8 Decennial Changes in Bricklayer's Real Wages[a] in London, 1750-1800 (percent)

1750-60	- 9.5
1760-70	-14.2
1770-80	- 0.5
1780-90	-11.1
1790-1800	-14.6

Source: L. D. Schwarz, "The Standard of Living in the Long Run: London, 1700-1860," Economic History Review, 2d ser., 38 (1985): 24-41.
[a] Five-year moving averages.

[51] Roman Sandgruber, *Österreichische Agrarstatistik 1750–1918* (Vienna: Verlag für Geschichte und Politik, 1978), p. 101.

[52] Roman Sandgruber, *Die Anfänge der Konsumgesellschaft: Konsumgüterverbrauch, Lebensstandard und Alltagskultur in Österreich im 18. und 19. Jahrhundert* (Vienna: Verlag für Geschichte und Politik, 1982), p. 158. In Sweden the intake of animal products in the eighteenth century was about half of what it had been in the sixteenth century. Mats Morell, "Eli F. Heckscher, the 'Food Budgets' and Swedish Food Consumption from the 16th to the 19th Century," *Scandinavian Economic History Review* 35 (1987): 67–107.

[53] F. W. Clements, "Some Effects of Different Diets," in S. V. Boyden, ed., *The Impact of Civilisation on the Biology of Man* (Toronto: University of Toronto Press, 1970), pp. 109–141. The protein and calorie intake of inmates in German charitable institutions declined at the end of the eighteenth century. In Prussia the per capita meat consumption was about 20 kg per annum during the first half of the nineteenth century. Hans J. Teuteberg and Günter Wiegelmann, *Der Wandel der Nahrungsgewohnheiten unter dem Einfluss der Industrialisierung* (Göttingen: Vandenhoeck und Ruprecht, 1972), pp. 106, 182.

[54] N.F.R. Crafts, *British Economic Growth during the Industrial Revolution* (Oxford: Clarendon Press, 1985), p. 40.

[55] Jackson, "Growth and Deceleration."

by farm labourers and their families in the south [of England] had sunk to negligible proportions."[56] In France on the eve of the revolution there were five or six million more mouths to feed than there had been in 1720; cereal production could not have kept up with these demographic demands either. As in England, starvation was not the main threat; rather, chronic malnutrition became the lot of perhaps as many as 30 to 40 percent of the French population. Dietary standards reached a nadir in the second half of the eighteenth century, with chestnuts becoming a staple for some communities for two or three months of the year.[57] In the early nineteenth century agricultural output per male worker in Denmark was declining at the rate of 0.1 percent annually.[58] In Sweden between 1750 and 1815 the number of landless peasants doubled.[59] In America the population was not subject to a Malthusian threat, since the land constraint was not binding. Consequently, the stature of American recruits did not change appreciably during the course of the eighteenth century.[60] Thus those societies in which population grew without access to virgin land were the ones that experienced diminution in nutrition and stature.

Population growth must have first exerted pressure on food intake within the family unit. After all, the extra population could not have been distributed evenly; rather, some families must have had one or two surviving children more than their counterparts would have had earlier. These were the families whose children began to suffer nutritional assaults early in life. Meat consumption had a high negative elasticity with respect to family size in late-eighteenth-century England.[61] Even in some modern populations the height of children declines with parity,

[56] John Rule, *The Labouring Classes in Early Industrial England, 1750–1850* (London and New York: Longman, 1986), p. 54.

[57] Olwen H. Hufton, "Social Conflict and the Grain Supply in Eighteenth-Century France," *Journal of Interdisciplinary History* 14 (1983): 303–331. According to a recent estimate, the consumption of at least 3 percent of the French population was at starvation level, and another 7 percent consumed insufficient nutrients even to participate in the labor force. Robert W. Fogel, "Biomedical Approaches to the Estimation and Interpretation of Secular Trends in Equity, Morbidity, Mortality, and Labor Productivity in Europe, 1750–1980," unpublished manuscript, Graduate School of Business Administration, University of Chicago, 1987, p. 38.

[58] Ester Boserup, "The Impact of Scarcity and Plenty on Development," *Journal of Interdisciplinary History* 14 (1983): 383–407.

[59] In 1750 the landless comprised 20 percent, and in 1850 40 percent, of the population. Sandberg and Steckel, "Overpopulation and Malnutrition Rediscovered."

[60] Kenneth Sokoloff and Georgia C. Villaflor, "The Early Achievement of Modern Stature in America," *Social Science History* 6 (1982): 453–481.

[61] Shammas, "English Diet," p. 259.

particularly among the lower classes.[62] Population growth also exerted pressure on family structure. In Hungary, with a decline in per capita income and a decline in the availability of housing stock per adult, nuclear families expanded in size, possibly in order to economize on rent.[63]

The cycles in human stature are not likely to be mere artifacts of the sample. Because cohorts of the 1750s entered the military in the 1770s and 1780s, prior to the French wars, the diminution in stature in the second half of the eighteenth century began prior to the mobilization, which forced the military to lower its minimum height requirement (Appendix A). Therefore, the decline in height after 1750 cannot be ascribed to the expansion of the army.

The size of the Habsburg army was about 170,000 between the 1750s and the 1770s.[64] In the subsequent decade its size rose by about 60,000 men, and in the 1790s increased by an equal amount, reaching 290,000 during the French wars. The increment of about 120,000 soldiers must not have been a great strain on an empire whose population was over 20 million.[65] (Moreover, about 20 percent of the soldiers were generally foreign, mostly from Germany.) These orders of magnitude are such that the Napoleonic Wars need not have placed sufficient demands on recruiting to alter substantially the social composition of the recruits, particularly in a society in which social differentiation had not advanced very far.[66]

[62] James M. Tanner, *Education and Physical Growth* (New York: International Universities Press, 1961); Wilton Marion Krogman, *Child Growth* (Ann Arbor: University of Michigan Press, 1972), p. 142. In contemporary Hungary the third cohort is on average one cm shorter than earlier ones. János Nemeskéri, Attila Juhász, and Balázs Szabady, "Az 1973. évi sorköteles fiatalok testi fejlettsége," *Demográfia* 20 (1977): 208–281.

[63] Tamás Faragó, "Paraszti Háztartás—és Munkaszervezet—Típusok Magyarországon A 18. Század Közepén. Pilis-Buda környéki birtokos paraszti háztartások 1745–1770 között," *Történeti Statisztikai Füzetek* 7 (1985): 1–187.

[64] Dickson, *Finance and Government*, vol. 2, p. 352.

[65] The number of males of military age must have been about 1/6 of the population, or about 3 million. Coale and Demeny, *Regional Model Life Tables*, p. 566; Gusztáv Thirring, *Az 1804. évi Népösszeirás* (Budapest: Hornyánszky Viktor, 1936), p. 17; Vinzenz Goehlert, "Die Ergebnisse der in Österreich in vorigen Jahrhundert ausgeführten Volkszählungen im Vergleiche mit jenen der neueren Zeit," *Sitzungsberichte der philos.-histor. Klasse der K. Akademie der Wissenschaften*, Vienna, 1854; Christopher Duffey, *The Army of Maria Theresa* (London: David and Charles, 1977), pp. 47, 205, 209; Mihály Horváth, *Horváth Mihály Kisebb Történelmi Munkái* (Pest: Ráth Mór, 1868), vol. 1, pp. 231, 237; Major Alphons Freiherr von Wrede, *Geschichte der k. und k. Wehrmacht* (Vienna: C. W. Seidel, 1898), Appendix 2, p. 35.

[66] In addition, one should recognize that the Habsburg army fought wars intermittently throughout the eighteenth century and casualties were often high. During the war with Prussia (1756–63), 125,000 men apparently perished. Between 1788 and 1815 Austria probably lost about 300,000 men in battle, i.e., 11,000 per annum. This loss might be

Other evidence supports the notion that the decline in stature was not caused by the expansion of the armed forces. If it had been, then one would expect that after the war the stature of the recruits would have reverted to the previous level. This did not happen. The only extant records for the first three decades of the nineteenth century pertain to Hungary. These data do not show any improvement in stature over the earlier birth cohorts[67] (Tables 2.1 and 2.2, and Figure B.2). The birth cohorts of the 1810s were the first to have been recruited under the universal conscription law of 1827, which mandated recruiting by lot.[68] The fact that this change had no appreciable effect on the mean height of the recruits is a good indication that the trends outlined above were not caused by the peculiarities of the recruiting practices. That is, neither the changes in the minimum height requirement nor changes in the social composition of the recruits account for the substantial decline in their stature during the second half of the century.

Yet another indication that the diminution in adult height is truly an indication of a reduction in nutritional status rather than changes in recruitment standards is the fact that the stature of the lower classes declined in many other parts of Europe. A recent study documents the contemporaneous decline in stature in Sweden.[69] In London, the stature of poor boys declined during the last quarter of the century.[70] Adult

---

contrasted with the approximately 200,000 men who became eligible for military service in the monarchy annually. Hence, recruitment demands of the French wars were probably not so great as to have caused a substantial diminution in average stature. Henrik J. Schwicker, "Magyarország s a Bajor Öröködési Háboru," *Századok* 12 (1878): 487–509. Wars spread disease, but that could not account for the fall in nutritional status during the second half of the century, because wars had been prevalent earlier as well. Austria fought Prussia throughout the 1740s, yet the birth cohorts of this decade were taller than those of the 1730s. Gaston Bodart, *Losses of Life in Modern Wars: Austria-Hungary; France* (Oxford: Clarendon Press, 1916), p. 133.

[67] $\bar{x}$ and $\bar{x}'$ decrease slightly, $\hat{x}$ increases to a small extent, but Θ declines substantially (Tables 2.1 and 2.2). After 1827 most of the recruits entered the military in their late teens or early twenties, and consequently most of the men measured after age 22 were probably ones who did not qualify younger. Because the taller men were taken at younger ages, the older recruits after 1827 are not the best indicators of the final height of a cross section of the population. For this reason it is important to examine the trend in the height of the younger recruits around the turn of the nineteenth century. That comparison, too, substantiates the notion that no major changes took place in the height of the recruits at that time (Table B.1).

[68] Because after 1827 recruitment was by lot, the military records thereafter reflect almost a random sample of the population (Appendix A). However, observations on those who were disqualified were still excluded from the records.

[69] Sandberg and Steckel, "Heights and Economic History."

[70] Roderick Floud and Kenneth Wachter, "Poverty and Physical Stature: Evidence on the Standard of Living of London Boys, 1770–1870," *Social Science History* 6 (1982):

male stature in Britain declined by 2.5 cm between the birth cohorts of 1762 and 1792.[71] The height of foreign soldiers in the Habsburg army ($\bar{x}$) from France, Lombardy, and Southern Germany declined; in four of the five samples, $\hat{x}$ also declined (Table 2.9). Thus the nutritional crisis was not confined to East-Central Europe; rather, it appears that population growth put a downward pressure on living standards throughout the European continent.

Table 2.9 Stature of Adult[a] Foreign Soldiers in the Habsburg Army, by Year and Place of Birth, 1720-1799 (cm)

Place of Birth	1720-1769			1770-1799		
	N	$\bar{x}$	$\hat{x}$	N	$\bar{x}$	$\hat{x}$
Unskilled						
France	197	174.7	173.3	216	169.3	164.5
Namur	186	174.6	172.6			
Luxemburg	743	173.7	171.1			
Tyrol	191	172.8	171.0			
Hainaut	520	174.2	170.1			
Brabant	471	172.5	169.2			
Germany	272	172.2	169.1			
Lombardy	200	170.9	168.0	786	166.2	164.9
Silesia	158	170.3	167.7			
Flanders	1243	171.8	167.5			
South Germany	965	171.5	166.3	208	169.9	167.6
Croatia	231	168.8	167.9			
Venice	192	168.5	167.5			
Skilled						
France	162	168.0	165.9			
Lombardy	484	169.9	164.3	726	167.3	164.1
South Germany	905	170.8	168.5	188	168.7	164.4

Source: See Table 2.1
[a] Over age 22.

422–452. This generalization is based on their Figure 1, in which thirteen-, fifteen-, and sixteen-year-old boys declined in stature between 1780 and 1800 and fourteen-year-old boys began to decline earlier. The smoothed version of their Figure 2 shows a rather different pattern for the thirteen- and sixteen-year-old boys, possibly because of the nature of the averaging procedure.

[71] Roderick Floud, Kenneth Wachter, and Annabel Gregory, "The Heights of the British since 1700," unpublished manuscript, Department of History, University of London, 1987, Table 4.1 C.

There are a number of indications that the diminution in stature that began in the 1750s stabilized toward the end of the century. The frequency distributions generally ceased shifting to the left and in some cases even reversed slightly (Figure B.1). The worst of the nutritional crisis appears to have passed. The argument will be presented in the next chapter that the economic reforms instituted by the government were instrumental in halting the deterioration in the standard of living of the population. Institutional change fostered industrialization and redistributed income in favor of the peasantry, providing a safety net that enabled the society, particularly its poorer elements, to overcome the impending Malthusian crisis. Before we proceed with that line of argument, however, we shall first examine other evidence corroborating the trends outlined above.

Height of Younger Soldiers

Until now the analysis has been confined to the terminal height of adult recruits, defined as being between 23 and 45 years of age. Of course, the height at every age prior to the cessation of growth can also be used as an indicator of nutritional status. For this reason one can examine the stature of those recruits who entered the military prior to achieving their final height. Evidence on younger soldiers begins with the birth cohorts of the 1740s; hence the rise in nutritional status cannot be documented with this part of the sample. The decline in stature, however, is quite evident.

In contrast to the adult pattern, the decline in height among the younger recruits does not begin consistently until the birth cohorts of the 1770s (Tables B.1, B.9, and B.10). The reason for this delay is to be found in the recruiting practices of the army (Appendix A). Relative to the 1740s, the share of young recruits in the total sample declined substantially in the 1750s and (with the exception of Hungarians) also in the 1760s (Table B.11). Evidently, the decline in nutritional status meant that in the 1750s and 1760s fewer 19- to 22-year-old men met the minimum height requirement than before and consequently were not accepted into the service.[72] Yet these rejects might have been accepted subsequently because by then they would have had more time to

---

[72] The sample was not designed specifically to obtain a random sample of the age distribution of the recruits. In order to do so, the sample would have had to have been restricted to the *Standestabellen*, which alone list the age at recruitment. The *Musterlisten* list only the age at which the current measurement applies. Yet I do not believe that the pattern found in Table B.11 is an artifact of my sampling procedure. In other words, I do not think that fewer records were obtained from the *Standestabellen* in the 1750s than in the 1740s.

grow and to reach a final height above the minimum requirement. Hence this peculiarity of the younger sample does not contradict the conclusion reached above on the basis of the adult soldiers, namely that the diminution in nutritional status began in the 1750s. In fact, the small number of younger soldiers born in the 1750s who ended up in the sample strongly suggests that there was a substantial slowdown in their rate of growth, which usually accompanies a decline in nutritional status. The decline in the rate of physical maturation brought with it a rise in the share of men in their late teens and early twenties who had not yet reached the minimum height requirement and were therefore not accepted into the military until they had more time to grow and reach their final height.

Evidence for the early nineteenth century exists only for Hungarian recruits. The indication is that, as among the adults, the diminution in stature was halted by the end of the eighteenth century, but a clear recovery during the first half of the nineteenth century is not evident. The frequency distributions, too, corroborate these generalizations (Figures B.3 and B.4).

Published statistics on the height of practically all young men, available beginning with the birth cohorts of the 1850s, can be used to test the hypothesis that the earlier military samples are fairly representative of the population at large. A comparison of the frequency distributions of the heights of recruits born in the 1850s, based on hundreds of thousands of observations, with those of earlier birth cohorts reveals no major differences between the two distributions. The absence of any substantial discrepancy in the height distributions after the enlargement of the sample, even with the inclusion of rejects (Figure B.13), indicates that the stature of the military samples prior to the birth cohorts of the 1850s was probably not very different from the stature of the whole male population.[73]

The Height Profile of Hungarian Soldiers

To provide further evidence that the nutritional status of the population deteriorated during the course of the eighteenth century, one can examine the tempo of growth of soldiers between the ages of eighteen and twenty-four. As mentioned in Chapter 1, biological indicators of nutritional well-being include terminal height, age at which this height is reached, height-by-age profile, and incremental growth at any one age. Other things being equal, the more nutrients available to satisfy biolog-

[73] The distributions do, however, indicate that the inclusion of the rejects in the sample expanded the left tail of the distribution markedly. Austria, *Militär-Statistisches Jahrbuch für das Jahr 1871* (Vienna: k. k. Hof- und Staatsdruckerei, 1873).

ical needs, the faster the human body grows. Examining height increments is important also because it provides longitudinal evidence on
growth profiles. That is, while previous data compared the heights of
different individuals over time, the records about to be examined consist
of multiple measurements on the same individual.[74] An advantage of
such a sample is that inferences drawn from longitudinal measurements
are generally more reliable than those derived from cross-sectional ones,
because the former data refer to the same individual over time.[75]

Soldiers entering the Habsburg army in the eighteenth century were
measured not only at induction but also several times thereafter. A sample of about 13,000 observations on Hungarian soldiers born between
1750 and 1800 was extracted from Hungarian regimental records.[76]
First and last name, village and county of birth, age, height, year of
recruitment, and whether the soldier had a skill were recorded. After the
list was alphabetized, multiple measurements on an individual were
identified by matching names, and in cases of misspelling by matching
other attributes of the soldier. Three thousand individuals with multiple
measurements were found.[77] These were divided into two groups: the
birth cohorts of the 1750s and 1760s, and the birth cohorts of the
1780s and 1790s.

Multiple height measurements of an individual were not always for
contiguous years. Height increments ΔH were found by subtracting the
height measured at a younger age from that at an older age: $\Delta H_{ij} = H_i
- H_j$, where $j = 18, \ldots, 23$ and $i = 19, \ldots, 24$, for $i > j$. $H_{20,19}$ is
therefore the growth between the ages of 19 and 20. The ΔHs were first
calculated for $i - j = 1$ (Table 2.10). The other cells (for those observations where $i - j > 1$) were calculated using the formula:

$$\Delta H_{i,i+1} = \Delta H_{ij} - \left(\sum_{n=j}^{i-2} (\text{mean } \Delta H_{n+1,n}) \right).$$

[74] These data are the oldest longitudinal records on the growth of young adults hitherto
examined.

[75] Another advantage is that this method eliminates the possibility that diminution in
mean height was caused by changes in measuring technique. Hence, one cannot argue
that the decline in stature was caused by soldiers being measured without their shoes in
the latter period, and with their shoes in the earlier one. However, this would not have
been likely, given that in Britain anthropometers were developed in the mid-eighteenth
century. Steegmann and Haseley, "Stature Variation in the British American Colonies,"
p. 414. See also Appendix A.

[76] Kriegsarchiv, Vienna, Austria: Musterlisten and Standestabellen, Infantry Regiment
19, Faszikel 1102–27, 1149–53.

[77] The total number of useful records was 6,949. Because they were few in number,
observations below age 18 and above 24 were not considered.

After the values along the principal diagonal, such as $\Delta H_{19,18}$ and $\Delta H_{20,19}$, were obtained, the other elements of the matrix were calculated (Tables 2.10 and B.12–B.14). For instance, an estimate of $\Delta H_{20,19}$ for 1750/60 was obtained by subtracting the calculated value of $\Delta H_{19,18}$ (1.17 in Table 2.10) from that of $\Delta H_{20,18}$ (1.34, not shown in the table). This procedure resulted in another estimate of $\Delta H_{20,19}$ (.17 for 1750/60) in addition to the one calculated along the diagonal (.95). These two values were averaged, using the number of observations as weights, in order to obtain the mean value for $\Delta H_{20,19}$ of .68 (bottom of Table 2.10).[78]

Table 2.10 Annual Height Increments of Unskilled Hungarian Soldiers, 1750-1799 (Variant A) (cm)

Age[b]	Birth Decade	Age[a]											
		19		20		21		22		23		24	
		N	ΔH	N	ΔH	N	ΔH	N	ΔH	N	ΔH	N	ΔH
18	1750/60	85	1.17	61	.17	55	.29	50	-.42	44	-.55	35	-.08
	1780/90	17	.93	32	.10	14	-1.68	2	2.46	8	2.92	12	.86
19	1750/60			115	.95	60	.87	57	.38	66	-.03	57	-.09
	1780/90			37	1.21	78	-.44	34	.21	14	3.81	30	2.51
20	1750/60					200	.61	64	.43	74	1.47	108	.38
	1780/90					121	.24	81	.26	29	.91	20	3.12
21	1750/60							191	.39	67	1.10	77	.80
	1780/90							128	.25	89	.15	31	1.55
22	1750/60									199	.41	31	.55
	1780/90									173	.34	98	-.06
23	1750/60											142	.39
	1780/90											177	.14
Average													
	1750/60	85	1.17	176	.68	315	.60	402	.26	450	.53	450	.37
	1780/90	17	.93	69	.70	213	-.14	245	.27	313	.56	368	.58

Source: Kriegsarchiv, Vienna, Musterlisten and Standestabellen, Infantry Regiment 19, Faszikel 1102-1127, 1149-1153.
Notes: N = Number of observations; ΔH = Estimate of height increment.
The values in the table refer to the growth increment during the year prior to the age in the top row.
[a] Age at the end of the observation period.
[b] Age at the beginning of the observation period.

[78] For the next column $\Delta H_{21,20}$ there are two estimates. The first one is: $\Delta H_{21,20} = \Delta H_{21,18} - (\text{mean } \Delta H_{20,19} + \text{mean } \Delta H_{19,18}) = 2.14 - (1.17 + .68) = .29$. The second one is: $\Delta H_{21,20} = \Delta H_{21,19} - \text{mean } \Delta H_{20,19} = 1.55 - .68 = .87$. These two estimates are

This process was continued until all elements of the matrix were estimated. Two variants of the calculation were made.[79]

Height increments of the recruits are calculated for the 1750/60s and 1780/90s. The growth velocity of men between the ages of 18 and 21 was greater in the middle of the century than at the end of the century (Table 2.11). In Variant A unskilled men grew 2.45 cm between ages 18 and 24 in the former period, but 1.49 cm in the latter period. In Variant B outliers have been eliminated. Estimated growth increments in the two periods are consequently less, 1.54 and 0.69 cm, but the difference between the two periods is almost identical to the one found in Variant A. In both variants the growth increment between ages 18

Table 2.11 Cumulative Growth of Hungarian Soldiers after Age 18, 1750-1800 (cm)

| | Variant A | | | | Variant B | | | | | |
| | Unskilled | | Unskilled | | Skilled | | All[a] | |
Age	1750-1769	1780-1799	1750-1769	1780-1799	1750-1769	1780-1799	1750-1769	1780-1799
19	1.17	0.93	0.56	0.54	0.53	0.39	0.55	0.51
20	1.85	1.63	1.12	0.57	0.97	0.38	1.09	0.54
21	2.45	1.49	1.54	0.69	1.42	0.83	1.52	0.69
22	2.71	1.76	2.03	0.92	1.56	0.93	1.95	0.90
23	3.24	2.32	2.25	1.22	1.98	1.36	2.10	1.22
24	3.61	2.90	2.36	1.65	2.19	1.63	2.23	1.63
Percent[b]	68	51	65	42	65	51	68	42

Source: Tables 2.10, B.12, and B.13.
[a] Both skilled and unskilled.
[b] Height increment between age 18 and 21 as a percentage of increment between age 18 and 24.

in turn averaged with the third value along the diagonal (.61) to obtain the mean for $\Delta H_{21,20}$ (.60) at the bottom of the table.

[79] In Variant A all ΔHs below -2 cm were discarded (95 observations) (Table 2.10). In Variant B all negative values (244 observations) and positive values that appeared unreasonable were also discarded (Tables B.12–B.14). The longer the time elapsed between the two dates of measurement, the larger is the filter, because there was more time for the soldier to actually grow. The positive ΔHs were discarded for $i - j = 1$ if $\Delta H > 4$ cm, for $i - j = 2$ if $\Delta H > 5$ cm, for $i - j = 3$ if $\Delta H > 6$ cm, and for $i - j > 3$ if $\Delta H > 7$ cm. This filter was adopted to screen out large positive growth increments that could be caused by measurement error, error in transcribing the data, or mistaken matching of the identity of soldiers.

and 21 in the 1780s and 1790s relative to the 1750s and 1760s declined by about 0.9 cm, that is, by 39 to 55 percent.[80] Not only were young men born in the 1780s and 1790s close to 4 cm shorter upon induction than those born in the 1750s and 1760s (Table B.9), but their rate of growth also continued to be slower until age 21.

As pointed out in the previous chapter, the higher a population's nutritional status, the earlier the cessation of biological growth. Hence the fact that the cohorts of the 1750s and 1760s grew less between the ages of 21 and 24 than did those born in the 1780s and 1790s is yet another indication that the former cohort's nutritional status was superior. While the earlier cohort grew 0.82 cm between the ages of 21 and 24, the later cohort grew 0.96 cm[81] (Table 2.11, Variant B). Hence the 1750/60s cohort grew faster at younger ages, and reached its final height earlier than the later cohort. By age 21 the earlier cohort had achieved 65 percent, but the later cohort only 42 percent, of the total growth increment between ages 18 and 24.[82]

Thus the diminution of the growth increments of Hungarian recruits aged eighteen or older who were born in the 1780s and 1790s confirms the notion of a decline in the nutritional status of the population in these decades relative to that of those born in the 1750s and 1760s (Figure 2.4). Not only were the birth cohorts of the 1780s and 1790s shorter at age eighteen than the birth cohorts of the 1750s and 1760s but, in spite of the considerable potential for catch-up growth, they also grew at a slower rate up to age 21 and reached their terminal height at a later age.

This finding corroborates the notion, suggested by the earlier results, that the nutritional status of the male population declined during the

[80] The rate of growth of the skilled recruits evinced the same pattern (Tables 2.11 and B.13). They grew 0.56 cm less between the ages of 18 and 24 in the 1780s and 1790s than they did in the 1750s and 1760s. This was a 26 percent decline in their height increments, similar to the one experienced by the unskilled population. In the 1750s and 1760s the growth of the skilled population after age eighteen deviated less than two millimeters from that of the unskilled population, and in the 1780s and 1790s the growth increments were identical for both samples.

[81] A similar pattern was obtained for the other variants of the calculation as well.

[82] The effect of changes in the minimum height requirement (MHR) on the growth increments between ages 18 and 24 was also examined. Lowering this requirement allowed recruits with an inferior nutritional experience to enter the army and could have had an influence on the above pattern. In order to compensate for changes in the MHR, those recruits who were shorter than 165.8 cm (63 Austrian inches) at the time of recruitment were eliminated. (This was the MHR at the outset and was subsequently lowered several times). The results remain the same: the rate of growth between ages 18 and 24 still declined at the end of the century (Table B.14). This indicates that the nutritional status of even the better nourished segment of the sample was deteriorating at that time.

Figure 2.4. Growth Increments of Hungarian Soldiers between Age 18 and 24 (Variant B)

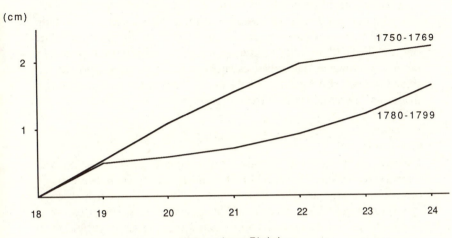

(cm)

1750-1769

1780-1799

Age at Last Birthday

second half of the century. Its importance lies in the fact that the data were longitudinal, and therefore pertain to the same individual over time. In contrast, the earlier results were based on the comparison of the height of different individuals. Thus an argument could have been advanced that the decline in stature was obtained only because at the end of the century more recruits were measured barefoot, i.e., without their boots, and therefore that the above results were obtained because of changes in the measuring procedure. Now this argument can no longer be advanced with credibility. By following the growth profile of the soldiers over time, the possibility that the slowdown in the rate of growth up to age 21 can be ascribed to any variation in the measuring technique used has been effectively eliminated.

Height by Occupation

The occupation of the recruits is given in the military records. Peasants were said to have no "profession." Recruits with some skills, such as carpentry or weaving, were distinguished from recruits without any skills at all. The cycles of the stature of the recruits in the two categories were practically identical.[83] There is little systematic difference between

[83] In the eighteenth century factory workers would not have been in the military, because the Habsburg Monarchy had only a small number of factories, and factory workers were generally exempt from military service (Appendix A).

the stature of recruits with some skills and those without. There seems not to have been a major divergence between the ways these two groups experienced the nutritional crisis at the end of the eighteenth century.[84] The longitudinal evidence presented in the previous section also indicates that there was virtually no difference between the growth profiles of the skilled and unskilled recruits (Table 2.11). This result is plausible, because recruits in the skilled category could have been born to unskilled parents and would not have enjoyed any nutritional advantages from their own skills during their growing years.

Stature of Troops Other Than the Infantry

Hitherto the trend in adult stature has been examined on the basis of infantry regiments, the backbone of the military. There were many other units in the army, however, such as the artillery, corps of engineers, heavy and light cavalry, border guards, and garrison troops.[85] Without the pretension of having taken a representative sample from these other units, but with the intention of nonetheless considering the trend in stature among some of them, a small sample was taken from the transport units and from the light cavalry (hussars) (Table 2.12). Among the transportation troops height was not as clearly advanta-

Table 2.12 Stature of Adult Soldiers in Various Military Units 1750-1800

Decade of Birth	Transport troops						Hussars			
	Moravia		Bohemia		Lower Austria		Hungary			
	N	$\bar{x}$	N	$\bar{x}$	N	$\bar{x}$	N	$\bar{x}$	$\hat{x}$	$\bar{x}'$
1750	16	165.9	39	165.4	7	166.3				
1760	54	164.6	95	165.0	35	166.3				
1770	75	164.0	112	165.0	38	165.3	20	167.2		169.5
1780							98	165.9		169.0
1790							391	165.6	164.6	168.8

Source: See Table 2.1

[84] A comparison of the stature of skilled and unskilled soldiers is rendered difficult by the fact that the $\bar{x}$s are biased by the minimum height requirement, and the $\hat{x}$s are not accurate enough for meaningful comparison of differences in stature, which are not likely to be more than a few millimeters.

[85] For instance, in 1782 the distribution of the troops among the various units was the following: infantry 56 percent, cavalry 13, artillery 3, frontier guards 23, and others 5 percent. Dickson, *Finance and Government*, vol. 2, p. 354.

geous as it was for the infantry, and therefore the minimum height requirement was lower and less stringently enforced. Because of the small number of observations, only the trend in $\bar{x}$ can be analyzed meaningfully. Although the diminution in height of the transport troops was much smaller than that of the regular infantry, it is nonetheless evident. This is an indication that even in units for which the minimum height requirement was never meant to apply, the quotas were increasingly filled by recruiting shorter men. The stature of hussars (both $\bar{x}$ and $\bar{x}'$) also evinces a downward trend. For the cavalry $\hat{x}$ is estimated as 164.6 cm (Table 2.12). This is close to the estimate of 163.0 cm for the infantry composed of the birth cohorts of the 1790s. Therefore the evidence on the soldiers in these two units is consistent with the finding on the infantry; the results discussed earlier cannot be said to have been obtained because the sample was limited to infantry troops.

Stature of Children

Because the adult sample is biased on account of the imposition of the minimum height requirement, various statistical procedures were used to analyze the data. To further explore the trend of the Habsburg population's nutritional status over time, evidence on the height of children and youth who were not subject to such requirements is examined. Since these data originated in different institutions and their collection was motivated by reasons other than the ones that led to the compilation of data on military recruits, the growth records of children become an important source for corroborating changes in adult stature over time. The results correspond to the cycles of human height reported above.

Three sources on the stature of boys have been found; they include some of the earliest extant data on the stature of youth.[86] The first source is the military academy Maria Theresia founded in the 1750s to train officers; 560 observations have survived on lower-aristocratic adoles-

[86] Only two sets of data concerning growth of children and adolescents in the eighteenth century were known previously; both pertain to the later decades. The first set comes from the Carlschule in Stuttgart, Germany. The second data set pertains to poor London boys recruited at a charitable organization called the Marine Society. James M. Tanner, *A History of the Study of Human Growth* (Cambridge, England: Cambridge University Press, 1981); idem, *Foetus into Man: Physical Growth from Conception to Maturity* (Cambridge, MA: Harvard University Press, 1978); Waltraud Hartmann, "Beobachtungen zur Akzeleration des Längenwachstums in der zweiten Hälfte des 18. Jahrhunderts" (unpublished Ph.D. dissertation, Goethe University, Frankfurt, 1970), pp. 87–119, and Table 10; Floud and Wachter, "Poverty and Physical Stature."

cents born in the 1730s and 1740s.[87] The second set of 366 observations stems from an orphanage, the Josephinische Waisenhaus, and contains information on children of various ages born in the 1760s and 1770s.[88] The third, and major, source of data is provided by the elementary schools run by the military for sons of ordinary soldiers.[89] About 25,000 records have been compiled from this source.[90]

Regression analysis indicates that the lower-aristocratic youth born in the late 1740s and early 1750s were taller than the earlier birth cohorts by as much as three to six centimeters[91] (equation 1, Table 2.13). Even though the number of observations at each age is small, the pattern is consistent at all ages and for all regions of the Monarchy. All of the increases in stature were attained before entering the academy, and hence cannot be attributed to changes in the diet at the institution. This finding is consistent with the conclusion reached above, on the basis of the increasing stature of adult recruits, that nutritional status was increasing in the 1740s.

The adult peasants were encountering difficulties maintaining their nutritional level by the 1750s; in contrast, sons of the lower nobility were not. This divergence between the trends in height of the upper and lower classes supports the notion espoused earlier that the trends in nutritional status were not caused by changes in the epidemiological environment; after all, there is no warrant for supposing that such a change might have had a differential impact on the various social classes. However, the difference in nutritional experience can be explained in terms of diverging trends in food intake. On the average, even the lower ranks of the nobility had more resources at their disposal than the landless peasantry, from whose ranks the army recruits were drawn. Therefore the nobility was less likely to be affected by food shortages than the lower classes.

On the contrary, what is actually surprising is that the stature of these

---

[87] Kriegsarchiv, Vienna: Theresianische Militärakademie, Faszikel 434.

[88] Kriegsarchiv, Vienna: Josephinisches Waisenhaus, Faszikel 3922. The orphanage was founded by Joseph II.

[89] Children entered the military school at all ages and usually remained in it for a number of years. Kriegsarchiv, Vienna: Erziehungshäuser, Musterlisten, Faszikel 3925, 3926, 3927. All data from Faszikel 3926 and 3927 have been recorded. From Faszikel 3925 the height of children born only in Galicia, Moravia, Hungary, Bohemia, and Lower Austria were recorded. Although serial measurements are available for many of the boys, these were not coded as longitudinal.

[90] Eighteen nationalities were distinguished. The name and religion, also available, were not recorded. Age is as of the previous birthday.

[91] Dummy variables have been entered into the regression for the age, year of birth, and place of birth of the boys.

Table 2.13 Regression Equations. Dependent Variable: Height of Boys (cm)

	Equations	
	1[a]	2[b]
Intercept	142.6[c]	106.0[c]
Birth Year		
1740/44	- 1.4	
1745/49	3.2[c]	
1750/59	5.6c	
Birthplace		
Moravia	1.1	-0.7
Bohemia	2.7[c]	
Silesia		2.3
Galicia	- 2.2	-6.6[c]
Styria		0.8
Hungary	0.3	0.7
Upper Austria		-5.2
Lower Austria	-0.4	-4.3
Italy		-0.3
Other		-0.6
Age		
7+		8.2[c]
8+		11.3[c]
9+		16.4[c]
10+		22.6[c]
11+	-10.4[c]	28.4[c]
12+	-7.2[c]	30.4[c]
13+	-3.0[c]	34.7[c]
14+		40.2[c]
15+	5.6[c]	46.6[c]
16+	9.5[c]	50.0[c]
F =	24[c]	121[c]
R^2 =	0.4	0.8
N =	556	480

Source: See Table 2.14

Notes: All independent variables are dummy variables; equation (1) intercept indicates height of a fourteen-year-old aristocrat born outside the six provinces before 1740; equation (2) intercept indicates height of a six-year-old orphan boy born in Bohemia.
[a]Habsburg aristocrats, 1735-1755.
[b]Orphans, 1760-79.
[c]Significant at the 1% level.

cadets responded at all to the favorable harvests of the time. One might have thought that the income of the nobility was sufficiently large that its food intake would not have been affected by changes in agricultural conditions. Yet nobility was a social rank, and should not be equated with high income. In Hungary, for example, a large share of the nobility was, in fact, impoverished, and often did not live at a higher standard than the landowning peasantry.[92] Moreover, the rise in the cadets' nutritional status becomes even less of an anomaly if one notes that the youth attending the military academy were recruited from the lower ranks of the nobility. They were generally the sons of those aristocrats who were not wealthy enough to educate their sons at their own expense, although boys whose fathers had served in government administration for twenty years or who were sons of "brave" officers were also admitted. In addition, Maria Theresia usually favored the poorer candidates.[93] In light of this selection bias, improvement in the nutritional status of birth cohorts of 1745–55 among the lower aristocracy becomes plausible.

Another consideration increasing the plausibility of the finding is that, even if the higher income of the nobility had enabled them to consume a greater quantity of food than the peasantry, in some ways their food might not have been of better quality. This must have been the case particularly among those noble children who were cared for by lower-class women and who therefore received diets resembling those of the rest of the population. In addition, aristocrats drank the same water, and were exposed to the same diseases that laid claim to nutrients, as the population at large.[94] For all of these reasons, the notion of a rise in the nutritional status of the lower nobility is not implausible, and corroborates the evidence presented earlier that nutritional status was increasing in the 1740s.

The notion that the stature of upper-class youth could rise is further supported by evidence from late-eighteenth-century Stuttgart, where the stature of aristocratic youth also rose. This could be an indication

[92] Only about half of the Hungarian nobility owned land by the middle of the eighteenth century. Many of the impoverished nobles became officials in the households of the higher nobility. Béla K. Király, *Hungary in the Late Eighteenth Century: The Decline of Enlightened Despotism* (New York: Columbia University Press, 1969), p. 35.

[93] Th. Leitner von Leitnertreu, *Geschichte der Wiener Neustädter Militärakademie* (Hermannstadt: n.p., 1852).

[94] Susan Cotts Watkins and Etienne van de Walle, "Nutrition, Mortality, and Population Size: Malthus's Court of Last Resort," *Journal of Interdisciplinary History* 14 (1983): 205–226.

that the increase in nutritional status among the upper classes, which had begun earlier, continued for the remainder of the century.[95]

The trend in the stature of sons of soldiers in the Austrian elementary schools also corresponds to the pattern found for the adult population. There was a consistent decline in stature at all ages between 1760 and 1800 (Figures 2.5 and B.5; Tables 2.14, B.15, and B.16). The difference between heights attained in the 1760s or 1770s and those of the 1780s ranged from 0.3 to 4.5 cm at various ages. The disadvantage of this sample is that its early part stems from an orphanage, while the data after the 1780s are from military schools, which were its successor.[96] However, the declining trend is not likely to have been caused by this attribute of the sample.[97] If one examines the military-school sample by itself one still finds that stature continued to decline until the birth cohorts of the early nineteenth century (Table 2.14). The decline was no longer substantial among the birth cohorts of the 1790s: it was generally less than one centimeter, with the exception of boys fifteen or older, whose height declined by as much as three centimeters. The boys' nutritional status did not reverse until those cohorts who were measured after the Napoleonic War (Figure 2.5). Therefore, the trend in the height of the Habsburg youth is similar to the one found for the military recruits: diminishing stature after the 1760s with stabilization by the turn of the nineteenth century. This corroborating evidence is quite important, because the children's records can be analyzed without the statistical transformations required by the nature of the data on the adult military recruits. Consequently, less uncertainty is associated with the results obtained.

Growth increments are themselves sensitive to nutritional status, especially during adolescence. The higher the nutritional status, the earlier and larger the adolescent growth spurt. The largest height increment of the youth of lower-aristocratic descent (1735–55) and orphans (1760s) was reached at age 15 (Table 2.15 and Figure B.6). The size of the maximum mean growth increment of the orphans born in the 1760s was almost 8 cm, i.e., even greater than that of the aristocrats.

During the last decades of the century, the adolescent growth spurt of boys attending military school was delayed. Compared with orphans born in the 1760s, who experienced their greatest growth increment on average between ages 14.5 and 15.5, boys born in the 1780s experi-

---

[95] Komlos, "Height and Social Status in Germany."

[96] Rechberger von Rechkron, *Das Bildungswesen im Österreichischen Heere* (Vienna: n.p., 1878), p. 35.

[97] About a third of the orphans' fathers were military officers, which was probably higher than in the military school part of the sample.

Figure 2.5. Height of Boys in the Habsburg Monarchy by Age and Decade of Birth, 1760–1815

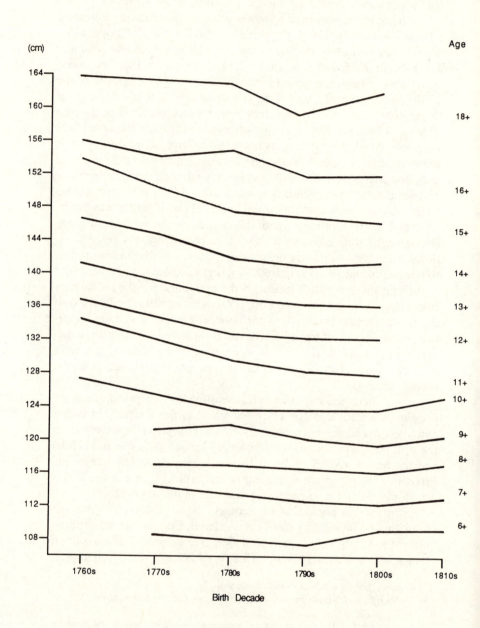

Table 2.14 Height of Boys in the Habsburg Monarchy,[a] 1735-1814 (cm)

Age at Last Birthday — ages 6–11

Year of Birth	6 N	6 H	6 s.d.	7 N	7 H	7 s.d.	8 N	8 H	8 s.d.	9 N	9 H	9 s.d.	10 N	10 H	10 s.d.	11 N	11 H	11 s.d.
1735/55[b]	20	108.7	5.4	29	114.2		38	117.3	4.3	44	121.9	6.1	50	127.6	5.3	30	131.5	6.4
1765/69[c]										11	119.5	6.3	18	123.7	6.8	27	134.4	7.5
1770/74[c]										17	122.3	4.6	12	123.9	4.5	15	130.8	5.5
1780/84[d]	19	107.8	5.1	108	112.1		217	117.0	4.7	263	120.6	5.1	316	124.0	5.7	72	129.2	5.4
1785/89[d]	94	106.9	4.9	234	112.1		263	116.1	5.1	496	119.8	5.3	422	124.0	5.9	312	128.7	6.0
1790/94[d]	164	107.8	4.6	401	111.8		700	115.9	5.4	659	119.4	5.7	649	123.6	6.1	634	128.2	6.3
1795/99[d]	99	109.1	4.7	274	112.1		436	116.2	5.3	699	119.6	5.5	986	123.8	5.9	387	127.8	6.3
1800/04[d]	118	109.2	4.4	311	112.9		344	117.1	4.6	196	121.1	4.9	27	125.5	4.5	1031	128.0	6.2
1805/09[d]																		
1810/14[d]																		

Age at Last Birthday — ages 12–18

Year of Birth	12 N	12 H	12 s.d.	13 N	13 H	13 s.d.	14 N	14 H	14 s.d.	15 N	15 H	15 s.d.	16 N	16 H	16 s.d.	17 N	17 H	17 s.d.	18 N	18 H	18 s.d.
1735/44[b]	55	134.2	7.2	114	138.4	7.2	88	142.7	7.8	49	148.9	8.1	22	156.2	3.8						
1745/55[b]	18	140.4	5.2	51	144.2	7.7	68	145.7	6.4	43	152.4	8.6	16	156.2	7.2						
1760/64[c]																					
1765/69[c]	41	137.0	6.7	40	141.4	6.7	32	146.2	6.3										9	163.7	5.5
1770/74[c]										20	154.0	6.5									
1775/79[d]							22	144.8	7.3	27	149.9	11.7	14	153.8	10.2	9	157.4	6.4			
1780/84[d]	188	132.5	6.5	238	137.3	6.3	242	141.1	6.8	30	148.6	9.4	110	154.8	7.5	9	161.2	4.5			
1785/89[d]	353	132.2	5.9	366	137.0	6.8	478	141.5	7.2	383	147.0	8.4	365	154.3	8.0	207	160.8	7.2	49	161.7	5.2
1790/94[d]	720	132.0	6.6	855	136.4	7.1	661	140.6	7.5	442	146.7	8.3	553	151.6	8.3	208	160.2	6.1	48	163.3	4.0
1795/99[d]	460	132.0	6.2	535	136.5	6.6	735	140.9	7.4	573	146.3	8.5	336	152.0	7.9	430	157.3	7.6	115	159.1	5.9
1800/04[d]										814	145.9	8.2				270	158.4	7.4	61	160.0	6.1
1805/09[d]	732	132.0	6.5	434	136.2	6.4	223	141.3	7.3	21	147.2	8.4	648	152.1	8.2	447	158.3	7.8	39	161.5	6.1

Source: Kriegsarchiv, Vienna. Standestabellen Erziehungshäuser Faszikel 3925, 3926, 3927; Josephinische Waisenhaus, Faszikel 3922; Theresianische Militärakademie, Faszikel 434. Notes: N = No. of observations; H = mean height; s.d. = standard deviation. [a]For a breakdown by place of birth see Table B.16; [b]Aristocrats; [c]Orphans; [d]Students in military schools.

Table 2.15 Mean Height Increment of Boys, Habsburg Monarchy, 1735-1814 (cm)

	7	8	9	10	11	12	13	14	15	16	17	18
					Age at Center of Increment Period							
1735/44[a]						4.2[d]	4.2	4.3	6.2			
1745/55[a]							3.8	1.5	6.7	3.8		
1760/74[b]	5.5	3.1	4.6		6.8	2.6	4.4	4.8	7.8	2.2	3.8[e]	3.8
1775/79[c]										3.9	5.5[f]	
1780/84[c]				4.2	7.1				3.8	6.2	6.0	0.9
1785/89[c]				1.6	5.3	3.3	4.8	3.8	5.9	7.3	5.9	3.1
1790/94[c]	4.3	4.9	3.6	3.4	4.7	3.5	4.8	4.5	5.2	4.9	5.7	1.8
1795/99[c]	5.2	4.0	3.7	4.2	4.2	3.8	4.4	4.2	5.7	5.7	6.4	1.6
1800/04[c]	4.0	4.1	3.5	4.2	4.2	4.2	4.5	4.4	5.0	6.2	6.2	3.2
1805/09[c]	3.0	4.1	3.4	4.2	4.2	4.0	4.2	5.1	5.9			
1810/14[c]	3.7	4.2	4.0	4.4								

Source: See Table 2.10.
[a]Aristocrats; [b]Orphans; [c]Boys in military schools; [d]1735/55;
[e]Estimated difference of mean height; [f]Average of 1770/79.

enced this at about age 16, and those born in the 1790s at age 17 (Figures B.7 and B.8). Corresponding to the delay in the adolescent growth spurt, the size of the peak height increment also fell over time (Table 2.15). By the turn of the nineteenth century the trend reversed (Figure B.9). The largest growth increment in the 1800s was reached between ages 16 and 17. Hence the adolescent growth spurt was delayed at the end of the eighteenth century by a full two years. The size of the maximum increment fell by 2.6 cm. Both of these results are consistent with the finding that the height-by-age schedule of the children was shifting down in response to a decline in nutritional status (Figure B.5). Therefore the trend in children's stature is yet another indication that the pattern outlined earlier on the basis of adult recruits is evidence of a real decline in nutritional status during the second half of the century and not some artifact of the sampling procedure, of the army's recruiting practices, or of the statistical techniques used to analyze the data.

The consistency of the evidence on the students with that drawn from the recruiting records can be checked by comparing the height of the eighteen-year-old boys with that of the adult soldiers. The boys in the military schools at age eighteen were between 159.1 and 163.3 cm tall. If one adds 0.5 cm to this height in order to account for the growth between ages 18 and 20, the results are very close to the height of the younger soldiers in the infantry units (Tables 2.11, 2.14, and B.9). Moreover, if one adds 1.6 cm to the height of the students in order to account for their growth until they reached their terminal height (Table 2.11), then their estimated final height is again within the range of estimates of the recruits' adult height (Table 2.1). In addition, Preece-Baines growth curves were fitted to the height measurement of the boys.[98] With the exception of one outlier, the estimated final height for the various birth cohorts was between 162.9 and 165.3 cm, in other words, within the above range. Thus the data set from the military schools is consistent, in the main, with the evidence on the soldiers.

International Comparisons

The terminal stature of the populations in the five provinces hitherto examined was in the range of 165–170 cm prior to the beginning of rapid population growth in the middle of the eighteenth century.[99] Soldiers in the Habsburg army born in France, Namur, Luxemburg, and Tyrol appear to have been above this range (Table 2.9). The height of Swedish soldiers, at 168.5 cm, was comparable in the 1740s, while British recruits, who were about 164 cm tall, were somewhat shorter.[100] Thus the stature of the population of the Habsburg Monarchy appears to have been within the European norm at mid-century.

The European nutritional trends, however, diverged considerably from the one in the British colonies of North America. There, after the 1720s the male population maintained the distinctly modern stature of 173 cm throughout the century.[101] Even slaves born in the New World were taller as adults than the European peasantry, implying that the former had more calories and protein in their diet.[102]

By the end of the eighteenth century the nutritional status of the Habsburg population relative to that of other lands appears to have deteriorated. Insofar as the American population maintained its stature, its nutritional advantage widened. While the nutritional status of the

[98] The estimates were kindly provided by Professor James Tanner of the University of London. The peak height velocities were between 5.4 and 7.2 cm, and the age of the adolescent growth spurt was between 15.4 and 16.2 years.

[99] In the sixteenth and seventeenth centuries the average height of men in Steyermark, estimated on the basis of the size of armaments, was apparently on the order of 160 cm; Oskar Stracker, "Körpermasse der Kinder und Jugendlichen im Jahre 1962," Österreichische Ärztezeitung 18 (1963): 1–24.

[100] Sandberg and Steckel, "Heights and Economic History"; Sokoloff and Villaflor, "Early Achievement of Modern Stature."

[101] Fogel, "Nutrition and the Decline in Mortality since 1700."

[102] Robert Margo and Richard H. Steckel, "The Height of American Slaves: New Evidence on Slave Nutrition and Health," Social Science History 6 (1982): 516–538.

other European populations also declined, the decline in some provinces of the Habsburg Monarchy was greater than elsewhere in Europe
(Table 2.9). Of the European populations sampled, none seems to have
been as short as the Bohemians or Lower Austrians born at the end of
the century, who ranged from 161 to 163 cm. By 1800 Swedish recruits
had lost a little over 2 cm from their stature, but at 166 cm they were
still far above the height of the Habsburg soldiers.[103]

In spite of increases in their stature, Habsburg aristocratic youth were
shorter than their German counterparts[104] (Table 2.16). The latter, in
turn, were shorter than English gentry boys attending the Sandhurst
Military Academy.[105] Hence the nutritional status of the upper classes
of different countries was not identical, perhaps because dietary customs
or, more likely, real incomes differed. However, the disease environ-

Table 2.16 Height of Boys Born in Germany and in the Habsburg Monarchy, 1745-1799.

| Age | German | | | Habsburg |
	Aristocrat 1760-1780	Middle Class 1760-1780	Peasant 1790s	Aristocrat 1745-1755
8	122.5	119.9		
9	128.3	121.7	116.3	
10	130.7	126.2	119.4	
11	134.6	132.0	123.9	
12	139.3	135.8	127.6	140.4
13	144.4	139.6	131.5	144.2
14	150.6	144.4	136.4	145.7
15	156.4	149.5	140.6	152.4
16	161.1	155.4	146.8	156.2
17	164.3	159.9	151.1	

Source: See Table 2.14; Hartmann, "Beobachtungen zur Akzeleration."

[103] Sandberg and Steckel, "Heights and Economic History."

[104] Hartmann, "Beobachtungen zur Akzeleration," pp. 87–119, and Table 10. A comparison of German and Habsburg aristocratic youth is not fully warranted because the
data pertain to individuals born a generation apart during a period when nutritional status
was changing rapidly in Europe. One might nevertheless note that until age 13 Habsburg
aristocrats born between 1745 and 1755 were about the same height as German aristocratic youth born between 1760 and 1780. Thereafter, German aristocratic youth experienced an earlier and greater adolescent growth spurt than Habsburg aristocratic youth,
whose height became closer to that of German middle class boys between the ages of
fourteen and eighteen.

[105] Roderick Floud, "Measuring the Transformation of the European Economies: Income, Health, and Welfare," unpublished manuscript, Department of History, University
of London, 1984.

ment was probably not sufficiently different across Europe to have accounted for such wide dissimilarity in nutritional status.

Class differences are vividly reflected in the stature of boys in various countries. Boys attending prestigious military schools in England, France, and Germany were much taller than the population at large (Table 2.17). In Germany aristocrats were taller than middle-class boys of the same age by three to seven centimeters throughout adolescence.[106] One important exception to this generalization is the stature

Table 2.17 Height of Boys of Selected Ages, Various Countries, by Year of Birth (cm)

	Age at Last Birthday in Years						
	6	10	13	14	15	16	18
1800 Habsburg Monarchy[a]	108	124	137	141	146	152	162
1760/80 German Middle Class[b]		128	140	144	150	155	163
1760/80 German Aristocrats[b]		131	144	151	156	161	167
1800 London Poor[c]			132	135	142	147	
1800 London Gentry [c]				157	163		
1800 France [d]						166	169
1800/60 United States Slaves[e]	103	125	141	147	153	158	166
1830/80 United States[f]						166	171
1900 Russia[g]					147	153	162
1920 Vienna[g]					152	155	160
1923 Vienna[g]					151	158	164
1981 Austria[h]	124	141		166			180

Sources: [a]Table 2.14; [b]Hartmann, "Beobachtungen zur Akzeleration"; [c]Roderick Floud, "Measuring the Transformation of the European Economies: Income, Health and Welfare," Department of History, University of London, 1984; [d]Jean Sutter, René Izac, and Tran Ngoc Toan, "L'Évolution de la Taille des Polytechniciens," Population (1958):373-406; [e]Richard Steckel, "A Peculiar Population: The Nutrition, Health, and Mortality of American Slaves from Childhood to Maturity,"; [f]John Komlos, "The Height and Weight of West Point Cadets: Dietary Change in Antebellum America," Journal of Economic History 47 (1987): 897-927 (stature at ages other than reported above were: 17: 169.6 cm; 19: 171.3 cm; 20: 171.8 cm); [g] Poor Jews; E. Nobel, "Anthropometrische Untersuchungen an Jugendlichen in Wien," Zeitschrift für Kinderheilkunde 36 (1924):13-16; [h] Österreichischen Statistischen Zentralamt. Note: twentieth-century dates refer to date of measurement.

[106] Hartmann, "Beobachtungen zur Akzeleration," pp. 9, 25.

of American slaves, who were taller than boys in the Habsburg Monarchy after age nine.[107] Only compared with that of London slum boys does the height of the Habsburg boys appear favorable.

By twentieth-century standards, boys of the Habsburg Monarchy were extremely stunted. At some ages they were well below the first centile of the modern height distribution. At age fourteen, for instance, they lagged ten centimeters behind West European norms established circa 1900.[108] Viennese children who lived through World War I were only slightly taller in 1920 than the Austrian boys of the eighteenth century[109] (Table 2.17). Compared with contemporary Austrian children, however, boys in the Habsburg military schools appear to have been tiny. They were between 16 to 18 cm shorter, a difference of about four years of growth for them. In fact, almost all populations in the world today are taller than the Habsburg boys of the eighteenth century.[110] One can find comparable heights only among some underdeveloped areas of Thailand, India, Burma, and Mexico.[111]

Cross-sectional Pattern

Whereas in modern market societies there is a positive correlation between height and per capita income, this was not always true in prior centuries.[112] In the eighteenth-century Habsburg Monarchy the correlation tended to be negative. The populations of Lower Austria and Bohemia, the most economically developed regions of the Monarchy, were generally the shortest, while those of Hungary and Galicia, the

[107] Richard H. Steckel, "A Peculiar Population: The Nutrition, Health and Mortality of American Slaves from Childhood to Maturity," *Journal of Economic History* 46 (1986): 721–742.

[108] At the turn of the twentieth century there were, however, still some European populations to whom the Habsburg boys were comparable, such as the poverty-stricken Jews of Russia.

[109] C. Pirquet, "Eine einfache Tafel zur Bestimmung von Wachstum und Ernährungszustand bei Kindern," *Zeitschrift für Kinderheilkunde* 6 (1913): 255; E. Nobel, "Anthropometrische Untersuchungen an Jugendlichen in Wien," *Zeitschrift für Kinderheilkunde* 36 (1924): 13–16.

[110] Children of Taipei, Hong Kong, Japan, Alaska, and South Korea, for instance, are all taller.

[111] Phyllis B. Eveleth and James M. Tanner, *Worldwide Variation in Human Growth* (Cambridge, England: Cambridge University Press, 1976), pp. 277, 307, 331, 388.

[112] Richard H. Steckel, "Height and Per Capita Income," *Historical Methods* 16 (1983): 1–7. Another indication of the validity of this assertion is the fact that heights in the American colonies were greater than in England in the eighteenth century, even though the relationship between American and English per capita income was just the opposite.

least developed provinces, were taller[113] (Tables 2.1 and B.2, and Figures 2.1 and 2.2). The height of Moravian soldiers, born in a province industrially more advanced than either Hungary or Galicia, but with a more productive agricultural sector, tended to fall in the upper end of the range. Hence, the recruits from the areas with a large agricultural sector, even if the economy was relatively underdeveloped, were well nourished by the standards of the time. The average height of the Hungarian birth cohorts of the 1740s, for example, falls into the 25th percentile of the modern height distribution. In contrast, the height of the Bohemian recruits is only in the third centile. Yet Bohemian GNP per capita exceeded Hungary's by at least 25 percent (Table 2.18).

Although stature in the eighteenth-century Habsburg Monarchy does not correlate well with per capita income, it does correlate better with per capita food production (Table 2.19). Per capita output of calories and of protein was greater in Galicia, Hungary, and Moravia than in Bohemia or Lower Austria, and the recruits born in the former set of provinces were also taller most of the time than those born in the provinces whose per capita calorie output was less. The calculation in Table 2.19 pertains to the 1780s, but the relative rankings were undoubtedly the same even earlier in the century.

The cross-sectional pattern thus indicates that propinquity to the source of food provided some nutritional advantages.[114] Individuals who bought their food had to pay for transportation costs and for the efforts of middlemen, whereas subsistence farmers did not. Animals driven to market consumed nutrients along the way, and when slaughtered provided extra-edibles that might not be consumed in the towns.[115] Moreover, prior to the age of refrigeration, the transport of food must have increased the likelihood of contamination and lowered

---

[113] In contrast to that of the peasants, the stature of youth of lower aristocratic descent in the first half of the eighteenth century did not generally depend on their place of birth (equation 1, Table 2.13). Those born in Bohemia were taller than average (by 2.7 cm). The overall pattern, however, implies that regional variation in stature among the aristocracy of the Habsburg Monarchy, even among the lower segment of this group, was not as widespread as it was among the peasantry during the early part of the eighteenth century.

[114] A similar cross-sectional pattern emerges in other data sets. In Vienna, for instance, domestic servants during the second half of the nineteenth century benefited from being close to nutrients in their employers' households, and gave birth to heavier babies than did women in other low status occupations. W. Peter Ward, "Weight at Birth in Vienna, Austria, 1865–1930," *Annals of Human Biology* 14 (1987): 495–506.

[115] As much as 18 percent of swine by weight is composed of such parts as the brain, blood, kidney, skin, and tongue. George Holmes, *Meat Situation in the United States*, United States Department of Agriculture, Report no. 109 (Washington, DC: 1916). These were eaten by the peasantry, but not to the same degree by the urban population.

Table 2.18 Gross National Product of Hungary and Bohemia circa 1789
(Millions of Gulden unless otherwise noted)

Product	Bohemia	Hungary	
		Local Prices	Bohemian Prices
Wheat	4.5	13.0	24.5
Rye	18.0	23.0	44.4
Barley	5.7	4.5	8.0
Oats	8.5	9.2	13.1
Meat	8.8	14.3	20.0
Wool	1.6	6.0	6.7
Other	3.0	7.0	10.0
Agriculture total	50.1	77.0	126.7
Industry			
Large	14	2	
Local	3	6	
Mining	1	2	
Industry total	18	10	
Services	6	4	7
Total GNP	74	91	144
Per Capita (Gulden)	25.6	13	20.5

Sources: Bohemian prices are actually prices in Klosterneuburg from Alfred Pribram, Materialen zur Geschichte der Preise und Löhne in Österreich (Vienna, 1938). Price of wheat is from Arthur Salz, Geschichte der Böhmischen Industrie in der Neuzeit (München, 1913). Hungarian prices are from Eckhart, A bécsi udvar (Budapest, 1922), p. 76. Bohemian industrial production is from Joseph Schreyer, Fabriken und Manufakturenstand in Böhmen (Frankfurt and Leipzig: 1799); and from Joseph Schreyer, Kommerz, Fabriken und Manufakturen des Königreichs Böhmen (Prague: 1790).
Note: Industrial production in Hungary is estimated to be about 10 percent of total output and services to be about 5 percent. Total Hungarian exports in 1780 were about 13 million gulden, i.e., between 10 and 14 percent of GNP, which seems plausibel. Eckhart, A bécsi udvar, p. 322.

its nutritional value. Therefore commercialization is likely to bring with it not only a monetary cost, but a cost in nutrients as well.

Many items of food are left out of the calculation presented in Table 2.19. A more detailed estimate, based on data pertaining to Bunzlau County, indicates that the major grains and meat provided most of the nutrients for the population and also that there were variations in food production even within a province (Table 2.20). Thus, while in Bohemia 1,829 calories were produced daily per capita in the four products enumerated in Table 2.19, in Bunzlau County only 1,056 calories were. Evidence from this county indicates that the four staples (wheat, rye, barley, and beef) provided about 80 percent of the total calories

Table 2.19 Per Capita Production of Nutrients in the Habsburg Monarchy by Provinces, circa 1789

	Lower Austria	Bohemia	Moravia	Galicia	Hungary
Poupulation (millions)	1.3	2.9	1.3	3.1	7.0
Grain (thousand tons)					
Wheat	25.0	86.4	73.3	124.9	470.0
Rye	148.6	434.1	204.8	343.8	1070.0
Barley	20.1	162.9	82.7	400.0	230.0
Total[a]	155.0	546.7	288.6	695.0	1416.0
Per Capita(kg)	119	189	222	224	202
Calories daily	1091	1736	2042	2084	1851
Protein daily (grams)	37.6	56.8	66.7	62.2	62.5
Livestock (thousands)					
Oxen	85	254	49	370	830
Cows	200	700	390	800	1500
Beef[b] (kg)	6.1	9.2	9.5	10.6	9.6
Total protein	39.6	59.7	69.7	65.6	65.6
Total calories	1153	1829	2138	2191	1948
Stature[c]($\hat{x}$) (cm)	162.4	161.4	163.9	163.3	163.4

Sources: Roman Sandgruber, Österreichische Agrarstatistik, 1750-1918 (Vienna: Verlag für Geschichte und Politik, 1978), pp. 163-165; Gyula Benda, Statisztikai adatok a magyar mezőgazdaság történetéhez (Budapest: Központi Statisztikai Hivatal, 1973), p. 119; Alfred Gürtler, Die Volkszählungen Maria Theresias und Josef II, 1753-1790; Bernice Watt and Annabel Merrill, Composition of Foods (Washington, DC: United States Department of Agriculture, Agricultural Handbook no. 8, 1963).

[a]Sum of grain production minus 20 percent for seed and losses; [b]Number of oxen and cows multiplied by 224 kg, divided by 8; [c] in the 1780s and 1790s (Table 2.1).

and 70 percent of the total protein consumption of the population. One can, therefore, increase the accuracy of the estimate of calorie and protein production in the Monarchy by inflating the results in Table 2.19 appropriately, thereby accounting for the products for which global statistics do not exist. The average production of nutrients with this adjustment, after per capita output is converted into output per adult-male equivalent, becomes about 3,000 calories and 105 grams of protein per day[116] (Table 2.21).

In order to convert these figures into estimates of ingested nutrients,

[116] According to an 1881 statistic, average protein intake in Hungary was 97 grams daily; Mihály Zafir, "Az 1881. évi Népélelmezési Statisztika mai Szemmel," Statisztikai Szemle 61 (1983): 1017–1034.

99

Table 2.20 Food Production in Bunzlau County, Bohemia, 1786

Food	Amount[a]	Per[b] Capita	Per Day Calories	Per Day Protein[c]
Grains				
Wheat	301			
Rye	360			
Oats	22			
Barley	11			
Total grain		106.0	964	33.2
Vegetables, Fruit				
Legumes	122	18.5	172	11.3
Garden produce[d]	130	19.7	12	0.6
Potatoes	19	3.3	6	0.2
Fruit	112	12.8	19	0.1
Meat[e]				
Sheep/mutton	90[f]	3.5	26	1.3
Beef/cattle	85[f]	8.5	86	2.7
Pork/swine	11[f]	0.8	10	0.2
Average[g]		115.7	1295	49.6

Source: Joseph Grünwald, Drey Abhandlungen über die physikalische Beschaffenheit einiger Distrikte und Gegenden von Böhmen (Prague and Dresden: Böhmische Gesellschaft der Wissenschaften, 1786), p. 114; Watt and Merrill, Composition of Foods.
[a] Thousands of metzen; [b] kilograms; [c] grams; [d] cabbage, hops, etc.; [e]1,000 heads; [f] Assuming that the slaughter ratio for swine and sheep was 50 percent and that the meat yield per swine was 40 kg and per sheep, 22 kg. For cattle weights, see Table 2.19; [g]For a population of 279,000.

the quantity of wasted calories should be subtracted. Evidence on this important variable is nonexistent for the eighteenth century, but, according to one source, it might have been as high as 20 percent of food production in late-nineteenth-century America.[117] Waste was probably less in East-Central Europe, because food was much more valuable there than in America.[118] In order to make some adjustment for this unknown quantity, ten percent has been deducted from production.

Deducting for waste thus leaves about 2,700 calories and 94 grams

[117] Merrill Bennett and Rosamond Peirce, "Change in the American National Diet, 1879–1959," Food Research Institute Studies 2 (1961): 95–119.
[118] Elizabeth A. Dowler and Young Ok Seo, "Assessment of Energy Intake: Estimates of Food Supply v Measurement of Food Consumption," Food Policy 10 (1985): 278–288.

Table 2.21 Estimate of Per Capita Daily Nutrient Consumption in the
Habsburg Monarchy, circa 1789

	Calories	Protein (gr)
Per capita[a]	1924	62.5
Adjustment[b]	451	24.4
Total per capita	2375	86.9
Per adult male equivalent[c]	2969	104.7
Ingested[d]	2700	94.0

Sources: Tables 2.19 and 2.20.

[a]For the products enumerated in Table 2.19; averages were weighted by
population size; [b]Data in Table 2.20 indicate that products enumerated in
Table 2.19 provided 81 percent of the calorie production and 72 percent of
the protein production in Bunzlau county. This relationship was assumed
to prevail in the other regions as well; [c]Assuming that adult males
consumed 25 percent more calories and 20 percent more protein than the
population on average; [d]Some indication of waste can be found in late-
nineteenth-century America in Massachusetts, Seventh Annual Report of
the Bureau of Statistics and Labor, Public Doc. no. 15 , 1886, part 3, p.
246.

of protein as the probable daily average nutrient intake per adult male.
This is very close to the 2,800 calories consumed daily by members of
22 English households in the late eighteenth century,[119] but considerably below, perhaps by as much as 1,000 calories, the average in antebellum America.[120] While the 2,700 calories might be acceptable for
populations not subject to excessive work regimens, living in a modern
epidemiological environment, and in which children attend school past
adolescence, it was not likely to have been adequate in the eighteenth
century, when the work intensity and the frequent disease encounters
laid claim to calories to a much larger extent than they do today. The
present recommended allowance for men engaged in heavy physical
work is 3,500 calories, but the requirement in prior centuries must have
been even greater.[121]

[119] Shammas's estimate of 2400 calories per adult male equivalent has now been revised
by Robert W. Fogel. Shammas, "English Diet," p. 256; Fogel, "Biomedical Approaches,"
p. 86.
[120] John Komlos, "The Height and Weight of West Point Cadets: Dietary Change in
Antebellum America," Journal of Economic History 47 (1987): 897–927.
[121] Shammas, "English Diet," p. 257; Freudenberger and Cummins, "Health, Work,

The average estimates also disguise the problem of how the consumption of nutrients was distributed within the society. According to a recent estimate for late-seventeenth-century England, 50 percent of the meat was consumed by just under 20 percent of the population.[122] Thus, many Europeans were living very close to the biological subsistence minimum by the late eighteenth century. Malnutrition was endemic.

The negative relationship between nutritional status and industrial development, which has been found among the different provinces of the Monarchy, holds up even within the province of Bohemia. In those four counties in which industrial production was most advanced, $\bar{x}$ is consistently lower after the 1740s than it is in the rest of the province.[123] Even within Bunzlau County itself the stature of recruits ($\bar{x}$) was smaller in manors where textile production was the most widespread (Tables B.5 and B.6). This cross-sectional pattern indicates that, in the first half of the century, underdeveloped regions that were not overpopulated and that had a large self-sufficient agricultural population, isolated from outside markets, were better nourished than those that had a more developed industrial sector.

The Polish and Hungarian men were initially better nourished, probably because their parents were, for the most part, engaged in subsistence agriculture, and hence did not pay market prices for agricultural produce. These provinces had higher land/labor ratios than the other areas under consideration, and few urban centers, which would have been a source of demand for their products.[124] Being isolated from markets by high transport and transaction costs, the subsistence peasant families had little choice but to consume all of their own food output[125] (Figure 2.6). Large estates working for the market did exist in Hungary, but even the peasants working on them generally had their own plots of land as well as some livestock, and were dependent on the market only

---

and Leisure," p. 4. This allowance is recommended for a "male engaged in heavy work" only 8 hours a day. World Health Organization, *Energy and Protein Requirements*, p. 77.

[122] Richard Stone, "Some Seventeenth Century Econometrics: Consumers' Behaviour," unpublished manuscript, Département d'Économétrie, Université de Genève, Switzerland, 1987, p. 31.

[123] Although $\bar{x}$ is a biased measure of $\hat{x}$, to the extent that the minimum height requirement is the same for the two truncated samples (and is equally enforced), then $\bar{x}_{r1}$ is less than or greater than $\bar{x}_{r2}$ as $\hat{x}_{r1}$ is less than or greater than $\hat{x}_{r2}$.

[124] Although Hungary's population was more than twice that of Bohemia, it had only one-tenth the number of towns Bohemia did in 1789. Alfred Gürtler, *Die Volkszählungen Maria Theresias und Josef II, 1753–1790* (Innsbruck: Wagner, 1909), Table 8.

[125] Local trade need not be ruled out entirely, but that must have been a very small segment of total consumption.

Figure 2.6. Food Consumption of Two Individuals—One Initially Self-Sufficient, A, and Another Integrated into the World Market, B

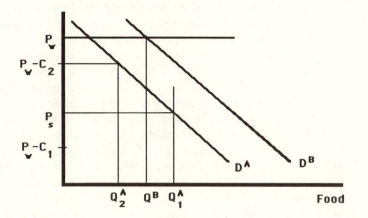

Legend:

P_w = World price of food

P_s = Shadow price of food for individual A in period 1

A = Superscript denotes self-sufficient individual in period 1 who becomes integrated into the market in period 2

B = Superscript denotes individual integrated into world market in both periods

D = Demand curve for Food

Q = Quantity of Food Demanded

1 = Subscript denotes initial period

2 = Subscript denotes final period

Y = Per capita real income

C = Transaction and information costs

Assume: $(P_w - P_s) < C_1$; $Y^A < Y^B$; $C_2 < C_1$

to a limited extent. In addition, the share of the landless in Bohemia and Lower Austria was greater than in the other provinces, and the level of urbanization was also higher.[126] In 1754 Moravia had 12 percent, while

[126] According to the census of 1785, 17 percent of the Bohemian labor force consisted of burghers and industrial workers. In Moravia their share was 11 percent, and in Hungary 6 percent. These figures probably do not include all workers engaged in domestic industry. Dickson, *Finance and Government*, vol. 1, pp. 46, 57.

Lower Austria had 23 percent of its population living in urban areas.[127] Vienna alone had 175,000 inhabitants at mid-century.[128]

In addition to population growth, the integration of the market must have contributed to the deterioration in nutritional status among the Hungarian and Polish peasantry. With the expansion of trade, their isolation broke down, and commodity flows tended to equilibrate nutritional status across the Monarchy. The creation of a customs union among Moravia, Bohemia, and Austria in 1775, enlarged in 1783 to include Galicia, accelerated the process of creating a unified market in foodstuffs. Hungary remained outside of the union but with a preferential status; this easing of trade restrictions tended, however, to equalize prices as well as incomes across the Monarchy. The integration of the market and the purchases of the army meant that a large agricultural sector no longer guaranteed the same comparative nutritional advantages as before.

There is considerable evidence that market integration proceeded in Hungary after the 1760s, with a concomitant increase in grain exports. While in the 1760s 1.2 million metzen of grain was exported, in 1771 and 1772 exports tripled, remaining at 2 million metzen for the rest of the decade. Cattle exports doubled between the 1740s and the 1770s.[129] Transport facilities, too, were improved, and by the end of the century Hungary was exporting between 5 and 14 percent of its grain output.[130] No doubt the Napoleonic Wars contributed to this process: the increased purchases of the army, even if stationed on foreign soil, were dependent on the grain-production capacity of Hungary and Galicia. In addition, the rise in cereal prices relative to transaction and information costs during the latter decades of the century made it profitable for merchants to penetrate new markets. In the 1760s Hungarian and Polish grain was sold as far away as Genoa or Tyrol. Of course, the harvest failures of the early 1770s in Bohemia also brought with them an increased reliance on grain deliveries from Hungary.[131] Since the large differences in nutritional status evident prior to mid-century were pred-

---

[127] Henyrk Grossmann, "Die Anfänge und geschichtliche Entwicklung der amtlichen Statistik in Österreich," *Statistische Monatschrift* (1916): 331–423.

[128] Goehlert, "Ergebnisse."

[129] Eckhart, *A bécsi udvar*, pp. 190, 318.

[130] Gyula Mérei, "A Magyar Királyság Külkereskedelmi Piaci Viszonyai 1790–1848 Között," *Századok* 115 (1981): 463–521; János Belitzky, *A Magyar Gabonakivitel Története 1860-ig* (Budapest: n.p., 1932), p. 99. For similar patterns in Russian agriculture see Kahan, *The Plow, the Hammer, and the Knout*, p. 59.

[131] Belitzky, *A Magyar Gabonakivitel Története 1860-ig*; István Kiss, "Der Agrarcharakter des Ungarischen Exports vom 15. bis 18. Jahrhundert," *Jahrbücher für Wirtschaftsgeschichte* (1978): 147–169.

icated on the existence of isolated markets, the process of market integration tended to equilibrate these differences in nutritional status, and therefore in human stature.

As a consequence, the heights of the populations across the various provinces tended to converge. In the 1740s and 1750s the range of differences in adult stature $(\hat{x})$ was close to five centimeters (Table 2.1), since food production per capita varied across the several provinces. By the birth cohorts of the 1780s the range had declined to about two centimeters (Figure 2.2). This is an indication that genetic differences among the various ethnic groups were not an important factor in the within-group variation in their stature.[132]

The stature of children in the military schools conforms to the pattern found for the soldiers insofar as the differences in their height across the various nationalities were very small at the end of the century (Table B.16). The heights of the boys of various nationalities might have been similar to one another also on account of the fact that they probably experienced the same army food for much, although not all, of their lives. The pattern is complex, however, because differences in the growth profile appear over time as well as at various ages. Among orphans born in the 1760s and 1770s, Galician boys alone were significantly shorter than average (Table 2.13, equation 2). Thereafter, only Carinthian and Croatian boys were consistently taller than average.[133] By the 1770s and 1780s the range of stature by place of birth of recruits was smaller than earlier.

Because in the middle of the eighteenth century large segments of the Habsburg population were isolated from the market, one should not expect market prices of food to correlate perfectly with fluctuations in stature. Since subsistence peasants did not buy or sell grain, their decisions were independent of price fluctuations in distant markets.[134] The quantity of food consumed is determined by the amount of output (Q_1^A in Figure 2.6). Hence in a nonmarket economy, output determines the amount consumed and its shadow price. Yet, aside from minor devia-

[132] Another reason that the degree to which height declined was inversely related to the level of height might have been that the elasticity of stature with respect to nutrients was not constant. Hence, populations that were shorter than average, such as the Bohemian and Lower Austrian ones, would have declined in stature less even for an equal decline in caloric or protein intake than the Hungarian or Polish populations, which had been in the 1740s among the tallest in the monarchy.

[133] Croatians were on average 2.4 cm taller than Bohemians. There are, however, only 412 Croatians in the sample. Boys of Bohemian, Lower Austrian, and Hungarian birth, whose statures were not consistently different from one another, comprised 40 percent of the whole sample.

[134] The price elasticity of demand with respect to the world price is zero.

tions, the downward trend in stature during the second half of the eighteenth century is in general agreement with the negative trend in the purchasing power of daily wages[135] (Table 2.3).

The decline in transaction costs can lead to a fall in food consumption among individuals who had previously been isolated from the market (Figure 2.6). Consider the demand for food from the point of view of two peasants A and B. A is a subsistence peasant, isolated from the world price by high transaction and transportation costs. In contrast, B is integrated into the world market and therefore faces the world price of food P_w. ($P_w - P_s$ is less than the cost of reaching the market.) Even though B's income exceeds that of A, the quantity of food consumed by A initially (Q_1^A) is greater than the quantity of food consumed by B (Q^B). That is, the subsistence peasant has a higher nutritional status even though his income is less than that of the commercial farmer. In the second period transaction costs fall; A becomes integrated into the world market, and as a consequence faces a new price of grain, $P_w - C_2$, which is greater than the shadow price P_s. As a consequence, he reduces his consumption of food to Q_2^A by selling food, and his nutritional status falls below that of B.

The effect of market integration on A's food consumption can also be analyzed from the point of view of his utility map (Figure 2.7). Self-sufficiency in the first period means that A consumes only food, and does not purchase any goods in the market.[136] Once the peasant is integrated into the market the relative price of food rises, inducing him to substitute away from food consumption and toward all other goods purchased in the market. The upshot is that while his utility rises, his food consumption, and therefore his nutritional status, falls.

The implications of the finding that nutritional levels depended to some extent on market integration might be explored further on the basis of a regional analysis of stature in Hungary over time. If the decline in stature was caused to some extent by the export of grain and cattle to the western half of the Monarchy, then one should expect that those areas would be affected most that had easy access to the Viennese market. Sample heights ($\bar{x}$) of the population of 43 Hungarian counties are consistent with the hypothesis formulated above. In the 1740s and 1750s the western counties of Hungary, closest to the Viennese market,

---

[135] A recent study of the British experience concludes that the association between stature and food prices was weaker than that between stature and harvest conditions. A. Theodore Steegman, Jr., "18th Century British Military Stature: Growth Cessation, Selective Recruiting, Secular Trends, Nutrition at Birth, Cold and Occupation," *Human Biology* 57 (1985): 88.

[136] This is usually referred to as a "corner solution."

Figure 2.7. Utility and Food Consumption of an Individual before and after Market Integration

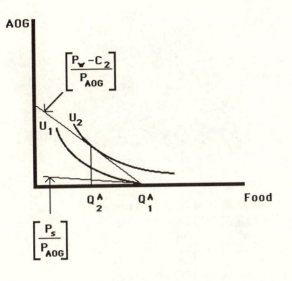

Legend: AOG = All Other Goods
For other symbols see Figure 2.6

were among the ones that tended to have the shortest recruits[137] (Figures 2.8 and 2.9). By the end of the century, however, the pattern was reversed, and the northeastern region had the shortest recruits[138] (Figure 2.10). That is, the regions that were first integrated into the Austrian market initially had the shortest populations. With the expansion of the market, the height of the rest of the population approached the level of western Hungary. Because of its low income, the population in the least-developed eastern region had by the end of the century difficulty maintaining its nutritional status. This supports the logic of equa-

---

[137] It is meaningful to compare values for $\bar{x}$, the sample height uncorrected for shortfall, if the minimum height requirement was enforced equally in all regions of Hungary. Yet even if it had not been, that very fact might be an indication that the county authorities were not able to meet their quotas unless the minimum height requirement was relaxed. In such a case $\bar{x}$ can be used as a convenient indicator of the geographic distribution of stature.

[138] In Brazil the rapid industrialization of the 1960s and 1970s was accompanied by a decline of 8 cm in the average height of military recruits. *Latin American Regional Reports, Brazil*, February 12, 1987, p. 5. In contemporary Hungary, stature decreases from west to east. Nemeskéri, Juhász, and Szabady, "Az 1973." p. 233.

Figure 2.8. Stature ($\bar{x}$) of Adult Hungarian Soldiers Born in the 1740s, by County of Birth

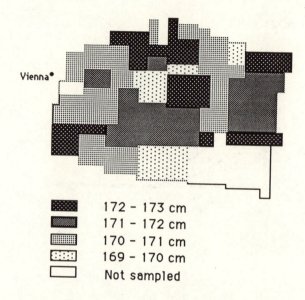

■	172 – 173 cm
■	171 – 172 cm
▦	170 – 171 cm
▦	169 – 170 cm
□	Not sampled

Figure 2.9. Stature ($\bar{x}$) of Adult Hungarian Soldiers Born in the 1750s, by County of Birth

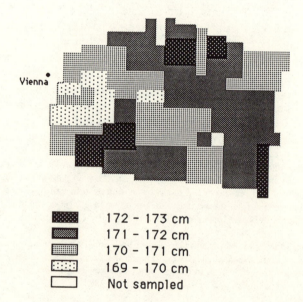

■	172 – 173 cm
■	171 – 172 cm
▦	170 – 171 cm
▦	169 – 170 cm
□	Not sampled

Figure 2.10. Stature ($\bar{x}$) of Adult Hungarian Soldiers Born in the 1780s and 1790s, by County of Birth

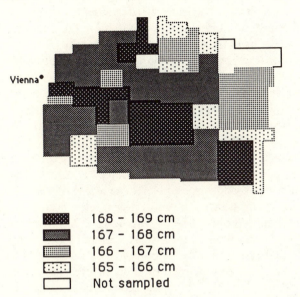

168 – 169 cm
167 – 168 cm
166 – 167 cm
165 – 166 cm
Not sampled

tion 1.4—namely, that in a commercial economy real money income does play an important role in determining nutritional status.

Thus the cross-sectional pattern indicates that self-sufficient agriculture had certain nutritional advantages, provided, of course, that the land/labor ratio was high enough to accommodate the population. Economic development for the Polish and Hungarian provinces brought with it integration into an economically more advanced market structure, which led to the export of nutrients and consequently to a decline in the nutritional status of the population.[139] Although trade can easily lead to decreased domestic consumption of food (Figure 2.7), the society might very well be a net gainer from the new trade arrangements, if they are considered either from the point of view of total income or in terms of utility. This textbook result, however, becomes a non sequitur if one considers that the gains and benefits might not be distributed

[139] This is not the same as immiserizing growth. Immiserizing growth occurs if the country experiences increased production in its export sector that significantly worsens its terms of trade. The net result is a decrease in welfare. Richard Caves and Ronald Jones, *World Trade and Payments: An Introduction*, 2d ed. (Boston: Little, Brown, and Co., 1977), p. 58. This was not the case in Hungary, because the agricultural sector was not growing quickly enough to have such consequences and because the relative price of agricultural products was rising, not falling.

evenly among the population and that the gainers generally do not compensate the losers. In this eighteenth-century society, interregional trade conferred benefits on a particular social stratum, which must have accentuated the skewing of the income distribution. On the other hand, the landless elements of the society, from whose ranks most of the soldiers were recruited, were probably among the losers: their nominal income did not keep pace with the persistent rise in the price of bread (Table 2.3). Insofar as it has been recently demonstrated that an increase in the degree of income inequality has a negative effect on stature,[140] the relationship between trade and stature outlined above becomes even more plausible.

From the point of view of an individual peasant, one can assume that the industrial goods exchanged in return for agricultural products were sufficient compensation in terms of value at the moment of exchange (Figure 2.7). This is by no means as clear if one considers the exchange from the family's point of view. The head of the peasant household might have been willing to sacrifice his children's nutrition in order to consume more industrial goods himself. In that case, the losses from trade would have been incurred by those members of the society who were not entitled to make any of the economic decisions.

Another possibility is that the peasant did not trade away food from current consumption, but drew on inventories that had been held as a safety net against future calamities.[141] Had this been the case, then the disadvantages of exchange would have become evident only subsequent to the sale of food, provided that the need for the inventory had not been perfectly anticipated; in that case a reduction in nutritional status would occur not contemporaneously with the exchange but thereafter. Since a fall in nutritional status is often accompanied by an increased susceptibility to disease and therefore leads to a decline in biological well-being, voluntary exchange could have led to a decline in welfare if the need for future inventories of grain had not been properly forecasted. This might very well have been the case in the early 1770s, when unusually adverse weather conditions throughout most of Europe culminated in a subsistence crisis of immense proportions in Bohemia.[142]

[140] Steckel, "Height and Per Capita Income," p. 6.

[141] A perfunctory glance at peasant inventories does give the impression that the stock of stored grain was decreasing during the second half of the eighteenth century. Private communication from Gyula Benda, Ethnographic Museum, Budapest, Hungary.

[142] Karl Přibram, *Geschichte der österreichischen Gewerbepolitik von 1740 bis 1860. Aufgrund der Akten* (Leipzig: Duncker und Humblot, 1907), pp. 125–149, 223. A French observer wrote in 1770 that it was the third consecutive winter of high grain prices; Fernand Braudel, *Civilization and Capitalism 15th–18th Century* (New York: Harper and

In a traditional (and segmented) labor market like that of the Monarchy, in which landless individuals were often bound by long-term contractual arrangements and in which the daily money wage appears to have been rather inflexible and set at a historically determined customary level, a rise in food prices posed a serious threat to the landless elements of society. Moreover, in these societies the number of landless peasants rose significantly at the time, both absolutely and relative to the population.[143] They were entering the labor market just at a time when real wages were falling and the industrial sector was not expanding quickly enough to absorb them. Hence, as the price of food rose, the economic position of a growing segment of the labor force continued to deteriorate. Nominal wages either remained constant, or at best lagged behind prices. In periods of severe crisis, when the price of bread rose greatly, the money wage might even decline. During the famine of the 1770s, for instance, Bohemian spinners were so desperate that reportedly they were willing to sell their labor at almost any price.[144]

Because of the increased demand for land, rents rose generally. In Germany and France, for instance, rents doubled during the second half of the eighteenth century.[145] An expanding population and rising grain prices meant that the value of the marginal product of land was increasing, which induced the landlords to raise rents. In spite of the Austrian government's efforts to counteract the improved market position of the landlords (see Chapter 3), entitlements to grain must have accrued disproportionately in the hands of the aristocracy. They were most likely the main beneficiaries of the expansion in international trade and they, along with merchants, could have captured most of the gains from trade.

This reasoning suggests that the process of economic development in such backward areas as Galicia and Hungary diverged in important respects from that in the western regions of the Monarchy. The share of

---

Row, 1981), vol. 1, *The Structures of Everyday Life: The Limits of the Possible*, p. 133. The difficulties in Bohemia were caused by two consecutive years of frost in May. Exporting grain to foreign countries was prohibited, and Hungarian grain was purchased at government expense and given to the peasantry; Henrik Marczali, *Világtörténelem-Magyar Történelem* (Budapest: Gondolat, 1982), p. 289.

[143] By the end of the eighteenth century, 44 percent of the adult male labor force was landless. Another 22 percent were landless, but were in line to inherit land from their father. Király, *Hungary in the Late Eighteenth Century*, p. 19; Dickson, *Finance and Government*, vol. 1, p. 57.

[144] The price of a bundle of yarn declined from 36 Kreuzer to 20 Kreuzer. Schreyer, *Kommerz, Fabriken und Manufakturen des Königreichs Böhmen*, vol. 1, p. 18.

[145] Jerome Blum, *The End of the Old Order in Rural Europe* (Princeton: Princeton University Press, 1978), pp. 163, 170.

skilled recruits in the total sample can be used as an indicator of the prevalence of the artisanal sector in the economy of the backward provinces.[146] In the 1740s skilled recruits from the agricultural regions of the Monarchy, such as Galicia, Hungary, and Moravia, composed about a fifth of all recruits, while in Bohemia and Lower Austria they were about a third. The demographic and economic processes that began to unfold in the 1750s caught these economies at different levels of development, and therefore their subsequent experiences diverged. While in Bohemia, Moravia, and Lower Austria the share of skilled recruits either remained constant or even rose, in some cases substantially, in the backward provinces of Hungary and Galicia, which were becoming integrated into the Monarchy's larger market, this share declined dramatically[147] (Table 2.22). This is an indication that these two societies were not capable of equipping new entrants into the labor force with the same amount of human capital as earlier. This could have come about either because the competition from the more advanced regions prevented the expansion of the artisanal sector in these regions or because the latter regions lacked sufficient resources themselves to expand the human capital stock as quickly as the population grew. In any event, this evidence is an indication of the difficulties these two societies encountered in responding successfully to the combined challenges of population growth and simultaneous integration into the more advanced market economies of the western provinces.

The share of agricultural output in total income was also an important determinant of stature even in the United States, where Southerners were 1.5 cm taller than men of the more industrial North, even though per capita income was greater in the North than in the South.[148] The same pattern held for England, the United States, and Ireland. Although England had the higher per capita income, its army was on average five centimeters shorter than that of the United States in the middle of the eighteenth century. During the first half of the nineteenth century per capita income was perhaps 25 percent lower in the United States than in Britain, yet the five-centimeter advantage in height was in America's favor.[149] Irish recruits into the Union army were also taller

---

[146] All artisanal occupations, such as weaver, blacksmith, and miller, are included in the skilled category. Peasants were considered to have no specific skill.

[147] In the nineteenth century Hungary's situation in this respect improved, in contrast to that of Galicia, which did not.

[148] Sokoloff and Villaflor, "Early Achievement of Modern Stature," p. 478.

[149] Kenneth Sokoloff, "The Height of Americans in Three Centuries: Some Economic and Demographic Implications," National Bureau of Economic Research Working Paper No. 1384, 1984; Robert Gallman, "The Pace and Pattern of American Economic

Table 2.22 Share of Skilled[a] Recruits in the Total Adult Sample, 1730-1800 (Percent)

Decade of Birth	Moravia	Bohemia (4 counties)	Bohemia (12 counties)	Hungary	Galicia	Lower Austria
1730	17	28	25	22		45
1740	18	31	32	23	20	34
1750	21	29	28	17	19	33
1760	24	34	23	15	12	42
1770	25	39	14	13	7	44
1780	23	44	30	16	7	39
1790	34	45	38	16	7	28

Source: Tables B.2 and B.3.
[a]All occupations are included in the skilled category. Peasants were listed as having no skills.

than soldiers born in England, although the English per capita income was certainly higher than that of the Irish.[150] Moreover, West Point cadets born in the 1830s who were sons of farmers were 1.3 percent taller than those cadets whose fathers were professionals.[151]

All this evidence corroborates the notion that being close to the supply of food had a positive effect on nutritional status, possibly because it meant that the transaction costs of obtaining food were lower. In addition, rural populations could have benefited from a lower exposure to disease than those who lived in an urban environment.

This relationship reappears, in an even more astounding form, in the late nineteenth century: although Bosnia-Herzegovina was certainly among the least developed parts of the Habsburg Monarchy, its population was nonetheless the tallest. In 1850 the tallest population in Europe was found in Dalmatia, also one of the least developed areas of the continent.[152] In Sweden the region with the tallest recruits was in the isolated North, where population density was the lowest.[153] The remote parts of Japan also had taller populations than those situated near urban markets.[154]

There are other episodes in which nutritional status deteriorated during the early stages of industrialization. In spite of a substantial decline in food prices and plentiful food supplies during the latter third of the nineteenth century, sustained industrial development in Montreal led to

---

Growth," in Lance Davis, Richard Easterlin, and William Parker, eds., *American Economic Growth: An Economist's History of the United States* (New York: Harper and Row, 1972), pp. 15–60. Estimates based on probate inventories indicate that per capita wealth in the thirteen colonies was only about a third of what it was in England. This estimate excludes slaves, as it ought to, because of the differences in economic systems. Jones's estimate of income diverges from the one made by Gallman, to which reference is made in the text, because she converted wealth to income without justification by dividing the wealth estimate of the colonies by an arbitrary number (3.5). Alice Hanson Jones, *Wealth of a Nation to Be: The American Colonies on the Eve of the Revolution* (New York: Columbia University Press, 1980), p. 68.

[150] Joel Mokyr and Cormac O Gráda, "Poor and Getting Poorer? Living Standards in Ireland before the Famine," *Economic History Review*, 2d ser., 41 (1988): 209–235. One study, however, did not find any noteworthy difference between Irish and English soldiers. Steegman, "Eighteenth Century British Military Stature."

[151] Komlos, "Height and Weight of West Point Cadets."

[152] Austria, *Militär-Statistisches Jahrbuch für das Jahr 1871*; idem, *Militär-Statistisches Jahrbuch für das Jahr 1910* (Vienna: k. k. Hof- und Staatsdruckerei, 1913).

[153] Sandberg and Steckel, "Heights and Economic History," p. 108. The tallest cadets in the West Point Military Academy in the antebellum period came from Tennessee, one of the more isolated states at the time. Komlos, "Height and Weight of West Point Cadets."

[154] Ted Shay, "The Level of Living in Japan, 1885–1938: New Evidence," unpublished manuscript, Department of Economics, Harvard University, 1986.

a marked deterioration in the nutritional status of poor women. Population pressure, which led to the elimination of many garden plots and stables in the working-class districts, meant that urban residents had to rely increasingly on cash to meet their food requirements.[155] This evidence attests to the profound difficulties inherent in the socioeconomic adjustments necessitated by rapid economic change, even if that change leads to economic development in the long run.

Part of the reason for these difficulties is that income distribution becomes more uneven during the initial stages of economic growth. Entitlements change. Even during famines, the problem is not always the lack of food. Often people starve because "of the inability to command food,"[156] due either to the skewed distribution of income or to transportation difficulties.

Because height is a good proxy for nutritional status, it can be used to measure the biological well-being of a population. The biological standard of living is a notion used to indicate the extent to which environmental circumstances are favorable to the functioning of the human organism. The concept encompasses such conventional variables as life expectancy, morbidity, fecundity, and general health. Moreover, insofar as food intake was an important component of total consumption in pre-industrial societies, height also measures the material well-being of a commercialized society.

An implication of the above evidence is that economic growth can be accompanied by a decline in nutritional status.[157] Hence the biological standard of living can diverge from the material standard of living during the early stages of industrialization. This was the experience of the landless elements among the Galician and Hungarian peasantry as a consequence of the rise in grain prices brought about by population growth and by the integration of the market with that of the more advanced parts of the Monarchy. This finding is in congruence with those theories that stress the initial disadvantages of free trade to the less developed partner.[158] Even if society as a whole gains from trade, espe-

[155] Ironically, reform legislation that limited the employment opportunities of women and children exacerbated the problem of low earning power. W. Peter Ward and Patricia C. Ward, "Infant Birth Weight and Nutrition in Industrializing Montreal," *American Historical Review* 89 (1984): 324–345.

[156] Amartya Sen, *Poverty and Famines: An Essay on Entitlement and Deprivation* (Oxford: Clarendon Press, 1981).

[157] As has been suggested by Gustav Ranis and John C. H. Fei, "A Theory of Economic Development," *American Economic Review* 51 (1961): 533–565.

[158] The adoption of beef cattle production for export in Guatemala has led to a decline in domestic beef consumption. "While production doubled between 1960 and 1972, beef consumption per capita declined by 20 percent." Gretel Pelto and Pertti Pelto, "Diet and

cially in the long run, the economic change induced by trade imposes burdens as well. The costs and benefits are not distributed evenly among the various segments of the population. The less advantageously placed members of the society have to bear the brunt of the burdens of economic development.

Thus per capita income was not the only significant factor determining the final height attained by a population; the relative price of food was also important. This pattern is not anomalous. Although income determines the position of the demand curve for food, an individual who buys food at (higher) market prices might consume less of it than a self-sufficient peasant isolated from the market by high transport and information costs, even if the income of the former is larger than that of the latter (Figures 2.6 and 2.7). These considerations, coupled with the above empirical finding, corroborate the notion (see equation 1.4) that height is not always a good measure of real income either in a nonmarket society or across populations that are at substantially different stages of economic development.

A recent study of birth weights in Montreal concludes that "malnutrition and [economic] development went hand in hand."[159] The same can be said of the Habsburg Monarchy's less developed regions. Yet the onset of the general decline in the standard of living preceded the rapid industrialization of the 1760s and 1770s. Maintenance of a minimum level of nutrition in the economically advanced provinces of the Monarchy was achieved with imports of agricultural products from Hungary and Galicia. The population in the western provinces continued to grow and escaped the Malthusian menace, in part by exporting its malnutrition, as it were, to the peasantry of the agricultural provinces of Hungary and Galicia.

Summary

The argument has been advanced that the cycling of human height can be used as a proxy for changes in nutritional status. The rise and subsequent decline in stature in East-Central Europe is not likely to have been caused by exogenous changes in the epidemiological environment, because there is absolutely no indication that the incidence of disease de-

Delocalization: Dietary Changes since 1750," *Journal of Interdisciplinary History* 14 (1983): 507–528.

[159] Ward and Ward, "Birth Weight in Montreal," pp. 326, 345. A similar pattern is evident in Scotland. Paul Riggs, "The Standard of Living in Britain's Celtic Fringe, c. 1800–1850: Evidence from Glaswegian Prisoners," unpublished manuscript, Department of History, University of Pittsburgh, 1988.

clined and then increased again after mid-century. Consequently, the rise and fall in nutritional status among the recruits is much more likely to have been caused by fluctuations in the food intake of the lower classes. Indeed, this pattern correlates well with conventional indicators of well-being such as real wages. The height of the recruits born in the five provinces of the Habsburg Monarchy shows the following pattern:

1. In the early eighteenth century nutritional status was higher in provinces that had a high land/labor ratio and a high share of national product originating in agriculture, and were isolated from the world market.

2. Nutritional status increased initially because of propitious harvest conditions. Real wages were relatively high and food intake rose correspondingly.

3. The increase in nutritional status brought about an acceleration in population growth which, however, ran into Malthusian ceilings.

4. The decline in the marginal product of labor in agriculture brought about a fall in real wages. Consequently food intake also declined, bringing about a fall in human stature beginning with the birth cohorts of the 1750s, and continued to decline during the second half of the eighteenth century. This experience fits well into the Malthusian model of population dynamics. In addition, the index of stature traces out a curve very similar to the graph of real wages: a rise and then a stabilization during the first half of the century, followed by a steep decline between 1750 and 1770.

5. The deterioration in nutritional status in the western provinces of the Monarchy was halted partly through institutional reforms, to be discussed in the next chapter, and partly by the import of nutrients from Galicia and Hungary.

6. In addition to population growth in Hungary and Galicia, the export of nutrients from these provinces, coupled with the large-scale food purchases of the army, contributed to the decline in nutritional status of the population there.

In sum, the argument has been advanced that the stature of the Habsburg population evinced cycles in the eighteenth century that can be interpreted in the light of our knowledge of economic and demographic processes. With this conceptualization the human biological system becomes, for the first time, fully integrated into its social and economic environment. The model outlined in this chapter will be expanded in Chapter 5 to explain the British experience, and generalized in Chapter

6 to encompass pre-industrial economic development in Europe as a whole.

The role of the government's reform program in counteracting the impending Malthusian crisis is outlined next. The institutional changes enacted, in turn, enabled the industrial sector of the western provinces to grow rapidly enough to raise incomes sufficiently to overcome the threat of a subsistence crisis of immense proportions. The beginning of the industrial revolution can therefore be seen as having played a role in the stabilization of economic conditions at the end of the eighteenth century.

CHAPTER 3

INSTITUTIONAL CHANGE
UNDER PRESSURE:
GOVERNMENT POLICY IN
AN ENLIGHTENED DESPOTISM

HAVING become aware of the diminution in the nutritional status of the population and the concomitant decline in the standard of living, the monarchs attempted from the 1750s on to overcome the bottlenecks hindering economic development. Their perception of the need for action was reinforced by a subsistence crisis of immense proportions in 1770–71 and by several jacqueries of an old-fashioned sort. Responding to these pressures, Maria Theresia and her son, Joseph II, worked persistently to overcome the power of the guilds, to limit the privileges of the aristocracy, and to reform those institutions constraining growth. Furthermore, a number of agricultural reforms in the 1770s and 1780s granted greater mobility to the peasantry, thereby fostering their entry into the industrial labor force as a means of defending their standard of living. The government also attempted to raise the peasantry's well-being by redistributing income in its favor at the expense of landlords. This program of economic reform could be brought about only because, compared with previous centuries, the state's financial, military, and bureaucratic powers had expanded sufficiently to enable it to influence the course of events significantly, and because it had sufficient wealth and credit at its disposal to overcome some of the initial difficulties of industrialization. Moreover, compared with previous centuries the social infrastructure had expanded greatly; there had also been considerable capital accumulation, both human and physical. Finally, government advisors had economic models with which to analyze the problems facing them. The institutional innovations of Maria Theresia and Joseph II led to a thorough restructuring of the Habsburg economy. The argument is advanced in this chapter that the economic reforms were instituted to a large extent as a response to the threatening crisis, and that the reforms, in turn, opened the way to industrialization.

Hitherto the economic reforms of Maria Theresia (1740–80) and her son, Joseph II (1780–90), have been explained by exogenous factors such as the humiliating loss of most of Silesia to Frederick the Great. The influence of enlightened thought on the empress, her son—later emperor—and their cameralist advisors was also interpreted as having been significant.[1] In contrast to the conventional wisdom, the present chapter considers institutional change to have been endogenous. The thesis is expounded that the governing elite responded to the deterioration in living standards among a large segment of the peasantry, whose well-being, as was shown in the previous chapter, declined significantly after the middle of the eighteenth century. The crisis threatened the stability, perhaps even the very existence, of the Monarchy. The destabilizing exogenous factor was population growth, similar to other instances noted by Douglass North.[2] Therefore the thesis formulated in this chapter fits into the model proposed by Ester Boserup and Julian Simon, in which increases in population density bring about technological or, as in this case, institutional innovations.[3]

Some scholars have noted that the demographic developments of the second half of the eighteenth century led to new agricultural practices because, given that the total quantity of arable land was constant, no

[1] In the most recent book on the topic, P.G.M. Dickson, *Finance and Government under Maria Theresia, 1740–1780* (Oxford: Clarendon Press, 1987), vol. 1, p. 15, the author argues that the government was "primarily concerned with the assertion of fiscal and military power, rather than the welfare of subjects." Yet throughout the book Dickson refers to "attempts to increase peasant well being," and to the fact that the monarchs ruled "for the benefit of their subjects." Ibid., vol. 1, pp. 127, 209.

[2] Karl Grünberg, *Die Bauernbefreiung und die Auflösung des gutsherrlich-bäuerlichen Verhältnisses in Böhmen, Mähren und Schlesien* (Leipzig: Duncker und Humblot, 1893–1894), vol. 1, pp. 158, 159; Douglass C. North, *Structure and Change in Economic History* (New York: Norton, 1981), p. 29. Among contemporaries, some argued that an increase in population would lead to an increase of well-being; others argued that the line of causation went the other way. Dickson suggests that ". . . population growth was beginning to lead to a faster increase in the poorer classes . . . , hence to exacerbate existing social tensions." *Finance and Government*, vol. 1, p. 14.

[3] Ester Boserup, *Population and Technological Change: A Study of Long-Term Trends* (Chicago: University of Chicago Press, 1981); Julian L. Simon, *The Economics of Population Growth* (Princeton: Princeton University Press, 1977).

other way out of the crisis existed.[4] In England private landowners en-
closed common lands, while in Austria the same pressing need for reform led to partial emancipation of the serfs. Placing the reforms clearly
within the context of economic circumstances makes the motivation of
the monarchs more comprehensible than had previous explanations.
The form of the response to the crisis in the Monarchy was in keeping
with the intellectual currents of the time and was quite similar to the
contemporary reforms attempted or undertaken elsewhere in continental Europe.[5]

The pressure that the declining welfare of the population exerted on
the leadership also enables one to understand the success with which the
monarchs were able to overcome parochial interests, the cornerstone of
the absolutist state. Without the threatening circumstances, the power
and privileges of the aristocratic oligarchy or of other vested interests
such as the Church or the guilds probably could not have been successfully curtailed.[6] Violating these interests meant, in a sense, that the monarchs were threatening some of the very pillars supporting the throne.
That they managed to balance the interests of various lobbies is in itself
a topic worthy of another study. The present task is to outline the reforms, to explore the motivation for institutional change, and to outline
its importance to subsequent economic development.

Policies that began to emerge in the 1750s, although a logical continuation of earlier efforts, constituted a watershed in the economic history
of the Habsburg Monarchy.[7] Although legal reforms were undertaken
during the first half of the eighteenth century, institutional change failed
to keep pace with the expansion of the market brought about by population growth. By the second half of the century the state began to respond vigorously to the challenge, because it "thought it was its duty
. . . to solve or attempt to solve these [problems] not consciously according to a plan all at once, but to the extent developments forced it to

[4] Wilhelm Abel, *Agrarkrisen und Agrarkonjunktur: Eine Geschichte der Land- und Ernährungswirtschaft Mitteleuropas seit dem hohen Mittelalter* (1935; reprint, Hamburg and Berlin: Paul Parey, 1966), p. 249.

[5] Jerome Blum, *The End of the Old Order in Rural Europe* (Princeton: Princeton University Press, 1978), p. 216.

[6] Mancur Olson, *The Rise and Decline of Nations: Economic Growth, Stagflation and Social
Rigidities* (New Haven: Yale University Press, 1982).

[7] One contemporary observer even put a precise date on the change in economic policy:
1752. Joseph Weinbrenner, *Patriotische Gedanken und Vorschläge über den gehemmten Ausfuhr Handel* (Vienna: n.p., 1781) as cited by Herman Freudenberger, "An Industrial Momentum Achieved in the Habsburg Monarchy," *Journal of European Economic History* 12
(1983): 339–350.

act . . . in its own interest, its need for power and the welfare of the state."[8]

Maria Theresia and her advisors recognized the gravity of the crisis, and realized that economic change was necessary to avert even greater difficulties in the future. Consequently, they endeavored to understand the preconditions of economic development and the institutional changes that were needed to bring them about. In spite of the inertia and inadequate size of the bureaucracy, and the opposition of groups that stood to lose from the reforms, such as the guilds, conservative segments of the aristocracy, and in some instances the provincial estates, the central government succeeded in creating, within a few decades, an environment propitious for economic change.[9] The government accomplished this feat by reducing or putting a ceiling on the rent of the peasantry, thereby supporting a redistribution of income in favor of the peasantry, or at least preventing a redistribution in favor of the nobility. In addition, it changed the legal and institutional framework in order to allow peasants greater access to the industrial sector, thus increasing the size of the national product and reversing the decline in the peasants' standard of living.[10]

---

[8] Karl Grünberg, *Franz Anton von Blanc, Ein Sozialpolitiker der theresianisch-josefinischen Zeit* (Munich: Duncker, 1921), p. 24. Dickson suggests in regard to the political reforms that they were "less the deliberate and far-sighted assertion of fundamental principles of government than desperate expedients provoked by the justified fear of total political collapse. The nightmare . . . recurred during the Bohemian famine . . . [and] peasant revolt of 1775 . . ." This view is also applicable to the economic reforms. Dickson, *Finance and Government*, vol. 1, p. 14.

[9] Grünberg, *Franz Anton von Blanc*, pp. 33, 40. In 1762 there were 7400 officials in the service of the monarch (not counting Hungary). In contrast, there were 13,000 civil servants in the service of local authorities, including manorial officials. Dickson, *Finance and Government*, vol. 1, p. 307.

[10] The effective formulation of mercantilistic policies designed to promote development, and their subsequent evaluation, required information. To gauge the extent of population growth a census was taken in 1754 and at regular intervals thereafter. To learn about the extent of economic activity, the compilation of systematic data on industrial activity began in the 1760s, although their collection had been requested as early as 1749. Henryk Grossmann, "Die Anfänge und geschichtliche Entwicklung der amtlichen Statistik in Österreich," *Statistische Monatschrift* (1916): 331–423. For the patent "Fabriquen und Manufacturen Aufnahme" from June 11, 1749, see Codex Austriacus Vol. 5, 1777, pp. 424–425, 446–448. Johann Slokar, *Geschichte der österreichischen Industrie und ihrer Förderung unter Kaiser Franz I* (Vienna: F. Tempsky, 1914), pp. 65, 104. By the middle of the 1820s the regular collection of industrial data had ceased. The institution of factory inspectors, responsible for collecting statistics, was dissolved in 1825. As a contemporary observed, the dominance of a liberal government economic policy rendered them superfluous. Since the government no longer intended to intervene actively in the economy, data collection was no longer necessary. Statistics of the profit tax adopted in 1813 replaced industrial data.

Ideological Background of the Reforms

For the formulation of policies fostering development, the monarchs relied on cameralist economic advisors whose opinions were often divided, particularly over issues which turned on a subjective evaluation of the state of the market.[11] They properly used various models of imperfect competition to conceptualize contemporary market structures. Eventually, however, with the expansion of the market, and under the influence of liberal economic thought from abroad, these advisors began to apply models applicable to perfectly competitive economies.

The motivation for formulating these policies was the desire to maintain the well-being of the population, one which, given the rigid institutional framework of the time, was finding it increasingly difficult to support itself exclusively from agriculture. The empress became aware of the deteriorating conditions of the peasantry through eyewitness accounts and through the accumulation of back taxes in Bohemia.

The humanitarian views of the enlightened monarchs and their advisors also disposed them to advocate legal reforms. Since Maria Theresia thought of herself as "mother of her peoples," and therefore believed that one of her foremost duties was to foster the alimentation of her subjects, she was concerned about developments that threatened the nutritional status of the peasantry. A description of conditions in the countryside was read in Vienna, according to a document from a cabinet meeting of 1769, "with astonishment, indeed, with true horror and . . . with ardent emotion."[12] This concern was manifested time and again.[13] In a letter to her daughter Marie Antoinette, Maria Theresia described the terrible suffering of the population in Bohemia during the subsistence crisis of 1771, and added, "you can imagine how very depressed I am over it."[14]

To be sure, the empress must have been motivated not only by her feelings of obligation,[15] but also by the conviction that the prolonged

[11] Joseph von Sonnenfels, *Politische Abhandlungen* (Vienna: 1777).

[12] Grünberg, *Franz Anton von Blanc*, p. 25; idem, *Bauernbefreiung*, vol. 1, p. 209. After returning from a tour of the Military Frontier in 1775, Joseph II "condemned the area as poverty-stricken" in "an excoriating report." Dickson, *Finance and Government*, vol. 1, p. 251.

[13] For instance, a 1764 instruction urged the provincial governments to conduct economic policy so as to increase the well-being of the inhabitants. Karl Přibram, *Geschichte der österreichischen Gewerbepolitik von 1740 bis 1860. Aufgrund der Akten* (Leipzig: Duncker und Humblot, 1907), p. 104.

[14] Paul Christoph, *Maria Theresia und Marie Antoinette: Ihr geheimer Briefwechsel* (Vienna: Cesam Verlag, 1952), p. 64.

[15] She wrote in another letter to her daughter, "We are in this world to do good to others; . . . we are not here for ourselves or for our pleasure, but to gain [entry] into

suffering of even a part of the population would lead to unrest, emigration, and even a serious confrontation that might threaten the existence of the state. Bloody clashes between peasants and the army occurred in rump-Silesia during the summer of 1766; 137 villages took part in another outbreak of disorder in the spring of the following year. Soon peasant revolts were breaking out in Moravia and Bohemia also; these were old-fashioned disturbances, in the course of which the peasants frequently refused to honor their labor obligations, or robot, to the lord of the manor.[16]

Such confrontations demonstrated that the government could not remain indifferent to the peasants' conditions. These manifestations of discord threatened stability directly, and eroded the ideology which maintained the cohesion of the absolutist social fabric.[17] Maria Theresia could not hope to remain in power unless she acted justly, that is, in congruence with expectations of the common law. Thus, as the vice regent of the Almighty on earth she was expected to persevere on behalf of the common weal. The political theories developed for the practice of enlightened absolutism allowed her to disregard particularistic considerations in pursuit of this goal: "A Prince, ordered by God to be leader and protector of a people, is justified in doing everything that the welfare of the state, entrusted to him, demands."[18] Hence, Maria Theresia could hardly remain idle in the face of the peasants' immiseration without breaking the implicit social contract and thereby undoing that socialization of the population on which tranquillity was based.

heaven where all strive and which one does not receive for free: one has to earn it." Ibid., p. 147.

[16] Grünberg, *Franz Anton von Blanc*, p. 44. According to one account, there were 16 jacqueries and 64 occasions on which the peasants refused to perform robot in 1775. Erika Weinzierl-Fischer, "Die Bekämpfung der Hungernot in Böhmen, 1770–72," *Mitteilungen der Österreichischen Staatsarchiv* 7 (1954): 478–514; Josef Petrán, "Der Höhepunkt der Bewegungen der untertänigen Bauern in Böhmen," *Acta Universitatis Carolinae. Philosophica et Historica* 3 (1969): 107–140.

[17] Ideology has important economic implications because it lowers the transaction costs of supervising the members of the society. North, *Structure and Change*.

[18] Sonnenfels, *Politische Abhandlungen*, p. 254. It is symbolic of this mentality that during the coronation ceremony in Bohemia, one of the two questions the archbishop of Prague asked a Habsburg monarch (except for Joseph II, who was not inclined to participate in such rituals) was: "Do you want to rule and defend the kingdom lent to you by God with the justice of your fathers?" With an affirmative response, the anointment followed. The other question was: "Do you . . . [in the familiar, Du, form] want to remain true to the Catholic religion?" G. N. Schnabel, *Statistische Darstellung von Böhmen* (Prague: n.p., 1826), p. 86. A recent article stresses Maria Theresa's sense of having a God-given responsibility for the welfare of her subjects. William J. McGill, "In Search of the Unicorn: Maria Theresa and the Religion of State," *Historian* 42 (1980): 304–319.

The influence of the Enlightenment can be seen in the government's response to the crisis. The ideas of the philosophes, such as the notion of natural right, had gained acceptance among many of the statesmen serving the Habsburg court. The doctrine of natural right implied that the peasants, too, had the right to partake of the general well-being. As one of the reform-minded bureaucrats put it: "the justification of an adequate subsistence for the peasantry is not based alone on the reason of state, but also on the natural rights of men and citizens."[19]

Moreover, the commitment of government officials to the ideas of the enlightenment seriously limited the options they were willing to consider. Had it not been for this orientation, the state surely could have dealt with its economic problems by other means. The forced colonization of southern Hungary could have been undertaken to relieve the population pressure in Bohemia, and the use of greater force to maintain tranquillity among the peasantry also had its advocates.[20] Although the state could have confiscated some of the aristocracy's land, it continued instead to respect private property, and the manors were considered the private property of the lords.[21] These options were disregarded because the Habsburg Monarchy was neither a modern dictatorship nor an Oriental despotism. As one reformer put it, the peasant was not "a slave in the Roman or Turkish Empire," and the idea that the peasant's freedom should be guaranteed was frequently mentioned.[22]

Government policymakers were influenced not only by new notions of natural right, but also by the pronatalist doctrines of mercantilism. That a state's power depended, to a large extent, on its population size was a fundamental tenet of mercantilism.[23] In a memorandum that Joseph II wrote to Maria Theresia in 1765, he argued that the principal aim of government should be to increase the size of the "population, that is the conservation and the augmentation of [the number of] subjects."[24] In fact, a frequent "litmus test" for adopting a policy, even in

[19] Blanc defined the subsistence minimum generously to include even the possibility of saving for times of need. Grünberg, *Franz Anton von Blanc*, pp. 22, 25.

[20] Ibid., p. 52.

[21] Grünberg, *Bauernbefreiung*, vol. 1, p. 154.

[22] Ibid., vol. 1, p. 20; Petrán, "Höhepunkt," p. 110.

[23] Hans Leo Mikoletzky, *Österreich, das grosse 18. Jahrhundert: von Leopold I bis Leopold II* (Vienna: Österreichischer Bundesverlag, 1967), p. 53. Karl Přibram, *Gewerbepolitik*, p. 42. Increased circulation of money was synonymous with an increased gross national product in the sense of the quantity equation. Joseph Sonnenfels, on becoming professor of finance at the University of Vienna in 1763, was the most ardent advocate of this viewpoint.

[24] Cited in Derek Beales, *Joseph II* (Cambridge, England: Cambridge University Press, 1987), vol. 1, *In the Shadow of Maria Theresa, 1741–1780*, p. 166.

religious matters, was whether it would foster population growth.[25] Urging guilds to allow journeymen to marry was one example of such a policy.[26] Since mercantilists did not know of the principle of diminishing returns to labor, they maintained a pronatalist orientation even in the face of the pauperization brought about by population growth.

Yet they did recognize that if the deterioration of the standard of living were allowed to continue, the population would be threatened and its further growth jeopardized. Hence, the notion was frequently expressed in bureaucratic correspondence that the aim of government policy was to increase opportunities in the industrial sector, thereby increasing the purchasing power of the monarch's subjects.[27] A directive in 1776 stated that the aim of the government was to "facilitate as much as possible the tasks of manufacturers, craftsmen, and similar workers to feed themselves by honest means."[28] Thus, the monarchs strove to adopt policies that would maintain the standard of living so that the population would continue to grow.

According to mercantilist thinking, population size determined not only the government's ability to tax, and hence its wealth, but also its military power, because the size of the military was a function of the financial strength of the state. The very existence of the Monarchy depended on its military power because of the constant threat posed by a number of predatory states.[29] Hence a standing army had to be adequately provisioned even in peacetime. The size of the army that could

[25] In 1777 Sonnenfels had urged the government, in order to promote marriage and therefore population growth, to place strict curbs on the entry of women and youth into monastic life. Sonnenfels, *Politische Abhandlungen*, pp. 254–255.

[26] Sonnenfels thought that the policy of encouraging marriages ought to be aimed at the "middle category" of the population. Sonnenfels, *Politische Abhandlungen*, pp. 241–242. Another step, which had Europe-wide ramifications, was the establishment of a *cordon sanitaire* within the military frontier separating the monarchy from the Ottoman Empire. This system was designed to increase population by protecting public health. Checkpoints were begun around 1740, but not until 1770 was the entire system introduced. The *cordon sanitaire* consisted of a series of watch posts with soldiers patrolling between them. Travelers were held in quarantine from 10 to 42 days depending on the circumstances. Imported goods were generally disinfected. Gunther E. Rothenberg, *Die Österreichische Militärgrenze in Kroatien, 1522 bis 1881* (Vienna: Herold, 1970), pp. 118–120.

[27] Státní ústřední archiv v. Praze (hereafter referred to as S.U.A.), Č.G. Commerz, 7, Fasc. 1, 1796–1805, folio 2–6. For an expression of concern over the standard of living by Count Leopold Kollowrat, president of the treasury, see Dickson, *Finance and Government*, vol. 2, p. 105.

[28] Přibram, *Gewerbepolitik*, p. 327.

[29] North, *Structure and Change*, pp. 205–206. According to a recent observer industrialization in one country will invite emulation in another, if for no other reason than to maintain a balance of military power. Gautham Sen, *The Military Origins of Industrialization and International Trade Rivalry* (London: Frances Pinter Publishers, 1984), p. 7.

be mustered depended partly on the size of the population from whose ranks soldiers were recruited and partly on the people's well-being, which determined the amount of taxes that could be collected to pay for the army. A growing and well-nourished population therefore had to be an important aim of economic policy. Hence, the declining welfare and health of the population posed an imminent threat to both tax revenues and state power.[30] In 1769 Maria Theresia expressed eloquently her awareness of the relationship between the peasantry's well-being and the maintenance of her power:

> The peasantry is the largest class among the state's citizens and therefore it is the foundation and the greatest support of the state. The peasants have to be maintained in such a condition that they can nourish themselves and their families and at the same time be able to contribute to the taxes. The private right of the manors have to be subordinated to this view.[31]

To be sure, some advisors cautioned that "diminishing the landlord's rights would be an outrageous interference in the sanctity of private property." Ultimately, however, they did not prevail.[32] The monarch and her advisors, while ostensibly maintaining their respect of the lords' rights, reinterpreted the meaning of private property in order to enable the government to intervene ever more energetically on behalf of the peasantry.[33] Franz Anton von Blanc, for instance, argued that contracts jeopardizing the subsistence of one of the parties had to be considered void, because no one could legally agree to his own destitution.[34] Thus the state could consider ways to alter the current relationship between the lords and the peasants without violating the sanctity of private property, since the agrarian *status quo* was threatening the existence of one of the contracting parties, namely the peasantry.

One should not conclude that maintenance of the tax base was the only, or even the primary, motive for the policies of Maria Theresia and Joseph II. Joseph believed that "the peasantry should not be protected only so far that they are always able to meet their tax obligations . . . but

[30] The land tax per holding in Bohemia was raised from 52 florin in the 1740s to 60 florin in the 1760s. Jaroslav Purš, "Struktur und Dynamik der industriellen Entwicklung in Böhmen im letzten Viertel des 18. Jahrhunderts," *Jahrbuch für Wirtschaftsgeschichte* (1965): 160–196.

[31] Grünberg, *Bauernbefreiung*, vol. 1, p. 71; idem, *Franz Anton von Blanc*, p. 31.

[32] Grünberg, *Bauernbefreiung*, vol. 1, p. 209.

[33] This new conceptualization of the lord-peasant relationship was similar to the changes in thinking that would enable the government to intervene on behalf of industrial workers in the course of the nineteenth century.

[34] Grünberg, *Bauernbefreiung*, vol. 1, p. 170.

the road to well-being should be opened for it."[35] In furthering economic development, the Habsburg Monarchy thus became, in modern terminology, an incipient welfare state, a notion by no means foreign to the mercantilist thinkers of the time.[36] Providing for the welfare of the people, to be sure, is one of the major aims of all governments, the others being protection and justice.[37] Therefore, in seeking their subjects' welfare the eighteenth-century Habsburgs were by no means unusual.

In sum, a combination of self-interest (maintaining power) and a feeling of responsibility for their subjects' standard of living accounts for the government's resolve to reform the industrial and agricultural laws. Institutional change, leading to industrial and agricultural advance, became the only escape from the dilemma posed by the peasants' immiseration.[38] Support of industrial activity in the distressed regions of the Monarchy loomed large in this program, because government advisors realized that industrial output was more elastic than agricultural output and consequently that it would be difficult to obtain greater tax revenues from the agricultural sector.[39]

For the rulers of the Habsburg lands, the proper formulation and conceptualization of the Monarchy's economic problems was rendered all the more necessary by the unfavorable outcome of the wars against Prussia in 1740–48 and 1756–63: the loss of all of the most industrially advanced province of the Monarchy, Silesia, with the exception of two small counties. According to one opinion, one-fourth of the weavers and spinners in the Monarchy had been lost as a consequence.[40] Some historians have contended that the loss of Silesia prompted the Monarchy to support industrialization in Bohemia.[41] Had that been truly the primary motivation, then reforms would have been limited to substitut-

[35] Ibid., vol. 1, p. 321.

[36] Alois Brusatti, *Österreichische Wirtschaftspolitik vom Josephinismus zum Standestaat* (Vienna: Jupiter, 1965), pp. 15, 20; Herman Freudenberger, "State Intervention as an Obstacle to Economic Growth in the Habsburg Monarchy," *Journal of Economic History* 27 (1967): 493–509. Freudenberger is a bit too skeptical of the effectiveness of Habsburg economic policy, but admits that the welfare motive was one of the aims of this policy.

[37] Walt W. Rostow, *Politics and the Stages of Growth* (Cambridge, England: Cambridge University Press, 1971), p. 11.

[38] Karl Grünberg noted in the nineteenth century that the government's concern for welfare led logically to agricultural reforms. Grünberg, *Bauernbefreiung*, vol. 1, p. 292. The point, however, has eluded subsequent historians. This is probably why government policy tended to exclude from the industrialization drive agriculturally more productive areas such as Hungary and Galicia.

[39] Přibram, *Gewerbepolitik*, p. 4.

[40] Ibid., p. 94.

[41] Purš, "Struktur und Dynamik," p. 169.

ing for the industrial labor force lost to Prussia. Indeed, reforms could have been limited to the linen industry alone, the principal industry of the lost territory. Moreover, the reforms began in the mid-fifties, at the outset of the second round of wars with Prussia, before the final fate of Silesia was known.[42] In any case, neither the monarchs nor any of the prominent advisors left behind evidence that could be interpreted to indicate that the loss of Silesia was a major consideration for enacting the reforms. Yet there are many indications that the maintenance of the peasantry's standard of living was of great concern to the members of the government.

Although humiliation suffered at the hands of Prussia was not the primary motivation for the sweeping reforms of the next four decades, it might have contributed to the adoption of the reforms by weakening the opposition. In the absence of such an external threat, an oligarchy whose power was based on land might have opposed more vehemently the reforms needed to transform the economic structure.[43]

Even that might be an overstatement, because many of the Bohemian aristocrats genuinely supported the monarchs in their effort to provide employment for their subjects. Like the monarchs themselves, these aristocrats were motivated to promote industrial activity in order to increase the well-being of their subjects. Count Waldstein put it succinctly: "I . . . have founded this factory in Oberleutensdorf, from purely Christian love and through the grace of God, so that my subjects would be able to make a living and have sufficient nourishment. They will be diverted from condemnable idleness, and will have no cause to find their bread with begging."[44] These factories were often unprofit-

---

[42] Grünberg, *Bauernbefreiung*, vol. 1, p. 193.

[43] Rostow, *Politics and the Stages of Growth*, p. 64.

[44] *Mitteilungen des Vereins für Geschichte des Deutschen in Böhmen*, vol. 71, p. 142, as cited by Arnošt Klíma, "Die Textilmanufaktur in Böhmen des 18. Jahrhunderts," *Historica* 15 (1967): 123–181; Herman Freudenberger, *The Waldstein Woolen Mill: Noble Entrepreneurship in Eighteenth-Century Bohemia* (Boston: Baker Library, Harvard School of Business Administration, 1963). Freudenberger, disagreeing strongly with the stereotype of the Bohemian nobility as reactionary, has repeatedly stressed the aristocracy's contribution before 1780 to the economic development of the Bohemian crownlands. Nowhere else in Europe, he argues, "can one find as many aristocrats in industry, providing as great a share of the output as in Bohemia and Moravia." Freudenberger, "Industrial Momentum," p. 347. For evidence that some of the nobility took an interest in scientific and technological, as well as industrial, progress, see Herman Freudenberger, "Progressive Bohemian and Moravian Aristocrats," in Stanley B. Winters and Joseph Held, eds., *Intellectual and Social Developments in the Habsburg Empire from Maria Theresia to World War I: Essays Dedicated to Robert A. Kann* (Boulder, CO: East European Quarterly, distributed by Columbia University Press, 1975), pp. 115–130.

able, and consequently have to be considered partly charitable undertak-
ings, brought into being out of *noblesse oblige*.[45]

The government's concern for their subject's livelihood actually became a commonplace of the language. By the late eighteenth century,
entrepreneurs requesting licenses from the government seldom failed to
point out the social benefits their undertaking would confer by providing subsistence for the poor, decreasing the number of beggars, or reducing the burden on poverty-stricken parents by giving their children
employment.[46]

One should note that the government's concern for maintaining the
tax base was motivated not only by the fear of declining ability to pay,
but also by its rapidly increasing expenditures. Needless to say the wars
against Prussia were expensive. By the end of the Seven Years' War, state
debt was approaching 300 million fl, perhaps three-fourths of GNP, and
the interest payments on the debt took almost half of the government's
net income of 35 million fl. Yet the fear of becoming a second-rate
power prevented the empress from reducing military expenditures.[47]
Nearly bankrupt, the government increased taxes, as did the other European powers in the eighteenth century. Net peacetime Habsburg revenue rose from 29 million fl in 1749 to 40 million by 1763 and to 50
million by 1784. This was about 12 percent of GNP. However, on a per
capita basis peacetime revenue remained "relatively stable after 1748."[48]
Except in Hungary, the government thereafter taxed noble land regularly, and increased indirect taxes which fell mostly on the middle class.[49]
The goal was to raise revenue without impinging on the well-being of
the lower classes: "The government's concern to spread the tax burden
fairly is shown by the exemption of peasants and the common people
from the . . . tax of 1759 . . . and by the half rate conceded to peasant

---

[45] Graf Joseph Kinsky, according to one observer, made not only his subjects "happy,"
by providing employment and nourishment for them, but his heirs as well. Others believed he had decreased his wealth by founding factories. Whether he actually did so is
unknown; however, one knowledgeable observer of the eighteenth century industrial
scene disagreed with this notion. He suggested that Kinsky might have suffered some
losses because people took advantage of him, but there was still plenty of wealth left for
his heirs. Joseph Schreyer, *Kommerz, Fabriken und Manufakturen des Königreichs Böhmen,
theils, wie sie schon sind, theils, wie sie es werden könnten* (Prague and Leipzig: Schönfeldisch
Meiznerischen Buchhandlung, 1790), vol. 2, p. 110.

[46] S.U.A. Č.G. Com., 1796–1805, 13/3–8, Box 613, and 1816–1825, 13/1, Box 894.

[47] Haus-, Hof-, und Staatsarchiv, Vienna, Zinzendorf Nachlass. Zinzendorf warned
against lowering the military budget, arguing that the consequent loss in prestige would
be unacceptable.

[48] Dickson, *Finance and Government*, vol. 1, p. 136; vol. 2, pp. 37, 102, 385.

[49] "The intention . . . was to tax landed revenue, . . . but to spare the peasantry and the
poor." Ibid., vol. 2, pp. 121, 151, 267.

inheritances liable for tax."[50] As a consequence the government avoided serious financial problems.[51]

Institutional Change in the Industrial Sector

During the second half of the eighteenth century, government intervention, aimed at mobilizing the economy, helped avert a full-blown Malthusian subsistence crisis. The government fostered industrialization by promulgating new laws, by subsidizing development directly, and by substituting for "missing prerequisites" of development, such as banks and entrepreneurship. In addition, it defended the peasantry from impersonal market forces by reformulating agricultural laws. In order to pursue these policies more effectively, new institutions, which would be free from parochial interests, were created within a centralized bureaucratic structure. To achieve the above aims, the institutional bottlenecks existing at mid-century had to be overcome.

The guild system was one of the institutions limiting industrial expansion.[52] Like modern craft unions, guilds constrained the entry of workers into certain occupations, and determined the production technology and the number of hours worked. Guilds also acted as cartels in limiting the production of goods in order to support a predetermined price and quality. The guilds promoted the well-being of their members by protecting them from outside competition. Because guilds limited industrial expansion, they might have functioned reasonably well at a time of slow demographic change, when the agricultural sector was capable of expansion, or at a time of excess demand for industrial labor. During the mid-eighteenth century, however, none of these conditions prevailed in the western parts of the Monarchy, and laws protecting the guilds' power became the major hindrance to further industrialization.

Complete abolition of the guilds was again considered.[53] Such a sweeping reform was, however, rejected; as in other areas, the government chose instead a cautious strategy of gradual change "to the extent that developments forced it to act."[54] Although this attitude was characteristic of the whole reform movement, by the end of Joseph II's reign

[50] Ibid., vol. 2, p. 129.

[51] Austrian credit was judged among the best in the Amsterdam capital market. James C. Riley, *International Government Finance and the Amsterdam Capital Market, 1740–1815* (Cambridge, England: Cambridge University Press, 1980), p. 133.

[52] Přibram, *Gewerbepolitik*, p. 346.

[53] Ibid., pp. 54, 75. The issue had also been raised in 1699. Arnošt Klíma, "Mercantilism in the Habsburg Monarchy—with Special Reference to the Bohemian Lands," *Historica* 11 (1965): 95–119; Freudenberger, "Industrial Momentum," p. 343.

[54] Grünberg, *Franz Anton von Blanc*, p. 24.

131

in 1790 the cumulative change had been considerable. Thus the power of the guilds, too, was gradually whittled away.

At first, industrial activity was allowed in rural areas, in 1731, as long as the master craftsman was incorporated into the guild of the nearest town.[55] This compromise seemed to maintain the guilds' authority in principle, while actually weakening them. Outside the city limits, such authority must have been difficult to exercise; yet before industrial development could proceed unfettered, the power of the guilds had to be curtailed further.[56]

A more effective strategy to circumvent the guilds' power was the granting of privileges to establish a factory.[57] The privilege was tantamount to a license to be outside guild jurisdiction, and it also protected the owner from competition.[58] At first privileges were granted sparingly, and did not seriously threaten the guilds. Yet by granting an exclusive privilege for producing goods not yet manufactured in the Monarchy, such as cotton textiles, the government was able to keep guilds entirely out of new industries that had not been under their control.[59] During Maria Theresia's reign the principle was enunciated that new industries not already organized into guilds would remain free of such corporate restrictions thereafter.[60]

[55] Přibram, *Gewerbepolitik*, p. 48.

[56] Similar action was taken by other governments elsewhere on the continent. Alan S. Milward and S. B. Saul, *The Economic Development of Continental Europe, 1780–1870* (London: George Allen and Unwin, 1973), p. 36. In the early 1730s the monarch also attempted without much success to weaken the guilds' authority to set limits on the number of master craftsmen. Arthur Salz, *Geschichte der Böhmischen Industrie in der Neuzeit* (Munich and Leipzig: Duncker und Humblot, 1913), p. 261.

[57] Gustav Otruba, *Österreichische Fabriksprivilegien vom 16. bis ins 18. Jahrhundert und ausgewählte verwandte Quellen zur Frühgeschichte der Industrialisierung* (Vienna: Böhlau, 1981), pp. 18, 20.

[58] Slokar, *Geschichte der österreichischen Industrie*, p. 1. With the founding of the cotton textile factory in Schwechat in 1726 under such a privilege, this branch of industry remained permanently free from guild restrictions. One might argue that between 1726 and 1763, or at least during part of that time, the charter had actually become a hindrance to the growth of the cotton textile industry. The large number of cotton textile factories founded shortly after Schwechat's exclusive patent lapsed indicate that by then the market had expanded sufficiently to support more than one factory. Přibram, *Gewerbepolitik*, p. 154. No doubt that stage had been reached earlier. The presumption is that the privilege was in effect longer than could be justified by infant-industry arguments. Without the charter, however, the guild system might have extended its influence over this sector as well. Hence the privilege can be seen as a second-best solution: the existence of an imperfection (the guilds) rendered suboptimal the case (no privileges) that would have been optimal in the absence of the imperfection. Under such circumstances, the second-best solution (privileges) might, in fact, have been the best feasible outcome.

[59] Přibram, *Gewerbepolitik*, p. 12.

[60] Slokar, *Geschichte der österreichischen Industrie*, p. 86.

In 1754 the government took another important step by dividing industrial enterprises into those producing for the local market and those producing for a distant market, either domestic or foreign.[61] The former were designated "police" industries; the latter became "commercial" industries and were placed entirely outside of guild restrictions. This action was again a compromise, an attempt to placate the guilds by appearing to support them in their traditional environment, while at the same time severely limiting the extension of their influence over industries working for foreign or interregional markets. This legal differentiation greatly limited the guilds' ability to expand their influence, because the guilds could not hinder growth in strategically important branches of industry. The commercial industries, after all, were the ones with a growth potential. Yet the new legislation was not an immediate threat to the guilds, because they were permitted to continue to determine the number of producers necessary to maintain equilibrium between local demand and supply. The number of masters producing for local consumption was still not allowed to increase unless, in the opinion of the guild, local conditions warranted it. From 1754 on, however, the number of masters working for distant markets could be determined entirely by market forces, thereby opening up the possibilities of increased employment outside of the agricultural sector.[62]

The most important step for encouraging industrial development was allowing the peasants to weave in their homes without any restrictions. In 1740 cotton weaving and spinning were permitted outside of towns.[63] Since the protoindustrial sector was then still rather small, the new law had significance mainly by setting a precedent. Also, in 1740, linen weaving was allowed freely in the two counties of Silesia that remained in Austrian possession.[64] In 1755 linen weaving was no longer

[61] Přibram, *Gewerbepolitik*, pp. 38, 104. Initially the central government enumerated commercial industries and continued to enlarge the list over time. Not until 1809 were the "police" industries enumerated. At that time the list included 97 occupations, including fish merchants and barbers. Slokar, *Geschichte der österreichischen Industrie*, p. 135. The municipalities granted licenses for these industries. In 1776, the right to grant licenses for commercial industries was delegated to the provincial authorities. Přibram, *Gewerbepolitik*, pp. 319, 329, 361, 514. The latter change in regulation probably did not become effective until 1781.

[62] While eager to promote industry, the authorities were also keenly aware of the importance of maintaining adequate food supplies; they wished to keep workers from being attracted to the industrial sector in sufficient numbers to cause agricultural shortages. Přibram, *Gewerbepolitik*, pp. 12, 243.

[63] Stephen Ritter von Keess and W.C.W. Blumenbach, *Systematische Darstellung der neuesten Fortschritte in den Gewerben und Manufacturen und des gegenwärtigen Zustandes derselben* (Vienna: Gerold, 1829–1830), vol. 1, p. 121.

[64] Přibram, *Gewerbepolitik*, pp. 57, 164.

restricted in Moravia and Bohemia: all persons regardless of gender living outside of towns were permitted to weave and spin linen in their homes. Thereafter, guilds had to compete with rural workers outside their control.[65] Other industrial activities were slowly emancipated from guild control: woolen textile weaving in 1764, woolen sock knitting in 1773, printing and dyeing of textiles in 1773.[66] Thus by the 1760s and 1770s all textile industries had been declared free professions, and the government had succeeded in isolating guilds sufficiently to open the way for industrialization.[67]

While linen textile guilds were abolished completely in 1784, other guilds were allowed to exist as long as they could compete without government protection. In some places, such as Reichenberg, the guild system continued to thrive. Yet all guilds came increasingly under government surveillance, and their restrictive practices were countered. For instance, masters weaving woolen textiles were allowed in 1765 to have as many looms and apprentices as they pleased, thereby relying more on market forces.[68]

Metal workers' guilds remained more powerful than textile guilds, although new opportunities were being created in that branch as well.

---

[65] Ibid., p. 268.

[66] In 1767 dyers could print textiles, and printers could dye, at least for their own use. In 1773 the printing and dyeing of textiles were still restricted by proof of competence, but six years later this stipulation was also lifted, because it had proven too difficult to enforce. (Jews were still excluded from dyeing and printing, because the authorities believed they would not use genuine dyes. They were allegedly able to circumvent the law by hiring Christian journeymen who became the ostensible owners of the enterprises.) Also in 1773, linen weaving and sock knitting were declared free professions for the rural population throughout Cisleithania. Přibram, *Gewerbepolitik*, p. 218. Slokar, *Geschichte der österreichischen Industrie*, p. 358. Otruba, *Österreichische Fabrikprivilegien*, p. 61. Similar edicts were issued in France at the time. Milward and Saul, *Economic Development*, p. 94. In 1762 peasants of Upper Normandy gained the right to manufacture cloth without joining a corporation. Gay L. Gullickson, "Agriculture and Cottage Industry: Redefining the Causes of Proto-industrialization," *Journal of Economic History* 43 (1983): 831–850. In 1770 Austrian women were allowed to produce silk goods. Journeymen in Vienna were so infuriated by this measure that they took to the streets. The journeymen were threatened with severe punishment if they continued to oppose the ordinance, since this step was seen as a means of protecting the family by increasing its income. Přibram, *Gewerbepolitik*, p. 217; Schreyer, *Kommerz, Fabriken und Manufakturen*, vol. 1, p. 230.

[67] Reforms favorable to industrial development were not confined to Austria. In Russia in the 1760s and 1770s legislation enabled the peasants to engage in domestic industries. The Parlement of Paris, too, supported domestic industries and distributed thousands of spinning wheels among the peasants. Blum, *End of the Old Order*, pp. 175–176.

[68] Similar steps were taken to free industrialists from the lord's monopsony rights. In 1775 the lord's fulling mill lost this privilege. Slokar, *Geschichte der österreichischen Industrie*, p. 317.

Thus journeymen, after six years of satisfactory performance, could no longer be denied master status.[69] From 1781 pig-iron production was deregulated, and three years later so were bronze foundries.[70] The glass industry was least affected by the reforms: only in 1835 was it freed completely from regulation. From 1818 on, however, glass factories could be founded even by those with no special education in the trade.[71]

The government was not content to foster industrialization merely by removing institutional bottlenecks; it took several additional steps as well. It promulgated quality ordinances for linen textiles in 1750 and for woolen cloth produced in Bohemia in 1758.[72] To protect and enhance the reputation of Bohemian cloth, the precise method of producing textiles was prescribed, inspection for proper quality was undertaken, and uninspected textiles were confiscated. In the absence of such legally-stipulated quality ordinances it might have been worthwhile in the short run for a producer to sell cloth of below-average quality, while claiming that it was Bohemian cloth of average quality. He would thereby make it more difficult for other Bohemian producers to sell their wares. Eventually, these laws fell into disuse, because the conviction developed that the weaver hurts only himself with the production of poor-quality cloth. Indeed, with the extension of the market, such negative externalities must have diminished, and by the 1780s most quality ordinances had become superfluous.

A large number of other steps were taken to promote economic development. As part of its industrial policy the government announced a prize in 1761 for the three best woolen cloth bolts manufactured.[73] In 1777, it lowered the weavers' tax burden at the lords' expense when it abolished the "wool-cent," paid to the manors. In 1787 usury laws were

[69] Přibram, *Gewerbepolitik*, p. 366.

[70] Slokar, *Geschichte der österreichischen Industrie*, pp. 445, 501.

[71] Ibid., p. 515. Yet the guilds seem not to have understood fully that the government was pursuing a policy inimical to their interests. Since they had no other avenue of redress, they continued to turn to the government for financial aid, but without success. For example, the clothmakers' guild of Humpoletz in Czaslau County, Bohemia, petitioned the Emperor on March 10, 1844, to help alleviate the unemployment of some of its members. It complained that the army did not purchase from them because their prices were above the market price. To lower their inventory, they were willing to reduce the price, but this did not help them because their quality was not up to par either. Their petition was rejected. In 1848 the National bank, however, granted the clothmakers' guild of Iglau a 20,000-fl loan, because they were terribly hurt by the cut off of their markets due to the Italian events. Unemployed men on the street were making threatening remarks. Without the loan, an insurrection was supposedly imminent. Kriegsarchiv, Vienna, Hofkriegsrath Akten, Monturs Commission, 1844 E 2/107 and 1848 E 2/69.

[72] Schreyer, *Kommerz, Fabriken und Manufakturen*, vol. 1, p. 32.

[73] Slokar, *Geschichte der österreichischen Industrie*, pp. 318, 323, 371.

abolished. Spinning schools were founded in Bohemia as early as 1755, but more frequently after 1764. All towns in Bohemia were ordered to open spinning schools, and learning this skill became mandatory for all children between the ages of 7 and 15. They were to receive a small per diem for support. In 1768 the government spent 12,000 fl to found a school for lace making in Prague. In 1786 it offered a subsidy of 12 fl for every loom suitable for weaving batiste linen put into service within the next six months. Batiste output was subsidized at a rate of 3 to 6 kreuzer per bolt.[74] In the early 1780s Joseph II imported flax seed from Riga and distributed it to the peasantry, thereby not only subsidizing the agricultural sector, but also helping to increase the supply of an important industrial raw material.[75]

Another instrument supporting the industrial sector was tariff policy. To induce import substitution, protectionist measures were introduced in 1764, aimed at foreign textiles in general, but Prussian-Silesian wool and linens in particular. Importing woolens was entirely prohibited.[76] The government saw this as part of the program of fighting prejudice against domestic goods.[77] In addition, the government adopted export subsidies for woolen cloth in 1768 in order to make the domestic product more competitive abroad. However, the one-florin subsidy per bolt, about 2 percent of value, seems not to have had appreciable effect.[78] In 1783 the export premium was doubled.[79] Until 1771, it had been possible for goods produced in the Monarchy, but exported as intermediate goods for the purpose of finishing, to be reimported under a special tariff. In that year the government abolished this privilege.[80] To diminish imports further, Jews were entirely forbidden to trade in foreign goods between 1764 and 1772.[81]

To foster domestic competition, while providing protection from for-

---

[74] Ibid., pp. 318, 319, 362. By 1789 there were 181 batiste weavers in Bohemia.

[75] Schreyer, *Kommerz, Fabriken und Manufakturen*, vol. 1, p. 3.

[76] Alfred Hoffmann, *Wirtschaftsgeschichte des Landes Oberösterreich* (Salzburg: Otto Müller, 1952), vol. 1, p. 32. Prussia retaliated by prohibiting glass and iron goods, imports from Austria. For a recent study of debates within the government over tariff policy during this period, see Helen P. Liebel, "Free Trade and Protectionism under Maria Theresa and Joseph II," *Canadian Journal of History* 14 (1979): 355–373.

[77] Přibram, *Gewerbepolitik*, p. 64.

[78] One florin had a silver content of 23.39 grams.

[79] Slokar, *Geschichte der österreichischen Industrie*, p. 318.

[80] Přibram, *Gewerbepolitik*, p. 209. In 1761 linen yarn was not allowed to be taken to Silesia for bleaching; this restriction was later lifted. Slokar, *Geschichte der österreichischen Industrie*, p. 360.

[81] This restriction was lifted because it was said not to have helped the Christian merchants, indicating how inelastic the supply of Christian entrepreneurs was at the time. Přibram, *Gewerbepolitik*, p. 238.

eign producers, the government in 1775 abolished tariff barriers that had hitherto hindered trade among the western provinces of the Monarchy. It thereby became one of the largest free-trade areas in Europe.[82] In 1784 prohibitive duties were placed on all industrial goods, thereby extending the level of protection from foreign competition. Factories, however, could import machinery with permission subject to a low tariff. The enactment of these tariffs was a sign that the market had expanded: officials thereby revealed their belief that the domestic supply of industrial goods sufficed to meet domestic demand, or at least that it was elastic enough to do so in the near future. The prohibitive system, which stayed in effect until the middle of the nineteenth century, was initially a great incentive to development; however, it probably remained in effect longer than was optimal.

In addition to tariff protection, factories enjoyed other kinds of government support. They were initially exempt from real estate taxes and, until 1812, from income taxes.[83] Their buildings could not be used for quartering soldiers. Workers were exempt from labor services they might have owed to the manor as peasants, and were also free from the draft until the Napoleonic Wars. Factories were allowed to attract skilled workers from abroad and to import those machines and raw materials not produced within the monarchy. They were also promised protection from competition, at least in the regions where they were located. Factories could subcontract work to the guilds. Labor contracts were enforced by making it illegal for a factory owner to hire any worker lacking a written letter of discharge from his previous employer.[84] By enforcing such contracts, the government prevented market failure that could have come about through the reluctance of entrepreneurs to invest in the on-the-job training of workers when the benefit of such investment might have accrued to someone else.

Although the monopoly of the Schwechat cotton textile factory was renewed for the last time in 1753, such monopolies were increasingly seen as hindering industrial progress. The market had expanded sufficiently by then to accommodate a larger number of enterprises. Hence the privilege came to resemble a mere license to produce without guild

[82] In Bohemia, Eger and its surroundings, as well as the county of Pilsen, remained outside the customs union until 1784. Eastern Galicia, acquired in 1772, was incorporated into the customs union in 1783, while western Galicia was incorporated in 1796. Slokar, *Geschichte der österreichischen Industrie*, p. 3.

[83] Ibid., p. 129.

[84] Příbram, *Gewerbepolitik*, p. 206. Slokar, *Geschichte der österreichischen Industrie*, p. 131. The fine for breaking this law was 50 florins. Schreyer, *Kommerz, Fabriken und Manufakturen*, vol. 2, p. 181.

restrictions, rather than an outright monopoly.[85] During the next decade the notion of a warrant for production in factories came into the bureaucratic language, although the word 'privilege' continued to be used as well.[86] The licensing procedure was deemed necessary to guard entrepreneurs from ruin through overproduction.[87] By the 1780s, however, very few exclusive privileges were granted, and only in cases in which existing industries would not be hurt, or if the entrepreneur used an entirely new technology. Thus the exclusive privilege came to resemble the modern form of a patent.[88]

Cloth factories were originally allowed to sell only to wholesale merchants. This limitation on their clientele was lifted in steps. In 1764 they were allowed to sell to the public on their own premises or at fairs, but not less than one bolt at a time.[89] Ten years later, the position of factories was further strengthened at the expense of merchants by allowing the former to sell retail at their premises without restriction.[90] The merchants' exclusive right to trade was further undermined by permitting larger factories to establish warehouses in the provincial capitals of the empire. Better capitalized enterprises could act as middlemen for smaller firms.[91]

These measures, enabling factory owners to profit at the expense of merchants, can also be interpreted as indicative of the inadequate size of the third sector. Had the number of merchants been sufficient, perhaps industrialists would not have been favored in this way, since they had no comparative advantage over merchants in this respect. The less than optimal size of the third sector can be explained in part by the strict government licensing procedure, which required that an applicant have 20,000 fl capital before becoming a wholesale merchant.[92]

The government's direct industrial promotion program started modestly, for only minimal funds were at its disposal for such purposes. Subsidies were initially financed by collecting a small sum of 2,000 fl per

[85] Přibram, *Gewerbepolitik*, pp. 72, 228.

[86] Otruba, *Österreichische Fabriksprivilegien*, p. 15.

[87] Since the government had more information at its disposal than the entrepreneur, this requirement sought to foster optimum allocation of scarce resources available to the economy. Yet industrial statistics were kept secret until 1790, even though their dissemination would have often eased the entrepreneurs' decision making. Přibram, *Gewerbepolitik*, p. 350.

[88] Ibid., p. 368.

[89] Slokar, *Geschichte der österreichischen Industrie*, pp. 142, 144.

[90] In 1783, this measure was extended by authorizing factories to sell retail in open stalls; this privilege was not limited to fairs. Přibram, *Gewerbepolitik*, pp. 332, 382.

[91] Ibid., p. 86.

[92] In Vienna the sum was 30,000 florins. In addition, non-Catholic merchants needed the emperor's permission to acquire real property. Přibram, *Gewerbepolitik*, p. 241.

year from the guilds. Certain minute fines were also allocated to this end. Beginning in 1755, a monthly "weaving-cent" was collected from rural Bohemian weavers to support development in the province's mountainous regions. In Moravia the annual tax amounted to only 17,000 fl.[93] The financial support initially granted to the industrial sector was thus minimal. Although the total sums spent by the government for industrial promotion are not known, they must have increased substantially. By 1770 they had reached one million fl.[94]

From the late 1770s, and even more so in the 1780s during Joseph II's reign, the government slowly but increasingly disassociated itself from the policy of granting loans and subsidies; requests were rejected regularly.[95] When the state did make loans, it acted like a private bank: it usually demanded collateral.[96] Instead of using loans or subsidies to foster industrialization, the state preferred to encourage more competition among producers; this new policy made sense in the context of the enlarged market of the 1780s.[97]

Protoindustrialization received further government incentive in the 1780s, when local authorities were granted the right to help small producers with loans or subsidies of between 200 and 500 fl, which could be dispensed without permission from higher authority. Artisans were also given financial aid to help them purchase tools required in their craft. The policy of supporting small producers had begun in the mid-1760s, with the distribution of looms and spinning rods among the peasantry, and with the aid given to itinerant masters who instructed peasants in spinning and weaving.[98] In carrying out such a policy, the state (in Gerschenkron's terminology) substituted for some of the "missing prerequisites of economic development" by acting as banker and entrepreneur.[99]

---

[93] Slokar, *Geschichte der österreichischen Industrie*, p. 66.

[94] It is also known that in 1780 loans of 680,000 florins granted during the previous two decades were still outstanding; however, the sum repaid by that time is not known. Bohemia and Lower Austria were the only two provinces receiving meaningful support; the above sum was divided equally between them. Přibram, *Gewerbepolitik*, p. 396. This sum might be compared with the 85,000 florins annual profit the government received from the industrial enterprises it owned.

[95] For instance, Joseph refused the petition of a factory owner for a loan, stating that if his factory were run well he would be able to procure private loans. Přibram, *Gewerbepolitik*, pp. 231, 267, 346, 390.

[96] Ibid., p. 399.

[97] Ibid., p. 346. According to one contemporary observer, industrial prosperity was evident in certain areas of Bohemia: instead of wooden houses, brick houses were being built.

[98] Přibram, *Gewerbepolitik*, p. 69.

[99] In this respect the directive was explicit. In fostering small firms, local governments

In addition, the government provided occasional support in times of calamity. In response to the economic crisis of the early 1770s, brought about by harvest failures, the government, acting in the true spirit of a welfare state, spent 100,000 fl to buy linen yarn and textiles to help support the suffering population. Merchants were also said to have bought linen yarn in order to keep spinners from starving.[100] With the recurrence of crisis in 1779, the government spent an even larger sum to aid the linen industry.[101] This policy continued into the nineteenth century.[102]

Industries requiring unskilled labor were fostered in rural areas. By supporting such labor-intensive industries, the government maximized employment even at the cost of efficiency, thus slowing the diffusion of technology into the Monarchy. Taking his reasoning from Montesquieu, Joseph von Sonnenfels argued in favor of preventing technological unemployment: "Since marriages thus depend chiefly on employment, and are with it either increased or decreased, so one must avoid everything that diminishes the quantity of employment."[103]

One need not view the government's financial support of industry with disdain just because it could not always recoup its loans. Many firms went bankrupt, and others might not have generated sufficient profits to meet their obligations to the state. Yet these funds were not wasted from the macroeconomic point of view, because positive externalities were still obtained even if the subsidized enterprise ultimately failed. Buildings erected, experience accumulated, skills disseminated, and information obtained about market conditions continued to benefit the economy as a whole.

The government took direct steps to regulate the incipient market, thereby economizing on the use of resources. Beginning in 1750, manorial estates assigned to yarn merchants districts in which they were given monopsony power (the exclusive right to purchase). Spinning was allowed even outside the already allocated spinning districts, affording newcomers the opportunity to acquire spinners. The yarn merchant

---

should not do more than a *merchant* would under similar circumstances; they were to emulate the behavior of entrepreneurs. Přibram, *Gewerbepolitik*, pp. 392, 393.

[100] Schreyer, *Kommerz, Fabriken und Manufakturen*, vol. 1, p. 18.

[101] Přibram, *Gewerbepolitik*, p. 232.

[102] In 1805, the government purchased 300,000 fl worth of linen goods to help the suffering weavers. Another 250,000 fl were granted as interest-free loans. Slokar, *Geschichte der österreichischen Industrie*, p. 368.

[103] Sonnenfels, *Politische Abhandlungen*, pp. 245–246. The fear of technological unemployment goes back to Roman times. John A. Garraty, *Unemployment in History* (New York: Harper and Row, 1978), p. 7.

licensed by the estate was responsible for the proper length of a bundle of yarn, and was threatened by the loss of his license and even by corporal punishment were he to cheat.[104]

This policy of granting monopsony rights was introduced to prevent market failure, which might have followed from the positive externalities associated with a merchant's efforts. The merchant organized the market initially, instructed the peasantry in the art of spinning, and often provided capital in the form of a spinning wheel. Had his investment not been legally protected from the encroachment of competitors who would otherwise have benefited from the initial investment, less than the optimal amount of effort might have been forthcoming. The government's policy aimed at equating social and private returns and was reasonable in the context of the economic environment prevailing at the time.

To ensure that yarn would be produced relatively cheaply, the government regulated spinners' wages in 1750. The policy was seen as maximizing employment because it would keep the price of the yarn low, but it also protected the peasants from excesses that might have come about because of the yarn merchants' monopsony power. Spinning was largely a part-time occupation of women and children, who had limited employment alternatives, especially during the winter, when agriculture required only a few hours of work a day.[105] Once spinning districts were apportioned, the wage would have been determined by bargaining between peasants, who were in excess supply, and the monopsonist outputter. In the absence of a minimum, the wage might have been determined by the marginal utility of leisure, which would not have been substantial among a population striving to stay alive. The wage might have been determined by the level of short-run subsistence, but could have been below the subsistence level in the long run.[106] Given the out-

[104] He was allowed to attach the name of the spinner to the bundle of yarn. Schreyer, *Kommerz, Fabriken und Manufakturen*, vol. 1, p. 22.

[105] In early twentieth-century Russia, peasants worked on average only three hours per day in February and two hours per day in October. A. V. Chayanov, *The Theory of the Peasant Economy* (1925; reprint, Homewood, IL: Irwin, 1966), p. 75.

[106] Subsistence is not a precise notion. Lloyd Reynolds, "The Spread of Economic Growth to the Third World: 1850–1980," *Journal of Economic Literature* 21 (1983): 941–980. Information on subsistence would not have been available to the population. How much food intake was needed to fight off certain diseases, for example, must not have been known. It does not help to think of the subsistence wage as the one that enables society just to reproduce itself in the steady state, because there is no guarantee that that wage will be unique. If by subsistence one means the ability to stay alive from one day to the next, then peasants were still above that level. The problem could perhaps be posed in terms of the wage's effect on life expectancy. Peasants were striving to maintain their

putter's greater bargaining power, the policy, in fact, could be seen as a measure protecting the peasantry.

Eventually, government regulation of spinning could have become inimical to the peasants' interest; however, the regulation remained in effect only long enough for the market to become organized. After two decades the district system for spinners was abolished, indicating that the enlarged market had rendered protection of the parties concerned superfluous. In addition, investments of the yarn outputters had been amortized over a long enough time for them to recoup their initial outlays. Further government regulation was therefore no longer required. The district system was abolished for linen yarn spinners in 1772, and shortly thereafter all districts were abolished; spinners were free to sell at will, or to sign long-term contracts with outputters.[107] Abolishing these rights indicates that by that time economic policies were being formulated in a more liberal spirit.[108]

A disadvantage of the institutional setting created by the government, aside from the many legal problems that arose when new factories or outputters encroached on someone else's spinning districts, was that once the spinning wage and districts had been established, they became part of the business culture. The fact that such districts continued to exist even after they were no longer mandated is indicative not only of the difficulty of disseminating information under incipient market conditions and of enforcing the law, but also of the dogged persistence of patterns of behavior and institutional forms. Even decades later, the spinning districts gave rise to many quarrels among outputters.[109]

The government also intervened in the labor market by attempting to decrease shirking among workers. To this end, it decreed that journeymen should be paid only for actual days worked rather than in a weekly lump sum, hoping that this regulation would call forth more effort.[110]

As part of the government's program of mobilizing society for the difficult task of defending the standard of living, religious orders without useful economic functions were disbanded. Monasteries were confiscated and sold or rented to businessmen at low rates. In 1773 the

---

standard of living. The actual wage would, no doubt, have been determined by bargaining. As the market expanded the wage would have risen through competition, had this institutional framework of spinning districts not existed.

[107] Přibram, *Gewerbepolitik*, pp. 219, 373. In 1776 monopsony powers granted to paper producers to purchase inputs and to leather merchants in Bohemia were abolished. Soap makers were granted monopoly rights within certain districts between 1772 and 1776.

[108] Přibram, *Gewerbepolitik*, p. 338.

[109] S.U.A. Č.G. Com., 1796–1805, 13/3, Box 613.

[110] That this decree was not appreciated by the workers is shown by the unrest in Vienna on July 8, 1805, caused by a similar decree. Přibram, *Gewerbepolitik*, pp. 247, 248.

Jesuit order was banished;[111] this was an indication of the rationalizing attitudes that Max Weber saw as a concomitant of economic development. The action taken against the monasteries was also symptomatic of the growth of antireligious sentiment, an influence of the Enlightenment on a once solidly Catholic country.[112]

By the late 1770s the market had expanded considerably. The government responded by relying more on free market forces, abandoning its exclusive dependence on mercantilistic policies. It no longer tried to overcome all difficulties associated with an underdeveloped market by specific directives from above. Instead of advancing the common weal by prescribing policy (to the minutest detail in some instances), the government was willing to allow individuals greater freedom of action to accomplish the same ends. In the 1780s, for example, provincial authorities were instructed a number of times to administer the laws in the spirit of free (domestic) trade.[113] The government's willingness to let market forces determine the relationship between spinner and outputter is just one manifestation of this spirit. The change in attitude was made possible by the diminution in the guilds' power, and by sufficient expansion of the market so that models of imperfect competition were no longer the only, or even the best possible, way to conceptualize economic processes. The market, of course, was still not perfectly competitive, but it was moving in that direction, and it made sense for policymakers to adopt liberal economic ideas more frequently in shaping policy.

Yet this was never meant to be a coherent plan, and deviations from the trend toward laissez-faire persisted. Thus, according to a 1789 directive, cotton weaving was to be discouraged in those places where linen production was already under way; instead, the former activity should be introduced into regions not yet producing textiles. Another policy that was reminiscent of the previous mercantilistic practice was the 100 fl premium given to foreign cotton weavers who immigrated into the country.[114]

[111] Přibram, *Gewerbepolitik*, p. 401. Such practices were not confined to Austria. Joel Mokyr, *Industrialization in the Low Countries, 1795–1850* (New Haven: Yale University Press, 1976), p. 39.

[112] Ernst Wangermann suggests that "scepticism and irreligion" became "fashionable in educated middle-class circles" during the years of Joseph II's church reforms. By the mid-1790s, such "rationalist ideas" had even come to be accepted by "a not inconsiderable number of people from the lower strata of Vienna's population." Ernst Wangermann, *From Joseph II to the Jacobin Trials: Government Policy and Public Opinion in the Habsburg Dominions in the Period of the French Revolution* (London: Oxford University Press, 1959), pp. 15, 19.

[113] Přibram, *Gewerbepolitik*, p. 361.

[114] Schreyer, *Kommerz, Fabriken und Manufakturen*, vol. 1, pp. 210, 223.

In the 1780s, partly in response to more liberal official policy, a large number of factories did come into being.[115] This phenomenon testified to the growth of the market: factories required a relatively large market in order to operate efficiently. In turn, they were able to capture economies of scale in production, and thereby produce at a lower cost than decentralized firms.

Although factories were no longer able to count on financial support regularly, some loans were forthcoming nonetheless.[116] The government granted a total of 250,000 fl in industrial subsidies in 1786 and 1787, but the following year, under the pressure of the Turkish war, the sum shrank to 40,000 fl. Thereafter subsidies were kept to a few thousand florins per annum.[117] Although outright subsidies had become minimal, the government continued to help the industrial sector overcome unanticipated difficulties. For instance, when the American Revolutionary War cut off the overseas markets of the Bohemian linen weavers, the government gave 50,000 fl quarterly for two years, partly as loans to merchants and partly as outright support for the unemployed.[118] Such a government-sponsored safety net fits well into the conceptualization of this absolutist monarchy as an incipient welfare state.

Large factories were allowed in 1787 to establish warehouses in all provincial capitals of the Monarchy. Thus began the distinction between "formally" privileged factories and the "simple" privileges granted to entrepreneurs who worked for a distant market, but were not permitted to establish warehouses elsewhere.[119] The criteria for acquiring the formal designation appear never to have been clearly formulated, which subsequently caused many difficulties.[120] Initially this regulation enabled larger factories to respond more quickly to distant

[115] Přibram, *Gewerbepolitik*, p. 374.

[116] Ibid., p. 271.

[117] Ibid., p. 401.

[118] Ibid., p. 390.

[119] Ibid., p. 383. Once the profit tax was introduced in 1813, formally privileged factories fell into different tax brackets from those of simple privileged ones. The former were divided into five categories, and in Vienna they paid a tax of 50 to 1,500 fl CM (i.e., in silver) per annum. In Prague, Brno, and Linz taxes were lower: from 40 to 1,000 fl. Simple privileged factories in Vienna were divided into ten categories and paid a tax of between 5 and 100 florins. Outside of Vienna, they paid from 3 to 50 florins in five gradations. Slokar, *Geschichte der österreichischen Industrie*, p. 129.

[120] The confusion in this regard is shown by Slokar's assertion that an entrepreneur did not need to possess a simple factory privilege before receiving a formal one. Slokar, *Geschichte der österreichischen Industrie*, p. 130. However, I do not know of a single instance in which this was not the case. In fact, the petitions usually emphasized that the petitioner already had a simple privilege.

market opportunities. In 1791 local or municipal authorities were given the right to grant simple privileges, thereby making it much easier to found factories. Formal licenses remained the prerogative of the provincial government.[121] In case of denial, the entrepreneur could petition higher authorities all the way to Vienna.

About 1800 this distinction, too, became blurred as factories with simple privileges were granted the right to maintain warehouses at other locations, not by law, but in practice.[122] Another manifestation of liberal tendencies was the fact that monopolies were no longer granted for goods produced for the common man but were still allowed for luxury goods. Such a policy indicated a desire to foster the market for mass-consumption goods.

A large share of workers in textile factories continued to be women and children. The ratio of the value of their marginal product to their opportunity cost was considerably greater than for men. In the textile factories, no great strength was required and women and children were dexterous enough to perform the required tasks, while in agriculture the reverse was true: strength was of more importance. Because of the acceleration in population growth, children made up a very large share of the population (about 34 percent); hence they were a great financial burden to their parents. Indeed, the government considered the employment of children a priority, and in petitions entrepreneurs tended to emphasize either that they employed children, or that they were willing to do so. This appeared all the more natural because children started to work at an early age in a pre-industrial setting as well.[123]

Religious toleration was yet another aspect of Joseph II's reforms, even though Roman Catholicism remained the state religion. After 1725, dispensation could be granted to Protestant industrialists living in Vienna; a tax similar to the one on Jews was, however, levied on them. While the tax on Protestants was abolished, the tax on Jews remained in effect until the mid-nineteenth century. In Bohemia, too,

---

[121] Přibram, *Gewerbepolitik*, pp. 515, 569.

[122] Slokar, *Geschichte der österreichischen Industrie*, p. 448. By 1820 it was especially easy to obtain access to the Viennese market.

[123] As one author put it recently, "The employment of women and children was . . . aggravated by industrialism, *but* it was not a new problem. . . . The women and children of the poor had always worked . . . often at harder labor, for longer hours, and . . . at a younger age." Gertrude Himmelfarb, *The Idea of Poverty* (New York: Knopf, 1983), p. 141. Steps to regulate the employment of children in Austria began in 1816, when the government stipulated that children working in factories should also go to school and visit doctors regularly. A decree of 1786, however, had mandated that children working in factories bathe at least once a week and be examined by a doctor twice a year. Slokar, *Geschichte der österreichischen Industrie*, pp. 8, 101, 102.

foreign Protestant manufacturers were allowed to settle as of 1725, though also with special permission and subject to an extraordinary tax.[124] In 1781 toleration of Protestants became general, and many foreigners immigrated to the Monarchy as a consequence. Their moving expenses were often paid by the Austrian government.[125]

In the 1780s Jews, too, became more integrated into the industrial structure. The degree of their toleration had varied from province to province ever since 1629, when they had received the right to trade at all markets. From 1709 on, Jews had been allowed to travel unencumbered and trade with products that they produced in royal free towns. They could buy and sell wool but were not allowed to own real property outside areas designated for them. Between 1726 and 1747 Jews had been allowed to become peddlers.[126] By 1781, Jews were allowed to live in the Czech and Polish provinces, in Hungary, and in Vienna, but nowhere else in Lower or Upper Austria or Steyermark.[127] Moravian Jews were confined to small towns; they could not live in Brünn, or in the six royal free towns. Although the toleration patents did not extend the Jews' permitted places of residence,[128] Joseph II did open a large number of professions to them in order to "increase their means of earning a living so that they would be discouraged from practicing usury and deceptive trade."[129]

However tainted with bias the justification of the reform might have been, the fact remains that the Jews' new legal position enabled them to become more active in the industrial sector. Many Jews became mer-

---

[124] Přibram, *Gewerbepolitik*, p. 147.

[125] Ibid., pp. 356, 403. While fostering skilled immigration, the law prohibited from 1752 onward the emigration of skilled glass workers. After 1761, those who turned in individuals intending to emigrate received a reward of 100 fl. This sum of money might be considered a measure of the negative externality of emigration. Slokar, *Geschichte der österreichischen Industrie*, p. 511.

[126] Christian D'Elvert, "Zur Geschichte der Juden in Mähren und der österreichischen Schlesien," *Schriften der historisch-statistischen Secktion der k. k. mährischen Gesellschaft zur Beförderung des Ackerbaues, der Natur- und Landeskunde*, vol. 30 (Brünn: Winiker, 1895), pp. 26, 179–181, 186.

[127] Ibid. In 1745 Maria Theresia had ordered the Jews to leave Bohemia because she suspected them of collaborating with her enemy, Frederick II. She had revoked this rescript in 1748 and extended their stay for a decade, partly because they were willing to pay 200,000 fl tax per year.

[128] Jews could petition to live in Lower Austria provided that they founded a factory, but only if it were in a rented building. Slokar, *Geschichte der österreichischen Industrie*, p. 260. For a more recent study of the intragovernmental debates that led to the toleration patent, see Paul P. Bernard, "Joseph II and the Jews: The Origins of the Toleration Patent of 1782," *Austrian History Yearbook* 4–5 (1968–69): 101–119.

[129] Přibram, *Gewerbepolitik*, p. 357.

chants and outputters. They might have enjoyed a comparative advantage because, according to at least one contemporary, they sold cheaper than the Christians.[130] Jews were well represented among shoemakers and tailors.[131]

Bohemian Jews had been allowed to practice most professions since 1748. With the important exception of cotton printing and dyeing firms, they could, with special permission, found factories; they were even allowed to hire Christian journeymen. To be sure, Jewish fortunes continued to fluctuate. From 1764 to 1772 Jews were forbidden to trade in foreign goods.[132] In 1765 they were again allowed to become peddlers in the Czech provinces, although peddling luxury goods among the rural population was still forbidden.[133] In 1781 all professions were opened to them, and they were allowed to learn trades from Christian masters.[134] In special cases they could purchase buildings for industrial uses, but even after the 1780s they still faced difficulties in acquiring real estate, except from the government.[135]

Some municipalities refused Jews permission to buy real estate from Christians or asserted that the town charter prohibited Jews from living within the town walls. In cases that were appealed, the higher authorities invariably intervened on the side of toleration. If no other compromise could be reached, Jews were allowed to rent buildings for production purposes, if not for domiciles.[136] In 1791 the Jews of Prague were allowed to buy houses outside of the ghetto for purposes of production,

---

[130] In 1769, 60 percent of Moravian merchants were Jews. Hofkammer Archiv, Vienna, Commerz, Rt. Nr. 796; Schreyer, *Kommerz, Fabriken und Manufakturen*, vol. 1, p. 133; vol. 2, p. 135. Jews came in contact, and established links, with the spinning and weaving peasantry, although they themselves did not practice these trades. To the extent that spinners' wages were set by the government, Jewish middlemen, practicing an occupation never particularly well-liked, were perceived as exploiting the peasantry, even though they were merely carrying out government policy. Animosity toward the Jews is shown by many reports blaming them for smuggling. Příbram, *Gewerbepolitik*, pp. 356, 357. Examples of complaints about Jews "monopolizing the market" abound. Letter from Trebitsch, April 18, 1848. Kriegsarchiv, Vienna, Hofkriegsrath Akten, Monturs Kommission, 1848 E 2/74. Slokar, *Geschichte der österreichischen Industrie*, p. 149.

[131] Some Jewish tailors started to produce ready-made suits for the Viennese market.

[132] Příbram, *Gewerbepolitik*, p. 238.

[133] Ibid., p. 380.

[134] Ibid., p. 358.

[135] Karl Grünberg, "Die Grundeigenthumsfähigkeit in den böhmischen Ländern vor 1848," *Schmollers Jahrbuch für Gesetzgebung, Verwaltung, und Volkswirtschaft* 21, reprinted in idem, *Studien zur österreichischen Agrargeschichte* (Leipzig: Duncker und Humblot, 1901), p. 113. Jews bought wool on forward contracts. Schreyer, *Kommerz, Fabriken und Manufakturen*, vol. 1, p. 132.

[136] S.U.A. Č.G. Com., 1796–1805, 13, Box 614.

and in 1801 Porges, a cotton textile printer, was allowed to buy land for a bleachery. By the early nineteenth century this became a general practice. Jews were allowed to own factory buildings, provided that repurchase right in case of cessation of production remained with Christians.[137]

With the death of Joseph II in 1790, industrial reform came to a halt. Successive administrations were preoccupied with foreign policy and military affairs during the Napoleonic wars. Though Joseph II's successors are often depicted as conservative, even reactionary, in many ways the economic outlook of Franz I was quite liberal: industrial freedom remained a cornerstone of his policy. Some scholars have interpreted the prohibition against the founding of factories in Vienna, in effect between 1802 and 1809, as reflecting an anti-industrial bias; in fact, it was an effort to keep the cost of living from rising in the capital, whose population had swollen. Outside Vienna, however, a liberal policy was maintained even during that interlude.[138] The idea of the propitious effects of free competition was often enunciated.[139] This is reflected in the words of a bureaucrat who wrote, in 1818, that "the liberal commercial policy of His Majesty aims at freedom of industry, with the removal of all ancillary considerations."[140]

The Agricultural System prior to the Reforms

As in the realm of industrial laws, the government proceeded cautiously, during the second half of the eighteenth century, to reform the agricultural system. Reforms were concentrated in Bohemia, Moravia, and Silesia, where economic circumstances were most pressing. In contrast, the lord-peasant relationship in Lower and Upper Austria had become less rigid during the course of the prior centuries, and consequently government intervention was less necessary there.[141]

The system of feudal land tenure still in effect in the eighteenth century was quite complex.[142] Although rural land was owned by free cities,

[137] Slokar, *Geschichte der österreichischen Industrie*, pp. 73, 261, 263.
[138] Ibid., pp. 49, 51, 63.
[139] Ibid., pp. 49, 136; S.U.A. Č.G. Com., 1816–1825, 1/1, Box 873.
[140] S.U.A. Č.G. Com., 1816–1825, 1/1, Box 873.
[141] Grünberg called such a system "Gemäßigtes Untertänigkeit." Grünberg, *Bauernbefreiung*, vol. 1, p. 209.
[142] It would be desirable if, in addition to describing the legal system prevailing in the countryside, one could complement it by describing actual conditions there. It would, for instance, be useful to explore the actual workings of manorial courts to be able to clarify our preconceived notions of how they functioned. Unfortunately, systematic analysis of this aspect of the past is not available at present for the Habsburg monarchy.

the Church, monasteries, and the monarch himself, most of the land, divided into manorial estates, was owned by lords. Initially aristocrats alone could buy estates, peasants alone could occupy land on the estates, and citizens of towns could do neither. The peasants, settled on the lord's land, had the right to its use, in effect renting it in exchange for labor obligations and many small payments in kind, such as spinning some yarn for the lord.[143] "The peasant worked the land without owning it."[144] Although peasants could purchase land, they seldom did, according to one observer, because then they would not be able to rely on the lord's help in case of calamity.[145] In addition, they seldom had the sufficient savings to purchase the rent outright. Borrowing was out of the question. Hence they continued to rent the land they worked.

Peasants were subjects of the landowner, not his property. Neither they nor their labor could be sold to other estates.[146] Peasants were not allowed to leave an estate without permission because the lords feared a labor shortage.[147] With population growth in the eighteenth century such anxieties became less realistic, and peasants were allowed to leave the estates after payment of a fee, about a five percent tax on their wealth, or if a diligent replacement was provided.[148] Peasants who had

[143] Grünberg, *Bauernbefreiung*, vol. 1, p. 340.

[144] Franz Mayer, "Die volkswirtschaftliche Zustände Böhmens um den Jahren 1770," *Mittheilungen des Vereins für Geschichte der Deutschen in Böhmen* (1876): 125–149.

[145] Grünberg, *Bauernbefreiung*, vol. 1, p. 100.

[146] Ibid., vol. 1, pp. 3, 28, 87. Peasants were bound to the soil, and when an estate was sold, they remained on the land. Recently Jerome Blum (*End of the Old Order*, p. 48) has suggested that peasants were, indeed, bought and sold. This assertion, however, rests on meager evidence. Blum cites Stark, who mentions the case of a locksmith allowed to leave an estate with his wife and children upon paying a fee of 53 Thaler. Werner Stark, "Die Abhängigkeitsverhältnisse der gutsherrlichen Bauern Böhmens im 17. und 18. Jahrhundert," *Jahrbücher für Nationalökonomie und Statistik* 164 (1952), p. 359. This, however, was the customary payment exacted from someone leaving an estate; it had nothing to do with the purchase or sale of a peasant. Grünberg, who studied that society more meticulously than anyone else, did not believe that peasants were bought and sold. In addition, in an environment in which peasant complaints were voiced frequently about almost every aspect of the peasant-lord relationship, it would be odd if such a system of buying and selling peasants had prevailed without any peasant complaints about it being voiced.

[147] This is similar to the system prevailing in the Soviet Union, in which individuals may not leave a particular locality without prior permission.

[148] One estate charged between 12 and 56 florins for permission to leave. This was by no means an insignificant sum, for there were villages in Bohemia in which, according to a contemporary, there were not two florins among all of the inhabitants. Yet there were rich peasants; some were said to buy grain futures from the less well-to-do prior to the harvest. Mayer, "Die volkswirtschaftliche Zustände Böhmens," pp. 134–137. Grünberg, *Bauernbefreiung*, vol. 1, pp. 8, 19. These payments resemble the ones citizens of Romania and East Germany have to make upon emigrating.

left their estates without permission were to be returned to their lords, and other lords who granted them asylum were threatened with a fine.[149] Day laborers who were not in possession of any land could leave the estate more easily, but only when their labor was not needed would permission be granted, on payment of a nominal 0.5 fl fee. Permission to marry someone living on another estate, however, could easily be obtained. The unemployed were also allowed to migrate.[150] Moreover, there were whole villages in which the movements of the peasants were exempt from restrictions, and in practice the legal prerogatives of the landlords often remained unenforced.[151]

Legal and administrative authority over all those living on manorial estates was vested in the lord of the manor, who delegated this authority to his bailiffs or stewards. Thus, the estate was a unit of local government as well as a form of private property and an economic entity.[152] In their capacity as local governments, the estates regulated marriage. This power was deemed all the more prudent as the burden of taking care of the poor and the orphans fell on the estates.[153] The poor were able to receive an advance of seed for planting in return for a share of the harvest.[154]

That the peasant was a subject of the lord and under his immediate legal jurisdiction ought not be construed to imply that the peasant was without legal protection. Peasants could sue their lords; this right had never been taken from them. The peasant could also appeal to higher authorities, even to the monarch.[155] If peasants brought suits against their lords, lawyers were available free of charge to represent them. That peasants could make use of this right is attested to by the references to their "litigious nature."[156]

In any event, lords and their bailiffs would surely have wanted to avoid capricious behavior in their own self-interest, since they relied on internalized socialization to maintain tranquillity. Transaction costs

[149] Grünberg, *Bauernbefreiung*, vol. 1, p. 12.

[150] Ibid., vol. 1, pp. 15, 19, 29.

[151] Tamás Faragó, "Paraszti Háztartás—és Munkaszervezet—Típusok Magyarországon A 18. Század Közepén. Pilis-Buda környéki birtokos paraszti háztartások 1745–1770 között," *Történeti Statisztikai Füzetek* 7 (1985): 1–187.

[152] Grünberg, *Bauernbefreiung*, vol. 1, p. 3.

[153] A fee of 0.5 florin was levied at the time of marriage. Grünberg, *Bauernbefreiung*, vol. 1, p. 18; John Komlos, "Poverty and Industrialization at the End of the 'Phase-Transition' in the Czech Crown Lands," *Journal of Economic History* 43 (1983): 129–135.

[154] Mayer, "Die volkswirtschaftliche Zustände Böhmens," p. 134.

[155] Maria Theresia received many anonymous memoranda about the distress of the peasantry. Grünberg, *Bauernbefreiung*, vol. 1, p. 191.

[156] Ibid., vol. 1, pp. 30–32, 209.

would otherwise have made the economic system prohibitively expensive to monitor, especially since police authority was weak.[157] The threat of vengeance on the part of the peasantry must also have been a deterrent to acting against the common law of the estate. Moreover, the actions of the lords must have been tempered by the threat that the peasants might run away. Hence, the lord had an incentive to maintain a semblance of justice as understood within the local culture. Of course, that is not to say that wherever possible lords and their bailiffs did not interpret particular situations in their own interest. The notion that the lord's behavior was constrained by the above factors is, however, often absent from discussions of the lord-peasant relationship.

The monarch often admonished the lords to act virtuously; this was actually codified in the edict of 1738. Although the lord could punish the peasant, the peasant's health or nourishment was not supposed to be endangered. Lords were to treat their subjects in a "fatherly" fashion, in a spirit of "Christian mildness." The edict threatened lords not only with fines, but also with loss of their estates, if they mistreated their peasants; furthermore, cruel lords could be declared ineligible for ownership of any estate. Bailiffs who acted unjustly could be fined and put in irons or jailed.[158] One such incident did take place in 1770 on a Bohemian estate with the worst reputation for exploiting the peasantry. Bailiffs of the lord were arrested and jailed by the central authorities; the lord had to compensate the peasants with 2,500 florins.[159]

Although peasants had some legal rights, the system of agrarian relations placed obstacles in the way of their economic advancement. In most cases the lord possessed both monopoly and monopsony rights; buying grain is an example of such manorial privilege, which lords often farmed out to merchants.[160]

The legal status of the peasantry fell into several categories. The *Angesessene* (settled peasants) occupied some land, or were cottagers, occupying only a house with a garden, or simply servants of the lord, working on the demesne, land which the lord planted on his own account.[161] *Angesessene* included those who occupied holdings set aside exclusively for the peasants' use (*Rustikalisten*) and those who rented that part of the land which the lord had retained for working on his own account (*Dominikalisten*). The latter were subject to lower tax rates.

The relationship between the *Dominikalisten* and the lord depended

[157] North, *Structure and Change*, p. 44.
[158] Grünberg, *Bauernbefreiung*, vol. 1, pp. 24, 31, 128; vol. 2, p. 37.
[159] Ibid., vol. 1, p. 199.
[160] Ibid., vol. 1, p. 42.
[161] Ibid., vol. 1, p. 50.

on the nature of the rental contract, with a usual length of between one and six years. Rents for these lands tended to be higher than for *rustikal* land, because the former were taxed at a lower rate and the lord paid the (extraordinary) taxes on them, not the peasant.[162]

Both categories were divided into those who had purchased their land (*Eingekauften*), and therefore had an outright title to it—a small minority—and those renting the land, without written contract (*Wirt bis weiter*). These were tenants at will (*Zeitbesitzer*), although customary law interpreted this as life tenancy; in fact, *rustikal* land could not be rented on any other terms except for life. Such tenancies were usually inherited; between 1770 and 1790 this practice was required expressly by law. Thereafter the peasant was again tenant-for-life, but in practice the land was almost always inherited.[163] In Bohemia peasant landholdings were often inherited by the youngest son, who compensated his siblings in money.[164] The land could not be easily subdivided. Even the *eingekaufte* peasants were not allowed to subdivide without the estate's permission.

No part of the lord-peasant relationship is more misunderstood than the labor obligations the peasant rendered to the lord in exchange for use of the lord's land. Rather than citing the mean, most writers quote the upper range of such obligations, which was rendered by peasants who occupied a full holding. The size of a holding varied inversely with the quality of the land.[165] In Moravia in 1800 a mere 4.6 percent of peasant families had a full holding.[166] The peasant family did not have to provide the labor itself, but could send hired labor to perform the obligation.

Some contemporaries and subsequent observers argued that the institution of providing labor services to the lord in exchange for the land was inefficient because the peasants lacked any incentive to perform ef-

---

[162] Ibid., vol. 1, p. 54.

[163] Ibid., vol. 1, pp. 50–54, 60, 268, 272, 364; Grünberg, "Die Grundeigenthumsfähigkeit," pp. 187, 192.

[164] Grünberg, *Bauernbefreiung*, vol. 1, p. 66.

[165] Blum wrote recently, for instance, that "a family in Austrian Silesia in the 1840s who had about 42 acres of land had to give its lord each year 108 to 144 days of labor service with a two-animal team, 28 days of hand labor. . . ." Such a family, Blum failed to note, would have been quite wealthy in contemporary terms. Blum, *End of the Old Order*, p. 74; John Komlos, "The End of the Old Regime in Rural Austria," *Journal of European Economic History* 14 (1985): 515–520.

[166] A full holding was the amount of land that was once deemed necessary to provide subsistence for a peasant family. Since land was worked more intensively by the eighteenth century, a full holding was by that time no longer a prerequisite for the survival of a family. Grünberg, *Bauernbefreiung*, vol. 1, p. 52.

fectively.[167] This allegation has never been investigated, but the presumption is that wage labor has to be supervised no less than robot labor; consequently, one should not expect very large gains from substituting wage for robot labor.

The robot obligations, as rents, were not as excessive nor as widespread as many have been led to believe. They were, in addition, scattered throughout the year. In Lower Austria, according to one eighteenth-century sample, approximately 28 robot days were due per peasant family on average; on a per capita basis it would have been even less. In Upper Austria such obligations had been mostly commuted to money payments by then.[168] The total labor dues owed by peasants to lords in the western provinces of the Monarchy in the 1840s was about 5 days per capita, which meant that per family about 25 days were due per annum.[169] Therefore, the labor obligations were, on average, less burdensome than historians have generally suggested.

Nonetheless, landlords were motivated to increase rents on their land in the eighteenth century in keeping with the rising demand for land. They found themselves locked into an unfavorable long-term contract. The lords began to encroach on the lands leased to the peasantry by subdividing them or by having the land revert to their own use. In some cases, lords forced a peasant to switch his landholding to another part of the manor.[170] In other cases more robot services were demanded than were actually due.[171]

Against the backdrop of this complex system of land tenure and institutions, which had evolved slowly out of the feudal past, the government decided to act cautiously yet resolutely to defend the peasantry's well-being. The task was complicated because the lord-peasant relationship varied substantially even from one manor to another. Interfering in local customs and rights was a delicate matter because the Crown could hardly afford to alienate the landlords, a powerful element of the social fabric.

---

[167] "Aber auch, wo die Frohnen ausgemessen sind, bleibt immer die nachtheilige Fulg: daß die Felder, welche durch Frohndienste bearbeitet werden, schlecht bestellt sind." Joseph von Sonnenfels, *Grundsätze der Polizey, Handlung, und Finanz* (Vienna: Joseph Edlen von Kurzbeck, 1787), part 2, p. 124.

[168] Roman Rozdolski, *Die Grosse Steur- und Agrarreform Josefs II. Ein Kapitel zur österreichischen Wirtschaftsgeschichte* (Warsaw: Panstwowe Wydawnictwo Naukowe, 1961), p. 193.

[169] John Komlos, *The Habsburg Monarchy as a Customs Union: Economic Development in Austria-Hungary in the Nineteenth Century* (Princeton: Princeton University Press, 1983), p. 236.

[170] Grünberg, *Bauernbefreiung*, vol. 1, p. 56.

[171] Mayer, "Die volkswirtschaftliche Zustände Böhmens," p. 134.

The Agricultural Reforms

The material condition of the peasantry was generally dismal from the point of view of a twentieth-century observer. An outmoded legal system, backward agricultural technology, and the scarcity of capital all depressed the peasantry's standard of living.[172] In addition, the acceleration of population growth burdened the peasantry ever more heavily, because their ability to expand production was greatly limited by the availability of land.

The government, however, did not take resolute action to ameliorate the peasant's lot until forced to do so periodically by unrest. All of the robot edicts were preceded by upheavals, and were accompanied by bloodshed. The 1738 edict followed the murder of a lord by his subjects. Similarly, the reforms of the 1770s were preceded by rioting.[173]

Although land redistribution in favor of the peasantry was discussed among the empress's advisors, reformers chose instead to seek more limited but more easily attainable solutions. Given the political strength of the landed oligarchy and the regional variations in the lord-peasant relationship, the most the reformers could hope to achieve in the short run was to regulate the peasantry's "indebtedness," that is, its labor obligations (robot). To alleviate the apprehension of the provincial estates, they were assured that the government had no intention of limiting their rights, but merely wanted to enumerate mutual rights and obligations, thereby making arbitration in case of dispute easier.[174] Codifying labor-service obligations was itself a small step forward. It would reinforce the claim of the central authorities that they had a right to oversee certain customary rights of the lords. However, a thorough reform was impractical because there was no feasible way to make the peasants better off without making the lords worse off. No matter how much the reform-minded government advisors wanted to improve the peasants' situation, the landlords remained, as a group, resistant to change; it is true, however, that many members of the aristocracy were willing to make sacrifices to improve the material lot of their subjects by supporting industrial development.[175]

Nonetheless, reducing the peasantry's labor obligations to the lords became a priority, because peasants would then have more time to devote to their own land, or if they did not own land then to devote their efforts to the "creation of other value." The reformers did not believe

[172] Grünberg, *Bauernbefreiung*, vol. 1, p. 209.

[173] Ibid., vol. 1, pp. 128, 169.

[174] Grünberg, *Franz Anton von Blanc*, p. 20.

[175] Ibid., pp. 25, 26, 30, 40; Grünberg, *Bauernbefreiung*, vol. 1, p. 205.

that this would inevitably lead to an increase in the total national product, nor did they think that the peasants' labor productivity was necessarily greater when they were allowed to dispose of their own labor freely than when they rendered obligations to the lord. Yet the government wanted to redistribute income by reformulating the peasants' labor dues because it did not believe that the lords ought to be allowed to deprive the peasants of sufficient time to ensure themselves at least the minimum of existence.[176] In addition, if the welfare of the peasantry could be raised through such redistribution, they would be dissuaded from emigrating, thereby preventing a diminution in the size of the population.[177]

A formidable obstacle to reform was posed by the fact that legally the manorial estates were deemed the property of the lords, who had administrative jurisdiction over the peasantry.[178] For the government to intervene on behalf of the peasantry, property rights had to be redefined or at least conceptualized so as to allow intervention. Furthermore, the landlords understandably opposed central-government efforts to impose a rent ceiling just at a time when the growing population was increasing the marginal product of the land. Rents were rising all over Europe, and landlords of the Habsburg Monarchy, too, wanted to capture at least part of the increased value of their land by increasing the labor obligations of the peasantry. Reform was difficult because all, including Maria Theresia, accepted the notion that "the lords as owners of the land had allowed the peasants use of it for as much services and payments in kind as . . . the net output of the land warranted."[179] The peasants were mere renters without rights to the land itself. In fact, since the fourteenth century the relationship of peasants to the land they occupied had been referred to merely as one of rental.[180] Consequently, determining the rent had been traditionally the private affair of the lords

---

[176] Grünberg, *Franz Anton von Blanc*, pp. 25, 27.

[177] Sonnenfels, *Politische Abhandlungen*, p. 238. In addition to defending the peasantry by redistributing income, the government also strove to increase agricultural production by increasing plowland and by encouraging a more intensive use of land already under cultivation. Grünberg, *Franz Anton von Blanc*, p. 26. Another way to increase a population's income was to allow more time for work; thus, many religious holidays were eliminated in 1754. Grünberg, *Bauernbefreiung*, vol. 1, p. 83.

[178] Grünberg, *Bauernbefreiung*, vol. 1, p. 256.

[179] Grünberg, *Franz Anton von Blanc*, p. 40. "Robot ist . . . ein Äquivalent für die der Unthertanen überlassene Bodennutzung." Grünberg, *Bauernbefreiung*, vol. 1, p. 340.

[180] Obligations included such stipulations as having to bring at harvest time enough of their own straw to bind the lord's grain into sheaves. Grünberg, *Bauernbefreiung*, vol. 1, pp. 184, 209.

and the peasants. Nonetheless, reasons of state necessitated reformulation of this tripartite relationship among lords, peasants, and state.

One of the government's goals was to prevent the lord's encroachment on *rustikal* land occupied by the peasant. This encroachment is often misinterpreted to mean that the land was expropriated from the peasantry. Instead of confiscating the land, the lords converted life-tenures into short-term leases. The peasant continued to work the land, but under less favorable tenure and financial arrangements. Peasants were rarely, if ever, expelled from the manor, because they were an important source of revenue; after all, industrious peasants did not grow "like mushrooms overnight."[181] The more flexible contract, of course, was to the lords' advantage in a period of rising population and rising demand for land, since it gave them the option of raising rents in the future. How prevalent this practice was is unknown, but one investigation found that 5 percent of the *rustikal* land was converted into *dominikal* land in this manner.[182]

In 1751 in Bohemia (in 1733 in Silesia and 1776 in Moravia), the government required that the redistribution of land among the peasantry as well as the conversion of *rustikal* into *dominikal* land have the prior approval of the county authorities. The law stipulated that lords were to compensate peasants who had suffered because of illegal manipulation of the lands they worked; this part of the law was said to have been enforced sparingly.[183] Eventually lords were not even allowed to purchase land from the peasantry, but in 1786 commoners were given the right to purchase manors.[184]

The government chose to support the peasants' claims not only to maintain its tax base, but also as part of its "welfare program."[185] The government intervened on behalf of the peasantry, for instance, by warning the lords not to incorporate peasant land into their own demesne. In this regard the interests of the peasantry and of the state coincided, because the tax rate on demesne land was lower in Bohemia than on peasant land. This was all the more important since not all of the taxes levied could be collected. The increase in arrears distressed

---

[181] Ibid., vol. 1, p. 258.

[182] Ibid., vol. 2, pp. 113, 325, 330.

[183] Ibid., vol. 1, p. 157, 190, 244, 253.

[184] Grünberg, "Die Grundeigenthumsfähigkeit," pp. 112, 133, 136. Peasants were thus able to expand their land holdings; they even acquired manors by forming companies. In 1805 there were 12 such manors in peasant hands in Bohemia; ownership was divided among 215 peasants. Eight of these manors were in Elbogen county.

[185] "Wohlfahrtsprogramme." Grünberg, *Bauernbefreiung*, vol. 1, p. 255.

officials sufficiently that a special investigator was sent to Bohemia.[186] The back taxes were indicative of a fall in per capita income as well as of increases in the obligations imposed on the peasantry. Worried about its revenues, the government ordered the estates not to "grieve" (kränken) the peasants with excessive demands, "but instead to do everything to maintain them in a condition so they can pay their taxes."[187]

However, it became apparent that the peasantry was difficult to defend without better knowledge of local circumstances. To overcome this obstacle, the government ordered Bohemian manors in 1771 to produce a protocol of peasant obligations to be examined by government commissioners.[188] In the meantime, the Crown undertook a major reorganization on its own estates, known as the Raab reforms, by commuting labor services and distributing land on favorable credit terms among its own peasants. All crown land was distributed to the peasantry.

Through the Raab system, peasants became outright owners of lands they had previously occupied. This reform was similar to mid-nineteenth-century laws known as the emancipation of the peasantry. The major difference between the two reforms was that under the 1775 law the state-peasantry bore the full burden of compensation. In effect, they were allowed to purchase on credit the land they had been renting.[189] Even if the reforms might not have meant an immediate gain for peasants living on government land, the next generation benefited greatly. During the inflation of 1811, peasants could repay their debts to the government in paper money of negligible real value. Therefore the Raab reforms meant that these peasants were recipients of a large income transfer.[190]

The Raab reforms fueled rural unrest because rumor spread that the monarch had ordered these reforms on all estates without exception. These political developments were superimposed on an already desperate economic situation for the Bohemian peasantry. The subsistence crisis of 1770–71, during which tens of thousands perished,[191] and the

---

[186] Ibid., vol. 1, p. 156. This investigator's suggestions were later incorporated into new agricultural laws related to the labor services of peasants.

[187] Ibid., vol. 1, pp. 122, 162.

[188] Ibid., vol. 1, p. 203.

[189] This reform also affected peasants living on manors belonging to royal free towns and on Jesuit-owned land—nationalized in 1773. There were 43 such manors in the Czech Crownlands. Ibid., vol. 1, pp. 221, 307.

[190] Ibid., vol. 1, p. 312.

[191] The famine death toll has been estimated at about one tenth of the population. That is probably an upper bound. Franz Martin Pelzel, *Geschichte der Böhmen* (Prague: Johann Adam Hagen, 1774), pp. 622–623.

peasant uprisings that followed put immense pressure on the government to choose sides between the angry peasantry and a powerful oligarchy. To avoid more bloodshed and for the additional reasons cited previously, Maria Theresia took the side of the multitude.

Even before completing the protocol, which was to list the obligations of the peasantry, Maria Theresia promulgated an agricultural regulation for Bohemia and Moravia in 1775. This was an important step toward improving the peasantry's lot.[192] The cottagers, who had very little land, gained perhaps the most; their rent was nearly halved. Those peasants who had previously worked between 78 and 104 days for the lord now had to work only 52 days; those previously obligated to provide 52 to 78 days to the lord had their rents reduced to 26 days; those whose obligations had been 24 days now owed only 13 days.[193]

The peasants in Bohemia who had previously purchased *dominikal* land from manors were allowed to break the contract and receive their money back if they wished.[194] The most important provision of the new law was that peasants of the Bohemian crownlands could choose between their old obligations and the new ones. This insured that they would not be worse off because of some peculiarity of local circumstances. Poorer peasants gained exemption from extraordinary robot.[195] The upper ceiling on labor services was set at three days a week for those occupying between a quarter and a full holding.

To ensure that the manors still had an adequate labor force despite the general reduction of rents, i.e., the labor services owed to the lords, the lords retained the right to claim the same amount of labor as they had prior to the new law, but had to pay cash for the difference between the previous level of robot services and the new one specified by the reforms. Wages were set by the government at 15 kreuzer per day during the summer, ten during the spring, and seven at other times.[196] This would have enabled the peasant to purchase about two pounds of beef for a day's work.[197] Under no circumstances, however, was a peasant to be required to work more than three days a week on *dominikal* land. This policy clearly meant a substantial income transfer to the peasantry.[198]

[192] Grünberg, *Bauernbefreiung*, vol. 1, p. 257.

[193] Ibid., vol. 1, pp. 177, 222–226. This listing of mutual obligations was not completed until 1778.

[194] In rump-Silesia only landlords had the right to void the contract.

[195] Grünberg, *Bauernbefreiung*, vol. 1, pp. 223–226.

[196] Sixty kreuzer was worth one florin.

[197] Alfred Přibram, *Materialien zur Geschichte der Preise und Löhne in Österreich* (Vienna: Ueberreuters, 1938), p. 462.

[198] Grünberg, *Bauernbefreiung*, vol. 1, p. 227.

After the reforms, lords could not raise rents. They were prevented from encroaching on *rustikal* land. Yet they were still obligated to provide building materials for the peasantry as the need arose, and to come to their aid in an emergency. Thereafter, however, the manors were able to charge for use of pasture land and firewood under certain circumstances, even if previously these had been free of charge.[199]

.The manor remained the court of first instance, but the lord himself could maintain his tenure as judge only to the extent it was sanctioned by the appellate court. The upper court could name an administrator of the court (*Gerichtsverwalter*) if it saw the need for it. The penalties manorial courts could order were limited to arrest or forced labor of not longer than eight days' duration. Fines were allowed only in case of financial damages caused by the peasant, and expulsion from the estate was allowed only if the peasant was caught smuggling. More severe penalties needed the approval of county authorities.[200]

Toward the end of his reign, Joseph II wanted to proceed even further to improve the lot of the peasantry. Laws that would have converted all labor services to money payment were formulated. In addition, he wanted to introduce a uniform system of taxation throughout his realm, applicable even to the *dominikal* lands of the lords. Under this system the maximum peasant burden, including all taxes and rent payments to the lord, would not exceed 30 percent of the peasant's gross output.[201] Since the government land tax was on average about 12 percent, the law would have left 18 percent for rent and local taxes.[202]

This reform was mostly Joseph II's work. It was formulated without achieving a consensus among the various factions at court. The provincial estates were not consulted. The peasants were only halfheartedly behind the proposal, because they were worried about their ability to acquire sufficient cash to meet the new financial obligations that such a reform would impose on them. In addition, the wages Joseph II specified in the new law were deemed too low by many peasants. After Joseph's death, therefore, the reforms were shelved. The old tax system remained in effect; the vacillation and uncertainty did bring about a few

[199] Ibid., vol. 1, pp. 239–240.

[200] Ibid., vol. 1, p. 287.

[201] This would have been a burden of about 40 percent of net output. Rozdolski, *Die Grosse Steur- und Agrarreform Josefs II*, p. 19.

[202] Grünberg, *Bauernbefreiung*, vol. 1, p. 323. For a study of agrarian reforms during the reign of Joseph II, and of the controversy within the government over these reforms, see Helen P. Liebel, "Count Karl von Zinzendorf and the Liberal Revolt against Joseph II's Economic Reforms, 1783–1790," in Hans-Ulrich Wehler, ed., *Sozialgeschichte Heute. Festschrift für Hans Rosenberg zum 70. Geburtstag* (Göttingen: Vandenhoeck und Rupprecht, 1974), pp. 69–85.

disturbances among the peasantry, especially among those who, antici-pating the new laws, had decreased their animal stock and fired their farm hands so that they would be able to start making cash payments to the lords.[203]

Summary

The argument was advanced in this chapter that the nutritional crisis induced the monarchs to slowly but persistently institute a long series of reforms fostering the expansion of the industrial sector. Moreover, the concern for the well-being of the peasantry led the monarchs to pre-vent the distribution of income from being determined by market forces. Instead they promulgated laws that strove to insure a subsistence minimum for the peasantry. Their genuine humanitarian concerns co-incided with their own self-interest, for their policy prevented a crisis of ideology from developing. After all, a social system can function smoothly only as long as the participants have internalized the rules of the society sufficiently so that excessive monitoring and coercion are not required. Ideology performs the function of lowering the transaction costs of enforcing the law. The ideology of enlightened absolutism in-cluded the notion that the monarch was responsible for the well-being of the people. It would have been difficult to keep within the bounds of this ideology and stand idly by while the peasantry was experiencing a considerable decline in its standard of living. To prevent the breakdown of civil order that would have followed such an erosion of the social contract, the monarchs intervened energetically in the nation's eco-nomic life, opening the way for industrialization. There was yet another reason for concern: domestic unrest might have allowed Austria's more efficient neighbors to exploit her problems and perhaps encroach on her territory.[204]

Questions of ideology aside, the monarchs did not welcome a de-crease in their tax base. Maintenance of their standing army, and in turn their power, depended on the ability of the peasantry to pay taxes. A fiscal crisis could be expected if the standard of living of the peasantry continued to deteriorate. The institutional changes brought about dur-ing the several decades subsequent to the onset of the nutritional decline can be understood only in the light of the threat this potential Malthu-sian crisis posed to the power of absolutist rulers. To maintain power, they had to reduce the excessive influence of the landed oligarchy on the

---

[203] Grünberg, *Bauernbefreiung*, vol. 1, pp. 334–352.
[204] North, *Structure and Change*, p. 44.

one hand and the guilds on the other, thus paving the way for economic development. They succeeded not only because they persevered and were willing to experiment with various approaches to counter the crisis, but also because the existence of an external threat rendered the aristocracy more pliable than it otherwise might have been.

In sum, population growth led to a decline in the standard of living as indicated by the diminution of human stature. This impending crisis, the last widespread threat to subsistence in Austria, induced the government to embark on a program of institutional reform. These reforms redistributed income in favor of the peasantry vis-à-vis the landlords and fostered the development of the industrial and commercial sectors. The changed economic circumstances and the new legal environment were propitious to further population growth, because the industrial sector was no longer constrained by diminishing returns to the same extent as the agricultural sector. In addition, capital accumulation and technical change could proceed, helping to overcome the capital-diluting effects of population growth and thereby permanently removing the Malthusian threat.[205] The schematic of this process, the "Austrian model" of the industrial revolution, is sketched in Figure 3.1.

The reforms were enacted slowly, over more than a generation, and the outcome was by no means optimal. While some reforms increased economic efficiency others did not. The new conceptualization of the property rights of the lord in the land was done for the sake of equity, not of efficiency. It did, however, contribute to the stability of the political system.[206] By redistributing income and by fostering economic development, the Habsburg monarchs weathered the Malthusian crisis. Insofar as a stable political order is a prerequisite for efficient production, redefining property rights could be thought of as leading to a more

---

[205] This is quite similar to the pattern found for Flanders in the eighteenth century: "the expansion of the rural industry . . . occurred in response to the growth of population, which tended to outrun the means of subsistence. . . . The development of the cottage industry made possible the acceleration of the rate of population growth." Franklin F. Mendels, *Industrialization and Population Pressure in Eighteenth-Century Flanders* (New York: Arno Press, 1981), p. 3.

[206] The Swiss economist, Sismondi, observed in 1819 that "by aiding a group that no doubt would have been oppressed had it been left undefended the state compensated for most of its vices. It did this for its own sake and its subjects, in the interest of stability for a large part of the population composed of peasants and land owners living in comfort who had been made happy. These subjects, aware of their happiness and fearing any change, had turned down each project of revolution or of conquest against the empire." Cited in Grünberg, "Die Grundeigenthumsfähigkeit," p. 170. Stein, the Prussian reformer, also held favorable views about the Austrian agricultural laws.

Figure 3.1. The "Austrian" Model of the Industrial Revolution

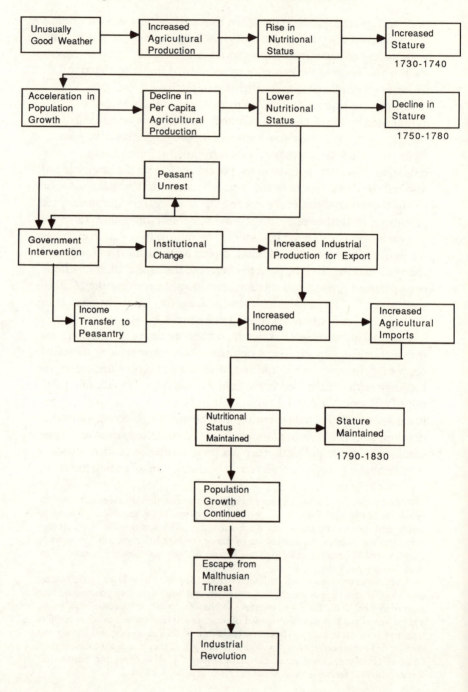

efficient economy than the one that would have prevailed without such redefinition.

Despite many criticisms that could be mentioned in connection with these reforms, it is amazing that they could be enacted at all, given the unequal distribution of privilege which prevailed. It was, in a sense, an advantage that all social groups did not have to be drawn into the bargaining process. Fortunately, the monarchs were sufficiently enlightened to advocate the well-being of the whole population vis-à-vis the vested interests.[207] This is, of course, quite contrary to the Marxist theory of the state, in which the institutions of a nonsocialist government represent the interest of the ruling class. The exploitation theory of the state does not fit well the Habsburg experience in the eighteenth century. To be sure, one could argue that the ruling class sacrificed power and wealth in the short run in order to be able to exploit the population in the long run. This argument admits that there existed real bounds on the extent of rent extraction from the peasantry in the short run. Eventually, however, the very process of industrialization set in motion in the second half of the eighteenth century eventually dissipated the power of the aristocracy. Hence, had their strategy been to exploit the peasantry in the long run at the expense of short-run sacrifices, such a strategy was unsuccessful.

The Habsburg experience might be conceptualized more fruitfully as conforming to North's notion of the neoclassical state, according to which protection and justice are traded for revenue and the state maximizes power or wealth. The maximization process in the Habsburg Monarchy did not lead to an optimum solution, because the process was fraught with uncertainties and constrained greatly by the existing legal system; the state itself was under constant external threat and threatened as well by internal political turmoil. The monarchs exhibited a bounded rationality, which entailed seeking solutions to economic problems within the given cultural milieu. They often made economically correct choices, but not invariably. The solution that ultimately emerged was not the most efficient by any means, but it was satisfactory, not extremist, and, consequently at least, acceptable to all parties concerned. In addition, it provided a framework within which the economy could evolve successfully for the subsequent half-century.

In evaluating the Austrian reforms, one should keep in mind that the statesmen, faced with a crisis, often vacillated among alternatives, and acted slowly and cautiously in their search for a satisfactory solution. It was to the monarchs' advantage that the society was much better

[207] Olson, *Rise and Decline of Nations*, p. 37.

equipped, intellectually and financially, than earlier societies, which also had been confronted with Malthusian crises. During prior episodes, when European societies had inched toward the Malthusian ceiling, they had encountered grave difficulties; the outcome in the eighteenth century was different. The industrial revolution eliminated the threat of another nutritional crisis, as the Malthusian ceilings were overcome.

After the death of Joseph II in 1790, institutional reform came essentially to a halt. Thereafter the government ceased to innovate; it continued, however, to administer the policies then in force. The achievements of the previous four decades were not reversed, although Joseph II's new tax law was not put into effect.[208] Guild hegemony and the industrial restrictions prevailing at mid-century were not restored, although these forces did attempt to reassert themselves.[209]

The market had expanded to such an extent that it would have been impossible, even if the government had attempted to do so, to reimpose the restrictions dismantled earlier. At first, the upheavals of the Napoleonic Wars distracted the government from active industrial promotion; by the time peace was restored, the market was developed sufficiently to continue to expand without having to rely on the central government's active support. In addition, demographic developments of the second half of the eighteenth century would, by themselves, have made a return to the old economic system impossible. The older mode of production could not have sustained a population that had doubled since the beginning of the reforms.

Further reforms were not undertaken to any significant degree, and perhaps for this reason some historians have labeled the regime of Franz I as reactionary. However, his predecessors had already successfully removed the major obstacles to economic development, and the preoccupation with a quarter century of war rendered active government support of industry unlikely in any event. Another reason why his reign ought not be thought of as backward-looking is that the liberal industrial policies and paternalistic notions of government formulated between 1750 and 1790 remained the cornerstone of policy, lingering on well into the nineteenth century.

At least in one sense, however, the legacy of the enlightened monarchs was undesirable. Although they changed many institutions, they were not prepared to institutionalize change. The ability of the Habsburg government to meet future challenges depended excessively on the personalities of the reigning monarch and of his entourage; this was the

---

[208] Přibram, *Gewerbepolitik*, p. 508.
[209] Ibid., p. 573.

weakness not only of Habsburg absolutism but of absolute monarchies in general. Maria Theresia and Joseph II were able to maintain the stability of their society. Yet as Mancur Olson points out, this very stability can eventually become a drawback, because it might lead to the accumulation "of networks of distributional coalitions."[210] Such coalitions barred reform of major proportions during the subsequent generations.

The heirs of Maria Theresia and Joseph II neglected institutional change, and the aristocracy was not inclined to give up any more of its power or wealth on its own accord. This was not of great importance during the first two decades of the nineteenth century, since war diverted society's attention. Even in the third decade the slow pace of further institutional change did not produce many obvious ill effects, since the economy continued to develop for decades before the fissures became appreciable. By the fifth decade of the century, however, the laws and institutions created by the enlightened despots were no longer in keeping with the economy's requirements. The unfavorable harvest conditions of the late 1840s exacerbated the population's lot. The unfortunate Ferdinand, on the throne when the outburst of 1848 began, was incapable of meeting the new challenges.

A century after the great reforms had started, a political revolution erupted. In 1848 aristocratic privileges were finally abolished de jure, though not de facto, and all feudal institutions that had survived the earlier reforms were now dismantled, save the most feudal of all institutions, the guilds, which persisted for yet another decade. The upheaval of 1848 was more costly in lives than the industrial revolution that came about in response to the reforms of Maria Theresia and Joseph II. Yet the earlier reforms had a much more profound effect on the daily lives of the multitude than did the reforms inaugurated in the wake of the revolution of 1848.[211]

[210] Olson, *Rise and Decline of Nations*, p. 145.
[211] Komlos, *Habsburg Monarchy as a Customs Union*, p. 109.

CHAPTER 4

CONCLUSION

THE PRESENT STUDY is an attempt to integrate anthropometric history into the mainstream of socioeconomic history. What emerges, I hope, is a version of "total" history, perhaps on the model of the Annales school, in which human biology plays a prominent role. This is accomplished by analyzing the various ways in which the nutritional status of the Habsburg population interacted with demographic, economic and even sociopolitical processes. Such a perspective, I have argued, enables one to synthesize the disparate strands of evidence into a coherent framework for understanding the industrial revolution in the Habsburg Monarchy. The resultant "Austrian" model will be shown in the next chapter to be applicable, with minor modifications, to the English case. Perhaps even more importantly, the framework can be extended to encompass the salient features of economic development in pre-industrial Europe as a whole. This view is presented in Chapter 6. The "Austrian" model is therefore actually a European model, but is given this name because it was formulated on the basis of Austrian evidence.

The notion of an industrial revolution has most often been associated with the British developments of the eighteenth century.[1] The argument advanced above deviates from this conventional wisdom by suggesting that Britain was neither the first nor the only nation to experience a profound expansion in industrial activity in the eighteenth

[1] Walt W. Rostow, *How It All Began: Origins of the Modern Economy* (London: Methuen, 1975), p. vii; Joel Mokyr, ed., *The Economics of the Industrial Revolution* (Totowa, NJ: Rowman and Allanheld, 1985), p. 44. For a critique of this conventional wisdom see Rondo Cameron, "A New View of European Industrialization," *Economic History Review*, 2d ser., 38 (1985): 1–23.

century.[2] The economic upswing that began after the middle of the century in the western provinces of the Habsburg Monarchy, contemporaneously with that of other parts of Europe, indicates that the economic forces at work there were, indeed, quite similar to the ones experienced elsewhere. As in the thirteenth century, and again in the sixteenth, economic expansion in the eighteenth century was a European phenomenon and was not confined merely to a few advanced nations. The boom of the eighteenth century, like the previous upswings of the Middle Ages and of the Renaissance, was triggered and fostered by the rapid growth of population.

This assertion, of course, should not be construed in such a way as to imply that the levels of development of these economies were close to one another. For instance, at the end of the eighteenth century Bohemian GNP per capita was only about a fifth of Great Britain's.[3] Structurally, too, the two economies were quite dissimilar. While only a third of Britain's GNP originated in agriculture, in Bohemia this share was twice as large[4] (Table 2.19). In spite of these great differences in the level of

[2] According to Herman Freudenberger ". . . the momentum generated by the accomplishments of the reigns of [Maria Theresia and Joseph II] carried Austrian industry into the twentieth century." See his "Industrialization in Bohemia and Moravia in the Eighteenth Century," *Journal of Central European Affairs* 19 (1960): 347–356.

[3] In 1801, British per capita GNP was 22 £. One should adjust this figure for items not included in the above calculation, such as rents on dwellings, government expenditure, etc. These components amounted to approximately 27 percent in Britain. Peter Mathias, *The First Industrial Nation: An Economic History of Britain, 1700–1914* (New York: Charles Scribner's Sons, 1969), p. 493. After reducing British income by 27 percent and by another 10 percent to extrapolate the 1801 figure back to 1790, it becomes 14.4 £. This was about 130 fl at the contemporary conversion rate of 9 florin = 1 £. Hence Bohemian GNP per capita was only a fifth of the British. Even if one allows for the possibility that the above exchange rate diverged from the true purchasing power parity, the gulf in the level of economic performance would still be much wider than that suggested by Paul Bairoch, "Europe's Gross National Product: 1800–1975," *Journal of European Economic History* 5 (1976): 273–340. Bairoch's assertion that GNP in Austria-Hungary in the early nineteenth century was 72 percent of the British GNP is not based on an actual calculation, but must be considered a mere guess. Bairoch also errs greatly by suggesting that per capita industrial output in Austria-Hungary in 1800 was 44 percent of Great Britain's. Paul Bairoch, "International Industrialization Levels from 1750 to 1980," *Journal of European Economic History* 11 (1982): 269–334. Per capita industrial output in Great Britain was 6.3 £ or 56.6 fl. N.F.R. Crafts, "British Economic Growth, 1700–1831: A Review of the Evidence," *Economic History Review*, 2d ser., 36 (1983): 177–199. However, according to the above calculation, Bohemian per capita industrial product, considerably greater than the average for Austria-Hungary, was 6.3 fl, that is, only about 10 percent of Great Britain's. For the exchange rate see Joseph-René Roelle, *Operations des Changes des Principales Places de l'Europe* (Lyon: Librairies Associes, 1775), p. 363.

[4] N.F.R. Crafts, "The Eighteenth Century: A Survey," in Roderick Floud and Donald McCloskey, eds., *The Economic History of Britain since 1700. Vol. 1: 1700–1860* (Cam-

development, however, both economies began to experience forces of expansion at about the same time, as indeed did most other European economies. It is true that each region participated in the upswing differently depending on its level of development, but they all participated in it to some degree.[5] There were, however, similarities as well. Textile production played a prominent role in both the Habsburg Monarchy and in Great Britain. Furthermore, the rates of transformation of both economies were comparable, even if not quite the same. Iron production in the Habsburg Monarchy, for instance, grew at a rate of 2 percent per annum, and cotton textile production at a rate of 4 percent per annum at the end of the century. This evidence must be interpreted as indicative of powerful expansionary forces, even if the comparable figures for England are twice as high.[6]

Yet between the first industrial census of 1766 and the last complete census of the eighteenth century in 1797 Bohemia's industrial labor force expanded at an annual rate of 4.6 percent. In contrast, the British rate was only 1.4 percent.[7] Similarly, the value of industrial product in Bohemia grew at a rate of 4 percent, while in Britain it grew at a rate of 1.8 percent per annum.[8] (In Moravia the rates of growth of the industrial sector were comparable to those of Bohemia.)[9] Thus the upswing of the second half of the eighteenth century in the Czech provinces was even more intense than it was in Great Britain, and began about the same time; Bohemia and Moravia did not lag behind in these respects.

To be sure, the great sectoral shifts in the Habsburg Monarchy were not accompanied by the same technological innovations as in England. While in England labor productivity in the industrial sector was rising, this appears to have been less likely in the Habsburg Monarchy. The reason for this is that in the latter lands the increment to the capital stock was not yet composed of the newer technologies, and, in any case, the

---

bridge, England: Cambridge University Press, 1981), pp. 1–16. The service sector, too, had a much more important role in Britain than in Bohemia.

[5] Even one of the most backward of European economies did so. Arcadius Kahan, *The Plow, the Hammer, and the Knout: An Economic History of Eighteenth-Century Russia* (Chicago: University of Chicago Press, 1985).

[6] John Komlos, *The Habsburg Monarchy as a Customs Union: Economic Development in Austria-Hungary in the Nineteenth Century* (Princeton: Princeton University Press, 1983), p. 99; N.F.R. Crafts, *British Economic Growth during the Industrial Revolution* (Oxford: Clarendon Press, 1985), p. 23.

[7] Státní ústřední archiv v. Praze, Prague, Czechoslovakia, Č.G. Commerz; Crafts, *British Economic Growth during the Industrial Revolution*, p. 16.

[8] Ibid., p. 22.

[9] Herman Freudenberger, "The Woolen-Goods Industry of the Habsburg Monarchy in the Eighteenth Century," *Journal of Economic History* 20 (1960): 383–406.

accumulation of human and physical capital might not have proceeded as quickly as the industrial labor force. The number of looms, for instance, grew at a slightly slower rate than the number of textile workers. While the number of master craftsmen increased by 3.1 percent per annum, the less skilled members of the work force, including not only journeymen but also apprentices and laborers, increased at a faster rate of 5.4 percent per annum.[10] In other words, the industrial sector did absorb a large number of new entrants, but probably only by equipping the new workers with less human and physical capital than before. Of course, the economy-wide gains in productivity must still have been substantial, if for no other reason than that the enormous sectoral shift in labor undoubtedly reduced or eliminated underemployment.

Nonetheless the intensity of the upswing as well as its duration signaled the beginning of a profound transformation of the economy of this region. Whether one prefers to label this phenomenon the beginning of the industrial revolution, as this author does, is ultimately of little importance. What is important to stress is the fact that this expansion, which began simultaneously in many European economies, was truly more than just a temporary upswing of the business cycle: it lasted, if one overlooks the period of the Napoleonic Wars, well into the twentieth century. The fundamental economic forces that were set in motion in the eighteenth century unleashed economic, demographic, and social processes that made this expansion, call it what one will, different from all that had preceded it. The difference was that economic growth was no longer constrained by Malthusian ceilings. With the exception of Ireland, the European economies were no longer subject to the kinds of subsistence crises which had followed in the wake of prior expansions.

To be sure, the rapid increase in industrial production after 1760 was interrupted by the French Wars. Between 1798 and 1807 the industrial labor force declined in Bohemia by about 6 percent and by another 28 percent by 1819. The late-eighteenth-century peak was not reached again until the acceleration of production in the mid-1820s.[11] However, the depression of the first quarter of the nineteenth century was caused by forces exogenous to the Habsburg economy. There is no reason why growth would have come to a halt if the upheavals of the war had not intervened. If one is willing to grant that, then the industrial expansion of the 1760s becomes as revolutionary as the British experience, even though it was temporarily interrupted in the first decades of the nine-

[10] The number of masters in the Moravian woolen-goods sector grew at a rate of 2.4 percent per annum, while other workers increased at a faster rate of 9.9 percent per annum. Freudenberger, "Woolen-Goods Industry," p. 404.
[11] John Komlos, *Habsburg Monarchy as a Customs Union*, Chapter 3.

teenth century. It should be considered revolutionary because of the intensity of the sectoral shifts and the rapid growth in output, and not because of the rate of technological change.

A crucial feature of the "Austrian" model (Figure 3.1) is that it conceptualizes the industrial revolution in terms of a process, rather than attempting to understand it in terms of comparative statics, as has been customary. Growth was not obtained through movements from one equilibrium position to another, but by slowly overcoming obstacles which had prevented the economy from reaching an efficient equilibrium. Once these obstacles were removed markets could adjust to the reforms, but not instantaneously. It took time for peasants to move off the land or to learn new trades, and for entrepreneurs to experiment with how to combine the factors of production most efficiently and to find ways to anticipate demand originating in distant markets. Hence during the period under discussion markets remained in disequilibrium. This meant that the marginal product of labor was not equated across all sectors of the economy, and great gains in output could be had by removing impediments which had previously restrained labor mobility. Disregard of this fundamental distinction has led to great confusion in the literature insofar as many economists have attempted to understand the industrial revolution by assuming that a perfectly competitive equilibrium prevailed continuously in all markets.[12]

In contrast to such theories I have argued that population growth in the Habsburg Monarchy led to a dramatic decline in the marginal product of labor in agriculture below what it was in industrial endeavors. This amounted to the beginning of a Malthusian subsistence crisis. When, in response to the impending crisis, the government cleared away the many impediments to the expansion of the industrial sector, great economic gains were obtained. Growth could occur because a transfer of labor from one sector to another brought with it an immediate rise in its marginal product per hour employed and also because seasonal utilization became more effective. In other words, underemployment was mitigated and, in addition, the labor force expanded through the recruitment of women and children.

During the first phase of expansion little additional capital was needed, because production was not centralized in factories; instead, the cottages of the peasants were converted into workshops. This of course meant that unemployed capital, e.g., buildings, was drawn into the pro-

[12] For examples of static models see Floud and McCloskey, *Economic History of Britain*; Richard Ippolito, "The Effect of the 'Agricultural Depression' on Industrial Demand in England: 1730–1750," *Economica* 42 (1975): 298–312.

duction process. Thus the industrial revolution could begin without that rise in the rate of saving which had so worried the economic historians of the previous generation. They believed that the marginal capital/output ratio remained constant during the industrial revolution. Yet there are good reasons for thinking that, at least in underdeveloped economies, it must have fallen.[13]

This conclusion implies that the Habsburg economy was inside its production possibility frontier in the middle of the eighteenth century. The production function, as usually drawn, separates the feasible areas of production from the unattainable region. The usual reflex is to assume that an economy is on the boundary, and consequently that the only way to increase output per capita is to shift the production function outward through physical or human capital accumulation, technological change, or the discovery of new resources. In contrast, I have argued that institutional constraints prevented the Habsburg economy from reaching its production possibility frontier. Consequently, large gains could be obtained from the elimination of these barriers. Even when the frontier had been reached, gains could still be had in per capita output as the labor force grew, because the small size of the industrial sector must have meant that the marginal product of labor was still rising (Figure 4.1).[14] In addition, once this process was set in motion, the rise in population densities brought about externalities that began to shift the production function itself. In sum, the industrial revolution began in Austria not with a shift of the production function, but with a move toward the most efficient production function. Institutional change, a fall in the marginal capital/output ratio, and the beneficial effects of population growth combined to raise aggregate per capita output. These aspects of the Austrian experience do not seem a sufficient reason to relegate it to second-class status.

Because Britain was without doubt much more developed than the Habsburg Monarchy, the market-expanding function of institutional change was less important there in the eighteenth century. Yet if one considers the underutilization of the labor power of women and children, and the institutional changes associated with the enclosure movement, one might accept the notion that Britain was perhaps not quite on its production frontier either just before the industrial revolution. It was not as far from it perhaps as was the Habsburg economy, but it could still gain from moving toward it. The starting point of the two

[13] Walt W. Rostow, *The Stages of Economic Growth: A Non-Communist Manifesto* (Cambridge, England: Cambridge University Press, 1971), p. 41.

[14] This is usually called the "first" stage of the production process. P.R.G. Layard and A. A. Walters, *Microeconomic Theory* (New York: McGraw-Hill, 1975), p. 212.

Figure 4.1. The Aggregate Production Function at the Beginning of the Industrial Revolution

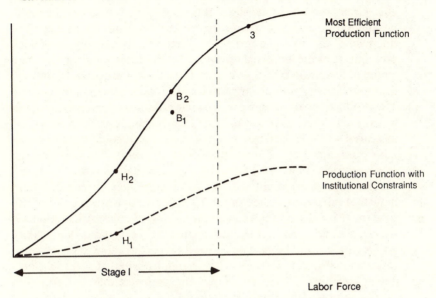

economies, H_1 and B_1, differed (Figure 4.1). Yet once the industrial revolution began, both economies started to move toward their most efficient production function (H_2 and B_2) and then along it, toward point 3. Meanwhile, the ongoing process of capital accumulation meant that the production function itself was shifting out, postponing the onset of diminishing returns to labor in the industrial sector. Of course, the British aggregate production function was no doubt shifting out faster than the Habsburg one, because technological change there was more rapid. Hence I do not argue that the processes of industrialization were precisely the same in the two economies, but that the dynamics of both processes can be conceptualized within a similar framework, and that both were an integral part of the post-1750 upswing in economic activity.

By making possible the exchange of industrial products for food from the less developed parts of the world, the industrial revolution eliminated the age-old Malthusian dilemma in Europe: population growth was no longer food-constrained. This was the crucial difference between the economic and demographic expansions of the eighteenth century and similar episodes that had occurred over prior millennia. Hungary, Galicia, Ireland, Russia, the West Indies, and the British colonies of

North America provided nutrients to the industrializing regions of Europe without which urban-industrial growth would have been unthinkable. Grain, meat, fish, and sugar imports became available to the urban populations to a greater extent than ever before. Although the high productivity of the domestic agricultural sector was beneficial, it was not a prerequisite of the industrial revolution, as Rostow suggested; the availability of food, however, was. The additional income generated through industrial activity could be used to import food from agricultural areas. The productivity of the agricultural sector did make a contribution, but it was even more important that the relatively high productivity of the industrial sector created purchasing power which could be used to acquire nutrients from abroad, provided, of course, that food-surplus areas were accessible. For this reason the fall in transportation costs and the rise in production in the New World were crucial to the European industrial expansion of the eighteenth century. For many regions of Europe the (Malthusian) food constraint was lifted by industrialization. Of course, the industrial sector did not produce food, but it did produce goods which could be exchanged for food on favorable terms of trade. International and interregional trade supplemented the nutrient-producing capability of domestic agriculture, and were therefore crucial to the dissolution of the Malthusian constraints. In prior centuries the negative effects of population growth (capital-dilution, greater propensity to transmit diseases) eventually overcame the positive effects (inducing technological and institutional change, lowering transaction costs). In eighteenth-century Europe this ceased to be the case. Because of the availability of nutrients, the Boserupian effects had a chance to overcome the Malthusian ones.

Once the food constraint was permanently lifted, economic growth could become self-sustaining in the sense that the population had a propensity to reproduce itself. Once the threat of starvation was no longer a factor, i.e., as long as there was sufficient food to maintain the increments to the population, economic growth would continue, and the beneficial effects of a rising population density, coupled with technological change and capital accumulation, meant that labor productivity could continue to rise. The eighteenth-century industrial revolution differs from previous expansions in that it brought with it the end of the Malthusian demographic regime.

Austria was not the only European country to experience rapid population growth during the second half of the eighteenth century. Population growth posed immense difficulties for many other societies as well. The response to population pressure differed depending on the level of economic development of the country and the degree to which policymakers were willing and able to take command of the situation. In the Habsburg Monarchy, as in several German states, the enlightened despots were able to avert a Malthusian crisis with mercantilistic policies that brought about institutional change on a large scale.[15] In these countries the market was sufficiently developed to respond favorably to government reforms, but not developed enough to have been able to expand without government intervention; there were too many imperfections for the private sector to overcome by itself. In addition, the aristocracy in these societies was not recalcitrant enough to resist the forces of change.

In England, the response to population pressure took an entirely different form from that in Austria. The market in England was larger, in fact large enough to benefit from the acceleration in population growth without active government support.[16] Moreover, the expansion of decreasing cost industries, of exports, and of nutrient imports could proceed quickly enough to maintain the population above subsistence level without massive government intervention in the market economy. Thus the dynamics of the English industrial revolution were similar to those of Austria's, but autonomous market processes played a more important role, and government intervention a much less important role, than in Austria.

In contrast, population growth in Ireland generated neither institutional change, as in Austria, nor a rapid expansion of the market, as in England. Attached to a more developed country, Ireland had to function within a set of policies designed for an advanced economy. It did not receive exceptional treatment from the government, and thus had to make do without the kind of reform program that saved the western provinces of Austria from disaster. Yet it could not follow the English model either, because its own economy was too underdeveloped to provide the expansion that would have been needed to maintain per capita income above subsistence. Instead, the poorer members of the society responded to population growth by abandoning their diversified diet. Although this strategy warded off the Malthusian threat in the short run, it was extremely risky. The outcome was the well-known disaster of the 1840s, which decimated the population.[17] This episode shows

[15] Herman Freudenberger, however, suggested that they promoted development in a fitful way. "State Intervention as an Obstacle to Economic Growth in the Habsburg Monarchy," *Journal of Economic History* 27 (1967): 493–509.

[16] Ester Boserup, *Population and Technological Change: A Study of Long-Term Trends* (Chicago: University of Chicago Press, 1981).

[17] Joel Mokyr, *Why Ireland Starved: A Quantitative and Analytical History of the Irish Economy, 1800–1850* (London: George Allen and Unwin, 1983).

clearly how precarious the balance between population growth and nutritional status was even as late as the nineteenth century. The inference is that it must have been even more so previously. The Irish experience also indicates that while laissez-faire policies often work well in an advanced economy, they might have disastrous consequences in an underdeveloped one.

The French response to population pressure was less successful than either the Austrian or the English. The French economy was not as well developed as the English, and, consequently, the population-induced economic expansion was insufficient to maintain the living standards of the population without massive government efforts to counter immiseration. Since France did not have hinterland equivalents of Ireland or Hungary, agricultural imports could not be expanded to the same degree as they were in England, Bohemia, and Lower Austria. The government vacillated, and when it did intervene, it did so more in keeping with physiocratic principles, which were not as appropriate for counteracting the destabilizing effects of population growth as were mercantilistic ones. "In 1764 and again in the period between 1774 and 1776, the [French] government formally abandoned paternalism and declared itself explicitly to be a proponent of laissez faire."[18] This was an acceptable position in England, but in France it caused difficulties. The adherence to physiocratic principles also made it difficult to redistribute income, because "if wealth lay in land and its produce, the owners of land had an inalienable right to maximize their profits through the free play of market forces. Enhanced agrarian revenues would then in the long term produce healthy state coffers." Yet in the short term this position "proved to be a grisly error."[19] The realm of theory was one thing; putting it into practice, however, dangerously destabilized the political structure, rendering an Austrian-type social compromise unattainable. The impending crisis was not averted; the result was, in 1789, a political upheaval of immense proportions. Thus the consequences of the eighteenth-century demographic boom were quite different in the various European economies.

In the Habsburg Monarchy the diminution in real income preceded the beginning of industrial growth in the eighteenth century. This finding is consistent with the thesis of those economic historians for whom the analysis of the relationship between industrialization and the standard of living began "with some set of exogenous changes (mainly pop-

[18] Olwen H. Hufton, "Social Conflict and the Grain Supply in Eighteenth-Century France," *Journal of Interdisciplinary History* 14 (1983): 303–331.
[19] Ibid., p. 319.

ulation growth) which would have had even more severe repercussions on the standard of living without the alternative of industrial development."[20] According to Arthur J. Taylor, ". . . the most powerful short-term influence on economic prosperity in the eighteenth century was the pressure of a rapidly expanding population."[21] François Crouzet put it this way:

> The decisive factor in the undoubtedly low standards of living and widespread poverty of the working classes in the eighteenth and early nineteenth centuries was the pressure of a rising population.[22]

In regard to the Swedish experience, Eli Heckscher observed that "progress in production was taken out . . . in the form of an increase in population, and not in raising the standard of living."[23] The English experience confirmed the Malthusian population dynamics:

> Before 1800, the situation developed much as Malthus had insisted it must: the faster population grew, the faster the price of food rose, the lower the standard of living fell, and the grimmer the struggle to exist became. As Malthus had postulated, there were indeed long, slow oscillations in the rate of population growth and in the standard of living.[24]

In contrast, for the pessimists "the analysis generally begins with the proposition that the transition to rapid economic growth could have been achieved with less cost to the working classes."[25] That, too, may have been true. In hindsight one might argue that the government could have intervened more energetically to better the lot of the under-privileged than it actually did. Society, however, was not prepared to respond more quickly to their plight by redistributing income on a grand scale. Yet the most pressing problems of life and death were in-

[20] R. M. Hartwell and Stanley Engerman, "Models of Immiseration: The Theoretical Basis of Pessimism," in Arthur J. Taylor, ed., *The Standard of Living in Britain in the Industrial Revolution* (London: Methuen, 1975), p. 213. See also Joel Mokyr, "Is There Still Life in the Pessimist Case? Consumption during the Industrial Revolution, 1790–1850," *Journal of Economic History* 48 (1988): 69–92. Mokyr argues that the standard of living probably stagnated during the first half of the nineteenth century.

[21] "Editor's Introduction," in Taylor, *Standard of Living*, p. lii.

[22] François Crouzet, *Capital Formation in the Industrial Revolution* (London: Methuen, 1972), pp. 63–64.

[23] E. F. Heckscher, "Swedish Population Trends before the Industrial Revolution," *Economic History Review*, 2d ser., 2 (1950): 266–277.

[24] Roger S. Schofield, "The Impact of Scarcity and Plenty on Population Change in England, 1541–1871," *Journal of Interdisciplinary History* 14 (1983): 265–291.

[25] Hartwell and Engerman, "Models of Immiseration," p. 213.

deed solved, and in Austria they were solved without a revolution. The success of the government in resolving these conflicts, given the entrenched power of the landed oligarchy, is in itself an admirable achievement.

Like many adherents of the pessimist school of historiography, contemporary observers pointed to the poverty of the hand-loom weavers as evidence of the suffering brought about by industrialization.[26] The pattern of the height data suggests, however, that such weavers were not poor because they wove; rather they wove because they were poor and because otherwise they would have been even poorer. Gertrude Himmelfarb recently summed up this and related issues:

> The 'standard-of-living' question . . . is generally discussed as if it were a question of industrialism alone, a measure of the social and economic costs and gains of mechanization and urbanization. In fact, . . . it was as much a product of such natural and political catastrophes as famine and war as of the industrial and agricultural revolution. It was also a product of the 'demographic revolution,' which itself was partly a consequence of industrialism and partly a cause or 'precondition' of it.[27]

Nutritional status is not identical with the material standard of living, but in the eighteenth-century Habsburg Monarchy it was a large component of it. Studying changes in human stature, therefore, provides insights not only into the changes in biological well-being but also into the trends in welfare in an economic sense. It is clear that the nutritional status, i.e., the standard of living, of the Habsburg population began to deteriorate, prior to the onset of widespread industrialization, as a consequence of population growth. The falling standard of living, in turn, led the government to embark on a program of institutional change that enabled many peasants, particularly in the western provinces of the Monarchy, to enter the industrial sector after the 1750s, at first as cottage workers in the employ of an outputter. Rural industrialization in Bohemia helped prevent the utter collapse of the local economy. Instead of causing a decline in the material standard of living, industrialization slowed its rate of diminution in Bohemia and also in Lower Austria. After the 1770s, with the beginning of industrialization, the stature of the lower classes stabilized. Instead of industrialism causing poverty, it

---

[26] An observer of the hand-loom weavers in England referred to them as a race "rigidly descending to the size of Liliputians." Cited by Roderick Floud and Kenneth Wachter, "Poverty and Physical Stature: Evidence on the Standard of Living of London Boys, 1770–1870," *Social Science History* 6 (1982): 422–452.

[27] Gertrude Himmelfarb, *The Idea of Poverty* (New York: Knopf, 1983), p. 135.

was the growth of the agricultural population which caused impoverishment of sufficient magnitude to force many peasants to engage in industrial activity. Industrialization, in turn, enabled the labor force to emancipate itself from the Malthusian menace which had threatened it periodically since time immemorial.[28]

The Bohemian and Lower Austrian experience indicates clearly that industrialization can be conceptualized as an antidote to the immiseration brought about by the beginning of the population explosion. To be sure, industrialization did not immediately bring about an improvement in living standards, but in East-Central Europe it did lead to a slowing down of the deterioration until it could be reversed. Industrialization meant that additional income was generated, which could be used to purchase nutrients from agricultural regions. The access to food supplies, in turn, removed the Malthusian constraints and enabled population growth to continue, even to accelerate.

If one were to ask hypothetically how this society would have fared without the response of industrialization, the answer would not be a simple one. One might conjecture that without industrialization, diminishing returns to labor in the agricultural sector would have continued to impinge on the nutritional status, and hence on the health, of the population until the Malthusian mechanism of positive checks had manifested itself once again. In other words, the standard of living initially would have declined faster than it actually did. After all, industrialization provided opportunities for employment that must have increased the income of workers who, otherwise, would have been under- or unemployed. Had the industrial sector not expanded sufficiently to provide an additional source of income and thereby act as a safety valve, population growth would eventually have been curtailed. However, the standard of living could not have declined indefinitely. If the rate of population growth had been moderated either by a rise in the crude death rate or a fall in the crude birth rate, then a homeostasis might have been achieved at a standard of living lower than that obtained with industrialization. It is more likely, however, that the decline in nutritional status would have been so dramatic in the absence of industrialization that the health of the population would have deteriorated until a subsistence crisis of immense magnitude ensued. By the early nineteenth century the population of the western half of the Monarchy could have

---

[28] The Malthusian positive checks still existed, but were no longer very powerful, in early-modern England. Negative checks, restraints voluntarily imposed in response to adverse economic developments, were operating well into the early nineteenth century. E. Anthony Wrigley and Roger S. Schofield, *The Population History of England, 1541–1871: A Reconstruction* (Cambridge, MA: Harvard University Press, 1981).

been weakened to such a degree that a catastrophe, similar to the ones weakening populations had experienced in earlier centuries, might have followed, as was the case in mid-nineteenth-century Ireland. There were signs of such a mortality crisis in Bohemia already in the 1770s. Although a catastrophe would no doubt have been a harrowing experience, for those who remained alive in its aftermath, the standard of living would clearly have improved and might even have exceeded temporarily the actual level achieved with industrialization. Therefore the view one takes on the effect of industrialization on the material standard of living depends, to a large extent, on the assessment of how probable a full-fledged Malthusian crisis in East-Central Europe actually was, and on how one might want to balance the pains suffered by the casualties of such a crisis with the gains in consumption by those who remained alive thereafter.

The point worthy of reiteration is that the immediate effect of industrialization in Bohemia and Lower Austria was to bring about a deceleration in the rate at which the population's standard of living was declining. Yet if there had truly been an immense mortality crisis and a Malthusian collapse, then the material standard of living would have been greater without industrialization than it was with industrialization for perhaps a few generations. Of course, both pessimists and optimists agree that in the long run industrialization raised the material standard of living substantially. The above findings suggest that a similar conclusion is warranted also for the short run as well. Only in the intermediate period of perhaps two generations might the standard of living have been lower with industrialization relative to the level that would have been obtained in its absence. This should not be construed as implying that industrialization lowered the standard of living; it did not. For the population alive it raised it. However in the absence of industrialization probably fewer people would have remained alive and therefore the amount of land, capital, and livestock available per capita to those who survived would have been higher for a few decades than it actually was.

Those who plan to explore further the relationship between the standard of living and industrialization in other regions of the globe should, therefore, keep in mind that it is insufficient to show a correlation between industrialization and a decline in the standard of living in order to construct a case for causation from the former process to the latter. The simultaneity of the onset of industrialization with a decline in the standard of living is not sufficient evidence that the former caused the latter. One must also explore the contemporaneous changes in the well-being of the rural population, and determine the beginning of the downturn of their standard of living as well. One should, furthermore, investigate the rate at which the deteriorating standard of living was falling and correlate that rate with the onset, pace, and extent of industrialization. In other words, the standard of living might have declined even after the onset of industrialization, but it might have done so at a slower rate than just prior to it, as appears to have been the case in Bohemia and Lower Austria. Lastly, more attention needs to be devoted to analyzing trends in well-being by gender, because recent evidence indicates that the standard of living of females can differ significantly from the experience of the male segment of the society.[29]

The case of the Habsburg Monarchy shows how widespread rural poverty was, and that immiseration of the rural population preceded the industrial revolution. Without industrialization, the effect of immiseration on the health of the population could have been catastrophic. In the Habsburg lands industrialization was a conscious response designed to ameliorate the pauperization that had begun to threaten this European society. The government's response to the impending nutritional crisis was a thorough revision of the agricultural and industrial laws. Institutional change, in turn, enabled the economy to expand sufficiently to counteract the deterioration in the standard of living. Without this Malthusian threat, such a broad range of government-initiated reform in a short period of time is unthinkable.[30]

In my previous book I sought to understand the salient features of the process of industrialization in a relatively backward economy, that of Austria-Hungary. I concluded that it began very early, in the 1820s, once the other European countries, and America too, had emerged from the post-Napoleonic depression. The rate of growth of the economy from the 1820s until World War I was relatively even. There were cycles of various intensities, to be sure, but there was no period worthy of being designated a "great spurt." Evidently this economy had not conformed to the major typologies of industrialization put forth by Rostow or Gerschenkron.

I had acknowledged the eighteenth-century antecedents of the persistent growth that began in the 1820s, but it was not until the present work that I became fully convinced of their significance. Previously I was not prepared to accept the notion that modern economic growth, or, if you will, the industrial revolution, began in a relatively backward

---

[29] Paul Riggs, "The Standard of Living in Britain's Celtic Fringe, c. 1800–1850: Evidence from Glaswegian Prisoners," unpublished manuscript, Department of History, University of Pittsburgh, 1988.

[30] For similar issues in Lombardy see: Alexander Grab, "The Politics of Subsistence: The Liberalization of Grain Commerce in Austrian Lombardy under Enlightened Despotism," *Journal of Modern History* 57 (1985): 185–210.

continental economy at the same time that it became evident in Great Britain. We have long been accustomed to thinking of British industrialization as not only unique, but also as having been the first truly revolutionary one.[31] The challenges to this vision have been of more recent vintage.[32] The present work, by defining the industrial revolution as the escape from the Malthusian trap, which enabled the population, and hence total product, to grow unconstrained thereafter, will—I hope— lay to rest the previous conceptualizations.[33] That fundamental change in the demographic regime, it seems to be worth stressing, is the essence of the industrial revolution of the eighteenth century, and the one characteristic that distinguishes it from prior economic upswings. Therefore this is a prominent feature of the "Austrian" model of the industrial revolution.

This view emphasizes that the upswing of the eighteenth century was a continuation of the expansion of the sixteenth century, an expansion which had been interrupted by the Malthusian crisis of the seventeenth. Moreover, the "Austrian" model stresses that the eighteenth-century boom, like previous booms, was not confined to any one country, but was quite general throughout Europe. Although this expansion was experienced in different ways by the various economies, and Britain's contribution was undoubtedly important, we should abandon the notion that the industrial revolution was a British monopoly. The Austrian economic and demographic expansion of the eighteenth century began at about the same time as the British one, and it transformed the economic and social structure as profoundly as in Great Britain. The intensity of the upswing in Austria was, in many ways, even greater.

Once anthropometric history had been woven into the study of the totality of Austria's eighteenth-century experience, it finally became possible to conceptualize the dynamics of economic development at the treshold of the industrial age. The discovery that the industrial advances in the Habsburg Monarchy had begun with the threat of a subsistence crisis brought with it an awareness, heretofore lacking, of the interconnectedness of demographic and economic processes in this epoch. Of course, by integrating for the first time human biology, via the nutritional link, into these processes, one gains more than just a conceptual-

---

[31] Phyllis Deane, *The First Industrial Revolution* (Cambridge, England: Cambridge University Press, 1965); Mathias, *First Industrial Nation*; Rostow, *How It All Began*.

[32] Patrick O'Brien and Caglar Keyder, *Economic Growth in Britain and France, 1780–1914* (London: George Allen and Unwin, 1978).

[33] Of course, this does not mean that the human population will never again face a crisis of immense proportions. If there ever is such a crisis on a continent-wide scale, however, it is unlikely that it will be caused by a shortage of nutrients.

ization of the industrial revolution. One also gains insights into the way market processes affected human beings at a certain stage of economic development. One learns that the biological standard of living can diverge significantly from the conventionally defined material standard of living under certain conditions.[34] In other words, the standard-of-living debate is given a new dimension. Thus anthropometric history opens up many new possibilities for understanding the processes of economic development, as well as the ways in which they affected the human beings who participated in them.

The "Austrian" model is extended in the following two chapters by first showing that it is applicable with minor modifications to the British experience as well. In Britain, too, population growth played a very important role in the economic expansion of the eighteenth century, and the demographic explosion also preceded the industrial revolution. In Britain, too, nutritional status and changes in nutritional status became important factors determining the outcome and pace of economic and demographic expansion. In Britain, too, the industrial revolution brought about an escape from the Malthusian trap.

In the final chapter I expand on the notion that the population-induced economic growth of the eighteenth century was a continuation of previous similar episodes. That is to say, the argument is advanced that the "Austrian" model is generalizable to the pre-industrial European experience. All major economic expansions of the millennium since the Dark Ages were accompanied by population growth, which was, however, constrained by Malthusian ceilings. The eighteenth-century expansion, i.e., the so-called industrial revolution, can be distinguished from prior industrial revolutions in that it successfully broke through the set of constraints that had limited prior expansions. Hence, the industrial revolution can be seen as a continuation of processes begun centuries before, and thereby becomes just one of the many cyclical expansions in the history of mankind. The essence of its uniqueness lies in the fact that during this upswing of economic activity the European societies were able to escape from the Malthusian trap, which had limited their prior development.

[34] John Komlos, "The Height and Weight of West Point Cadets: Dietary Change in Antebellum America," *Journal of Economic History* 47 (1987): 897–927; Gustav Ranis and John C. H. Fei, "A Theory of Economic Development," *American Economic Review* 51 (1961): 533–565.

EXTENSIONS

CHAPTER 5

THE "AUSTRIAN" MODEL AND
THE INDUSTRIAL REVOLUTION
IN ENGLAND

THE ARGUMENT is advanced in this chapter that the "Austrian" model of the industrial revolution is also applicable to the English experience of the eighteenth century. The framework outlined in the previous chapters linked economic and demographic processes through the nutritional status of the population. A rise in nutritional status led to population growth, which, in turn, was followed by a decline in the standard of living of sufficient magnitude that it put pressure on the political system for institutional change. In Austria the reforms that came in the wake of the crisis opened the way for industrialization, enabling economic forces to halt the deterioration in the well-being of the population. With minor changes, this model is useful in understanding the classical industrial revolution in England as well.

The British variant of the "Austrian" model substitutes the expansion of the market for institutional change in the causative chain. The market in England was sufficiently developed that it did not need the active intervention of the government in order to benefit from higher population densities. In contrast, the Austrian economy, with its many imperfections, could not have reaped the full benefits of population expansion without effective government action.

In the 1730s the English economy, like the Austrian one, reached an important conjuncture. Compared with prior centuries, both economies had a larger accumulation of capital and a larger urban sector, capable of expanding commerce and production, than ever before. In addition, their populations were relatively well nourished; benefiting even

187

more from the propitious harvest conditions of the decade, they were about to procreate at a rate unsurpassed within recent memory. The acceleration in population growth had a market-expanding effect in a Boserupian fashion, thereby triggering the industrial revolution, the roots of which, however, extended back into the distant past.[1] Thus the factors that have been regarded as crucial in unleashing the industrial revolution, such as the rise in the rate of saving, are less important within this framework than the acceleration in the growth of a well-nourished population in a relatively developed economy. The level of development reached in England was such that the economy could benefit from the rise in population density without significant capital-diluting effects, and without impinging drastically on the ability of the labor force to feed itself. To be sure, population growth had accelerated in prior centuries as well, but earlier the other factors, mentioned above, were not present to the same degree. Previous episodes of population growth had run into Malthusian ceilings;[2] in the eighteenth century, however, this constraint dissolved, and the Malthusian demographic regime was overtaken by a Boserupian one.[3]

Dating the Demographic Revolution in England

Recent annual estimates of the English population render the task of dating the demographic revolution in England possible.[4] The test is based on changes in the birth rate, because in the eighteenth century the increase in fertility was more important than the decline in mortality in

[1] Eric L. Jones, *The European Miracle: Environments, Economies, and Geopolitics in the History of Europe and Asia* (Cambridge, England: Cambridge University Press, 1981); Ester Boserup, *Population and Technological Change: A Study of Long-Term Trends* (Chicago: University of Chicago Press, 1981).

[2] For the Malthusian nature of the seventeenth-century crisis, see Jack Goldstone, "State Breakdown in the English Revolution: A New Synthesis," *American Journal of Sociology* 92 (1982): 257–322.

[3] For the structural change in demographic regime at mid-century, see Jack Goldstone, "The Demographic Revolution in England: A Reexamination," *Population Studies* 40 (1986): 5–33.

[4] E. Anthony Wrigley and Roger S. Schofield, *The Population History of England, 1541–1871: A Reconstruction* (Cambridge, MA: Harvard University Press, 1981), pp. 162, 176, 179. The authors themselves are uncertain on the dating of the demographic revolution. They suggest that the 1710s is one possible candidate, because after that decade ". . . a rising trend clearly sets in again." Yet they do not see this as a sign "of the onset of powerful population growth. . . ." From the mid-1740s, they note, births began to pull consistently away from deaths: ". . . natural increase remains relatively low during the first half of the eighteenth century. . . . From the mid-eighteenth century the surpluses of births over deaths grow rapidly."

bringing about the acceleration in population growth. A recursive-residual test is used to date the structural change in the English demographic regime.[5] This procedure uses ordinary least-squares regression to estimate the initial relationship on a data base, the size of which is at least one more than the number of independent variables. The initial estimate is then used to forecast one period ahead. After each forecast the error (residual) is calculated, and the data base is increased by one observation. In turn, another forecast is made and compared with the actual value of the dependent variable. Thereafter, another forecast error is calculated. This process is continued until the data are exhausted. To test the null hypothesis that the regression coefficient vector is constant over time, the cumulative sums of the standardized forecast residuals (CUSUM) are analyzed. Since residuals of the moving OLS regressions are assumed to be normal white noise, under the null hypothesis a visual inspection may reveal systematic patterns of under- or overprediction that signal a structural change, that is, a departure from the model.[6] The model to be tested is: $B = \gamma \exp[rt] + \epsilon$, where B is the number of births per annum, γ is a constant, e is the base of the natural logarithms, r is the rate of growth of B, t is time, and ϵ is the usual error term. Using this model one can determine if, and when, after 1670, the growth rate began to depart from a constant path. Structural change occurs when the CUSUM departs permanently from its expected value of zero. The cumulative sum of the one-step-ahead recursive residuals indicates a systematic propensity to underpredict beginning in the early 1730s (Figure 5.1). The fact that CUSUM never reaches zero again thereafter implies that the structural change in the English demographic regime occurred in that decade.

Analysis of the data by conventional means corroborates the above finding. Population was increasing already in the 1720s, but the increment to births in excess of deaths was sporadic, and in 1728/29 an ab-

---

[5] The recursive residual test was performed using the B34S program. Houston Stokes, "The B34S Data Analysis Program: A Short Write-up," Working Paper Series, Report FY 77–1, revised 14 July, 1981, College of Business Administration, University of Illinois at Chicago Circle. This test is more powerful than the Chow test, since the investigator is not burdened with having to search for the appropriate demarcation by dividing the sample into various periods of differing lengths and running regressions over these periods. R. L. Brown, J. Durbin, and J. M. Evans, "Techniques for Testing the Constancy of Regression Relationships over Time," *Journal of the Royal Statistical Society*, Ser. B, 37 (1975): 149–192. For another study using this technique see John Komlos, "Financial Innovation and the Demand for Money in Austria-Hungary, 1867–1913," *Journal of European Economic History* 16 (1987): 587–606.

[6] The drawback of the recursive residual test is that in the presence of autocorrelation it can be unreliable.

Figure 5.1. Plot of Cumulative Sum of the Recursive Residuals, Births in England, 1670–1809

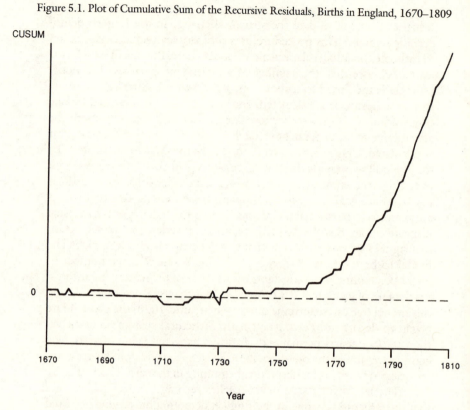

solute decline was evident. After the devastating winter of 1729/30 the pattern changed dramatically. The number of births in 1730 was high, near the previous all-time peak. Yet because during the previous winter death rates had also been very high, population did not begin to increase until the next year. Thereafter the number of births exceeded the number of deaths consistently for nine years. The increment to population during that interval was in excess of 300,000 individuals (5.7 percent), an increase not experienced since the beginning of the seventeenth century. In the 1720s the average crude birth rate (CBR) was approximately the same as the average crude death rate (CDR); in the 1730s, however, the former exceeded the latter by 5.8, and continued to do so in the 1740s by 3.6. The average annual number of births in the 1730s was 10 percent higher than in the 1720s, and 17 percent higher than in the 1710s. In addition, the gross reproduction rate reached 2.4 in the 1730s (an all-time high), and the net reproduction rate was the highest since 1581. In addition, the threat posed by subsistence crises to population growth was rapidly waning: 1741 and 1742 were the last two years when the number of deaths exceeded the number of births.[7]

To estimate the number of excess births in the 1730s, the above equation was run on quinquennial data for 1670–1729.[8] The estimated time trend was:[9] $B = 724.5 \exp[0.0152t]$. Comparison of the forecasts using this estimated trend with the actual number of births suggests that there were 126,000 more births in the 1730s than predicted.[10] Thus the population increased by a large margin in that decade.[11] This became the generation that played such an important role in the industrial revolution. The causes of this baby boom will now be explored.

The Rise in Nutritional Status

Several factors reinforced one another in the 1730s to bring about the structural change in the demographic regime in England. Although population had been growing slowly since the 1690s in conjunction with the gradually warming climatic trend, in 1730 population had not yet exceeded the level of 1657. While the size of the population was still at the mid-seventeenth-century level, the persistent advances in agricultural yields[12] meant that the English population must have been at a nutritional peak. Livestock production had been on the rise, and its

[7] A number of other factors were conducive to population expansion. One was the decline in infanticide; another was the decline by about 6,000 in the number of emigrants in the 1730s. Wrigley and Schofield, *Population History*, pp. 176, 179, 183, 218; Jim Beattie, "The Pattern of Crime in England, 1660–1800," *Past and Present* 62 (1974): 47–95.

[8] Wrigley and Schofield, *Population History*, p. 495.

[9] Both estimated coefficients were significant at the 0.01 level. $R^2 = .66$, D.W. $= 2.17$. The number of births is in thousands, and $t = 1$ for 1670–1674.

[10] Excess births can also be estimated on a monthly basis. The cumulative number of births in excess of the number predicted by an exponential trend is 133,000 in the 1730s and 13,400 in the 1740s.

[11] The demographic upturn was not confined to England. In Sweden, the 1720s and most of the 1730s witnessed a low death rate of about 21 per 1,000. It subsequently increased, however, and did not return to the level of the 1730s during the next century. Population growth exceeded 1.1 percent per annum in the 1720s and 1730s. Economic conditions in France were similar. "After 1720," writes Le Roy Ladurie, "things pick up again more or less everywhere and the prosperity that goes with recovery becomes established. Then after 1750 . . . there is a boom." Having stagnated for three and a half centuries, French agricultural output was "propelled . . . upward" once again. E. F. Heckscher, "Swedish Population Trends before the Industrial Revolution," *Economic History Review*, 2d ser., 2 (1950): 266–277; Emmanuel Le Roy Ladurie, *The Territory of the Historian* (Chicago: The University of Chicago Press, 1979), pp. 13, 89, 201, 232.

[12] Robert C. Allen, "Inferring Yields from Probate Inventories," *Journal of Economic History* 48 (1988): 117–126.

quality, too, was probably improving. Legume cultivation, as well as the share of wheat in cereal production, was increasing.[13] As a consequence, per capita food consumption could have increased between 1660 and 1740 by as much as 50 percent.[14] The fact that real wages were higher in the 1730s than at any time since 1537 indicates what a high standard of living was reached.[15] The increase in grain exports, from 2.8 million quintals in the first decade of the eighteenth century to 6 million by the 1740s, is also indicative of the availability of nutrients.[16]

The remarkably good harvests were brought about by the favorable weather conditions of the 1730s. In England the first four decades of the eighteenth century were much warmer than the last decades of the previous century (Table 5.1).[17] Even small differences in temperature may have important consequences for production. Length of the growing season, pasture output, and hence livestock and milk availability can all be affected.[18] Meat production is particularly sensitive to the quality of the pasture.[19] Bountiful harvests, and the greater availability of food that resulted, were a boon to population growth[20] not only in En-

[13] Eric L. Jones, "Agriculture and Economic Growth in England, 1660–1750: Agricultural Change," *Journal of Economic History* 25 (1965): 1–18; Mark Overton, "Estimating Crop Yields from Probate Inventories: An Example from East Anglia, 1585–1735," *Journal of Economic History* 39 (1979): 363–378. The latter article provides regional evidence that grain yields were increasing up to the 1730s.

[14] R. V. Jackson, "Growth and Deceleration in English Agriculture, 1660–1790," *Economic History Review*, 2d ser., 38 (1985): 333–352.

[15] Wrigley and Schofield, *Population History*, p. 643.

[16] A. H. John, "Agricultural Productivity and Economic Growth in England, 1700–1760," *Journal of Economic History* 25 (1965): 19–34.

[17] Sweden, too, enjoyed mild winters between 1721 and 1735. In France, the "miserable seventeenth-century reality" was not entirely over until after 1730. In Holland, winter temperatures between 1699 and 1757 were more than one degree lower than during most of the seventeenth century. The variability of the weather was also smaller. Gustaf Utterström, "Climatic Fluctuations and Population Problems in Early Modern History," *Scandinavian Economic History Review* 3 (1955): 3–47; LeRoy Ladurie, *Territory of the Historian*, p. 9; idem, *Times of Feast, Times of Famine: A History of Climate since the Year 1000* (Garden City, NY: Doubleday, 1971); Jan de Vries, "Measuring the Impact of Climate on History: The Search for Appropriate Methodologies," in Robert I. Rotberg and Theodore K. Rabb, eds., *Climate and History: Studies in Interdisciplinary History* (Princeton: Princeton University Press, 1981), pp. 19–50; Helmut Landsberg, "Past Climates from Unexploited Written Sources," in Rotberg and Rabb, *Climate and History*, pp. 51–62.

[18] Reid A. Bryson and Christine Padoch, "On the Climates of History," in Rotberg and Rabb, *Climate and History*, pp. 3–17.

[19] Robert J. McFall, *The World's Meat* (New York: Appleton and Co., 1927), p. 56.

[20] Winter temperatures can also affect population growth. A study of pre-industrial Swedish mortality concluded that ". . . warm winters have especially beneficial effects on survival." This is plausible, since the poor could not afford adequate protection through clothing and housing during severe winters. The weather could have had an effect on mortality rates directly, since damp houses were harmful to the respiratory organs, partic-

Table 5.1   Index of Price of Consumables, Real Wages and Mean Temperatures in England

Decade	Price Index	Real Wages	Temperature
1670	116.3	77.3	8.6
1680	92.4	85.1	8.7
1690	132.4	80.7	8.1
1700	99.0	92.9	9.2
1710	109.8	89.7	9.1
1720	100.0	100.0	9.4
1730	85.7	113.1	9.5
1740	83.3	105.9	8.2
1750	101.4	103.8	9.0
1760	111.7	100.0	8.9
1770	131.0	94.0	9.3
1780	135.5	101.9	8.8

Sources: Brian R. Mitchell and Phyllis Deane, <u>Abstract of British Historical Statistics</u> (Cambridge, England: Cambridge University Press, 1971), p. 486; Gordon Manley, "Central England Temperatures: Monthly Means 1659 to 1973," <u>Quarterly Journal of the Royal Meteorological Society</u> 100 (1974): 389-405; E. Anthony Wrigley and Roger S. Schofield, <u>The Population History of England,1541-1871: A Reconstruction</u> (Cambridge, MA: Harvard University Press, 1981), p. 643.

gland,[21] but also in many other regions of Europe.[22] As a consequence of high yields[23] the price of consumables declined by 14 percent in the 1730s relative to the 1720s. Wheat cost 30 percent less in the 1730s than it did in the 1660s.[24]

ularly those of infants. Zvi Eckstein, T. Paul Schultz, and Kenneth I. Wolpin, "Short-Run Fluctuations in Fertility and Mortality in Pre-Industrial Sweden," *European Economic Review* 26 (1984): 295–317; Le Roy Ladurie, *Times of Feast*, p. 291; Gustaf Utterström, "Some Population Problems in Pre-industrial Sweden," *Scandinavian Economic History Review* 2 (1954): 103–165.

[21] John, "Agricultural Productivity"; H. J. Habakkuk, "English Population in the Eighteenth Century," *Economic History Review*, 2d ser., 6 (1953): 117–133; Gordon Manley, "Central England Temperatures: Monthly Means 1659 to 1973," *Quarterly Journal of the Royal Meteorological Society* 100 (1974): 389–405.

[22] Utterström, "Some Population Problems"; Patrick R. Galloway, "Long-Term Fluctuations in Climate and Population in the Preindustrial Era," *Population and Development Review* 12 (1986): 1–24. Japan, however, was an exception. There population reached 26.1 million in 1721 and only 26.9 million in 1846. Susan Hanley, "Population Trends and Economic Development in Tokugawa Japan," unpublished Ph.D dissertation, Yale University, 1971, p. 29.

[23] Overton, "Estimating Crop Yields"; G. E. Mingay, "The Agricultural Depression, 1730–1760," *Economic History Review*, 2d ser., 8 (1955): 323–338.

[24] The price of animal products remained constant. John, "Agricultural Productivity."

The increase in wheat consumption was particularly important because wheat was less susceptible to mold than rye.[25] In addition, increased consumption of legumes made a substantial contribution to the quality of proteins available in cereals, because the mix of proteins found in them complement one another.[26]

There is direct evidence that the nutritional status of many populations was, indeed, improving in the early part of the eighteenth century, because human stature was generally increasing in Europe as well as in America (see Chapter 2). This is a strong indication that protein and caloric intake rose. In the British colonies of North America, an increase in food consumption—most importantly, of animal protein—in the beginning of the eighteenth century has been directly documented.[27] Institutional menus also indicate that diets improved in terms of caloric content.[28]

Changes in British income distribution conform to the above pattern. Low food prices meant that the bottom 40 percent of the distribution[29] was gaining between 1688 and 1759, but by 1800 had declined again to the level of 1688.[30] This trend is another indication that a substantial portion of the population that was at a nutritional disadvantage was doing better during the first half of the eighteenth century than it did earlier, but that the gains were not maintained throughout the century.

As a result of better nutritional conditions, marriages took place at younger ages: from 1650 to 1699, 24 percent of the women were married at age 21 or younger; from 1700 to 1749, 28 percent were. This indicates that many girls in their late teens and early 20s were deciding to marry at younger ages. Their decision to marry might very well have been influenced by the age at which they reached menarche, and con-

[25] Rye is most likely to produce ergot, especially during cold winters. Mary Kilbourne Matossian, "Death in London, 1750–1909," *Journal of Interdisciplinary History* 16 (1985): 183–197; idem, "Mold Poisoning and Population Growth in England and France, 1750–1850," *Journal of Economic History* 44 (1984): 669–686; idem, "Climate, Crops, and Natural Increase in Rural Russia, 1861–1913," *Slavic Review* 45 (1986): 457–469.

[26] Martha Weidner Williams, "Infant Nutrition and Economic Growth in Western Europe from the Middle Ages to the Modern Period," unpublished Ph.D. dissertation, Department of Economics, Northwestern University, 1988, chapter 2.

[27] Sarah McMahon, "Provisions Laid Up for the Family: Toward a History of Diet in New England, 1650–1850," *Historical Methods* 14 (1981): 4–21.

[28] Carole Shammas, "The Eighteenth-Century English Diet and Economic Change," *Explorations in Economic History* 21 (1984): 254–269.

[29] Including paupers.

[30] Peter Lindert and Jeffrey Williamson, "Reinterpreting Britain's Social Tables, 1688–1913," *Explorations in Economic History* 20 (1983): 94–109. Growth of per capita real output showed a similar pattern: it was faster in the first half than in the second half of the century (0.19 vs. 0.14 percent per annum).

sequently by their nutritional status.[31] The increase in nutritional status would have brought about a decline in the age at menarche, and an earlier entry into the marriage market could very well have been linked to their having reached sexual maturity earlier (see Chapter 1).

The rise in nutritional status must also have increased fecundity and thus conceptions both in and out of marriage. The steady rise in prenuptial pregnancies during the course of the century is consistent with this notion. While at the end of the seventeenth century 15 percent of the brides were pregnant, a century later 35 percent were.[32] Because of the rise in prenuptial pregnancies, age-specific marital fertility between the ages of 15 to 24 increased.[33] A nutrition-related increase in the desire for sexual contact could also have reinforced the effect of a rise in fecundity.[34]

The Generation of the 1730s Matures

The argument has been expounded that exogenous changes in weather conditions caused a structural change in the English demographic regime in the 1730s. A well-nourished population benefited from the additional nutrients brought about by good harvest conditions. Population growth accelerated in consequence of the rise in nutritional status because the marriage rate, as well as birth and death rates, were all nutrition sensitive.

The age structure of the population changed suddenly in the 1730s. The number of children under age five in 1736 reached 13.5 percent of the total population, its highest proportion since the sixteenth century. The demographic upsurge had echo effects in twenty-year intervals as the generation of the 1730s matured and procreated. Hence in the 1750s there was an unusually large number of young adults in the population: the share of those between the ages of 15 and 24 rose to 18.5 percent. (That had happened only three times during the previous century.) Thus the share of the population at risk of becoming pregnant

[31] John Komlos, "The Age at Menarche in Vienna: The Relationship between Nutrition and Fertility," *Historical Methods* 22 (1989), forthcoming.

[32] Although the number of women who were one or two months pregnant at the time of their marriage remained at 8 to 9 percent of all brides, the number who were pregnant longer increased greatly, from 7 to 26 percent. Twelve points of the 19-percentage-point increase must have taken place during the two decades after 1755.

[33] E. Anthony Wrigley and Roger S. Schofield, "English Population History from Family Reconstitution: Summary Results, 1600–1799," *Population Studies* 37 (1983): 157–184.

[34] Wrigley and Schofield, "English Population History," pp. 168–169.

peaked in the quinquennia of 1756 and 1771, and therefore the number of births also reached high levels then.[35]

As cohorts of the 1730s came of age, the number of persons looking for mates simultaneously became unusually large.[36] This might have influenced the marriage age by lowering the cost of finding a partner. Besides economic opportunities, the age at marriage could have depended on two other factors—the age at which the decision was made to begin looking for a partner and the time required to find one. The former factor might have been influenced by nutrition, through the age at menarche, and the latter factor might have depended on the size of the cohort seeking mates. The likelihood of finding someone acceptable with a given expenditure of effort must have increased as the density of the population of marriageable age increased. Improvements in transportation and increased spatial mobility could have reinforced this effect. In some parishes in Nottinghamshire, "between 1670 and 1700, the proportion of extra-parochial marriages was 10.8 percent . . . between 1770 and 1800 it was 26 percent."[37] By thus reducing search costs, the increase in the size of the marriage market in the 1750s could have led to a further decline in the age at marriage; it might also explain the decline in celibacy.

To be sure, members of a large birth cohort all entering the job market at the same time could also experience difficulties finding employment. By the eighteenth century, however, the British economy was sufficiently advanced that the market-expanding effects of a higher population density, by creating opportunities not available before, could counterbalance the problems of increased competition in the labor market.

Thus the momentum of population growth could continue even as real wages began to fall and food prices increased even more dramatically (Table 5.1). Marital fertility was maintained, partly because the increased labor-force participation rates of women and children provided opportunities to defend the customary standard of living and thereby obviated the need to adjust vital rates. In addition, enough nutrients were available to forestall by one or two decades the beginning of positive checks, which otherwise would have put downward pressure on further population growth. Since nutritional status is transferable to

[35] Wrigley and Schofield, *Population History*, pp. 529–530.

[36] As in Sweden; Utterström, "Some Population Problems," p. 149.

[37] J. D. Chambers, "The Course of Population Change," in David V. Glass and David E. C. Eversley, eds., *Population in History: Essays in Historical Demography* (Chicago: The University of Chicago Press, 1965), pp. 327–334.

some extent between generations,[38] the diminution in the nutrients available to children of the generation of the 1730s was partly offset by the fact that their parents were well nourished.

Agricultural productivity was high and increasing, but it could not keep pace with the demands placed upon it by the acceleration of population growth. Although England had been a nutrient-surplus economy until then, exports of food now ceased. Luckily England could depend on her colonies and on Ireland for imports of nutrients. Beef imports from Ireland tripled, and butter and pork imports also increased greatly in the 1750s and 1760s.[39] In effect, the English society was able to postpone the Malthusian threat at Ireland's expense, with profound consequences for the Irish peasantry.

The English population in the 1750s continued to procreate at the traditional rate. There was not yet any reason why these adults should not have reproduced as before. Couples of the 1750s could not have known the size of their cohort and therefore could not have foretold that the externalities of their collective action would ultimately lead to an even more substantial rise in food prices. As a consequence of this inability to predict the future course of events, population growth persisted.

The ingredients of a Malthusian crisis were accumulating. While the population growth rate reached 0.83 percent per annum (1760–1801), agricultural output grew at only half that rate. In prior centuries a subsistence crisis would probably have ensued, but by the eighteenth century the economy was sufficiently advanced to overcome the threat.[40] This is why it was so important that the society started the process of rapid economic growth from a high nutritional base, even with surplus nutrients and with the availability of food imports. This advantage meant that the English population could increase and still have sufficient time to allow the beneficial effects of population growth to work themselves through the economy and generate market-expanding forces.

One prerequisite of population growth was thus at hand in the 1730s: a high level of per capita nutritional intake relative to the minimum required for sustaining life. This was important, because to some degree nutritional status can be transferred between generations, and

---

[38] Animal experiments suggest that intergenerational transfer of malnutrition is significant. Robert W. Fogel, Stanley L. Engerman, and James Trussell, "Exploring the Uses of Data on Height: The Analysis of Long-Term Trends in Nutrition, Labor Welfare, and Labor Productivity," *Social Science History* 6 (1982): 401–421.

[39] Brinley Thomas, "Escaping from Constraints: The Industrial Revolution in a Malthusian Context," *Journal of Interdisciplinary History* 15 (1985): 729–753.

[40] Ibid., p. 730.

because most new entrants into the labor force could then enter the industrial or commercial-urban sector without risking an irreversible deterioration in the society's nutritional status. Although nutrient intake did diminish by approximately 20 percent between 1740 and 1790,[41] the high level of 'stored-up nutrition' meant that the population could grow and nutritional status could decline for some time before the decline posed an imminent threat to the biological system. Since food shortage tends also to destabilize the political system, the adequate food supply meant that this problem did not impose a constraint on economic development.[42] Hence, English society had sufficient time for the market to expand in response to the increasing population density, before the negative checks began to restrain the further expansion of population.

The Industrial Revolution

The course of the industrial revolution after the 1760s is too well known to need reiteration. The point requiring emphasis here is that the increase in population density had a market-expanding effect, because technological change, capital accumulation, commercialization, expansion of the industrial sector, the enclosure movement, and changes in industrial organization were all sensitive to population size.[43] The increase in population density meant that transaction costs between buyers and sellers declined, and that the cost of acquiring information, crucial for production as well as for marketing, was similarly lowered. It also meant that the generation and transmission of knowledge became easier. Economies of scale could be captured in production that were not feasible earlier, and as output expanded, positive externalities were obtained, which lowered production costs further.[44] In addition, English industry might have been on that section of its aggregate production function where the marginal product of labor was rising. All of these benefits of increased population size undoubtedly contributed to the acceleration of total factor productivity toward the end of the century.[45]

[41] Jackson, "Growth and Deceleration"; Shammas, "English Diet," p. 263.

[42] Boserup, *Population and Technological Change*; Julian L. Simon, *Theory of Population and Economic Growth* (Oxford: Basil Blackwell, 1986).

[43] Julian L. Simon, *The Ultimate Resource* (Princeton: Princeton University Press, 1981).

[44] These effects are explored more fully in Joel Mokyr, "Demand vs. Supply in the Industrial Revolution," *Journal of Economic History* 37 (1977): 981–1008.

[45] N.F.R. Crafts, "The Eighteenth Century: A Survey," in Roderick Floud and Donald

The demand for industrial products increased even though per capita demand might have remained constant or even declined.[46] Increased aggregate demand could have meant that critical thresholds were met for the commercialization of some branches of industry, thereby inducing a switch from household to market production. The subsequent economic expansion broke the nexus that had existed between real wages and population growth, because the marginal product of labor was constant in the industrial and commercial sectors rather than diminishing as in agriculture. Moreover, the economic opportunities created in the expanding industrial sector enabled family formation to proceed unhindered by the difficulties that would have otherwise beset a large cohort searching for jobs.

It took time for these economic consequences of population growth to have a beneficial effect on production; English society was able to gain the necessary time only because it started the process of expansion from a high nutritional base, and could acquire nutrients from abroad. Once the process of growth gained momentum population could expand further, no longer constrained by diminishing returns and Malthusian ceilings. The industrial revolution was under way.

English society had achieved a high level of urbanization by 1750: a fifth of the population lived in urban areas. During the century and a half preceding 1750 nearly half of the increment to population had accrued to the urban sector.[47] This is an indication that the agricultural sector was sufficiently developed to support a large industrial and commercial sector without jeopardizing the availability of nutrients. By reducing transaction and information costs, which might counteract the market forces of expansion in a rural economy, urbanization contributed to the intensity of the economic expansion. The large share of the population living in urban areas meant that capital accumulation, knowledge creation, expansion of commerce, technological innovation, financial sophistication, and industrial production could all proceed at a faster rate than ever before.

The last time prior to the eighteenth century that population growth had accelerated to this extent was in the sixteenth century. The level of

McCloskey, eds., *The Economic History of Britain since 1700. Vol. 1: 1700–1860* (Cambridge, England: Cambridge University Press, 1981), pp. 1–16.

[46] Elizabeth Gilboy, "Demand as a Factor in the Industrial Revolution," in R. M. Hartwell, ed., *The Causes of the Industrial Revolution in England* (London: Methuen, 1967), pp. 121–138.

[47] E. Anthony Wrigley, "Urban Growth and Agricultural Change: England and the Continent in the Early Modern Period," *Journal of Interdisciplinary History* 15 (1985): 683–728.

urbanization then was only five percent.[48] Starting from such a low level of development, an escape from the Malthusian constraint was unlikely. During the succeeding two centuries the transportation system was improved, and the urban infrastructure was also expanded. The concomitant growth in commerce brought into Europe's reach agricultural regions that could provide nutrients during periods of rapid population growth. In the sixteenth century neither Ireland, the American colonies, nor Eastern Europe could deliver edibles to Western Europe to the same degree as in the eighteenth century.[49] Population growth in the fifteenth and sixteenth centuries was therefore followed by a large number of mortality crises. Between 1540 and 1625 there were on average two years per decade in England when the crude death rate was more than 10 percent above trend. Between 1730 and 1800, however, the average was only one per decade. Prior to 1730 there were only four decades without such episodes, yet the 1730s and 1750s both went by without experiencing such a rise in the crude death rate.[50]

The increase in population density in the 1760s and 1770s led both to the expansion of the market and to an increased demand for technological change.[51] Threatened by an impending crisis brought about by an acceleration in population growth, societies often scurry to find technological solutions.[52] The fact that population growth coincided with the well-known technological breakthroughs of the industrial sector in England after mid-century fits well into a Boserupian framework.

In addition, there is a relationship between nutrition and mental capacity. Medical and psychological evidence indicate a link between protein-calorie malnutrition, especially in the very early stages of life, and stunted brain growth and lowered intellectual ability.[53] Experiments, too, have demonstrated that malnutrition causes a reduction in brain

[48] Ibid., p. 688.

[49] Boris Nikolaevich Mironov, "In Search of Hidden Information: Some Issues in the Socio-Economic History of Russia in the Eighteenth and Nineteenth Centuries," *Social Science History* 9 (1985): 339–359.

[50] Wrigley and Schofield, *Population History*, pp. 333–34.

[51] Boserup, *Population and Technological Change*.

[52] Julian L. Simon and Gunter Steinmann, "The Economic Implications of Learning-by-Doing for Population Size and Growth," *European Economic Review* 26 (1984): 167–185.

[53] Williams, "Infant Nutrition," Chapter 2; M. B. Stoch and D. M. Smythe, "Fifteen-Year Developmental Study on Effects of Severe Undernutrition during Infancy on Subsequent Physical Growth and Intellectual Functioning," *Archives of Disease in Childhood* 51 (1976): 327–336; Ancel Keys *et al.*, *The Biology of Human Starvation* (Minneapolis: The University of Minnesota Press, 1950), vol. 1, pp. 863, 885; Robert Balazs *et al.*, "Undernutrition and Brain Development," in Frank Falkner and James M. Tanner, eds., *Human Growth: A Comprehensive Treatise*, 2d ed. (New York and London: Plenum Press, 1986), vol. 3, pp. 415–473.

weight, number of nerve cells, and learning capacity.[54] Stunted children in several third world countries did not test as well as taller children in visual-kinesthetic performance.[55]

Consequently it should not be considered a mere coincidence that the generation of inventors responsible for the crucial innovations during the initial stage of the industrial revolution was born during a period when the nutritional level was relatively high.[56] The fact that the generation of the 1730s and 1740s was well fed during childhood must have been a contributing factor in its ability to perceive a large number of relationships that had eluded previous generations. In addition, the fact that English society responded with relative ease to the whole complex of challenges posed by the process of industrialization, and was capable of absorbing the new technologies to the extent it did, indicates that favorable cognitive development was diffused throughout the society, and was not restricted to a few inventive geniuses.

Another reason why a relatively high nutritional status is important to the process of industrialization is that it can influence both labor-force-participation rate and work intensity. Even though nutritional status in England was on average higher than in, for instance, France, nonetheless, according to a recent estimate 3 percent of the population probably did not consume sufficient calories to do any work at all, and the balance of the bottom 20 percent could perform just 6 hours of light work daily.[57]

The above arguments should not be construed in such a way as to make the weather conditions of the 1730s a prerequisite for the industrial revolution. Rather, the level of population density reached in the 1750s was one of the factors contributing to the acceleration in aggregate output. No doubt, in the absence of the unusually propitious environmental conditions it would have taken longer to reach the critical

[54] Angeles Menendez-Patterson, Serafina Fernández, Jose Florez-Lozano, and Bernardo Marin, "Effect of Early Pre- and Postnatal Acquired Malnutrition on Development and Sexual Behavior in the Rat," *Pharmacology, Biochemistry and Behavior* 17 (1982): 654–664; Nevin Scrimshaw, "The Value of Contemporary Food and Nutrition Studies for Historians," *Journal of Interdisciplinary History* 14 (1983): 529–534.

[55] Joaquin Cravioto and Ramiro Arrieta, "Nutrition, Mental Development, and Learning," in Falkner and Tanner, *Human Growth*, pp. 501–536.

[56] James Watt was born in 1736; Edmund Cartwright in 1743; and Sir Richard Arkwright in 1732.

[57] In contrast, the situation in France, with a mean energy intake of about 400 calories less than the English circa 1790, was much worse. There the bottom 10 percent of the population lacked enough energy for regular work, and the next decile could do only 3 hours of light physical labor per day. Robert W. Fogel, "Biomedical Approaches to the Estimation and Interpretation of Secular Trends in Equity, Morbidity, Mortality, and Labor Productivity in Europe, 1750–1980," unpublished manuscript, Graduate School of Business Administration, University of Chicago, 1987.

level of population densities that triggered the acceleration of industrial output. The other ingredients of the industrial revolution, such as the large capital stock, the size of the commercial-urban sector, the agricultural improvements, and the accessibility of the New World's nutrients, were all achieved during the course of the prior centuries. The conjunction of these factors rendered the industrial revolution a possibility in the eighteenth century. The weather conditions of the 1730s and the concomitant rise in nutritional status have been emphasized because without them the industrial revolution would have been delayed.

The real price of food began to rise in the 1770s, and without doubt the nutritional status of the population, especially that of its poorer segments, began to deteriorate. The stature of poor London boys, for example, was declining during the last decades of the eighteenth century.[58] In prior centuries such episodes no doubt would have culminated in a subsistence crisis, followed by Malthusian checks to further population growth. There were signs that in the 1770s preventive checks were becoming more important, as the proportion of celibate women in the population rose and the crude marriage rate declined.[59] Yet the age at first marriage continued to decline, because the relationship between that age and food prices, crucial for the generation of the 1730s, had been broken.[60] By the 1770s industrial employment opportunities theretofore nonexistent meant that the labor-force-participation rate of women and children could rise. Contributions of children to family income could offset to some degree the decline in the parents' real wages, and underemployment could also decline. Opportunities to work in the industrial and commercial sectors meant that the number of hours worked could be increased to defend a target level of income, a possibility not as readily available in agriculture. In other words, the marginal product of labor was more elastic in industrial pursuits than in agriculture. Thus, the implications of rising food prices for English vital demographic rates during the 1770s and thereafter were very different from what they had been for earlier generations. The economy was already undergoing a momentous transformation, with profound implications for demographic structure. The Malthusian dynamics belonged to the past, even if episodes of hunger persisted.[61]

Wrigley and Schofield have suggested that the rising fertility of the

---

[58] Roderick Floud and Kenneth Wachter, "Poverty and Physical Stature: Evidence on the Standard of Living of London Boys, 1770–1870," *Social Science History* 6 (1982): 422–452.

[59] Wrigley and Schofield, *Population History*, pp. 260, 425.

[60] Goldstone, "Demographic Revolution."

[61] Walter Stern, "The Bread Crisis in Britain, 1795–96," *Economica* 31 (1964): 168–187.

late eighteenth century was a delayed response to the prosperity of the 1730s and 1740s. There has been some skepticism expressed about the plausibility of such long-term effects.[62] Yet the argument put forth here suggests that their finding is plausible in the light of a process that can account for the several generations of elapsed time between the high real wages of the 1730s and the high fertility of the second half of the century.

Summary

The thesis has been expounded that the "Austrian" model is useful in understanding the dynamics of the British economic expansion of the eighteenth century, which is universally referred to as the industrial revolution. The formulation posited a mechanism that linked several structural changes in the economic-demographic regime. The sequence of the model is as follows: (1) prior to 1730 the population of England was essentially in a food-controlled (Malthusian) homeostatic equilibrium, living "close to the tyranny of nature";[63] (2) the favorable weather conditions of the 1730s and the concomitant good harvests destabilized this equilibrium by improving the population's nutritional status, resulting in a baby boom; (3) the increased population density, once the cohorts of the 1730s matured, created market opportunities that fostered economic development; (4) the industrial expansion created opportunities for employment,[64] which meant the end of the Malthusian relationship between population growth and nutritional status; (5) hence population growth and economic expansion could continue without limits.

Thus the upsurge in population growth in the 1730s was the proximate cause of the industrial advances during the second half of the century. By the early eighteenth century, the adverse weather conditions characteristic of the seventeenth century were at an end. Population grew correspondingly. Compared with annual average births of 156,000 in the 1680s and 1690s and 162,000 during the first two de-

---

[62] Peter Lindert and Jeffrey Williamson, "English Workers' Living Standards during the Industrial Revolution: A New Look," *Economic History Review*, 2d ser., 36 (1983): 1–25; Joel Mokyr, "Three Centuries of Population Change," *Economic Development and Cultural Change* 32 (1983): 183–192. There has been an attempt to shorten the effect of real wages on fertility. Jack Goldstone believes that a 20-year lag is more appropriate; see his "Demographic Revolution"; see also Martha L. Olney, "Fertility and the Standard of Living in Early Modern England: In Consideration of Wrigley and Schofield," *Journal of Economic History* 43 (1983): 71–77.

[63] Peter Mathias, "Preface," in R. Max Hartwell, ed., *The Causes of the Industrial Revolution in England* (London and New York: Methuen, 1967), p. 7.

[64] Goldstone, "Demographic Revolution," p. 13.

cades of the eighteenth century, the number of births in the 1730s jumped to 192,000 per annum.[65]

The high nutritional standards attained by the generation of the 1730s and the availability of food imports after mid-century meant that the economy gained time to develop before a nutritional crisis became imminent. This is not to be construed as implying that the unusually good harvests of the 1730s were a precondition for population growth. Yet, without the bountiful harvests of the 1730s, it would have taken much longer to reach the critical mass needed to bring about the market-expanding effects of population growth.

The greater population densities achieved by the 1750s fostered the division of labor, expanded decreasing cost industries, increased both the number of potential inventors and the demand for industrial goods, and, by enlarging the market, made technological and institutional change, such as enclosures, more profitable.[66] With the expansion of the industrial sector, economies of scale were obtained, and labor was no longer faced with the prospect of diminishing returns to its efforts, as was the case in the agricultural sector. Although the standard of living was declining, expansion of the industrial and commercial sectors sufficed to prevent the recurrence of a Malthusian crisis. The beginning of the industrial revolution meant that the Malthusian demographic system was overtaken by the Boserupian one.

The industrial revolution did not mean that aggregate output or output per capita had to grow dramatically. In fact, a number of scholars have recently emphasized how slow growth in such quantitative indicators was. By slow they no doubt mean relative to rates obtained in subsequent centuries. Yet compared with earlier achievements the growth must have been dramatic, in duration if not in intensity. Moreover, previous episodes of population growth had invariably led to subsistence and demographic crises. The essence of the eighteenth-century transformation was not the intensity of the upsurge after 1760, but its duration, and the fact that it could proceed without bringing about a subsistence crisis of major proportions.

Others have pointed to the importance of the good harvests of the 1730s, and of a productive agricultural sector in general, to the onset of

[65] Harvey Leibenstein has recognized that a population might be displaced from its equilibrium state because of a fortuitous increase in average income brought about by favorable weather conditions. If the displacement is large enough, the "system may become unstable and average income may explode." See his *A Theory of Economic-Demographic Development* (Princeton: Princeton University Press: 1954), pp. 31, 66, 102, 194.

[66] Simon S. Kuznets, *Modern Economic Growth: Rate, Structure and Spread* (New Haven: Yale University Press, 1966).

the industrial revolution.[67] Until now the issue has been analyzed in terms of a static framework by assuming that "lower grain prices implied a higher real income for consumers of these commodities, and therefore led to an expansion of industrial demand." Such static effects were arguably inconsequential, because the producers' loss essentially offset the consumers' gain.[68] This line of reasoning, however, is not helpful in understanding dynamic economic processes such as the industrial revolution. The same should be said about exploring the causes of the revolution in terms of the comparative statics of demand and supply. In contrast, the argument expounded in this chapter suggests that the major effect of the good harvests of the 1730s was to bring into being a large number of well-nourished human beings.[69] As this generation entered the labor force, aggregate output was bound to increase faster than it had earlier. By the subsequent generation of the 1770s per capita demand might have fallen, but aggregate demand could still increase, because the number of consumers was larger than ever before. This, in turn, had supply effects, because the enlarged market induced a decline in the cost of production. In this dynamic model, the supply and demand effects are intertwined, and static effects wane in significance.

The model of the industrial revolution outlined above proposes a framework that integrates population growth via the nutritional link into a dynamic process of economic development. Such a model synthesizes the Malthusian with the Boserupian worldview by arguing that by the eighteenth century, economic and nutritional circumstances were propitious for overcoming the Malthusian constraints. The essence of the industrial revolution in this view is not the rates of growth that were achieved, but the fact that for the first time many European societies escaped from the Malthusian trap. Given that the "Austrian" model is useful in analyzing the English experience, in the next chapter the argument is expanded further by suggesting that the dynamics of this conceptualization capture well the salient features of pre-industrial economic and demographic developments in Europe as a whole.

[67] John, "Agricultural Productivity"; Paul Bairoch, *Révolution industrielle et sous-développement* (Paris: Société d'édition d'enseignement supérieur, 1963), p. 30. Bairoch suggests that agricultural progress was the basis of demographic progress in the eighteenth century. He sees the high level of nutrition as a crucial factor, but does not suggest that the demographic revolution was the proximate cause of the industrial revolution. He believes that the industrial revolution and the demographic revolution started at about the same time.

[68] Richard Ippolito, "The Effect of the 'Agricultural Depression' on Industrial Demand in England: 1730–1750," *Economica* 42 (1975): 298–312.

[69] Of course one should also consider the foreign exchange earnings on the grain exports of the 1730s and 1740s, which Ippolito assumes did not matter.

CHAPTER 6

PRE-INDUSTRIAL ECONOMIC GROWTH: A GENERALIZATION OF THE "AUSTRIAN" MODEL

HAVING outlined the dynamics of the industrial revolution in the Habsburg Monarchy, and having argued in the previous chapter that the same conceptualization is useful in understanding British economic growth in the eighteenth century, I now turn to expanding the model. In this chapter I suggest that the salient features of pre-industrial European economic development conform, in the main, to the framework abstracted from the Habsburg experience. The essence of the "Austrian" model is that the industrial revolution was preceded by population growth, which, in turn, brought with it not only the benefits of a higher population density, but also the threat of a Malthusian nutritional crisis. By asserting that both of these forces were evident simultaneously, the model synthesizes the Malthusian and Boserupian worldviews. The argument is now advanced that episodes of population expansion in prior centuries also carried with them these opposing tendencies. The great economic expansions of the Middle Ages and of the sixteenth century were both population driven. Whereas in earlier centuries the Malthusian effect eventually gained the upper hand, by the eighteenth century the European economies were sufficiently well developed that the Boserupian effect could dominate. The mathematical version of the model is presented in Appendix C.

Hitherto the industrial revolution was considered either as a sudden break with the past, or as an outgrowth of processes that had begun in the Middle Ages or even earlier. The present conceptualization synthe-

207

sizes these two views by arguing that the industrial revolution can be thought of as part of a process of economic development begun centuries, perhaps millennia earlier. Yet these same processes could give rise to discontinuities in the growth of many economic and demographic variables during the second half of the eighteenth century. There is, in other words, no inherent contradiction between the evolutionary nature of the economic development that culminated in the industrial revolution and the manifest discontinuity in the rate at which output, the labor force, and output per capita grew in its wake. The industrial revolution should be thought of not as a structural break with the past, but as an integral part of the economic experience of the previous millennia.[1]

From the economic point of view the period extending from the Neolithic agricultural revolution to the industrial revolution can be considered as a unity, because the economies were overwhelmingly agricultural throughout this epoch. The economy of hunters and gatherers which preceded it, as well as that of the twentieth-century industrial world which followed in its wake, can both be characterized by a significantly different production relationship from that of the agricultural societies of the intervening millennia. In the nineteenth century the demographic regime was no longer Malthusian, and the European economy was becoming less and less agricultural. Moreover, scientific knowledge was applied in earnest to solve technological and economic problems. These characteristics made the new economy fundamentally different from the structure that had prevailed during the prior centuries. Douglass North suggests in this regard that "the First Economic Revolution created agriculture and 'civilization'; the Second created an elastic supply curve of new knowledge which built economic growth into the system. . . . Both economic revolutions deserve the title because

---

[1] Carlo Cipolla, *The Economic History of World Population* (1962; reprint, Baltimore: Penguin Books, 1970); Eric L. Jones suggests in *The European Miracle: Environments, Economies, and Geopolitics in the History of Europe and Asia* (Cambridge, England: Cambridge University Press, 1981), p. 225, that industrialization was "not a thunderstorm that suddenly arrived overhead but a growth deeply rooted in the past." In a similar vein, Jan De Vries suggests that ". . . the middle of the nineteenth century—one might say the beginning of the railway age—is a worthier candidate for the title of threshold to the era of universal urbanization" than "the conventional use of 1800 as a dividing line." *European Urbanization, 1500–1800* (Cambridge, MA: Harvard University Press, 1984), p. 44. Daniel Christ likewise argues that ". . . without the preceding millennial rise of the West, the story of England's industrial revolution would have been entirely unthinkable." "The Rise of the West," *American Sociological Review* 50 (1985): 181–195. For another study emphasizing the continuity of economic processes in Europe, see David J. Herlihy, "The Economy of Traditional Europe," *Journal of Economic History* 31 (1971): 153–164.

they altered the slope of the long-run supply curve of output so as to permit continuing population growth without the dismal consequences of the classical economic model."[2]

From the point of view of the demographic system, too, the ten millennia separating the two revolutions can be considered as a unity, because population growth was slow and setbacks were frequent. Prior to the Neolithic agricultural revolution population grew perhaps at a rate of 0.0015 percent per annum. Although this rate was extremely slow, it nevertheless meant that population doubled every 50,000 years. After the agricultural revolution the rate of population growth increased perhaps by a factor of 24, to 0.036 percent per year, a rate maintained until the beginning of our time. Thereafter growth accelerated again to 0.056 percent per year until the middle of the eighteenth century, when it increased by a factor of ten.[3]

Moreover, I shall argue that the industrial revolution of the eighteenth century was an integral part of the epoch that preceded it, that it grew out of this epoch, and that hence it ought not to be seen as a great discontinuity. North, too, suggests that the industrial revolution "was the evolutionary culmination of a series of prior events."[4] Although not reaching as far back as North does into the Neolithic past, Rondo Cameron's view reinforces the notion of continuity in economic development. He argues that the events of the eighteenth century were the consequence of "a long, drawn out process, in no sense inevitable, which scarcely deserves the epithet 'revolutionary.' "[5]

[2] Douglass C. North, *Structure and Change in Economic History* (New York: Norton, 1981).

[3] Ansley J. Coale, "History of the Human Population," *Scientific American* 231 (September 1974): 40–51; John D. Durand, "The Modern Expansion of World Population," in Thomas R. Detwyler, ed., *Man's Impact on Environment* (New York: McGraw-Hill, 1971), pp. 36–49, reprinted from *Proceedings of the American Philosophical Society*, 111 (1967): 136–145; idem, "Historical Estimates of World Population: An Evaluation," *Population and Development Review* 3 (1977): 253–296; Colin McEvedy and Richard Jones, *Atlas of World Population History* (New York: Penguin Books, 1978); Jean-Nöel Biraben, "Essai sur l'évolution du nombre des hommes," *Population* 34 (1979): 13–25; Robert M. Schacht, "Estimating Past Population Trends," *Annual Review of Anthropology* 10 (1981): 119–140. For several centuries the population growth rate in the western Mediterranean region was −0.0013 per annum. McNeill attributes this decline to epidemiological disaster. William H. McNeill, *Plagues and Peoples* (Garden City, NY: Anchor Press, 1976), p. 115.

[4] North, *Structure and Change*, p. 162.

[5] Rondo Cameron, "The Industrial Revolution: A Misnomer," *The History Teacher* 15 (1982): 377–384; idem, "A New View of European Industrialization," *Economic History Review*, 2d ser., 38 (1985): 1–23.

EXTENSIONS

The Malthusian Assumptions

The epoch under consideration was essentially Malthusian in the sense that there was an incessant contest between population growth and society's resource base, which included natural as well as reproducible capital.[6] The present consensus is that in the pre-industrial world, population growth was essentially food controlled.[7] With the capital stock and improved land growing slower than population, and with technological progress sporadic, rapid population growth led to diminishing returns to labor, and eventually resulted in a nutritional crisis. Yet population tended to reproduce, because there were long periods during which subsistence was above the critical level. Indeed, North noted that as long "as the standard of life was above a certain level, there was a tendency for man to increase in numbers."[8]

Hence prior to the eighteenth century the human population had a tendency to increase, but as it did, food output per capita eventually declined because of diminishing returns to labor, until the available nutrients did not suffice to sustain a healthy and growing population. In addition, exogenous climatic variations affected food output and thereby had an impact on the nutritional status of the population.[9] The severity of these climatic shocks depended to some extent on the degree to which the nutritional status of the population had already deteriorated.[10] Malthusian positive checks (mortality crises) maintained a long-

[6] Harvey Leibenstein, *A Theory of Economic-Demographic Development* (Princeton: Princeton University Press, 1954), p. 8; Thomas R. Malthus, *An Essay on the Principle of Population*, (1798; reprint, New York: Norton, 1976).

[7] Roger S. Schofield, "The Impact of Scarcity and Plenty on Population Change in England, 1541–1871," *Journal of Interdisciplinary History* 14 (1983): 265–291; Ronald Demos Lee, "Population Homeostasis and English Demographic History," *Journal of Interdisciplinary History* 15 (1985): 635–660; Zvi Eckstein, T. Paul Schultz, and Kenneth I. Wolpin, "Short-Run Fluctuations in Fertility and Mortality in Pre-Industrial Sweden," *European Economic Review* 26 (1984): 295–317; Peter Lindert, "English Population, Wages, and Prices: 1541–1913," *Journal of Interdisciplinary History* 15 (1985): 609–634; Paul M. Hohenberg and Lynn Hollen Lees, *The Making of Urban Europe, 1000–1950* (Cambridge, MA: Harvard University Press, 1985), p. 78; Thomas McKeown, *The Modern Rise of Population* (New York: Academic Press, 1976).

[8] North, *Structure and Change*, p. 83.

[9] Patrick R. Galloway, "Long-Term Fluctuations in Climate and Population in the Preindustrial Era," *Population and Development Review* 12 (1986): 1–24.

[10] Carl E. Taylor, "Synergy among Mass Infections, Famines, and Poverty," *Journal of Interdisciplinary History* 14 (1983): 483–501; Robert W. Fogel, "Nutrition and the Decline in Mortality since 1700: Some Preliminary Findings," in Stanley L. Engerman and Robert Gallman, eds., *Long-Term Factors in American Economic Growth*, National Bureau of Economic Research, Studies in Income and Wealth, vol. 51 (Chicago: The University of Chicago Press, 1987), pp. 439–555.

run equilibrium between population size and the food supply. To be sure, not all diseases are nutrition sensitive, but the devastation wrought by epidemics frequently depended on population densities as well as on the experience of the society in dealing with previous calamities. It is true that negative checks, what Malthus called "moral restraint," also played a part in maintaining a balance between the human population and the resource base. These controls, however, were adopted relatively late in human experience, and were not always effective in maintaining homeostasis.

Crises followed by periods when human nutritional status was above the level of subsistence gave rise to cycles. Although the secular trend of economic activity was ever upward, the cycles testify to the continued existence of the "Malthusian population trap": population could not grow beyond an upper bound imposed by the resource and capital constraints of the economic structure in which it was imbedded.[11] The "escape" from this trap did not occur until the aggregate capital stock was large enough and grew fast enough to provide additional sustenance for the population, which thereby overcame the effects of the diminishing returns that had hindered human progress during the previous millennia. After escaping from the Malthusian trap, population was able to grow unchecked. In historical terms, this escape corresponds to the industrial and demographic revolutions. Through the accumulation of capital, the food-producing sector could accelerate production sufficiently quickly to outpace population growth. Removal of the nutritional constraint, at least for the developed part of the world, resulted in a population explosion.[12]

The warrant for using the Malthusian model comes from investigations that outline the evolution of the population and the economy during the last thousand years. Numerous studies document the "incessant contest" between population growth and the society's resource base.[13] "Before 1800, the situation developed much as Malthus had insisted it must: the faster the population grew, the faster food prices rose, the

[11] For a description of the Malthusian dynamics see H. J. Habakkuk, "English Population in the Eighteenth Century," *Economic History Review*, 2d ser., 6 (1953): 117–133.

[12] Thomas McKeown, "Food, Infection, and Population," *Journal of Interdisciplinary History* 14 (1983): 227–247; Stephen J. Kunitz, "Speculations on the European Mortality Decline," *Economic History Review* 36 (1983): 349–364.

[13] Michael M. Postan, *The Medieval Economy and Society: An Economic History of Britain in the Middle Ages* (London: Weidenfeld and Nicolson, 1972); Wilhelm Abel, *Agrarkrisen und Agrarkonjunktur: Eine Geschichte der Land- und Ernährungswirtschaft Mitteleuropas seit dem hohen Mittelalter* (1935; reprint, Hamburg and Berlin: Paul Parey, 1966); idem, *Massenarmut und Hungerkrisen im vorindustriellen Europa* (Hamburg and Berlin: Paul Parey, 1974).

lower living standards fell, and the grimmer the struggle to exist became. As Malthus had postulated, there were indeed long, slow oscillations in the rate of population growth and in the standards of living."[14] Overpopulation contributed greatly to the utter collapse of the European economy in the fourteenth century, when the number of Europe's inhabitants suddenly declined by about a third. The plague might have been the proximate cause of this collapse, but the epidemic attacked a nutritionally weakened population. In fact, "in the course of the thirteenth century . . . agricultural yield, tended to fall off [in England as] . . . land was nearing exhaustion."[15] In some places the population decline began well before the outbreak of the epidemic. By the early fourteenth century, the poor were allegedly dying by the millions from hunger,[16] and in Great Britain cannibalism was even recorded. "The steadily increasing overpopulation in the thirteenth century must have led to malnutrition. . . . The high mortality . . . can only be explained as the result of prolonged undernourishment."[17]

The expansion of European commerce during the prior centuries, itself related to increased population size, also contributed to the onset of the plague, because the introduction and transmission of the disease depended critically on the frequency of shipping and the level of urbani-

[14] Schofield, "Impact of Scarcity and Plenty."

[15] Georges Duby, "Medieval Agriculture, 900–1500," in Carlo Cipolla, ed., *The Fontana Economic History of Europe* (London: William Collins and Sons, 1972), vol. 1, *The Middle Ages*, pp. 175–220; L. R. Poos, "The Rural Population of Essex in the Later Middle Ages," *Economic History Review*, 2d ser., 38 (1985): 515–530; Galloway, "Long-Term Fluctuations," p. 20. Climatic deterioration also hampered population growth: the increased frequency of volcanic eruptions and a decline in solar activity caused a decrease in mean temperatures; a succession of wet years during the second decade of the fourteenth century contributed to the decline in agricultural output even prior to the outbreak of plague. C. U. Hammer, H. B. Clausen, and W. Dansgaard, "Greenland Ice Sheet Evidence of Post-Glacial Volcanism and Its Climatic Impact," *Nature* (Nov. 20, 1980): 230, as cited by Mary Kilbourne Matossian, "Volcanic Activity and Disease in Europe, 1550–1900," unpublished manuscript, Department of History, University of Maryland, 1986; John A. Eddy, "Climate and the Role of the Sun," in Robert I. Rotberg and Theodore K. Rabb, eds., *Climate and History: Studies in Interdisciplinary History* (Princeton: Princeton University Press, 1981), pp. 145–167.

[16] Emmanuel Le Roy Ladurie, *Times of Feast, Times of Famine: A History of Climate since the Year 1000* (Garden City, NY: Doubleday, 1971), pp. 8, 12, 13; David J. Herlihy, *Medieval and Renaissance Pistoia: The Social History of an Italian Town, 1200–1430* (New Haven: Yale University Press, 1967), p. 69. On cannibalism in Germany see: Hans J. Teuteberg and Günter Wiegelmann, *Der Wandel der Nahrungsgewohnheiten unter dem Einfluss der Industrialisierung* (Göttingen: Vandenhoeck und Ruprecht, 1972), p. 70.

[17] B. H. Slicher van Bath, *The Agrarian History of Western Europe, A.D. 500–1850*, translated by Olive Ordish (London: Edward Arnold, 1963), p. 89.

zation.[18] The spread of the epidemic, too, was a function of population densities. "Opportunities for transfer of disease from one host to another multiply with increased human density, so that, if and when the critical threshold is surpassed, infection can suddenly develop into runaway hyperinfection."[19] A possible reason that the black death was less severe in Eastern Europe than in the Northwest was that population density in the former region was lower.[20] Hence, the fact that the collapse of the European population at the end of the Middle Ages occurred at a time when population densities there were higher than ever before ought not to be considered accidental.[21]

Moreover, population growth tended to be conducive to urbanization, and this brought with it the difficulty of producing and transporting sufficient food for the urban sector. Consider that Rome had a population of 150,000 in 200 B.C. and within the next 300 years reached 650,000.[22] The problem of food procurement, given the agricultural technology of the time, must have increased greatly. Pirenne noticed that population growth in the Middle Ages resulted in a "detaching

[18] "For ports, the rate of gain of rats would depend on the frequency of arrival of ships. . . . Persistence of populations of rats would have required frequent arrivals of ships from the Mediterranean, where rats were widely distributed." They were present there already in ancient times. "During Roman times, frequent voyages and large port cities encouraged the establishment of rats in Britain and other European countries. But in the early Middle Ages the decline in shipping resulted in the extinction of rats in most cities of the north. . . . But the increase in shipping and the size of ports in Columbian times released an avalanche of rats. . . ." David E. Davis, "The Scarcity of Rats and the Black Death: An Ecological History," *Journal of Interdisciplinary History* 16 (1986): 455–470.

[19] McNeill, *Plagues and Peoples*, p. 23; McKeown, "Food," p. 243.

[20] Hohenberg and Lees, *Making of Urban Europe*, p. 9.

[21] Yet one should not view the relationship between population densities and demographic crises in a deterministic fashion. A leading French historian has pointed out that "there are some very considerable examples, lasting over several centuries, of rural civilizations departing a long way from this 'position of equilibrium,' to return to it gradually later on." Emmanuel Le Roy Ladurie, *The Territory of the Historian* (Chicago: The University of Chicago Press, 1979), p. 95.

[22] After the eleventh century, commercialization and urbanization of Europe also proceeded at a faster rate than population growth itself. The growth of Paris was just as spectacular as the decline of Rome had been. The population of Paris was 20,000 in the tenth century; in 1200 it was already 110,000 and by 1300 was, at 228,000, the largest city in Europe. Yet in 1600 its population was still only 250,000. Tertius Chandler and Gerald Fox, *3000 Years of Urban Growth* (New York: Academic Press, 1974), pp. 302, 375. On the ecological problems in the Roman Empire see David J. Herlihy, "Attitudes Toward the Environment in Medieval Society," in Lester J. Bilsky, ed., *Historical Ecology: Essays on Environment and Social Change* (Port Washington, NY: Kennikat Press, 1980), pp. 100–116; Charles R. Bowlus, "Ecological Crises in Fourteenth Century Europe," in Bilsky, *Historical Ecology*, pp. 86–99.

from the land of an increasingly important number of individuals."[23] Hence urbanization in the Middle Ages, too, must have brought with it the intrinsic problem of feeding the part of the population no longer on the land.

Urbanization had many positive effects on economic development, but it also exacerbated the precarious balance between the food supply and population size. At such a conjuncture climatic variation could have a potent effect on the availability of nutrients. Small changes in weather conditions could then produce great variations in the food supply available to the urban sector. Hence the European population was regularly decimated, but after each demographic crisis the nutritional status of the population could improve. The livestock available on a per capita basis must have increased, which meant that protein intake could rise. The population could reproduce and recover once again to its previous levels.

Marked improvements in the diet after the black death, particularly increases in the intake of animal protein, brought about a recovery of the population during the course of the fifteenth century, and production grew correspondingly.[24] Thereafter, "the race between population and production was on again." While the recovery of the fifteenth century was quicker than the previous one of the early Middle Ages, by the sixteenth century the "Malthusian scissors" were opening up again. French tithe statistics confirm that the ceiling on grain output reached during the fourteenth century was not surpassed in either the sixteenth or the seventeenth centuries.[25] Presumably, the European societies were not yet capable of accumulating resources quickly enough to emancipate the population from the Malthusian menace.

The rapid population growth of the sixteenth century culminated in

[23] Henri Pirenne, *Medieval Cities: Their Origins and the Revival of Trade*, translated by Frank Halsey (Princeton: Princeton University Press, 1925; paperback ed., 1969), p. 114. Herodotus pointed to the vulnerability of towns in the Ancient World by stating: "the cities that were formerly great have most of them become insignificant; and such as are at present powerful, were weak in olden time." De Vries, *European Urbanization*, p. 121; Hohenberg and Lees, *Making of Urban Europe*, p. 9.

[24] Ch. Dyer, "Changes in Nutrition and Standard of Living in England, 1200–1500," in Robert W. Fogel, ed., *Long-Term Changes in Nutrition and the Standard of Living* (Berne: 9th Congress of the International Economic History Association, 1986), pp. 35–44; Teuteberg and Wiegelmann, *Der Wandel der Nahrungsgewohnheiten*, p. 64.

[25] Emmanuel Le Roy Ladurie and Joseph Goy, *Tithe and Agrarian History from the Fourteenth to the Nineteenth Centuries: An Essay in Comparative History*, translated by Susan Burke (Cambridge, England: Cambridge University Press, 1982), p. 73. By the end of the sixteenth century, a cooling trend in the weather was having an unfavorable effect on agricultural production. Le Roy Ladurie, *Times of Feast*, pp. 9, 21, 58, 158; Galloway, "Long-Term Fluctuations"; Le Roy Ladurie, *Territory of the Historian*, pp. 12, 25, 88.

the crisis of the seventeenth century. Although the effect of population pressure was no longer as severe as it had been in the fourteenth century,[26] the plague did strike some parts of Europe again.[27] The economies of Germany, France, Hungary, and Spain were perhaps hurt more by the crisis than those of Holland and England, which got through the century relatively unscathed.[28] The famine of 1693, one of the worst to visit Western Europe since the Middle Ages, "turned France into a big, desolate hospital without provisions."[29] Population pressure was mitigated by the creation of market channels with East European grain markets, which had not existed in the fourteenth century. Preventive checks became more prevalent as a means of keeping population growth within manageable bounds.[30] The conclusion is inescapable: in pre-industrial Europe diminishing returns to agricultural labor often imposed an effective constraint on further population growth.[31]

Although the seventeenth century witnessed the last prolonged demographic crisis in Europe, in the eighteenth century, too, a Malthusian crisis threatened in the wake of an acceleration in population growth. The fact that nutritional status was deteriorating is shown by the declining height of men born after mid-century.[32] In contrast to prior centuries, a crisis was averted in the eighteenth century, either because the economy was strong enough to overcome the threat or, as in the Habsburg domains, because the central authorities had sufficient financial resources to come to the aid of the destitute, and had the organizational capability to bring about institutional change, a prerequisite for absorbing the growing labor force into the economy.

A certain organizational sophistication in disaster management was needed to enable the government to avert an impending crisis. Maria Theresia, for instance, sent substantial aid to the poverty-stricken peas-

[26] Le Roy Ladurie, *Times of Feast*, p. 90.

[27] George Alter, "Plague and the Amsterdam Annuitant: A New Look at Life Annuities as a Source for Historical Demography," *Population Studies* 37 (1983): 23–41.

[28] North, *Structure and Change*.

[29] Le Roy Ladurie, *Times of Feast*, p. 90.

[30] E. Anthony Wrigley and Roger S. Schofield, *The Population History of England, 1541–1871: A Reconstruction* (Cambridge, MA: Harvard University Press, 1981).

[31] W. A. Coale and Phyllis Deane, "The Growth of National Incomes," in H. J. Habakkuk and Michael M. Postan, eds., *Cambridge Economic History of Europe* (Cambridge, England: Cambridge University Press, 1965), vol. 6, *The Industrial Revolution and After: Incomes, Population and Technological Change*, pp. 1–55.

[32] In prior centuries, human stature had also fluctuated with the availability of the food supply. Helmut Wurm, "The Fluctuations of Average Stature in the Course of German History and the Influence of the Protein Content of the Diet," *Journal of Human Evolution* 13 (1984): 331–334.

ants of Bohemia during the subsistence crisis of 1770–71. In more backward countries the impact of the crisis was more severe. In Moldavia, for example, as late as 1770 three hundred thousand died of the plague.[33]

Rondo Cameron has pointed to the cycles outlined above as characteristic of European economic development, referring to them as logistics because of their similarity to the elongated S-shaped curve described by the mathematical formula with this name. Population grew in each of these logistics, separated by periods of decline or deceleration. He suggests that these logistics provide a "convenient framework for a history of European economic development." He points to the phenomenon of diminishing returns becoming evident during the decelerating phase of each of the logistics, at which time "conditions of life were becoming increasingly difficult." Cameron concludes "that mankind has repeatedly postponed the Malthusian dilemma by means of technological and institutional innovations that have increased the supply of food."[34]

Over time the cycles became less severe and of shorter duration. Four hundred years elapsed between the apex of population in A.D. 200 and the nadir reached in A.D. 600. The next apex took another 700 years to reach. The following cycle was considerably shorter—300 years, from 1300 to 1600. The subsequent cycle lasted about a century and a half. At last, the downturn could be averted in the second half of the eighteenth century, because European societies had become sufficiently sophisticated to mobilize resources to overcome the threat, and the accumulated capital stock was large enough, and grew quickly enough, to enable the population to grow unhindered. The overall pattern, in which the severity of the cyclical downturns diminished over time until they vanished entirely, indicates that the ability of socioeconomic and political structures to cope with the rising population increased slowly until the eventual breakthrough of the eighteenth century.

Capital Accumulation

In addition to the Malthusian demographic regime, another important feature of the pre-industrial European economic system was the accumulation of capital and technology in the long run, a feature re-

[33] In Bengal, ten million people perished through famine in 1769 and 1770. Jones, *The European Miracle*, pp. 29, 32, 139.

[34] Rondo Cameron, "The Logistics of European Economic Growth: A Note on Historical Periodization," *Journal of European Economic History* 2 (1973): 145–148; idem, "Economic History, Pure and Applied," *Journal of Economic History* 36 (1976): 3–27.

cently emphasized by E. L. Jones. He referred to the propensity of productivity to increase slowly but incessantly as "technological drift."[35] Under the concept of capital one should include not only human and physical capital in the usual senses but also knowledge, broadly conceived, as well as the creation of institutions that improved the efficiency of markets, because the latter could lower the costs of production, shift the production function, and thereby raise productivity. Jones argues that improvements in the routine administration of government and the creation of a legal framework consistently applied are very important aspects of the long-term European growth record.[36] Institutions conducive to growth contribute greatly to "the progress and retrogression of societies."[37] Of course, institutions can also raise transaction costs and even create bottlenecks. Yet the essence of the European experience over time has been the creation of an institutional infrastructure that fostered development. Clearly, developing efficient property rights is part of this record, since a legal system conducive to economic development is an important feature of economies that grow.[38]

Human capital should, in addition to education, include such gains made by the human species as the increased immunity and resistance to disease that were acquired slowly through recurrent exposure. When an infection attacks a population previously unexposed to the disease, the epidemic can assume immense proportions; however, many diseases subsequently cause the production of antibodies, thereby providing a safeguard against future attacks. An example is provided by the decline of the Roman population, which was devastated by the arrival of smallpox or measles. By the sixteenth century, however, in Europe these diseases afflicted mainly children, and no longer devastated the adult population, as they had upon their first arrival. With the expansion of commerce and European contact with the rest of the world, the "likelihood of a really devastating disease encounter" in Europe was reduced. Increased resistance to diseases raised labor productivity, and therefore was tantamount to a large-scale increase in the accumulated stock of human capital. One reason why human-capital formation in Africa was more difficult than in Europe was that African populations had to face a different disease environment: "many of the parasitic worms and pro-

---

[35] Jones, *The European Miracle*, p. 69.

[36] North, *Structure and Change*, pp. 59, 167.

[37] Douglass C. North and Robert P. Thomas, *The Rise of the Western World: A New Economic History* (Cambridge, England: Cambridge University Press, 1973).

[38] Economic organization was getting more efficient not only in early modern times, but even during the long period between the origins of agriculture and the decline of the Roman Empire. North, *Structure and Change*, p. 64.

tozoa that abound in Africa do not provoke . . . the formation of antibodies in the bloodstream."[39]

Another factor to stress is that capital depreciation was not an important aspect of the European experience. The capital stock, as defined here, includes organizational know-how, knowledge about how to manipulate the environment, and immunity from certain diseases, and these seldom depreciated over time. Knowledge does not diminish by being used, as do physical resources. "The accumulation in the stock of knowledge has largely been irreversible throughout history," observes North, "but human economic progress has not: the rise and decline of . . . entire civilizations, are certainly indisputable."[40] In addition, Jones has argued that the European capital stock was quite immune to destruction through natural disasters, partly because "geophysically and climatically, Europe is quieter than most other parts of the world."[41]

Of course, one can cite examples of capital destruction even in the European context. Yet Jones's argument is that in Europe, accumulation was much more important than capital depreciation. In Europe capital was not systematically destroyed, and that is an important way in which Europe differed from the Orient.[42] Although there were exceptions, the European instinct was to accumulate, and the political and geophysical environment favored such accumulation.

Boserupian Episodes

In contrast to the Malthusian view, some scholars emphasize the beneficial effects of population growth by arguing that such growth fosters technological change in the long run.[43] Population growth leads to ur-

[39] McNeill, *Plagues and Peoples*, pp. 3, 12, 23, 223. The drawback in conceiving of capital stock so broadly is that it defies quantification, although some proxies, such as the number of books printed, could be constructed to quantify knowledge. Yet because of lack of data, even ordinary, reproducible capital cannot be measured for the years prior to the eighteenth century. Hence this problem is moot: currently, all capital eludes measurement for the pre-modern period.

[40] North, *Structure and Change*, p. 59.

[41] Jones, *The European Miracle*, p. 61.

[42] Is it a mere coincidence that cities proliferated in the Middle Ages in areas that had previously belonged to the Roman Empire, or did the existence of an infrastructure, even in a dilapidated state, lower the cost of European urbanization? Hohenberg and Lees, *Making of Urban Europe*, p. 27. In 1500, 71 percent of European cities with a population in excess of 10,000 were located in the formerly Romanized world. De Vries, *European Urbanization*, p. 28. The spread of forests in Europe in the late fourteenth and early fifteenth centuries indicates that agricultural capital built up by earlier generations deteriorated. Yet subsequently it was easier to clear the forests again than it had been initially.

[43] Ester Boserup, *Population and Technological Change: A Study of Long-Term Trends* (Chicago: University of Chicago Press, 1981); idem, *The Conditions of Agricultural*

banization, which fosters the creation of knowledge.[44] Higher population densities, because they lower transaction costs, are conducive to the widening of the market, which in turn leads to market integration and further division of labor. In addition, as the market for a product grows enterprises can grow in size, thereby capturing economies of scale and enabling externalities to be captured, resulting in decreasing average costs for whole industries. Population pressure can induce governments to institute reforms that foster production. Hence in the long term, population growth can be quite conducive to economic growth.

In the European experience, population growth and economic growth were intertwined. During the three major phases of economic expansion—in the Middle Ages, during the sixteenth century, and during the eighteenth century—population grew rapidly. In contrast, during the crisis of the seventeenth century European population declined or stagnated.

A Synthesis

These three strands of thought can now be synthesized within the framework of the "Austrian" model. Population tended to grow until the food supply became limited or until population densities increased the probability of epidemics, given the state of public health and the medical technology of the time. Although a crisis eventually ensued, the incessant process of capital accumulation meant that the European societies faced each subsequent crisis with a higher capital/labor ratio than previously. The nutritional or epidemiological crisis might decimate the population, but left the stock of animals untouched. Hence, the decline in population density increased the amount of food available per capita, and demographic crises were followed by long periods of rising nutritional status and population growth.

Growth (Chicago: Aldine Publishing, 1965); Julian L. Simon, *Theory of Population and Economic Growth* (Oxford: Basil Blackwell, 1986); Gunter Steinmann, "A Model of the History of Demographic-Economic Growth," in Gunter Steinmann, ed., *Economic Consequences of Population Change in Industrialized Countries. Proceedings of the Conference on Population Economics Held at the University of Paderborn, West Germany, June 1–June 3, 1983. Studies in Contemporary Economics*, vol. 8 (Berlin: Springer-Verlag, 1984), pp. 29–49.

[44] Simon Kuznets noticed that high population densities foster the creation of knowledge. He suggested that "creative effort flourishes in a dense intellectual atmosphere, and it is hardly an accident that the locus of intellectual progress . . . has been preponderantly in the larger cities, not in the bucolic surroundings of the thinly settled countryside." Simon S. Kuznets, "Population Change and Aggregate Output," in *Demographic and Economic Change in Developed Countries: A Conference of the Universities-National Bureau of Economic Research* (Princeton: Princeton University Press, 1960), p. 329.

Thus the cycle continued. Population growth fostered urbanization, knowledge creation, and the expansion of the market, but the degree to which it could continue was constrained by the availability of nutrients. Because agricultural technology was slowly improving, and because trade was bringing new agricultural regions within reach of Northwest Europe, each episode of population growth led to higher population densities than ever before. These episodes fostered the expansion of the market, even if a crisis might ensue. The cycle of population growth, capital accumulation, market expansion, and crisis, followed by population growth again, could proceed until by the eighteenth century the European societies were sufficiently advanced to break out of the Malthusian trap.

The industrial revolution can therefore be conceptualized as an "escape" from the Malthusian demographic trap. It was a period of both economic and demographic expansion similar to the ones that Europe had experienced in prior centuries. In the eighteenth century, however, a major subsistence crisis could be averted, because the supply of nutrients sufficed to maintain a growing population. This was achieved not only because domestic agriculture was more productive than during the previous expansionary phase (in the sixteenth century), but also because East European and colonial food supplies were available to a greater degree than ever before.[45]

This framework retains the Malthusian effects of population growth, but superimposes on them "Boserupian episodes," during which rapid population growth had positive economic effects. In the meantime capital accumulation led to slow shifts in the production function and to rising labor productivity. Each episode of population growth led to a Malthusian crisis, but each subsequent crisis was faced with a larger resource base, thereby increasing the probability that the accumulated stock of capital would eventually suffice to overcome the Malthusian threat. Although the Malthusian effect dominated during the pre-industrial epoch, the Boserupian effect did eventually gain the upper hand: the Malthusian ceiling was permanently lifted during the industrial revolution.

Summary

This conceptualization stresses, as does Jones, the importance of the slow but persistent accumulation of capital through time, which ulti-

---

[45] Arcadius Kahan, *The Plow, the Hammer, and the Knout: An Economic History of Eighteenth-Century Russia* (Chicago: The University of Chicago Press, 1985), p. 59.

mately enabled the Europeans to emancipate themselves from the Malthusian menace. Once the food constraint was lifted for Europeans, population growth could proceed, leading to further economic gains; this process had important feedback effects. Thus economic growth became "self-sustaining" after the industrial revolution, differing from the previous upswings only in that the nutritional constraint was no longer binding, and therefore population could expand unhindered by positive checks. While slow population growth had hindered economic expansion prior to the eighteenth century, in the nineteenth this was no longer a factor. Thousands of years of very slow economic growth could be followed by a period of extremely rapid growth without any fundamental transformation in the relations of production and reproduction. Although there was no structural break in the economy, output and per capita output could grow faster for a longer period of time than ever before.

Yet the saving rate did not need to increase for output to expand exponentially. For the economy to escape permanently from the Malthusian constraint, two criteria had to be satisfied. First, the level of capital stock had to be sufficiently large so that enough nutrients could be produced or imported to sustain a growing population increasingly concentrated in the urban-industrial sector. Moreover, productivity in the industrial sector had to be sufficiently high to enable its products to be exchanged for nutrients through international trade on favorable terms. Once this level of performance was reached, enough food could be obtained to maintain the nutritional status of a growing population above the minimum needed for subsistence. The capital-diluting effect of population growth could be overcome by a rise in the rate at which the capital stock grew, but initially this increase was brought about not by a rise in the rate of saving, but through a rise in the share of the population producing capital. Thus it was important that the eighteenth-century growth in population started from a high technological base and with a large segment of the population already in the urban sector.

The notion that the share of the population in the commercial-industrial-urban sector must fall within a critical range at the time of escape is intuitively plausible. If the share of population in this sector were too large, the food-producing sector could not have produced enough nourishment to maintain the nutritional status of the population. If, however, the share of the population in the nonagricultural sector were below a threshold level, then capital could not be augmented fast enough to overcome the capital-diluting effect of population growth. Once these critical conditions were met in the eighteenth century, the economy was poised for an escape from the Malthusian trap.

221

In this model the industrial revolution is conceptualized as the culmination of a process begun millennia before, rather than as a fundamental break with prior developments. Population growth is seen as having had both positive and negative economic consequences. On the one hand, population growth led to a deterioration of nutritional status and consequently to innumerable subsistence crises, which temporarily hindered further growth. Yet over time the capital stock was augmented, which was of great value to subsequent generations. In spite of recurrent setbacks, the non-nutrient-producing population was able to expand in the long run precisely because each new phase of population expansion began with a greater stock of accumulated capital. Hence, over many cycles both population and capital stock increased. Eventually, with the accumulation of capital and the increase of the share of the population in the urban-industrial sector, the stock of capital grew fast enough to overcome the Malthusian constraints permanently. The industrial revolution was under way. Population growth was therefore the proximate cause of the industrial revolution, but the achievements of the previous millennia were the preconditions for sustaining the economic momentum brought about by the rise in population. (A mathematical version of this model capable of simulating the salient features of European economic development, as outlined above, is presented in Appendix C.)

The industrial revolution of the eighteenth century, in the words of David Landes, "lifted beyond visible limits the ceiling of Malthus's positive checks."[46] The industrial revolution, like the previous population expansions of the thirteenth and sixteenth centuries, coincided with the beginning of a subsistence crisis. By the eighteenth century, however, the accumulated stock of capital and the high rate of urbanization sufficed to enable the European societies to break out of the Malthusian trap and reverse the decline in nutritional status. While this model is Malthusian, it nonetheless allows the effects of population growth to be other than capital diluting in the long run. By synthesizing the Malthusian and Boserupian worldviews, the model integrates the industrial revolution into the economic and demographic processes of the preindustrial world.[47] Almost half a century ago, Sir John Hicks anticipated

---

[46] David S. Landes, *The Unbound Prometheus: Technological Change and Industrial Development in Western Europe from 1750 to the Present* (Cambridge, England: Cambridge University Press, 1969), p. 41.

[47] For other syntheses of the Malthusian and Boserupian ideas see Ronald Demos Lee, "Malthus and Boserup: A Dynamic Synthesis," in David Coleman and Roger Schofield, eds., *The State of Population Theory. Forward from Malthus* (Oxford: Basil Blackwell, 1986); Frederic L. Pryor and Stephen B. Maurer, "On Induced Economic Change in Precapitalist

the "Austrian" model of the industrial revolution when he noted in an obscure footnote that ". . . one cannot repress the thought that perhaps the whole industrial revolution of the last two hundred years has been nothing else but a vast secular boom, largely induced by the unparalleled rise in population."[48]

Societies," *Journal of Development Economics* 10 (1982): 325–353; Warren Robinson and Wayne Schutjer, "Agricultural Development and Demographic Change: A Generalization of the Boserup Model," *Economic Development and Cultural Change* 32 (1984): 355–366.

[48] John R. Hicks, *Value and Capital: An Inquiry into Some Fundamental Principles of Economic Theory*, 2d ed. (Oxford: Clarendon Press, 1939), p. 302.

APPENDIX A

RECRUITING PRACTICES OF
THE HABSBURG ARMY

THE CONSCRIPTION SYSTEM in the Habsburg Monarchy can be traced to the beginning of the Thirty Years' War. Johann Albrecht von Waldstein's system, instituted in 1625, prescribed no legal duration of service for infantry; the term of service was fixed by contract between recruitment officers and recruits by means of a renewable "Capitulation." Upon enlistment the recruit received a sum determined by agreement.[1] These contracts were normally for six months to one year. Subsequently the length of the service varied, but most often was for a period of six years.

Because of the difficulties of providing men for a standing army under the Waldstein system, a reserve system was introduced in 1753.[2] A reserve corps of 24,000 was envisioned,[3] and a census of the population was ordered in order to ascertain the number of eligible men.[4] A two-tier system of recruiting existed. The provincial estates had quotas to fill which were apportioned among local lords. In addition, volunteers

---

[1] Wrede, Major Alphons Freiherr von, *Geschichte der k. und k. Wehrmacht* (Vienna: C. W. Seidel, 1898), vol. 1, p. 95. Kriegsarchiv, Vienna, Austria: *Instruction für die kriegs-Commissarische Beamte* (April 30, 1749) mentions a "Muster Instruction" of 1698.

[2] Wrede, *Geschichte der k. und k. Wehrmacht*, p. 99. Kriegsarchiv, Vienna, Austria: Franz Hübler, *Handschriften*, vol. 2 (1749), p. 172. All unpublished documents cited hereafter are from Kriegsarchiv, Vienna, Austria.

[3] Franz Hübler, *Sammlung der im Jahre . . . an die k. k. österreichische Armee ergangenen Politisch, Ökonomischen und Justiz-Militär-Gesetze* (1753), vol. 3, p. 106. Most of these men were to come from Bohemia. This indicates that the court was aware of the under-employment prevailing there.

[4] *Auszug der Conscriptions- und Werb-Bezirks-System für Niederösterreich* (1781), p. 4.

were actively sought throughout the Monarchy as well as in the German states.

In 1771 a more modern system, one of conscription-by-recruitment district, was established;[5] the district system remained intact, in the main, until the dissolution of the Monarchy after World War I. The manorial estates chose according to their own discretion the recruits needed to fill the quota allotted to them by the district commander.[6] They were, however, to follow certain guidelines, such as exempting married men to the extent possible in times of peace.

In 1804 a ten-year term was introduced for the infantry, and a permanent bureaucracy responsible for conscription was also created. The latter was accomplished by turning primary responsibilities for recruitment over from the company commander to the conscription office.[7]

In 1827 the recruitment districts were reorganized, and conscription by lottery instituted. The lottery system operated every third year for those between the ages of 19 and 29. Men who had committed a crime could be drafted outside of this system by administrative decision.[8]

In November 1858 the recruitment districts were again reorganized, and the number of exemptions was reduced.[9] With the creation of the Dual Monarchy in 1867, the Monarchy was divided into eighty military "enlargement" districts and two naval districts.[10]

Exemptions

Exemptions from military duty were granted regularly throughout the period. They were designed to keep the economically most important segments of the society within the production process.[11] As a consequence, in the eighteenth century the army was composed, in the main, of the lower classes of the population.[12] This, however, does not imply

[5] Hübler, *Handschriften*, vol. 6 (1771), p. 175.

[6] *Militär Impressen*, 27 III, 1771, 364/1. By 1795, 104,000 men were being drawn for the Army from the entire Monarchy. *Protokoll Register*, 1795.

[7] Wrede, *Geschichte der k. und k. Wehrmacht*, pp. 103–104; for wording of decree enacting this change, see *Protokoll Register*, 1788 A 317.

[8] Wrede, *Geschichte der k. und k. Wehrmacht*, pp. 105, 106; Alois Graf von Ugarte, Joseph Freiherr von der Mark, und Franz Graf v. Woyna, *Über das Conscriptions- und Recrutierungs-System* (Vienna: n.p., 1804), p. 8.

[9] Ferdinand Schmid, *Das Heeresrecht der österreichisch-ungarischen Monarchie* (Vienna: F. Tempsky, 1903), p. 5.

[10] Austria, *Militär-Statistisches Jahrbuch für das Jahr 1871* (Vienna: k. k. Hof- und Staatsdruckerei, 1873), p. 24.

[11] Hübler, *Handschriften*, vol. 7 (1773), pp. 138, 139; vol. 10 (1779), p. 4.

[12] Gunther E. Rothenberg, "The Austrian Army in the Age of Metternich," *Journal of Modern History* 40 (1968): 155–165.

that the army was an employer of last resort. Beggars and men without subsistence were not allowed to enlist unless a manor had selected them and they otherwise qualified.[13] In 1749 citizens of towns and peasants in possession of land or their only sons were exempt.

Settled peasants (*Ansässige*) on both *rustikal* and on *dominikal* land were exempt from military service, as was one of their sons, regardless of the size of their land holdings. Those peasants, however, who rented land on short-term contracts were not exempt.[14]

Joseph II prescribed categories for exemption in 1780: nobility; clergy; bureaucrats; factory owners and foremen; coal, iron, and salt-peter miners; and settled peasants. (In Hungary only the higher nobility were exempt, due to the large number of poor nobles.) In some cases persons wishing to be exempted had to pay a fine. For example, for conscripts wishing to enter the priesthood the diocese paid 200 fl.[15] The exemption of settled peasants from recruitment was reaffirmed in 1790.[16]

Jews, too, were exempt until the 1780s. However, by the end of that decade, Jews could serve in the fighting forces.[17] Afterwards, Jews also had a quota to fill, but exemptions could be purchased at a price of 140 fl (about two years' income). A subsequent instruction warned that not only the sons of poor Jews were to be sent to the army, but also the sons of wealthier ones.

Workers in the industrial sector were also exempt from the draft in numerous cases. Miners had been exempt since the seventeenth century. Maria Theresia reaffirmed this regulation, but during the Napoleonic Wars only those who were actually working in the seams enjoyed the exemption. Persons engaged in industries that did not work exclusively for the local market (so-called commercial industries) were exempt as long as they were engaged full time in this occupation.[18] Factory workers were regularly provided with exemptions, as stipulated in the privilege granted to owners of factories. In 1780–81, exemptions for skilled personnel and foremen in factories and commercial industries were

---

[13] The justification for this policy was that the proper measures had already been taken to maintain the standard of living of the population. *Protokoll Register*, 1780, K 249. The manors were permitted to send foreigners, instead of locals, to the army. *Protokoll Register*, 1783, D 293.

[14] *Militär Impressen*, 27 III, 1771, 364/1; and 10 III, 1773, 370.

[15] *Auszug*, 1781, p. 25.

[16] *Protokoll Register*, 1790 A 211. A similar regard for the needs of agriculture is shown by a decision, in 1788, that recruitment in Hungary should be postponed until the completion of the harvest. *Protokoll Register*, 1788 G 2608.

[17] Wrede, *Geschichte der k. und k. Wehrmacht*, p. 103; *Protokoll Register*, 1788 A 317.

[18] *Militär Impressen*, 10 III, 1773, 370.

standardized. Yet in 1794 bleachery apprentices in Prague were denied an exemption, and the owner was directed to hire people who had been rejected for military service.

The law of 1804 defined more precisely the various exemptions from military service. Under this law, master craftsmen, wholesalers, town dwellers, and artisans such as weavers were exempt. Among factory workers, foremen and skilled workers, who were difficult to replace, were similarly exempted. In the mining sector, foremen and skilled workers in iron, salt, saltpeter, powder, and foundry-works were also exempted.[19] Industrial enterprises were encouraged to hire men who had been rejected for military duty. In 1822, the granting of licenses for industrial firms was denied to individuals eligible for military service as long as conscription quotas were not filled; this decision caused considerable friction, since men were liable for duty until their fortieth year. In 1827, factory workers lost their exemptions unless they provided proxies. Miners and urban skilled workers continued to be exempt.[20] Following the revolution of 1848, the nobility lost its exempt status.

Nonetheless, the exemptions from 1827 to 1867 still included religious leaders of all denominations, officials, peasant landholders who worked their own land, students and professors of higher education, teachers, and the only sons of aged parents in cases in which these parents were unable to support themselves.[21]

Minimum Height Requirements

Minimum height standards fluctuated from the second half of the eighteenth century onward, and were redefined in the major revisions of the conscription law. The issue of the minimum height requirement was discussed early in Maria Theresia's reign. Soldiers in the reserve infantry of 1753 had to be at least 5 feet 3 Austrian inches (165.8 cm) tall. In 1756 the minimum height in the regular infantry was 163.1 cm;[22] in

---

[19] Ugarte, *Über das Conscriptions- und Recrutierungs-System*, p. 8.

[20] Johann Slokar, *Geschichte der österreichischen Industrie und ihrer Förderung unter Kaiser Franz I* (Vienna: F. Tempsky, 1914), pp. 20, 65, 96, 117, 442.

[21] Franz Hübler, *Militär-ökonomie-system der k. k. österreichischen Armee* (Vienna: J. Geistinger'schen Buchhandlung, 1820), vol. 1, pp. 341–43; vol. 2, pp. 17, 22, 28, 36, 43, 148, 153, 294, 295, 318.

[22] *Protokoll Register*, 1756, pp. 2581, 2598. As late as 1758, it was this minimum height that Hungarian and other regiments were admonished to meet. See *Protokoll Register*, 1758, p. 477. Tall men were preferred in the army because they were stronger, had greater stride, could reach further with the bayonet, and could load the musket more easily than shorter men. James M. Tanner, *A History of the Study of Human Growth* (Cambridge, England: Cambridge University Press, 1981), p. 98.

1758, however, a minimum height of 165.8 cm was reestablished for the infantry.[23] This became the ideal standard thereafter, even if exceptions were often made, and even if it was gradually lowered over time, albeit reluctantly, and with a great deal of hesitation.[24] In 1758, the issue of whether individuals 0.66 cm lower than 165.8 cm could be accepted into the army was discussed at a meeting of the Council of State, with the participation of Count Chotek.[25] This discussion indicates how seriously the issue was taken by the military. In 1760 there was a controversy over whether men who were 1.32 cm under the minimum should be accepted.[26] The authorities decided to enforce the minimum height requirement flexibly at this time and allowed men to be recruited who were 2.63 cm below the minimum.[27] In the subsequent year individuals slightly below the minimum could be recruited if they were otherwise "fit for service."[28] The Court War Council actually urged recruiting officers not to be "precise" about the minimum height requirement, but instead to look at whether the potential recruit was capable of field service, whether he had strong limbs, and whether he was capable of further growth.[29] Yet there were profound reservations about relaxing the requirement excessively. In 1760 the provincial estates were warned that any recruit shorter than the minimum of 165.8 cm must be at least 163.1 cm tall.[30] In 1761 the provincial estates were reprimanded for having committed the error of making the exception the rule and accepting men 163.1 cm tall on a regular basis.[31] The warning was subsequently repeated.[32]

The degree of flexibility in enforcing the minimum height requirement continued to be an issue often disputed. In 1777 the existence of exceptions to the minimum height requirement was explicitly acknowledged: it was conceded that the standard would be overlooked at times.

[23] *Protokoll Register*, 1758, 764; 1759, 248. As contradictory as it may seem, in the same year the minimum height requirement of 163.1 cm was still mentioned. *Protokoll Register*, 1758, 477.

[24] Hübler, *Handschriften*, vol. 3 (1753), p. 93; vol. 3 (1760), p. 38; vol. 7 (1773), p. 138. Under the Josephinian charter of 1780, the minimum height was kept at 5 feet, 3 (Austrian) inches (165.8 cm); *Auszug*, 1781, 5, p. 21. Measurements have been converted to the metric system. One Austrian inch (zoll) is 2.633 cm. There were 12 zoll in an Austrian foot.

[25] *Protokoll Register*, 1758, 2049.

[26] *Protokoll Register*, 1760, 1956.

[27] *Protokoll Register*, 1760, 2037.

[28] *Protokoll Register*, 1761, 1051.

[29] *Protokoll Register*, 1761, 37; 1762, 2277; 1763, 3, 10, 47, 66.

[30] *Protokoll Register*, 1760, 1860.

[31] *Protokoll Register*, 1761, 1390.

[32] *Protokoll Register*, 1762, 628.

Examiners were advised, for instance, not to apply the minimum height requirement rigorously to young men.[33] Yet in 1779 a regulation warned that it was not permissible to accept anyone more than 2.63 cm below the minimum height requirement.[34] In 1782 two men were recruited who were below the 165.8 cm minimum, not because of mismeasurement, but because an exception was made in their case. The recruiting officers were allowed to keep them, but were admonished not to allow this practice to continue.[35] In the same year, in response to the query to the Court War Council whether a man 1.3 cm below the minimum should be allowed to reenlist, it was stated that, although the practice should be avoided in the future, the particular recruit in question, who "had been very highly praised," should be permitted to reenlist.[36] In 1783 it was decreed that those who were 163.1 cm but were likely to grow in the future could be recruited.[37]

The degree of flexibility of the central authorities in this regard continued to fluctuate. Authorities were ordered in 1783 not to take recruits from Galicia, Hungary, or Transylvania who were below the 165.8 cm minimum.[38] In 1787 it was stated that no one who was shorter than 165.8 cm, not even youth capable of further growth, should be allowed to enter the military; such youth could neither handle a long rifle nor cope with the stress of war, and would just end up in a hospital.[39]

Yet the regulations were generally more lenient with those young men who, in the opinion of the recruiting officer, would continue to grow. This tendency was expressed as early as 1769 and repeated often thereafter.[40] In 1788 a decree stated that those young men between 160.5 and 163.1 cm who would certainly grow further could be recruited.[41] The recruiting of young men 160.5 cm tall who were capable

---

[33] *Protokoll Register*, 1777 A 1702.

[34] *Protokoll Register*, 1779 K 64.

[35] *Protokoll Register*, 1782 D 1531. There seem to have been other cases where, despite stern warnings, disregard of the minimum was tacitly permitted. In 1783, a memorandum stated that a foreigner shorter than 5 feet should not have been recruited. It seems, however, that he was not discharged. *Protokoll Register*, 1783, D. 293.

[36] *Protokoll Register*, 1782 D 836.

[37] *Protokoll Register*, 1783 G 3841.

[38] *Protokoll Register*, 1783 D 325.

[39] *Protokoll Register*, 1787 G 3052.

[40] *Protokoll Register*, 1787 G 3052. A similar policy was adopted in Great Britain. "Lads . . . who are well-limbed and likely to grow, may be taken as low as five feet four inches." From the Military Order of 1786. Vernon Vymon Kellogg, *Military Selection and Race Deterioration: A Preliminary Report and Discussion* (Oxford: Clarendon Press, 1916).

[41] *Protokoll Register*, 1788 G 4926.

of further growth again received the stamp of official approval in 1790 and in 1791.[42]

In 1790 it was decreed that all recruits could be below the minimum height requirement by 2.63 cm.[43] The following year a directive stated that this flexibility was allowed only in time of war,[44] and in 1792, during the French Wars, the authorities reissued the decree that men 163.1 cm could be recruited, provided they were otherwise strong enough.[45] Yet in 1796, still a period of wartime exigency, the prior 165.8 cm minimum was again being maintained (in principle), at least in Galicia; it was vitiated in practice, however, by the proviso that anyone from that province could be accepted without regard to height if he was strong enough.[46] In 1804 the minimum height standard for infantrymen was lowered to 160.5 cm, provided the recruit was otherwise fit for service.[47] However, recruits with strong physical build, and those still not having reached their terminal height, could be admitted if they were at least 157.9 cm tall.[48] In 1809 standards were lowered to 157.9 cm, provided that taller men were unavailable. In 1815 the standard was raised once again to 160.5 cm.[49]

After 1827, the minimum height was 160.5 cm, although slightly shorter recruits could be admitted if they qualified otherwise. With the revised army law of 1858, the minimum height of recruits was lowered still further, to 158 cm; with the universal conscription law of 1868, the minimum height standard became 155 cm. Thus, height standards, which were themselves flexibly enforced, were lowered over the course of a century by 11 cm.

[42] Hofkriegsrath Akten, 1790, 47.32; *Protokoll Register*, 1791 G 2661, G 5557. That the "capable of further growth" clause was taken seriously is shown by the decision in 1792 to discharge Franz Wick, who had failed to grow as expected because of sickness. *Protokoll Register*, 1792 D 2064.

[43] *Protokoll Register*, 1790 A 211.

[44] *Protokoll Register*, 1791 G 7923. Apparently in wartime, or even earlier, a lower standard might have prevailed. It was asserted in 1783 that a recruiting officer, who had been accepting men barely 5 feet tall because of a writing error in the circular, should have checked if the minimum stated was the correct one rather than simply "relying on his memory of the military campaign" (zur Erinnerung des Feldkrieges). *Protokoll Register*, 1783 D 763.

[45] *Protokoll Register*, 1792 G 7776; Hübler, *Handschriften*, vol. 20 (1792), p. 372; vol. 21 (1792), p. 170.

[46] *Protokoll Register*, 1796 D 2866.

[47] Hübler, *Handschriften*, vol. 29 (1807), p. 334.

[48] Ugarte, *Über das Conscriptions- und Recrutierungs-System*, p. 13.

[49] Hübler, *Handschriften*, vol. 33 (1809), p. 7; vol. 38 (1813), p. 467; vol. 40 (1815), p. 784.

Recruitment Problems

When local recruiting authorities encountered difficulty finding enough recruits who could meet the current minimum height requirement, they exerted pressure on the higher authorities to lower that minimum. In 1759 recruiters in the non-Habsburg lands of the Holy Roman Empire complained that the then current 165.8 cm minimum was too high; more men could be recruited, they argued, if the minimum were lowered to 163.1 cm.[50] In the town of Iglau, Moravia, in 1779, not even nine recruits could be found who were above 163.1 cm. The officials sought permission to enlist men who were between 160.5 and 161.8 cm tall.[51]

In 1759 the recruiting authorities of Gömör County in Hungary suggested that it would be better if the 165.8 cm minimum were not so strictly enforced.[52] In 1790 Graf Palffy insisted that it would take too long to find recruits who were 165.8 cm tall.[53] A recent study points out how, during the Austro-Turkish War (1788–90), the Hungarian counties, responsible for recruiting, pressed for a relaxation of height requirements in order to meet the conscription quotas more easily.[54] In 1794, in time of war, Hungarian recruiting authorities asked if men as short as 157.9 cm could enter the army; the reply from Vienna was negative.[55]

Occasionally the local authorities misinterpreted the minimum height standard. In 1783 one regiment mistakenly enforced a 171.0 cm minimum height requirement.[56] In 1796 recruiters in Galicia were reprimanded for believing that the minimum height requirement was 168.4 cm.[57] With frequent changes in policy and often ambiguous directives, it is no wonder that confusion often prevailed at the local level.

Regional Variation in Minimum Height Requirements

The minimum height requirement varied not only over time, but also across regions. In 1777 youth from Transylvania who were 0.66 cm

[50] *Protokoll Register*, Nov. 21, 1759, 184.
[51] *Protokoll Register*, 1779 K 54.
[52] *Protokoll Register*, 1759, 466.
[53] *Protokoll Register*, 1790 G 323.
[54] Horst Haselsteiner, *Joseph II und die Komitate Ungarns* (Vienna: Böhlaus, 1983), p. 122.
[55] *Protokoll Register*, 1792 G 2018.
[56] *Protokoll Register*, 1782 D 763; 1783 D 17.
[57] *Protokoll Register*, 1796 D 2866.

less than the minimum of 165.8 cm could be recruited "if they showed a promise of certain growth." The recruiting officers were directed to be more flexible in borderline cases.[58] In 1783, however, local authorities were reminded not to take any more men from Hungary or Transylvania who were under the minimum height requirement.[59] In 1787 men from Hungary or Transylvania who were not more than 2.63 cm below the minimum height requirement were to be accepted into the military;[60] shortly thereafter, however, a new directive ordered strict adherence to the 165.8 cm minimum.[61] This decree was issued in time of war, when greater flexibility might have been expected. In 1790 less rigidity was shown toward Transylvanian recruits: the 165.8 cm minimum was reduced to 163.1 cm for those who seemed capable of further growth.[62]

The recruiting pattern for Italy and for the Austrian Netherlands was somewhat different from that of the rest of the Monarchy. By 1781, men from these provinces who were below the minimum were being recruited.[63] In 1783 the authorities in Vienna reversed themselves and stated that, although those 163.1 cm tall had been taken in the past from these areas, the 165.8 cm standard should henceforth be the rule. Men shorter than the minimum height requirement recruited prior to this order were to be sent to those Austrian regiments that did not have too many foreigners.[64] The order was repeated in 1785.[65] In 1790, however, Italians who were only 157.9 cm tall were being accepted, although this practice was ordered to be stopped in the same year.[66]

Standards elsewhere also varied. In 1784, however, the minimum standard for the Austrian Netherlands was fixed at 163.1 cm.[67] In Vorderösterreich, young men without subsistence shorter than the minimum height requirement "who showed promise of growth" were ordered to be accepted in 1781 in order to prevent emigration.[68] As early as 1790, men from Silesia who were only 163.1 cm could be accepted.[69]

[58] *Protokoll Register*, 1777 E 1193, E 1324.

[59] *Protokoll Register*, 1783 D 325.

[60] *Protokoll Register*, 1787 G 2922.

[61] *Protokoll Register*, 1787 G 3543.

[62] *Protokoll Register*, 1790 G 323.

[63] A decree of that year warned against sending such recruits to regiments formed from recruits from the Holy Roman Empire, and ordered that such actions should be reported to the *Hofkriegsrat*. *Protokoll Register*, 1781 D 1850.

[64] *Protokoll Register*, 1783 D 323.

[65] *Protokoll Register*, 1785 D 1407.

[66] *Protokoll Register*, 1790 D 602, D 915, D 3161.

[67] *Protokoll Register*, 1784 G 3345, G 3758.

[68] *Protokoll Register*, 1781 G 1839.

[69] *Protokoll Register*, 1790 G 1131.

Treatment of foreigners was often less stringent than that of Habsburg subjects. In 1786 young men from Prussian Silesia who were below the minimum height requirement, but who showed promise of further growth, could be recruited with the payment of a 6 gulden bounty.[70] In 1781 there was some concern about too many men under the minimum stature entering the regiments from the Holy Roman Empire; authorities were warned against sending too many recruits from Italy or the Austrian Netherlands who were below the minimum to Austrian regiments.[71] In 1783, however, permission was given to recruit men from the Holy Roman Empire who, although only 163.1 cm tall, seemed capable of further growth.[72] According to a report in 1786, the average height of one regiment had decreased because of short recruits from the Holy Roman Empire.[73] In 1787 it was explicitly stated that the minimum height requirement should not be so strictly enforced for recruits from the German states. Such recruits, unlike recruits from Hungary or Transylvania, were not "directly facing the enemy" (i.e., across the Turkish border), but would instead remain behind in camp. The report asserted that recruits from the Holy Roman Empire had more time to grow to reach the minimum standard before they would face military action, and consequently the men had to be only 163.1 cm tall at the time of recruitment.[74] In addition, recruits at that height could be accepted even if it was clear that they had already reached their final height, provided that less bounty was paid.[75] Two men below the minimum height requirement were allowed to join the army on the assumption that they would still grow (a hope that did not materialize) and were allowed to reenlist. By 1792, recruits from the Holy Roman Empire who were only 157.9 cm tall could be accepted.[76]

Frenchmen, mostly prisoners of war taken into the Habsburg army, were held to higher standards: a minimum requirement of 171.0 cm was decreed for them in 1791 and again in 1792; it was briefly lowered to 165.8 cm, and then raised again in 1793 to 171.0 cm.[77] In 1794 it

[70] *Protokoll Register*, 1786 D 751-2. Complaints were voiced in the reports of one regiment that the height of the regiment had declined as a consequence of too many small men having been recruited in the Holy Roman Empire.

[71] *Protokoll Register*, 1781 D 1850.

[72] *Protokoll Register*, 1783 D 5, D 361.

[73] *Protokoll Register*, 1786 D 751-2.

[74] *Protokoll Register*, 1787 G 3513, G 3543.

[75] Hofkriegsrath Akten, 1787, 47.538.

[76] *Protokoll Register*, 1792 G 6707.

[77] *Protokoll Register*, 1791 G 6945; 1792 G 779, G 1588, G 1646; 1793 G 2004, G 4285.

was decreed that French-speaking recruits from Alsace had to be 171.0 cm, whereas German-speaking Alsatian recruits could be 165.8 cm.[78]

Minimum Height Requirements
by Branch of the Military

Different branches of the military were subjected to different degrees of stringency in the application of the minimum height requirement. The grenadiers, within the infantry, had the greatest minimum height requirement; a 1780 regulation, however, instructed the infantry to avoid taking too many tall soldiers for the grenadiers, because the carbineers needed them too.[79]

The authorities were particularly cautious about relaxing the minimum height standard for recruits to the artillery. An order of 1783 stated that individuals under 165.8 cm tall, even with good attributes, could be accepted "only in special cases," for which the brigadier's approval was necessary; the artillery, it was explained, demanded "above all, strong, fully grown men."[80] There was an ongoing rivalry between the artillery and the infantry. The artillery corps was repeatedly warned not to "select those of greater height" as long as there were men 165.8 cm tall available. Men 165.8 cm tall should all be chosen before those who were 168.4 cm tall, and all those 168.4 cm tall before those 171.0 cm tall were chosen.[81] Yet the artillery at times deliberately chose tall recruits, despite the infantry's protests.[82] When the artillery took a man 176.3 cm tall from the infantry, the commander sent a sharp note to the Court War Council: they did not have a sufficient number of tall men themselves. The artillery was instructed again not to deliberately choose taller than average men, because doing so would make an entire infantry regiment too short.[83] Like the artillery, the dragoons and the uhlans maintained a higher standard than the infantry. As late as 1809, the minimum height of dragoons remained 165.8 cm, and that of the uhlans, 163.1 cm.[84]

The *Frey Corps* (militia), however, was permitted to have a lower height standard. Their stature was deemed not as important as it was

---

[78] *Protokoll Register*, 1794 G 6524.
[79] *Protokoll Register*, 1780 K 195.
[80] *Protokoll Register*, 1783 J 240.
[81] *Protokoll Register*, 1786 A 931, D 751-2.
[82] *Protokoll Register*, 1787 A 372.
[83] *Protokoll Register*, 1786 A 456, D 751-2.
[84] Hübler, *Handschriften*, vol. 32 (1808), p. 1407; vol. 33 (1809), p. 415.

for the regular field regiments; therefore, recruits only 158 cm tall were accepted.[85]

The *Staabs infanterie* do not seem to have been subjected to a rigid height minimum either. In 1793 men from Moravia who were below the minimum height requirement were being sent to the *Staabs infanterie*.[86] In 1796 the *Staabs infanterie* with the Rhine Army received 13 recruits from Moravia and Galicia who were not even 158 cm tall.[87]

The infantry composed the largest segment of the army. In 1848 the infantry numbered 315,000, while the artillery, cavalry, and other support corps numbered altogether 86,000 men.[88]

Age of Eligibility

Age of eligibility for recruitment varied over time. In 1749 the reserve corps accepted men between the ages of 18 and 30. From 1781 to 1804, the minimum age of service was 17, and the maximum age, 40; from 1804 to 1827 the minimum age was 18; from 1827 to 1852, it was 19; and after 1831 the maximum age was 45. With the 1868 law the minimum age was raised to 20.

Method of Measurement

According to Hübler, the 1749 instruction stated that height was to be determined by having the recruit "stand under the measuring instrument."[89] This language, however, was not found in the original document,[90] but appears to have been Hübler's interpretation of the meaning of the instruction. This interpretation is supported by the fact that the population census was to note the height of the male population, but expressly as a mere estimate.[91] That is, when the height was to be estimated rather than measured the instructions specified it explicitly. The 1753 law as well as later instructions mention measurements, and since the height was determined to the nearest 1/4 zoll (that is, 0.66 cm)

[85] *Protokoll Register*, 1792 G 2272. The Freikorps were dissolved in 1801.

[86] *Protokoll Register*, 1793 G 3509.

[87] *Protokoll Register*, 1796 D 4129.

[88] Rothenberg, "Austrian Army," p. 161.

[89] Hübler, *Militär-ökonomie-system*, 1820, vol. 2, p. 321: "stellt der einen für den Feuergewehrstand bestimmten Mann unter das Mass." In Weimar in 1779 men were measured with proper measuring instruments and without shoes. Tanner, *Study of Human Growth*, p. 100.

[90] *Instruction für die kriegs-Commissarische Beamte*, April 30, 1749.

[91] In the census the height was to be recorded as small, average, or large. Hübler, *Handschriften*, vol. 16 (1784), p. 465.

and at times even more accurately, one can be reassured that the measurements were not mere estimates.

A later regulation stipulated that every recruiting post had to have an accurate measuring instrument "so that the height of the recruits could be determined accurately." This was all the more important because recruits received an amount of money on enlistment that depended on their height. For this reason recruits were measured twice,[92] and then annually thereafter. When a mistake arose regarding the accuracy of a measurement, the authorities ordered that the accuracy of the measuring instrument be checked.[93]

The type of measuring instrument used varied over time. In 1761, recruiting authorities in Steyermark were sent a wooden measuring stick.[94] In 1824, however, the Austrian military authorities ordered a metal measuring stick.[95]

The soldiers were measured without boots, but probably in socks. According to one report, even the hair of the men was loosened in order to provide a more accurate measurement.[96] An order of 1787 states clearly that "the men should be measured without shoes or stockings." One might also note that according to the instructions a doctor was to inspect the recruit before he was measured. Since his feet had to be inspected by the doctor it is reasonable to suppose also on this ground that his measurement took place without shoes.[97] The earliest regulation of 1753 stated that "by the usual measurement . . . such a height should be determined, that a man, as he stands with shoes or boots is

---

[92] Hübler, *Handschriften*, vol. 32 (1808), pp. 1407, 1415; vol. 33 (1809), p. 7. In Hungary, the sum paid to recruits (Werbgeld) was the following in 1809:

For the I. Klasse (5′ 5″ or taller):	45 fl.
For the II. Klasse (5′ 4″ – 5′ 5″):	35 fl.
For the III. Klasse (5′ 3″):	30 fl.
For the IV. Klasse (5′ 2″):	25 fl.
For the V. Klasse (5′ 1″):	15 fl.
For those 5′ 0″:	3 fl.

Werb-Instruction für das Königreich Ungarn, January 6, 1809, p. 7; found in Hofkriegsrath Akten, 01 29-8. When someone received too much money for his height, an effort was made to find out who was responsible for the mistake. If the recruiting officer (*Werbehauptmann*) was responsible, he had to pay back the amount that had been mistakenly given to the recruit. *Protokoll Register*, 1782 D 679, D 1244.

[93] *Protokoll Register*, 1782 D 679.

[94] Hofkriegsrath Akten, 1761, August 21, 513.

[95] Karl Ritter von Bundschuh, *Handbuche über das bei der k. k. österreichischen Armee bestehende Militär-Ökonomie-System*, Supplement (Prague: n.p., 1824), p. 79.

[96] Hofkriegsrath Akten, 1770, 74/843.

[97] Hofkriegsrath Akten, 1787, 47.539, p. 15.

able to look into the musket next to his feet . . . this height should be 165.8 cm."[98] But these measurements were not recorded, because the earliest extant records with height information appear sporadically in the late 1760s, and more regularly in the 1770s. By then the recruits were measured without boots.

Accuracy of Measurements

The army was instructed not to select only the tall men from the population. As a consequence, that portion of the recruits' height distribution that was above the minimum requirement probably reflects accurately the underlying population distribution of that social class from which the recruits were generally drawn. Great effort was made to ensure accurate measurement of the soldiers.[99] The *Feldkriegs Commissarische Beamte* was responsible for the measurement. The measurements had to be taken seriously, because the officers responsible for them bore the financial burden in cases of discrepancy. This meant that the recruiting officer would not only have to reimburse the treasury the money received by a recruit who subsequently was found not to qualify, but would also have to pay the costs associated with his recruiting process. Records survive of an incident in which a recruiting officer who falsified the height of two recruits was reprimanded but pardoned by the Court War Council, and the two recruits were allowed to remain in the army because they "do not have other defects."[100] In a similar case the Court War Council ordered an investigation into the accuracy of the measuring stick so that the recruiting officer would not be punished unjustly.[101] No evidence was found of a recruiting officer actually having been fined.[102] According to one report of 1770 there were 5 cases out of a sample of 44 in which the initial measurement of the soldier was found to be inaccurate upon subsequent measurement. In two cases, the discrepancy amounted to 1 cm; in three cases, the two measurements dif-

[98] Hübler, *Handschriften*, vol. 3 (1753), p. 93; *Protokoll Register*, 1761 G 7495. Note that a musket was about 142 cm long.

[99] Two errors are reported in *Protokoll Register*, 1783 D 2193. One contemporary report frankly acknowledged two inevitable sources of error: in the morning a person was taller than in the evening, and if someone who barely met the minimum height requirement suddenly "lost the desire to be a soldier," he could easily make himself slightly shorter. *Protokoll Register*, 1784 D 748.

[100] *Protokoll Register*, 1782 D 1531.

[101] *Protokoll Register*, 1783 D 679 D 861.

[102] A recruiting lieutenant for the Holy Roman Empire, however, might have been fined for accepting two men below the minimum height requirement. *Protokoll Register*, 1782 D 1244.

fered by 0.66 cm. This implies an average error per measurement of less than one millimeter. The authorities responded to this finding by sending the officials a more accurate measuring device, one made of solid material.[103] This episode, as well as the large body of correspondence on this and related issues, indicates that the measurements were taken seriously by contemporaries and can therefore be used with confidence.

[103] Hofkriegsrath Akten, 1770 74/843.

APPENDIX B

SUPPLEMENTARY TABLES AND FIGURES

Table B.1 Height of 21- and 22- Year-Old Soldiers by Year and Place of Birth, 1740- 1950 (cm)

Place of Birth

Decade of Birth	Moravia			Bohemia			Hungary			Galicia			Lower Austria		
	N	$\bar{x}$	$\hat{x}$	N	$\bar{x}$	$\hat{x}$	N	$\bar{x}$	$\hat{x}$	N	$\bar{x}$	$\hat{x}$	N	$\bar{x}$	$\hat{x}$
1740	66	168.8		189	169.8	164.2	254	170.7	167.6				35	169.6	
1750	100	171.8		208	170.2	166.4	872	169.8	167.0	89	169.7		42	168.3	
1760	336	170.9	167.4	568	168.9	165.7	3897	170.4	167.8	161	171.8		198	168.7	164.1
1770	551	167.3	166.7	392	166.4	164.9	1133	168.2	165.3	29	170.3	168.0	209	166.7	163.0
1780	659	166.8	161.9	1655	166.4	164.1	3334	167.2	164.9	349	167.5		353	168.0	163.7
1790	653	165.0	162.3	926	167.2	161.8	2967	166.1	161.2	101	167.2	161.7	263	166.5	161.1
1800							182	167.0	163.5						
1810							304	166.7	163.2						
1820	128	164.5		171	165.0	159.6	238	166.3	163.7				251	166.5	160.2
1830	1183	166.0	163.7	2611	165.8	159.4	860	165.7	163.4	1564	164.8	160.6	1192	165.4	161.8
1840				128	166.2		437	165.2	161.1	336	164.6	161.4	824	166.2	160.4
1850									162.5[a]				134	167.2	
1860	71	165.7		128	166.3		63	166.6	163.8[a]				671	166.6	
1870									164.4[a]				2406	166.8	
1880													2383	167.0	
1890									165.0[a]	1553	168.1				
1900							1250		166.2[b]						
1910							285		168.4				170	169.1	
1920							381		169.6				378	169.7	
1930									170.1[a,c]						
1940									170.6[a,c]						
1950									172.2[a,c]						

Source: See Table 2.1 and A 18 Éves sorköteles Fiatalok Testi Fejlettsége. Biologiai Egészségi Állapota (Budapest, 1983).
[a] Based on actual measurement of all draftees; [b] 23-year-olds; [c] One cm has been added to 18-year-old height.

Table B.2 Regression Equation. Dependent Variable: Height of Soldiers Taller Than the Minimum Height Requirement[a]

Constant[b]	170.5[d]
Age	
17	-2.0[d]
18	-1.5[d]
19	-1.0[d]
20	-0.7[d]
21	-0.5[d]
22	-0.5[d]
Urban[c]	-0.1
Skilled	0.0
Place of birth	
Galicia	0.0
Moravia	0.0
Bohemia (4 counties)	-0.6[d]
Bohemia (12 counties)	-0.1
Lower Austria	-0.3[d]
Decade of birth	
1730	0.6[d]
1740	1.1[d]
1750	0.9[d]
1760	0.8[d]
1780	-0.1[d]
1790	0.1
1800	0.0
1810	0.3[e]
1820	0.2[e]
1830	0.3[d]
1840	0.7[d]
R^2	0.04
F	150[d]
N	97025

[a]165.8 cm; [b]Constant refers to a rural unskilled soldier over the age of 22 born in the 1770s; [c]Vienna, Prague, Reichenberg, Brno, Lemberg, Cracow, Buda, Pest, Pressburg; [d]coefficient significant at the 1 percent level; [e]coefficient significant at the 5 percent level.

Table B.3 Height of Adult[a] Rural Unskilled Soldiers in the Habsburg Monarchy, by Decade and Place of Birth, 1730-1849 (cm)

Decade of Birth	Place of Birth														
	Moravia			Bohemia			Hungary			Galicia			Lower Austria		
	N	$\bar{x}$	$\hat{x}$	N	$\bar{x}$	$\hat{x}$	N	$\bar{x}$	$\hat{x}$	N	$\bar{x}$	$\hat{x}$	N	$\bar{x}$	$\hat{x}$
1730	360	169.8	166.3	231	170.5	165.3	582	170.4	167.9	17	169.4		36	170.0	
1740	1056	172.1	166.6	729	170.9	164.9	2008	171.4	169.6	120	172.0		130	170.5	
1750	2151	170.7	166.4	1561	169.5	164.5	7556	170.7	166.6	661	171.5	168.9	367	169.0	164.0
1760	1330	170.2	168.5	1573	168.6	162.7	5611	170.4	166.0	796	170.6	167.1	453	168.9	167.4
1770	770	167.3	163.1	2306	167.5	161.4	3340	167.7	163.8	1444	168.6	163.7	457	166.9	161.0
1780	1540	167.5	162.8	1816	166.8	161.7	4889	167.8	163.7	1238	168.2	164.2	694	166.5	161.8
1790	406	168.2	165.0	675	167.0	160.8	7361	167.1	164.1	505	169.0	168.5	1149	166.2	162.8
1800							323	166.1	163.7						
1810							310	166.3	165.0						
1820	112	165.4		83	165.3		210	166.4	163.7	215	164.2		101	166.2	
1830				74	166.1		82	167.3		644	165.4				
1840							101	163.4		82	165.2				

Source: See Table 2.1.
Notes: N = number of observations; $\bar{x}$ = sample mean; $\hat{x}$ = estimated population mean.
[a] Between the ages of 22 and 45. For standard deviations see Table B.8.

Table B.4 Height of Adult[a] Skilled or Urban Soldiers in the Habsburg Monarchy by Decade and Place of Birth, 1730-1839 (cm)

Decade of Birth	Moravia			Bohemia			Hungary			Galicia			Lower Austria		
	N	$\bar{x}$	$\hat{x}$	N	$\bar{x}$	$\hat{x}$	N	$\bar{x}$	$\hat{x}$	N	$\bar{x}$	$\hat{x}$	N	$\bar{x}$	$\hat{x}$
1730	73	170.7		102	170.4		165	169.9	165.3				30	170.1	
1740	228	171.3	167.4	366	170.7	165.5	615	171.4	168.5	30	171.6		67	171.1	
1750	573	170.6	165.8	588	170.3	164.6	1500	170.9	168.5	151	171.5	168.9	177	169.8	
1760	422	170.3	164.0	672	169.0	165.9	983	170.1	167.8	106	170.3		330	166.5	162.3
1770	262	167.2	163.9	898	167.0	163.1	492	168.2	163.7	107	168.4		352	166.4	162.9
1780	472	167.5	165.5	1169	166.2	161.5	960	168.3	165.7	96	167.9		433	166.8	166.4
1790	206	167.3	165.8	523	166.8	161.0	1408	167.6	164.8	37	169.6		439	165.3	161.1
1800							110	167.8							
1810							71	168.0							
1820	60	165.8		132	165.9		65	167.7		30	164.7		66	165.6	
1830	65	166.4		557	165.0		31	165.6		64	165.8		30	166.5	

Source: See Table 2.1.
[a]Between the ages of 23 and 45
Note: For standard deviations see Table B.8.

Table B.5 Height of Adult[a] Rural Unskilled Bohemian Soldiers by Region of Birth, 1730-1799 (cm)

Decade of Birth	4 Counties[b]				12 Counties[c]				Selected Manors[d]	
	N	x̄	s.d.	x̂	N	x̄	s.d.	x̂	N	x̄
1730	114	170.4	3.9		100	170.5	4.5			
1740	342	171.1	4.6	165.7	365	170.7	4.8	165.2		
1750	789	169.3	3.8	164.7	745	169.7	4.4	164.1		
1760	777	167.9	4.4	164.1	771	169.4	4.9	163.1	263	167.4
1770	641	166.2	5.1	164.5	1638	168.0	5.3	161.6		
1780	1029	165.8	4.3	161.6	764	168.0	4.9	163.5	490	165.3
1790	254	165.9	3.3	162.0	296	168.7	5.7	166.2		

Source: See Table 2.1.

[a]Between the ages of 23 and 45; [b]Leitmeritz, Bunzlau, Königgrätz, Bidschow; [c]All other counties except Prague; [d]The most proto-industrial areas of Bunzlau County include the following manors: Friedland, Reichenberg, Böhmisch-Aicha, Gross Skal, Semil, Kost, Morchenstern, Klein Skall, Swigau, Grafenstein.

Table B.6 Height of Adult[a] Skilled or Urban Bohemian Soldiers by Region of Birth, 1730-1799 (cm)

Decade of Birth	4 Counties[b]				12 Counties[c]				Selected Manors[d]	
	N	$\overline{x}$	s.d.	$\hat{x}$	N	$\overline{x}$	s.d.	$\hat{x}$	N	$\overline{x}$
1730	44	170.5			34	170.5	3.2			
1740	153	171.4	4.3	168.1	175	169.9	3.8	165.3		
1750	328	170.0	4.4	164.3	291	170.6	4.7	164.6		
1760	408	168.9	3.8	166.1	229	169.3	5.0	162.9	138	168.1
1770	416	166.6	5.0	164.1	431	167.9	4.9	162.7		
1780	806	165.7	4.9	161.7	321	167.6	4.9	164.9	393	165.0
1790	205	166.8	3.8	165.3	178	168.2	5.3	165.0		

Source: See Table 2.1.
[a]Between the ages of 23 and 45; [b] Leitmeritz, Bunzlau, Königgrätz, Bidschow; [c]All other counties except Prague; [d] For list of manors see Table B.5.

Table B.7 Change in Sample Mean Height ($\Delta \bar{x}$) of Adult[a] Soldiers from Previous Decade (cm)

Decade	Moravia	Bohemia[b]	Bohemia[c]	Hungary	Galicia	Lower Austria	Sweden
Rural Unskilled							
1740	+2.3	+0.6	+0.7	+1.0	+2.6	+0.5	+0.2
1750	-1.4	-1.1	-1.9	-0.7	-0.5	-0.7	-1.4
1760	-0.5	-0.7	-0.9	-0.3	-0.9	-0.9	-1.0
1770	-2.9	-1.4	-1.6	-2.7	-2.0	-2.0	+1.2
1780	+0.2	+0.1	-0.4	+0.1	-0.4	-0.4	-0.6
1790	+0.7	+0.2	-0.3	-0.7	+0.8	+0.3	-0.4
				Cumulative Change			
1750-1800	-3.9	-2.9	-5.1	-4.3	-3.0	-4.3	-2.0
Skilled							
1740	+0.6	-1.2	+0.9	+1.5		+1.0	
1750	-0.7	+1.3	-1.4	-0.5	-0.1	-1.3	
1760	-0.3	-1.3	-1.1	-0.8	-1.2	-3.3	
1770	-3.1	-1.4	-2.3	-1.9	-1.9	-0.1	
1780	+0.3	-0.3	-0.9	+0.1	-0.5	+0.4	
1790	-0.2	+0.6	+1.1	-0.7	+1.7	-1.5	
				Cumulative Change			
1750-1800	-4.0	-1.1	-4.6	3.8	2.0	5.8	

Source: Tables B.3-B.6; Swedish data from Lars Sandberg and Richard Steckel, "Heights and Economic History." [a]Between the ages of 23 and 45; [b]Twelve counties; [c]Four counties.

Table B.8 Sample and Estimated Standard Deviations of the Height of the Adult Soldiers

Decade of Birth	Moravia A		Moravia B		Bohemia A		Bohemia B		Hungary A		Hungary B		Galicia A		Galicia B		Lower Austria A		Lower Austria B	
	s.d.	ŝ	s.d.	ŝ	s.d.	ŝ	s.d.	ŝ	s.d.	ŝ	s.d.	ŝ	s.d.	ŝ	s.d.	ŝ	s.d.	ŝ	s.d.	ŝ
1730	4.6		3.7	5.9	3.4		4.3	7.3	4.1	6.6	4.8	6.3					3.6		4.0	
1740	4.6	6.9	4.8	7.8	4.3	7.1	4.7	7.8	4.5	6.2	4.6	6.0	2.3		3.7		3.7		3.6	
1750	4.3	6.8	4.0	6.2	4.6	7.4	4.2	6.7	4.5	6.0	3.6	6.9	3.5	4.9	3.9	5.3	4.2	5.3	4.7	7.7
1760	5.4	8.6	4.6	7.6	4.3	6.1	4.7	7.6	4.4	5.9	4.0	6.7	3.9		5.0	7.0	5.1	7.5	5.7	6.8
1770	5.4	7.2	5.6	7.8	5.0	7.0	5.3	8.5	4.8	7.1	4.7	6.8	4.6		5.0	7.4	4.8	6.8	5.3	8.4
1780	5.0	6.0	4.9	7.4	5.0	7.2	4.8	7.2	4.8	6.3	4.8	7.2	4.5		4.4	6.7	4.3	4.8	5.0	7.2
1790	5.3	6.4	6.5	8.3	4.5	7.2	4.7	8.0	5.0	6.7	4.2	7.0	4.2		4.5	5.0	4.1	6.2	4.9	6.5
1800									4.5		4.4	6.0								
1810									5.1		4.7	6.1								
1820	4.1		4.6		5.1		5.5		8.6		4.6	6.0			4.8	7.1	5.4			
1830	4.8				5.0		5.4		4.5		4.7		5.2		4.3	7.0	5.5		4.7	
1840											4.4									

Source: See Table 2.1
s.d. = standard deviation of the sample height distribution; ŝ = estimated standard deviation of the population's height distribution; A = skilled; B = unskilled.

Table B.9 Height of 19- and 20-Year-Old Soldiers, 1740- 1849 (cm)

Decade of Birth	Moravia			Bohemia			Place of Birth — Hungary			Galicia			Lower Austria		
	N	x̄	x̂	N	x̄	x̂	N	x̄	x̂	N	x̄	x̂	N	x̄	x̂
1740	133	168.8		278	169.0	165.1	581	169.8	166.3				76	169.1	
1750	91	170.1		246	169.8	165.4	375	169.6	168.3	83	169.7		54	169.9	
1760	216	171.3		247	169.9	166.2	3255	169.9	166.4	74	170.9		136	169.7	
1770	619	166.1	162.8	631	167.0	162.8	1634	168.1	164.3	52	168.8		406	165.4	162.6
1780	1050	166.2	162.6	1741	165.6	161.5	3098	166.9	163.3	92	166.4		436	167.4	163.9
1790	1413	164.0	163.2	1520	165.8	161.3	1471	165.2	161.0	68	166.8		125	166.5	
1800							304	167.1	163.5						
1810							484	166.4	163.9				49	165.8	
1820	121	165.4		192	166.7		591	165.9	160.6				519	166.8	160.2
1830	115	166.0		445	166.0	162.8	231	165.1	161.5	388	164.2	160.4	322	166.3	160.7
1840													822	167.0	165.5

Source: See Table 2.1

Table B.10 Height of 19-to 22-Year-Old Bohemian Soldiers by Region and Decade of Birth, 1760-1839 (cm)

Decade of Birth	4 Counties Skilled			4 Counties Unskilled			12 Counties Skilled			12 Counties Unskilled			Selected Manors Skilled		Selected Manors Unskilled	
	N	$\bar{x}$	$\hat{x}$	N	$\bar{x}$	$\hat{x}$	N	$\bar{x}$	$\hat{x}$	N	$\bar{x}$	$\hat{x}$	N	$\bar{x}$	N	$\bar{x}$
Age 19 or 20																
1760	57	170.4		93	169.9					56	169.4					
1770	170	167.7	165.9	387	166.7	163.0				41	167.4					
1780	540	165.5	161.2	937	165.1	161.7				223	167.7	160.2	554	165.5	868	165.2
1790	533	166.4	161.4	722	165.6	161.5				133	165.2					
1830	101	166.7		30	166.2											
Age 21 or 22																
1760	147	168.7		316	168.7	164.5							58	167.7	83	168.7
1770	122	165.4		224	166.3	165.7										
1780	448	165.9	165.3	634	165.7	163.7	147	167.7		418	167.6	164.9	310	165.2	419	165.8
1790	214	167.5	164.0	283	167.4	162.2	102	167.5		168	166.9	162.6				
1830	888	165.5	160.9	271	167.2	163.7	535	165.2	158.5	395	165.5					

Source: See Table 2.1 and B.5

Table B.11 Share of Young[a] Soldiers in the Total Sample, 1740-1799

Decade of Birth	Place of Birth				
	Moravia	Bohemia	Hungary	Galicia	Lower Austria
1740	26	30	24		57
1750	10	17	12	17	15
1760	21	26	52	21	30
1770	53	24	42	5	43
1780	46	53	52	25	41
1790	77	67	34	24	20

Source: Tables 2.1, B.1, and B.9.
[a]19- to 22-Year-Old Soldiers.

Table B.12 Height Increments of Unskilled Hungarian Soldiers, 1750-1799 (Variant B) (cm)

												Age[a]	
		19		20		21		22		23		24	
Age[b]	Birth Decade	N	ΔH	N	ΔH	N	ΔH	N	ΔH	N	ΔH	N	ΔH
18	1750/60	81	.56	55	.65	44	.74	45	.32	37	-1.15	28	-.73
	1780/90	17	.54	30	-.30	12	-.35	-	-	72	.84	92	.43
19	1750/60			107	.50	54	.60	49	.83	62	-.58	51	-.62
	1780/90			38	.19	76	.19	32	.20	9	2.09	27	2.53
20	1750/60					87	.30	90	.70	61	1.31	94	.45
	1780/90					113	.12	82	.26	29	.74	17	2.06
21	1750/60							186	.34	62	.59	67	.58
	1780/90							122	.21	88	.06	28	-.06
22	1750/60									189	.28	29	.12
	1780/90									166	.15	97	-.03
23	1750/60											131	.10
	1780/90											166	.17
Average													
	1750/60	81	.56	162	.56	285	.42	370	.49	411	.22	400	.11
	1780/90	17	.54	68	.03	201	.12	236	.23	299	.30	344	.43

Source: See Table 2.10.

Notes: N = Number of observations; ΔH = Estimate of height increment.
[a] Age at the end of the observation period.
[b] Age at the beginning of the observation period.

Table B.13 Height Increments of Skilled Hungarian Soldiers, 1750-1799 (Variant B) (cm)

Age[b]	Birth Decade	19		20		21		22		23		24	
		N	ΔH	N	ΔH	N	ΔH	N	ΔH	N	ΔH	N	ΔH
18	1750/60	21	.53	5	.26	8	.76	12	.28	12	.10	4	1.00
	1780/90	5	.39	7	-.01	4	.61	1	.49	2	4.00	1	4.56
19	1750/60			20	.49	8	.38	8	.17	14	.41	10	-.10
	1780/90			-	-	-	-	3	.62	2	2.89	2	1.10
20	1750/60					33	.39	16	-.02	14	.87	20	.47
	1780/90					19	.42	13	-.25	-	-	2	.98
21	1750/60							36	.15	9	.74	9	-.68
	1780/90							26	.20	14	.51	9	.20
22	1750/60									36	.27	9	.31
	1780/90									26	.09	10	-.36
23	1750/60											34	.27
	1780/90											34	.21
Average													
	1750/60	21	.53	25	.44	49	.45	72	.14	85	.42	86	.21
	1780/90	5	.39	7	-.01	23	.45	43	.10	56	.43	48	.27

Source: See Table 2.10.

Notes: N = Number of observations; ΔH = Estimate of height increment.
[a]Age at the end of the observation period.
[b]Age at the beginning of the observation period.

Table B.14 Height Increments of Hungarian Soldiers,[a] 1750-1799 (Variant B) (cm)

		Age[b]											
		19		20		21		22		23		24	
Age[c]	Birth Decade	N	ΔH	N	ΔH	N	ΔH	N	ΔH	N	ΔH	N	ΔH
18	1750/60	82	.67	36	.44	34	.94	50	.49	45	-.48	22	-.73
	1780/90	8	.66	20	-.36	13	-.09	1	.53	6	2.33	6	.43
19	1750/60			110	.55	46	.47	45	.55	73	-.01	56	-.62
	1780/90			22	.21	63	.20	25	.29	1	1.30	17	2.53
20	1750/60					118	.45	89	.30	59	1.05	91	.45
	1780/90					58	.24	77	.10	28	.44	13	2.06
21	1750/60							196	.35	67	.72	57	.58
	1780/90							62	.20	73	.19	26	-.06
22	1750/60									206	.32	34	.12
	1780/90									90	.23	69	-.03
23	1750/60											147	.10
	1780/90											107	.17
Average													
	1750/60	82	.67	146	.52	268	.52	380	.38	450	.34	407	.09
	1780/90	8	.66	42	-.06	134	.19	165	.17	204	.34	238	.45

Source: See Table 2.10.

Note: Sample is restricted to those recruits whose initial height measurement exceeded 165.7 cm.
N = Number of observations; ΔH = Estimate of height increment.
[a] Skilled and Unskilled; [b] Age at the end of the observation period;
[c] Age at the beginning of the observation period.

Table B.15   Regression Equation.

Dependent Variable: Height of Boys, 1760-1815 (cm)

Intercept	109.6[a]
Decade of Birth	
1760	2.8[a]
1770	-0.5
1790	-1.5[a]
1800	-1.6[a]
1805	-1.5[a]
1810	-0.7[a]
Birthplace	
Moravia	-0.6[a]
Silesia	-1.7[a]
Galicia	-1.2[a]
Styria	-1.0[a]
Hungary	0.2
Upper Austria	-1.0[a]
Lower Austria	0.2
Other	0.2
Carinthia	0.6[a]
Italy	0.0
Germany	-0.3
France	-0.5
Tyrol	-0.8[a]
Transylvania	0.4
Croatia	2.4a
Age	
7+	4.4[a]
8+	8.4[a]
9+	12.0[a]
10+	15.9[a]
12+	24.0[a]
13+	28.4[a]
14+	33.0[a]
15+	38.3[a]
16+	44.6[a]
17+	50.3[a]
18+	52.3[a]
R^2	0.08
F	3251[a]
N	25,071

Source: See Table 2.14
Note: Intercept indicates height of a six-year-old Bohemian boy born in the 1780s. Independent variables are all dummy variables.
[a]Significant at the 1 percent level.

Table B.16 Height of Boys by Age and Place of Birth, Habsburg Monarchy, 1790- 1815 (cm)

Age at Last Birthday

Place of Birth	7 1790s	7 1800s	7 1810s	8 1790s	8 1800s	8 1810s	9 1790s	9 1800s	10 1790s	10 1800s	11 1790s	11 1800s	12 1790s	12 1800s
Moravia		112.0			116.0	117.2	119.5	119.3		123.0	129.6	127.6	132.1	131.7
Bohemia	112.5	113.4	113.4		116.5	118.2	120.4	119.7	124.0	123.9	127.8	128.0	131.7	131.9
Silesia										123.7		126.6		
Galicia		110.9			115.2			118.0		122.3		126.5	130.2	131.5
Other	110.7	112.1			116.0	116.1		120.8	124.2	124.8	128.2	129.2	132.3	132.9
Steyermark								119.0		123.5		127.4		132.3
Hungary		110.4	113.0		115.8	116.0	120.6	119.1	124.7	123.8	128.0	128.9	132.5	133.1
Lower Austria					116.4		120.6	119.4	126.0	124.1	130.2	127.8	133.3	131.9
Germany							119.4		123.9		127.6		131.5	
Transylvania					116.3			119.9		123.4		128.4		133.2

Place of Birth	13 1790s	13 1800s	14 1790s	14 1800s	14 1810s	15 1790s	15 1800s	15 1810s	16 1790s	16 1800s	16 1810s	17 1790s	17 1800s	17 1810s
Moravia	136.5	135.9	140.0	140.0		145.0	145.6	144.5	154.2	151.6	152.0	159.2	157.9	157.9
Bohemia	135.7	136.3	140.7	141.4		148.1	146.3	146.1	155.0	151.8	152.5	161.6	157.6	
Silesia		136.5												
Galicia			140.1	140.2			144.8	145.9		150.4				
Other	136.2	136.9	141.4	142.0			146.5	148.3		152.3	153.0		157.2	158.9
Steyermark														
Hungary	138.5		142.0	142.0			147.5	146.2	156.5	152.4	151.2		158.7	
Lower Austria	137.5	137.0	140.3	140.9			147.7	145.8		151.4				
Germany	136.4		140.6											
Transylvania		135.1					146.8			151.1				

Source: See Table 2.14

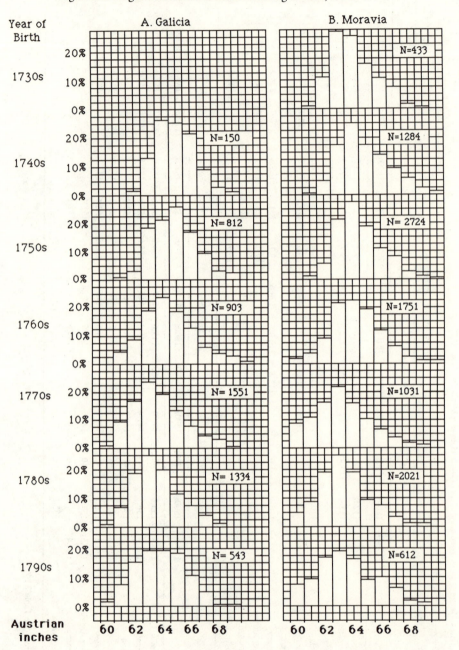

Figure B.1. Height Distribution of Adult Habsburg Soldiers, 1730s–1790s

Figure B.1. (*cont.*) Height Distribution of Adult Habsburg Soldiers, 1730s–1790s

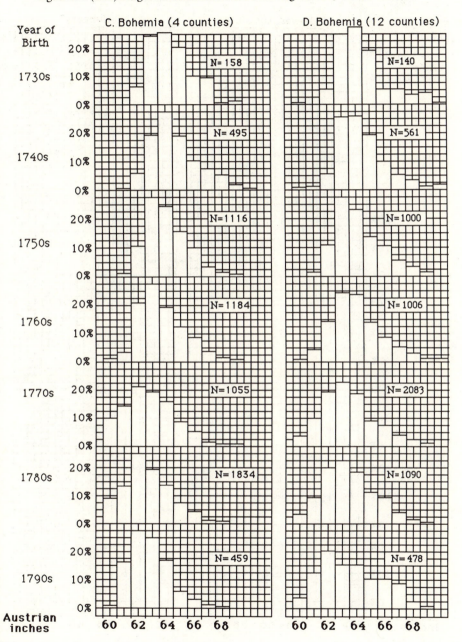

Figure B.1. (*cont.*) Height Distribution of Adult Habsburg Soldiers, 1730s–1790s

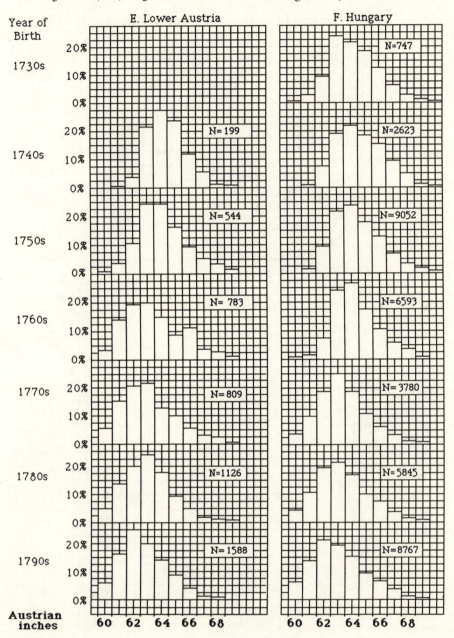

Figure B.2. Height Distribution of Adult Habsburg Soldiers, 1790s–1840s

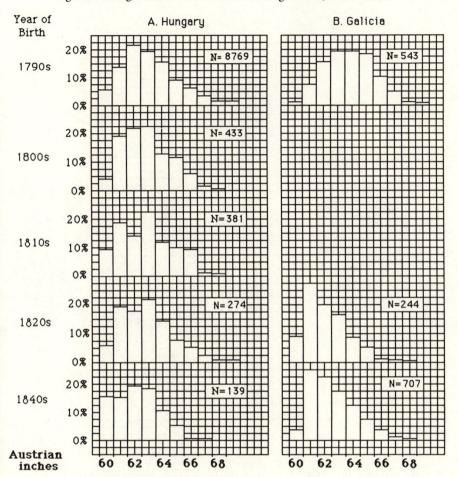

Figure B.3. Height Distribution of Habsburg Soldiers, Ages 21 and 22 Years

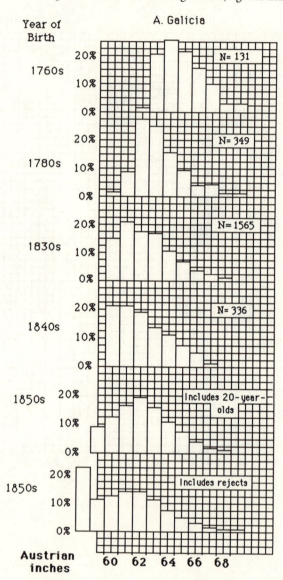

Figure B.3. (*cont.*) Height Distribution of Habsburg Soldiers, Ages 21 and 22 Years

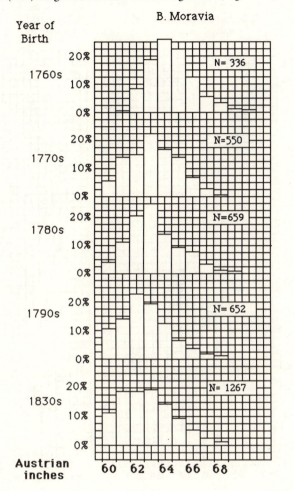

B. Moravia

Year of Birth

1760s — N= 336

1770s — N=550

1780s — N=659

1790s — N= 652

1830s — N= 1267

Austrian inches: 60 62 64 66 68

Figure B.3. (*cont.*) Height Distribution of Habsburg Soldiers, Ages 21 and 22 Years

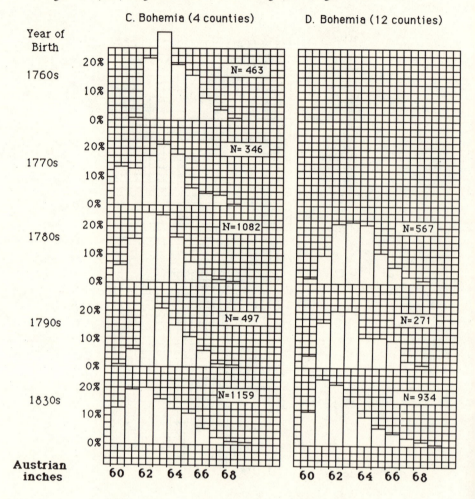

Figure B.3. (*cont.*) Height Distribution of Habsburg Soldiers, Ages 21 and 22 Years

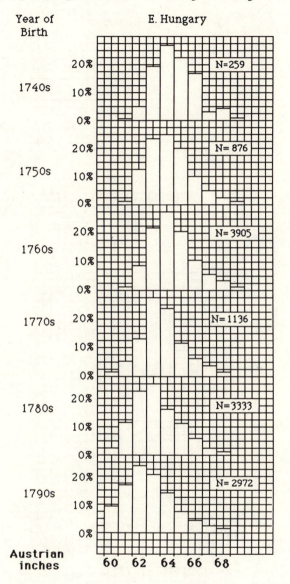

Figure B.3. (*cont*.) Height Distribution of Habsburg Soldiers, Ages 21 and 22 Years

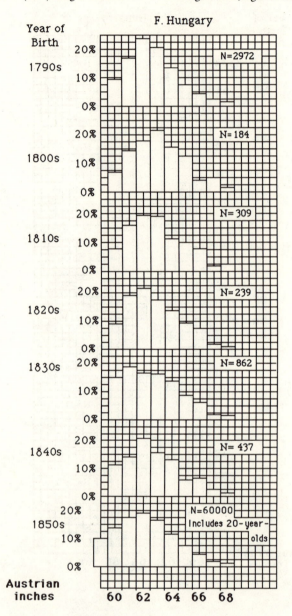

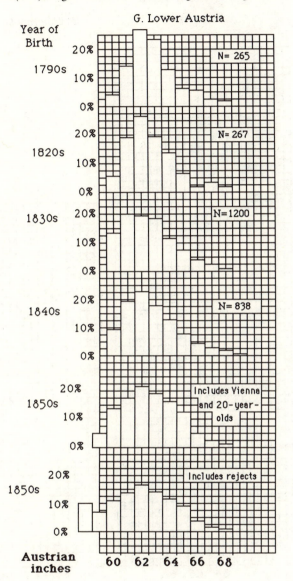

G. Lower Austria

Year of Birth

1790s   N= 265

1820s   N= 267

1830s   N=1200

1840s   N= 838

1850s   Includes Vienna and 20-year-olds

1850s   Includes rejects

Austrian inches   60   62   64   66   68

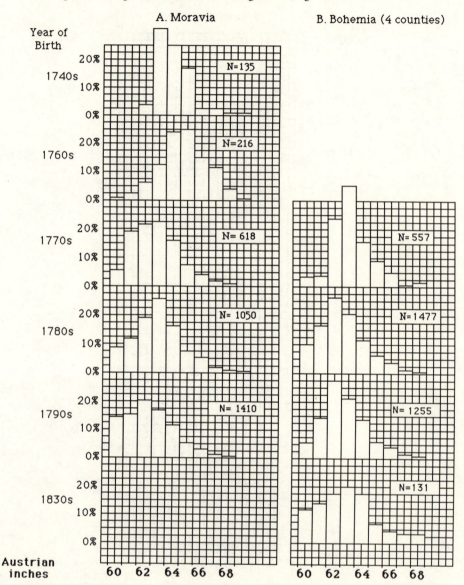

Figure B.4. Height Distribution of Habsburg Soldiers, Ages 19 and 20 Years

Figure B.4. (*cont.*) Height Distribution of Habsburg Soldiers, Ages 19 and 20 Years

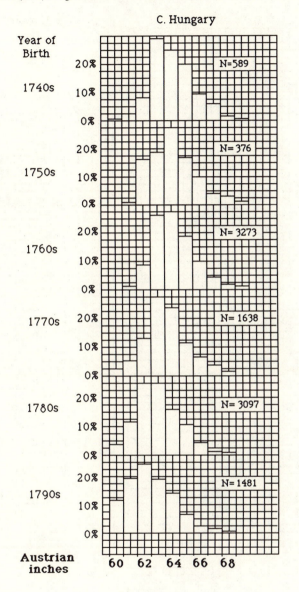

C. Hungary

Figure B.4. (*cont.*) Height Distribution of Habsburg Soldiers, Ages 19 and 20 Years

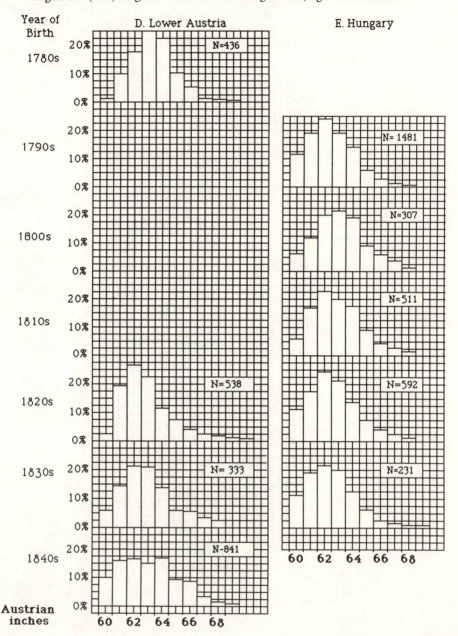

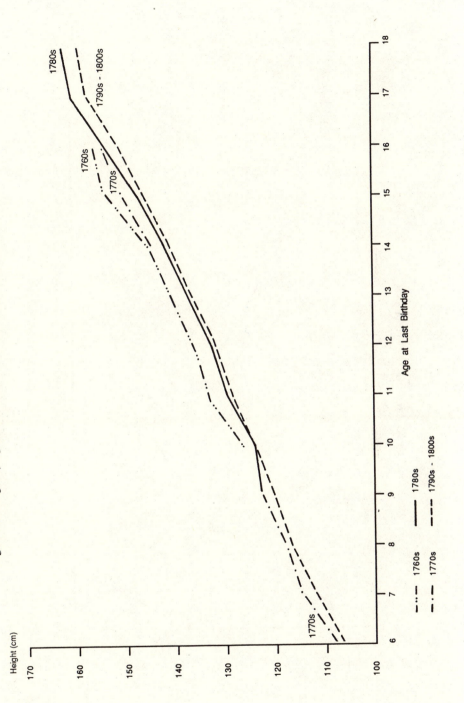

Figure B.5. Height by Age Profile of Boys in the Habsburg Monarchy, 1760–1790

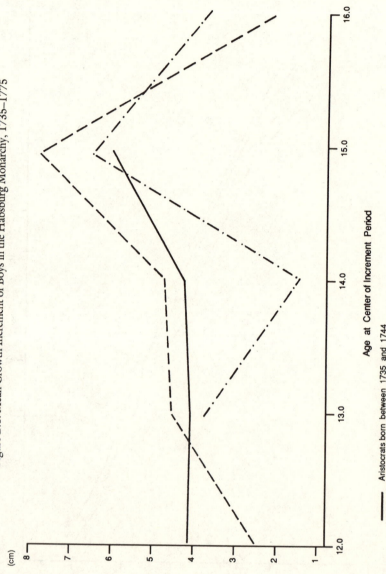

Figure B.6. Mean Growth Increment of Boys in the Habsburg Monarchy, 1735–1775

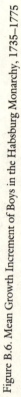

Age at Center of Increment Period

——— Aristocrats born between 1735 and 1744
—·—· Aristocrats born between 1745 and 1755
– – – Orphans born between 1760 and 1775

Figure B.7. Mean Growth Increment of Boys in the Habsburg Monarchy, 1760–1789

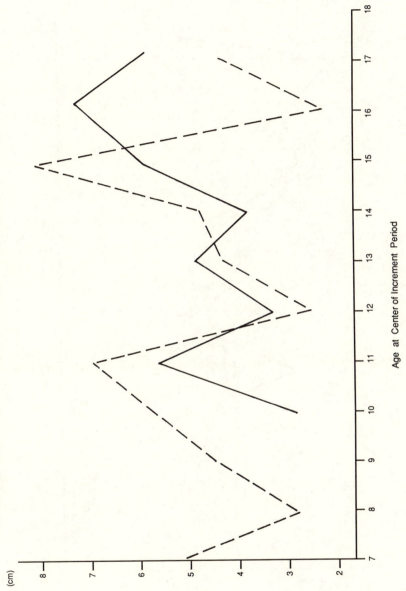

(cm)

Age at Center of Increment Period

- - - Orphans born between 1760 and 1775
——— Students in military boarding schools born between 1780 and 1789

Figure B.8. Mean Growth Increment of Boys in the Habsburg Monarchy, 1780–1799

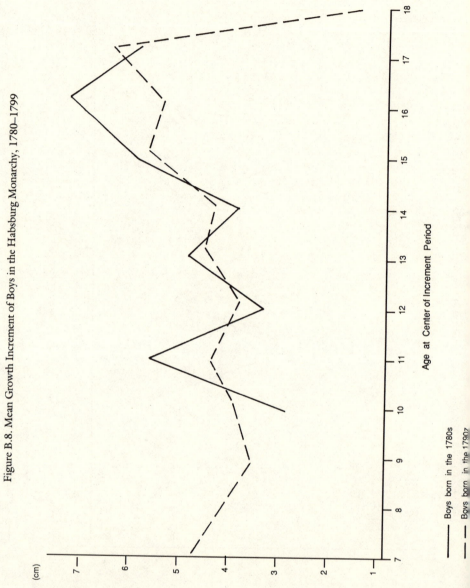

(cm)

Age at Center of Increment Period

——— Boys born in the 1780s

– – – Boys born in the 1790z

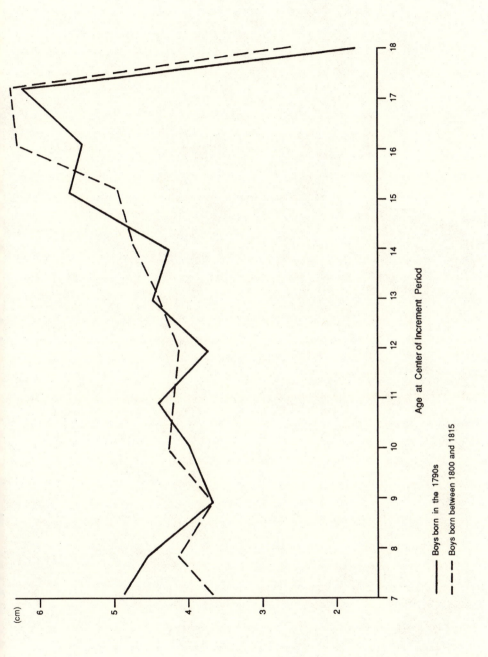

(cm)

Age at Center of Increment Period

—— Boys born in the 1790s

--- Boys born between 1800 and 1815

A SIMULATION OF THE "AUSTRIAN" MODEL OF THE INDUSTRIAL REVOLUTION (WITH MARC ARTZROUNI)*

A FORMAL VERSION of the "Austrian" model of the industrial revolution, elaborated in Chapter 6, is presented in this appendix. An attempt is made to capture the salient features of pre-industrial economic development by specifying functional relationships on the basis of the evidence outlined there. We propose a nonlinear stochastic model capable of simulating the stylized pattern of economic and population growth from the Neolithic agricultural revolution through the industrial revolution. This epoch can be considered as a unit because, throughout the period, the agricultural sector dominated the economy, and population growth was slow and intermittent. In these respects the structure of the pre-industrial economy was essentially invariant with respect to time. The goal is to synthesize the Malthusian and Boserupian notions of the effect of population growth on economic development in order to argue that the escape from the pre-industrial Malthusian trap, i.e., the industrial revolution of the eighteenth century, can be thought of as having grown out of a process begun millennia earlier.

The industrial revolution is commonly thought of as a great discontinuity brought about by a sudden surge in technical progress, but the "Austrian" model substitutes for this another paradigm: the industrial revolution can be thought of as the culmination of an evolutionary pro-

* This appendix was written in collaboration with Marc Artzrouni, Department of Mathematics, Loyola University of New Orleans.

cess. This characterization is in keeping with recent evidence that the rate of economic change during the second half of the eighteenth century was not as dramatic as previously thought.[1] With the use of simulation techniques one can demonstrate that the industrial revolution can be obtained through slow but persistent accumulation, as emphasized by the "Austrian" model. The goal is to show that a time-invariant process can lead to discontinuous growth.

The model is Malthusian because prior to the industrial revolution capital stock, technology, resource base, and improved land generally grew slower than the population. Consequently population growth invariably led to diminishing returns to labor and eventually resulted in a subsistence crisis. On this Malthusian framework we superimpose a "Boserupian process" which enabled population growth to exert beneficial influence on economic development in the long run.[2] During most of the period under consideration the former process dominated but was eventually overcome by the latter. Because the European economies incessantly augmented their capital stock, the society faced each new crisis with a greater stock of capital per capita than previously. Consequently, the probability that the Malthusian constraints would be ultimately overcome increased over time. After the Boserupian process became dominant, per capita output and population growth could continue without the threat of a nutritional crisis. This is the escape from the Malthusian trap, which we conceptualize as the demographic and industrial revolutions of the eighteenth century. The discontinuity in the values of the variables of the model is obtained within the framework of a time-invariant dynamic process without resorting to discontinuous shifts of the production function in the eighteenth century and without a fundamental structural change in the economy—the explanations often invoked.

To be plausible, the model should conform to the following salient features of the past:

[1] Rondo Cameron, "The Industrial Revolution: A Misnomer," *The History Teacher* 15 (1982): 377–384; idem, "A New View of European Industrialization," *Economic History Review*, 2d ser., 38 (1985): 1–23; N.F.R. Crafts, "British Economic Growth, 1700–1831: A Review of the Evidence," *Economic History Review*, 2d ser., 36 (1983): 177–199; Jeffrey G. Williamson, "Why Was British Growth So Slow during the Industrial Revolution?" *Journal of Economic History* 44 (1984): 687–712; C. Knick Harley, "British Industrialization before 1841: Evidence of Slower Growth during the Industrial Revolution," *Journal of Economic History* 42 (1982): 267–289.

[2] Ester Boserup, *Population and Technological Change: A Study of Long-Term Trends* (Chicago: The University of Chicago Press, 1981); Julian L. Simon, *Theory of Population and Economic Growth* (Oxford: Basil Blackwell, 1986).

1. The population and total product should grow slowly and cyclically until the very end of the simulation;
2. The stock of capital should rise slowly, but rise nonetheless, throughout the period;
3. Per capita output should stagnate until the end of the period under consideration;
4. There should be periodic subsistence crises caused by diminishing returns to labor;
5. Per capita output and population should rise quickly at the end of the period without a change in the economic structure.

The proposed model resembles the usual neoclassical growth models.[3] These models introduce exogenous disembodied technical change, which shifts the production function at a given rate. However, this class of models has not been capable of simulating the evolution of actual economies, which seldom grow in a steady state. Another approach considers technical change as endogenous. With such models population growth leads to increased consumption per capita by inducing technological change or learning-by-doing.[4]

The model includes randomly determined demographic catastrophes in conjunction with a Malthusian mechanism that simulates the dynamics of economic and population growth from 7000 B.C. to A.D. 1900. We emphasize the role of Malthus's positive checks in determining population growth and disregard "moral restraint," because the former was much more important during the nine-thousand-year period under discussion. Only at the end of the period did negative checks gain in significance, and even then Malthusian subsistence crises continued to persist into the eighteenth century. Hence we concentrate on Malthus's positive checks and leave the inclusion of negative checks to subsequent versions of the model.

[3] A. K. Dixit, *The Theory of Equilibrium Growth* (London: Oxford University Press, 1976); Robert Solow, "Technical Change and the Aggregate Production Function," *Review of Economics and Statistics* 39 (1957): 312–320.

[4] Boserup, *Population and Technological Change*; Julian L. Simon, "The Present Value of Population Growth in the Western World," *Population Studies* 37 (1983): 5–21; Julian L. Simon and Gunter Steinmann, "The Economic Implications of Learning-by-Doing for Population Size and Growth," *European Economic Review* 26 (1984): 167–85; Gunter Steinmann, "A Model of the History of Demographic-Economic Growth," in Gunter Steinmann, *Economic Consequences of Population Change in Industrialized Countries. Proceedings of the Conference on Population Economics Held at the University of Paderborn, West Germany, June 1–June 3, 1983. Studies in Contemporary Economics*, Vol. 8 (Berlin: Springer-Verlag, 1984), pp. 29–49.

Formal models of long-term economic growth have not been proposed to date. Scholars have frequently viewed the industrial revolution as a great discontinuity, and have sought explanations for it in regional conditions, technological change, or abrupt changes in the saving rate.[5] In contrast, others have stressed the evolutionary nature of economic, institutional, and human development, and have argued that economic growth was neither as rapid nor as obviously discontinuous as previously imagined.[6] Our model provides a formal synthesis of the work of this latter group of scholars.

The Model Specification

In our model $t = 0$ corresponds to the beginning of the period under consideration (7000 B.C.). The unit of time is the decade, and thus the variable t represents the number of decades after 7000 B.C.; $t = 890$ is A.D. 1900, end point of the period being studied.

The economy is assumed to consist of two sectors: a sector producing only nutrients and a sector producing all other goods (AOG) (including capital). The outputs $Q_A(t)$ and $Q_I(t)$ of the two sectors at period t are described by Cobb-Douglas production functions with constant returns to scale:

$$Q_I(t) = C_1 K(t)^{\alpha_1} P_I(t)^{\alpha_2} \qquad (C.1)$$
$$Q_A(t) = C_2 K(t)^{\beta_1} P_A(t)^{\beta_2} \qquad (C.2)$$

where $K(t)$ is the aggregate capital stock in period t, and $P_I(t)$ and $P_A(t)$ are the workers in the two sectors in period t. Total population is $P(t) = P_I(t) + P_A(t)$. We assume that the labor force participation rate is unity.

C_1, C_2, α_1, α_2, β_1, β_2 are positive constants; $\alpha_1 + \alpha_2 = \beta_1 + \beta_2 = 1$. The per capita output of nutrients $S(t)$ is given by

$$S(t) = Q_A(t)/P(t). \qquad (C.3)$$

S^* is defined as the biologically determined subsistence minimum. When $S(t) < S^*$ the population is in a Malthusian subsistence crisis.

The aggregate capital stock is accumulated through the following process:

[5] Walt W. Rostow, *The Stages of Economic Growth: A Non-Communist Manifesto* (Cambridge, England: Cambridge University Press, 1960).

[6] Cameron, "New View"; Douglass C. North, *Structure and Change in Economic History* (New York: Norton, 1981); Douglass C. North and Robert P. Thomas, *The Rise of the Western World: A New Economic History* (Cambridge, England: Cambridge University Press, 1973).

$$K(t + 1) = K(t) + \lambda_i Q_I(t), \quad i = 1, 2 \qquad (C.4)$$

where λ_i is the rate of saving net of depreciation; λ_1 is the rate prevailing when the society is in a nutritional crisis, i.e., $S(t) < S^*$, and λ_2 is the rate when the society is not in a crisis, i.e., $S(t) \geq S^*$. Hence, the saving rate oscillates between λ_1 and λ_2. For the sake of simplicity we assume that the rate of saving is higher when the society is above the level of subsistence than when it is below this level. Saving is assumed to equal investment. Our model is not sensitive to changes in the process that leads to capital accumulation, as long as there is some way to augment the capital stock.[7]

Capital in this model includes not only land, as well as human and physical capital, but also knowledge broadly conceived, and the creation of those institutions that were conducive to production because they improved the efficiency of markets. The development of efficient property rights, for instance, created a part of the European institutional infrastructure that contributed greatly to the minimizing of market imperfections. Land improvements are conceptualized as part of the output of the capital-producing sector.

An idiosyncratic aspect of the model is the fact that the total capital stock enters both production functions. (This is tantamount to assuming that the ratio of industrial to agricultural capital stock remained constant.) We resort to this simplification because there is no historical warrant that would enable us to intuit the relative size and relative growth rates in the two sectors during such a long period. Allocating the capital stock at an arbitrary rate between the two sectors would have added nothing to the model's conceptualization. In any case, the accumulation of knowledge, the increased sophistication of social organization, and many of the great scientific and geographic discoveries of the past often advanced production in both sectors. These intangibles as well as social overhead capital cannot be partitioned in principle.

Another important task is to model the dynamics of population growth in accordance with the Malthusian hypotheses. Our model postulates that the growth rate of the population is r^* (per decade) as long

---

[7] Instead of a step function we have tried a logistic function whose slope depended on $S(t) - S^*$. We have also tried a rate of saving that grows at a constant rate. Both of these specifications produced results very similar to the one reported here. If the saving rate is high relative to population growth, even when the population is in a nutritional crisis, then capital will accumulate quickly, and the escape occurs soon after the onset of the process. Of course, if the rate of saving is too low, then population will grow faster than the stock of capital and there will not be any escape at all. There is no historical warrant for preferring one savings mechanism over another except insofar as to suggest that the rate of depreciation, in Europe at least, was small.

as $S(t) \geqslant S^*$. It appears to be a reasonable approximation of reality that as long as subsistence was above a critical level, population tended to reproduce. As a stabilizing mechanism, whenever per capita nutritional intake $S(t)$ drops below S^*, the population is subject, in a random fashion, to lowered growth rates, which can become negative and can even take on disastrous proportions. As the population declines, $S(t)$ increases and eventually becomes larger than S^* (eq. C.3). A cycle is completed and the growth rate is again r^* per decade until the next crisis. Hence, the model yields oscillations of $S(t)$ about S^*, and captures the "incessant contest" between population growth and available resources. If $S(t) \geqslant S^*$ for any period t after t_0, then the population has escaped the Malthusian trap, and can grow exponentially without constraint. In the next section we implement this simulation model by specifying numerical values for the parameters.

Because so much is not yet known about pre-industrial economic development, we had to make a number of arbitrary assumptions on the size of parameters such as the elasticities of the factors of production. We have experimented with various combinations of these parameters, and have found that our results are not sensitive to reasonable changes in our assumptions. Our basic thesis, that the industrial revolution can be conceptualized as having grown out of a long process of development, is not sensitive to small changes in our model.

Implementation of the Model

We assume the following values for the parameters:

$$\beta_1 = \beta_2 = \alpha_1 = \alpha_2 = 0.5; \tag{C.5}$$
$$C_1 = 2.5; C_2 = 0.213; \lambda_1 = 0.02; \lambda_2 = 0.05; r^* = 0.05. \tag{C.6}$$

The value $r^* = 0.05$ is arbitrary. We have chosen it because it was approximately the "escape rate," i.e., the rate of population growth that prevailed at the beginning of the industrial revolution. The value S^* was fixed at 0.07, in conjunction with an initial value $K(0)$ of the capital stock equal to 0.4. The parameter values above, obtained by trial and error, are not intended to be realistic; indeed, we cannot claim to simulate plausibly the historical values of those economic variables about which very little is actually known. We should stress, however, that our results are not sensitive to the values of the chosen parameters. The initial values influence, in the main, only the length of the process and the size of the population at any one time.

The initial value $P(0)$ was six million in 7000 B.C. and that of the capital-producing population was assumed to be zero. We let $r(t)$ be the growth rate of the population at period t; then

$$P(t + 1) = [1 + r(t + 1)] P(t). \qquad (C.7)$$

As we have seen, if $S(t) \geqslant S^*$, then $r(t + 1) = r^* = 0.05$ and

$$P_A(t + 1) = (1 + r^*) P_A(t) \qquad (C.8)$$
$$P_I(t + 1) = (1 + r^*) P_I(t). \qquad (C.9)$$

If, however, $S(t) < S^*$, then we determine the growth of the population by a random process. The growth rate becomes

$$r(t + 1) = r(t) - \epsilon_t, \qquad (C.10)$$

where ϵ_t is a positive random variable determined by a two-step Monte Carlo–type simulation.[8] The probability that a disturbance will occur depends on the degree to which the nutritional status of the population has deteriorated below the level of subsistence. If there is a disturbance, its size, too, is a function of the severity of the nutritional crisis, and also of the length of time elapsed since the beginning of the crisis. Indeed, $r(t + 1)$ of eq. C.10 decreases with t and may eventually become negative. As a consequence of these randomly generated negative shocks, population during a crisis is susceptible to small fluctuations as well as to those catastrophic collapses known to characterize populations of the past.

Finally, we specify the allocation of the population between the two sectors of the economy when the population is in a Malthusian crisis. In such a case $S(t) < S^*$, and the population can either continue to grow or decline depending on the size of the random disturbances, that is, depending on whether $r(t + 1)$ of eq. C.10 is still positive. If the population continues to grow, then we assume that equations C.8 and C.9

---

[8] At first we determine whether there will be a catastrophe ($\epsilon_t > 0$) or not ($\epsilon_t = 0$). Specifically, we recall that $S^* - S(t) > 0$, and define

$$U(t) = \frac{1}{1 + 4 \exp(-400(S^* - S(t)))}.$$

Observe that $U(t)$ approaches 1 as $S^* - S(t)$ becomes larger. We now draw a random number $\eta(t)$, uniformly distributed between 0 and 1. Then $\epsilon > 0$ if $\eta(t) \leqslant U(t)$, and $\epsilon_t = 0$ if $\eta(t) > U(t)$. Hence, the probability of a crisis occurring increases with the severity of the crisis $[S^* - S(t)]$. When $\epsilon_t > 0$, we proceed to determine the magnitude of ϵ_t.

If $\epsilon_t > 0$, a random number $\mu(t)$ is drawn from a truncated (the positive side) normal distribution with mean 0 and variance 1. We then assume that ϵ_t is proportional to $\mu(t)U(t)$. In addition, ϵ_t increases with $y(t)$, the number of decades the population has been in a crisis; ϵ_t is given by

$$\epsilon_t = 0.1 \, \mu(t) \, [U(t)][1 + \exp(0.15(y(t) - 5))].$$

hold as long as the average product of labor in the agricultural sector is above the level of subsistence: $(Q_A/P_A) \geqslant S^*$. If the average product of labor falls below subsistence, then we postulate that half of the increment to population enters the AOG sector and half enters the nutrient-producing sector (eqs. C.11 and C.12). Motivated by the survival instinct, the labor force migrates into the AOG sector because the only way to reverse the crisis is to expand the sector that contributes to capital accumulation. (The nutrition-producing sector is, in a sense, satiated.) These are the Boserupian episodes, during which rapid population growth becomes conducive to capital accumulation.

$$P_A(t + 1) = P_A(t) + 0.5 \, [P(t + 1) - P(t)] \quad \text{(C.11)}$$
$$P_I(t + 1) = P_I(t) + 0.5 \, [P(t + 1) - P(t)] \quad \text{(C.12)}$$

If, however, the population in a Malthusian crisis begins to decline, that is, if the negative shocks are sufficiently large so that the population growth rate becomes negative, then we also assume that half the decrease comes out of each of the two sectors (equations C.11 and C.12).[9]

Because initially P_I is zero, the AOG sector starts during the first crisis, when part of the excess population enters the AOG sector. Subsequently the random shocks might devastate the population, and P_I can become zero again. The cycle then repeats, but with a greater accumulation of capital.

As a consequence of migration, the population in the AOG sector oscillates with a greater amplitude than the population of the subsistence sector. This phenomenon is in keeping with the notion that urban population was highly susceptible to catastrophic epidemics.[10] (The Black Death in fourteenth-century Europe, and more generally endemic outbursts of bubonic plague, cholera, smallpox, etc., are well documented examples of such epidemics in early modern Europe.)

The model is now completely specified. The derived variables $Q_I(t)$, $Q_A(t)$, and $S(t)$ are functions of the primary variables $K(t)$, $P_A(t)$, and $P_I(t)$. The simulation provides plausible trajectories for the population, capital stock, and per capita food production in keeping with the stylized facts outlined in the introduction (Figures C.1–C.3). We do not, however, purport to replicate all nuances of Europe's demographic and economic experience. Indeed, our aim was not to reproduce the actual

[9] We have experimented with various shares of the population increase entering the respective sectors without jeopardizing the results, including the one in which all the population change was absorbed by the capital-producing sector.

[10] Paul M. Hohenberg and Lynn Hollen Lees, *The Making of Urban Europe, 1000–1950* (Cambridge, MA: Harvard University Press, 1985).

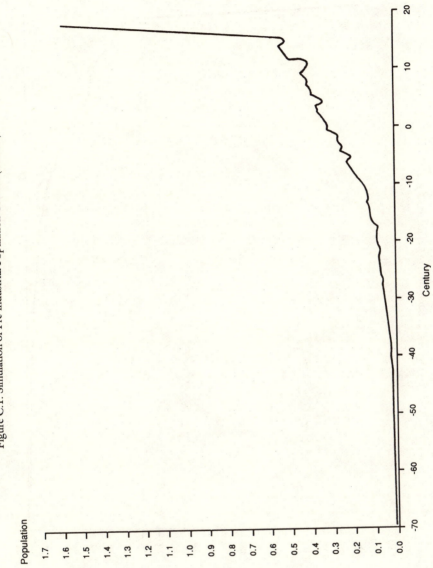

Figure C.1. Simulation of Pre-industrial Population Growth (billions)

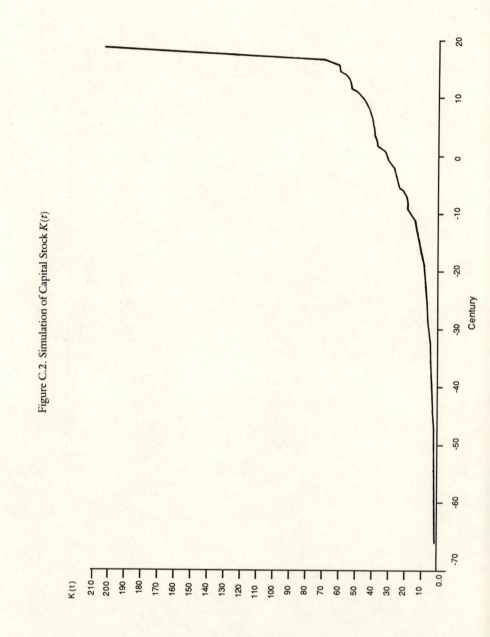

Figure C.2. Simulation of Capital Stock $K(t)$

population cycles of the past, because those were, we believe, partly the outcome of a random process. Hence, they were just one of the many possible outcomes that could have been obtained. Because of the stochastic process, the escape need not be obtained on every run. The probability of an escape depends on the parameters chosen for the model, and since these were chosen arbitrarily, the notion of the likelihood of obtaining an escape cannot have historical significance. The results are not sensitive to reasonable variations of the equations, constants, or variables. The initial values of the parameters have little effect on the salient features of the model's dynamic aspects. They control both the values of the variables at a point in time and the duration of the process.

Per capita output $S(t)$ of the subsistence sector oscillates about $S^* = 0.07$ until the time of escape (Figure C.3). Because of capital accumulation $S(t)$ eventually remains larger than S^* (see eq. C.3) and departs from its equilibrium value, thus resulting in the escape from the Malthusian trap which we conceptualize as the industrial revolution: per capita output becomes large enough to allow the population and total product to grow unhindered.

Summary

Our purpose was to conceptualize within a mathematical framework the dynamics of economic and population growth posited by the "Austrian" model of the industrial revolution. In addition, we wanted a computer model capable of simulating an industrial revolution, that is to say, one that is capable of reproducing a stagnating economy through hundreds of iterations, but that nonetheless would be capable of suddenly growing unhindered. We accomplished this by positing a time-invariant economic-demographic model that captures the salient features of Europe's passage into modernity. The stylized economy consists of two sectors, one producing only nutrients and the other everything else, including capital. Population grows, but under rather adverse, Malthusian conditions. When the nutritional status of the population deteriorates, randomly generated positive checks begin to pose an effective constraint on further population growth. During a subsistence crisis the population is eventually decimated. Because of the ongoing process of capital accumulation (eq. C.4), even with a very low saving rate, each new phase of population expansion begins with a greater stock of accumulated capital than previously, despite recurrent setbacks. This process enables the population in the AOG-producing sector to expand in the long run. In sum, over many cycles both population and capital stock increase. Thus the model emphasizes the fact that slow

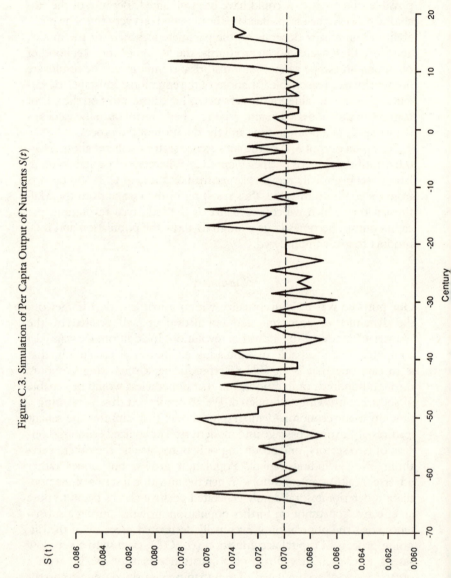

Figure C.3. Simulation of Per Capita Output of Nutrients $S(t)$

but persistent accumulation was an important reason for the success of Europe's economic development.

With the growth of capital the productivity in the nutrient-producing sector rises, and an ever increasing share of the population can be maintained in the AOG sector, the sector that also produces capital. The rate at which the capital stock grows increases not through a rise in the rate of saving but through a rise in the share of the population that produces capital. Eventually the abundance of nutrients enables a critical share of the population in the AOG sector to be reached. As a consequence, the rate of capital accumulation can proceed sufficiently quickly to overcome the Malthusian constraints.

The model posits a mechanism capable of resolving the paradox between the continuity and the discontinuity of pre-industrial economic processes. The simulation is able to replicate the salient features of economic and demographic growth in this period (Figure C.1). Even under worst-case assumptions—a low saving rate and a population constantly decimated—we show that society can escape from the Malthusian trap and generate a sustained increase in output after an extended period of fluctuations and slow growth. The industrial revolution is therefore conceptualized not as a break with the past, but as the culmination of a demographic-economic process begun millennia before. The model emphasizes that the important feature of the industrial revolution was not the rapid growth in total output, but the fact that the Malthusian constraints on population growth finally vanished.

There is no contradiction in conceiving of the economic-demographic framework as having remained stable during this epoch even though some of the variables grew unconstrained at the end of the period. The crux of the model is that the slow and intermittent accumulation through time enabled humanity ultimately to emancipate itself from the Malthusian menace. In this way we integrate the Malthusian and Boserupian views of the effect of population growth on economic development. The implication of this model is that one can account for the unprecedented increase in output during the industrial revolution without resorting to discontinuous shifts in the production function. One does not need to think of the industrial revolution as a period of structural change, or what Abramovitz and David have poetically called "technologically induced traverses," that is, "disequilibrium transitions between successive growth paths."[11]

It is true that the capital stock has to grow fast enough during the

[11] Moses Abramovitz and Paul David, "Reinterpreting Economic Growth: Parables and Realities," *American Economic Review* 63 (1973): 428–439.

industrial revolution to accommodate a growing population. Yet the rate of growth of the capital stock is more important than the saving rate itself. One should distinguish between the two parameters, because the rate of growth of the capital stock depends on the size of the labor force engaged in the AOG sector as well as on the saving rate. Another useful insight provided by the model is that the nutritional status at the beginning of the industrial revolution is a crucial factor in obtaining a permanent escape from the Malthusian trap. There is a trade-off between the level of nutritional status and the minimum rate of capital accumulation that is required for a successful escape. Thus the higher the level of nutrition the lower the rate of capital accumulation needs to be for the industrial revolution to be successful.

In sum, we have posited a plausible model that conforms to five basic features of economic growth in pre-industrial Europe. This is the first growth model capable of tracking the demographic experience of the world, and of simulating the demographic-industrial revolution of the late eighteenth and early nineteenth centuries without discontinuous shifts in the production function. Instead, our model is able to generate the industrial revolution with a time-invariant process through the slow but persistent accumulation of capital. Population growth is therefore the proximate cause of the industrial revolution in the model, but the achievements of the previous millennia were the preconditions to sustaining the economic momentum precipitated by the rise in population.

BIBLIOGRAPHY

Archival Sources

Hadtörténeti Levéltár, Budapest, Hungary.
  Kiegészitő parancsnokságok és bevonulási központok, állitási lajstromok. 1867–1945.
Kriegsarchiv, Vienna, Austria.
  Hofkriegsrath Akten.
  Protokoll Register.
  Militär Impressen.
  Instruction für die kriegs-Commissarische Beamte. April 30, 1749.
  Werb-Instruction für das Königreich Ungarn.
  Auszug der Conscriptions- und Werb-Bezirks-System für Niederösterreich. 1781.
Hübler, Franz. *Handschriften*, vols. 1–40.
———. *Sammlung der im Jahre . . . an die k. k. österreichische Armee ergangenen Politisch, Ökonomischen und Justiz-Militär-Gesetze*, vol. 3, 1753.
Musterlisten and Standestabellen, 1770–1819.
Grundbücher, 1820–1867.
Stellungslisten, 1867–1913.
Theresianische Militärakademie, Faszikel 434.
Josephinisches Waisenhaus, Faszikel 3922.
Erziehungshäuser, Musterlisten, Faszikel 3925, 3926, 3927.
Haus-, Hof-, und Staatsarchiv, Vienna, Austria.
  Zinzendorf Nachlass.
Hofkammer Archiv, Vienna, Austria, Commerz.
State Archives, Prague, Czechoslovakia.
  Státní ústřední archiv v. Praze, Č.G. Commerz.

Published Sources

A 18 Evés Sorköteles Fiatalok Fejlettsége Biologiai, Egészségi Állapota. A Központi Statisztikai Hivatal Népességtudományi Kutató Intézetének és a Magyar Tudományos Akadémia Demográfiai Bizottságának Közleményei, 1983, No. 53.

Abel, Wilhelm. *Agrarkrisen und Agrarkonjunktur: Eine Geschichte der Land- und Ernährungswirtschaft Mitteleuropas seit dem hohen Mittelalter.* 1935. Reprint. Hamburg and Berlin: Paul Parey, 1966.

———. *Massenarmut und Hungerkrisen im vorindustriellen Europa.* Hamburg and Berlin: Paul Parey, 1974.

Abramovitz, Moses, and Paul David. "Reinterpreting Economic Growth: Parables and Realities." *American Economic Review* 63 (1973): 428–439.

Adams, Donald. "The Standard of Living during American Industrialization: Evidence from the Brandywine Region, 1800–1860." *Journal of Economic History* 42 (1982): 903–917.

Allen, Robert C. "Inferring Yields from Probate Inventories." *Journal of Economic History* 48 (1988): 117–126.

Alter, George. "Plague and the Amsterdam Annuitant: A New Look at Life Annuities as a Source for Historical Demography." *Population Studies* 37 (1983): 23–41.

Amelar, Richard D., Lawrence Dubin, and Patrick C. Walsh. *Male Infertility.* Philadelphia: W. B. Saunders and Co., 1977.

Anderson, Michael. *Population Change in North-Western Europe, 1750–1850.* London: Macmillan Education Ltd., 1988.

Appleby, Andrew. *Famine in Tudor and Stuart England.* Stanford, CA: Stanford University Press, 1978.

Apter, Dan, and Vihko Reijo. "Early Menarche, a Risk Factor for Breast Cancer, Indicates Early Onset of Ovulatory Cycles." *Journal of Clinical Endocrinology and Metabolism* 57 (1983): 82–86.

Aron, Jean-Paul, Paul Dumont, and Emmanuel Le Roy Ladurie. *Anthropologie du conscrit français.* Paris: Mouton, 1972.

Ashton, T. S. *An Economic History of England. The 18th Century.* 1955. Reprint. London: Methuen & Co, 1972.

Austria. *Militär-Statistisches Jahrbuch für das Jahr 1871.* Vienna: k. k. Hof- und Staatsdruckerei, 1873.

———. *Militär-Statistisches Jahrbuch für das Jahr 1910.* Vienna: k. k. Hof- und Staatsdruckerei, 1913.

Aymard, Maurice. "Toward the History of Nutrition: Some Methodological Remarks." In Robert Forster and Orest Ranum, eds., *Food and Drink in History*, pp. 1–16. Baltimore: The Johns Hopkins University Press, 1979.

Bairoch, Paul. "Europe's Gross National Product: 1800–1975." *Journal of European Economic History* 5 (1976): 273–340.

———. "International Industrialization Levels from 1750 to 1980." *Journal of European Economic History* 11 (1982): 269–334.

———. *Révolution industrielle et sous-développement.* Paris: Société d'édition d'enseignement supérieur, 1963.

Balazs, Robert, *et al.* "Undernutrition and Brain Development." In Frank Falkner and James M. Tanner, eds., *Human Growth: A Comprehensive Treatise.* 2d ed. Vol. 3, pp. 415–473. New York and London: Plenum Press, 1986.

Beales, Derek. *Joseph II*. Vol. 1, *In the Shadow of Maria Theresa, 1741–1780*. Cambridge, England: Cambridge University Press, 1987.

Beattie, Jim. "The Pattern of Crime in England, 1660–1800." *Past and Present* 62 (1974): 47–95.

Belitzky, János. *A Magyar Gabonakivitel Története 1860-ig*. Budapest: n.p., 1932.

Bellagio Conferees. "The Relationship of Nutrition, Disease, and Social Conditions: A Graphical Presentation." *Journal of Interdisciplinary History* 14 (1983): 503–506.

Benda, Gyula. *Statisztikai adatok a Magyar mezőgazdaság történetéhez, 1767–1867*. Budapest: Központi Statisztikai Hivatal, 1973.

Bennett, Merrill, and Rosamond Peirce. "Change in the American National Diet, 1879–1959." *Food Research Institute Studies* 2 (1961): 95–119.

Berg, Alan. *Malnourished People: A Policy View*. Washington, DC: Publications Department, The World Bank, 1981.

Berlanstein, Lenard R. *The Working People of Paris, 1871–1914*. Baltimore: The Johns Hopkins University Press, 1984.

Bernard, Paul P. "Joseph II and the Jews: The Origins of the Toleration Patent of 1782." *Austrian History Yearbook* 4–5 (1968–69): 101–119.

Bilsky, Lester J., ed. *Historical Ecology: Essays on Environment and Social Change*. Port Washington, NY: Kennikat Press, 1980.

Biraben, Jean-Nöel. "Essai sur l'évolution du nombre des hommes." *Population* 34 (1979): 13–25.

Blum, Jerome. *The End of the Old Order in Rural Europe*. Princeton: Princeton University Press, 1978.

Bodart, Gaston. *Losses of Life in Modern Wars: Austria-Hungary; France*. Oxford: Clarendon Press, 1916.

Boldsen, J. L., and D. Kronberg. "The Distribution of Stature among Danish Conscripts in 1852–56." *Annals of Human Biology* 11 (1984): 555–565.

Bongaarts, John. "Does Malnutrition Affect Fecundity? A Summary of the Evidence." *Science* 208 (1980): 564–569.

Boserup, Ester. *The Conditions of Agricultural Growth*. Chicago: Aldine Publishing, 1965.

———. "The Impact of Scarcity and Plenty on Development." *Journal of Interdisciplinary History* 14 (1983): 383–407.

———. *Population and Technological Change: A Study of Long-Term Trends*. Chicago: The University of Chicago Press, 1981.

Bowlus, Charles R. "Ecological Crises in Fourteenth Century Europe." In Lester J. Bilsky, ed., *Historical Ecology: Essays on Environment and Social Change*, pp. 86–99. Port Washington, NY: Kennikat Press, 1980.

Braudel, Fernand. *Civilization and Capitalism 15th–18th Century*. Vol. 1, *The Structures of Everyday Life: The Limits of the Possible*. New York: Harper and Row, 1981.

Braun, Rudolph. *Industrialisierung und Volksleben: Die Veränderung der Lebensformen in einem Industriegebiet vor 1800*. Zürich: E. Rentsch, 1960.

Bresel, Jo Ann. "Impact of Malnutrition on Reproductive Endocrinology." In W. Henry Mosley, ed., *Nutrition and Human Reproduction*, pp. 29–60. New York and London: Plenum Press, 1978.

Brinkman, Henk Jan, J. W. Drukker, and Brigitte Slot. "Height and Income: A New Method for the Estimation of Historical National Income Series." *Explorations in Economic History* 25 (1988): 227–264.

Brown, R. L., J. Durbin, and J. M. Evans. "Techniques for Testing the Constancy of Regression Relationships over Time." *Journal of the Royal Statistical Society*, Ser. B, 37 (1975): 149–192.

Brudevoll, J. E., K. Liestol, and L. Walloe. "Menarcheal Age in Oslo during the Last 140 Years." *Annals of Human Biology* 6 (1979): 407–416.

Brusatti, Alois. *Österreichische Wirtschaftspolitik vom Josephinismus zum Standestaat*. Vienna: Jupiter, 1965.

Bryson, Reid A., and Thomas Murray. *Climates of Hunger: Mankind and the World's Changing Weather*. Madison: The University of Wisconsin Press, 1977.

Bryson, Reid A., and Christine Padoch. "On the Climates of History." In Robert I. Rotberg and Theodore K. Rabb, eds., *Climate and History: Studies in Interdisciplinary History*, pp. 3–17. Princeton: Princeton University Press, 1981.

Bundschuh, Karl Ritter von. *Handbuche über das bei der k. k. österreichischen Armee bestehende Militär-Ökonomie-System*. Supplement, Prague: n.p., 1824. II. Supplement, Prague: n.p., 1852.

Cameron, Rondo. "Economic History, Pure and Applied." *Journal of Economic History* 36 (1976): 3–27.

———. "The Industrial Revolution: A Misnomer." *The History Teacher* 15 (1982): 377–384.

———. "The Logistics of European Economic Growth: A Note on Historical Periodization." *Journal of European Economic History* 2 (1973): 145–148.

———. "A New View of European Industrialization." *Economic History Review*, 2d ser., 38 (1985): 1–23.

Carmichael, Ann. "Infection, Hidden Hunger, and History." *Journal of Interdisciplinary History* 14 (1983): 245–265.

Carr, Lois G., and Lorena S. Walsh. "Inventories and the Analysis of Wealth and Consumption Patterns in St. Mary's County, Maryland, 1658–1777." *Historical Methods* 13 (1980): 81–104.

Caves, Richard, and Ronald Jones. *World Trade and Payments: An Introduction*. 2d ed. Boston: Little, Brown, and Co., 1977.

Chambers, J. D. "The Course of Population Change." In David V. Glass and David E. C. Eversley, eds., *Population in History: Essays in Historical Demography*, pp. 327–334. Chicago: The University of Chicago Press, 1965.

Chandler, Tertius, and Gerald Fox. *3000 Years of Urban Growth*. New York: Academic Press, 1974.

Chayanov, A. V. *The Theory of the Peasant Economy*. 1925. Reprint. Homewood, IL: Irwin, 1966.

Christ, Daniel. "The Rise of the West." *American Sociological Review* 50 (1985): 181–195.

Christoph, Paul. *Maria Theresia und Marie Antoinette: Ihr geheimer Briefwechsel.* Vienna: Cesam Verlag, 1952.

Cipolla, Carlo M. *Before the Industrial Revolution: European Society and Economy, 1000–1700.* 2d ed. New York: Norton and Co., 1980.

———. *The Economic History of World Population.* 1962. Reprint. Baltimore: Penguin Books, 1970.

———. *Guns, Sails and Empires: Technological Innovations and the Early Phases of European Expansion 1400–1700.* 2d ed. New York: Minerva Press, 1966.

Clarke, George, *et al.* "Poor Growth prior to Early Childhood: Decreased Health and Life-Span in the Adult." *American Journal of Physical Anthropology* 70 (1986): 145–160.

Clarkson, Leslie. *Death, Disease and Famine in Pre-Industrial England.* New York: St. Martin's Press, 1976.

Clements, F. W. "Some Effects of Different Diets." In S. V. Boyden, ed., *The Impact of Civilisation on the Biology of Man,* pp. 109–141. Toronto: University of Toronto Press, 1970.

Coale, Ansley J. "History of the Human Population." *Scientific American* 231 (September 1974): 40–51.

Coale, Ansley J., and Paul Demeny. *Regional Model Life Tables and Stable Populations.* Princeton: Princeton University Press, 1966.

Coale, H.S.D., Christopher Freeman, Marie Jahoda, and K.L.R. Pavitt, eds. *Models of Doom: A Critique of the Limits to Growth.* New York: Universal Books, 1973.

Coale, W. A., and Phyllis Deane. "The Growth of National Incomes." In H. J. Habakkuk and Michael M. Postan, eds., *Cambridge Economic History of Europe.* Vol. 6, *The Industrial Revolution and After: Incomes, Population and Technological Change,* pp. 1–55. Cambridge, England: Cambridge University Press, 1965.

Coleman, D. C. "Proto-Industrialization: A Concept Too Many." *Economic History Review,* 2d ser., 36 (1983): 435–448.

Corvisier, André. *L'armée française de la fin du XVIIᵉ siècle au ministère de Choiseul. Le Soldat.* Paris: Presses Universitaires de France, 1964.

Crafts, N.F.R. "British Economic Growth, 1700–1831: A Review of the Evidence." *Economic History Review,* 2d ser., 36 (1983): 177–199.

———. *British Economic Growth during the Industrial Revolution.* Oxford: Clarendon Press, 1985.

———. "The Eighteenth Century: A Survey." In Roderick Floud and Donald McCloskey, eds., *The Economic History of Britain since 1700. Vol. 1: 1700–1860,* pp. 1–16. Cambridge, England: Cambridge University Press, 1981.

———. "English Workers' Real Wages during the Industrial Revolution: Some Remaining Problems." *Journal of Economic History* 45 (1985): 139–144.

Cravioto, Joaquin, and Ramiro Arrieta. "Nutrition, Mental Development, and Learning." In Frank Falkner and James M. Tanner, eds., *Human Growth: A*

Comprehensive Treatise. 2d ed. Vol. 3, pp. 501–536. New York and London: Plenum Press, 1986.

Crouzet, François. *Capital Formation in the Industrial Revolution*. London: Methuen, 1972.

————. *The Victorian Economy*. New York: Columbia University Press, 1982.

Davis, David E. "The Scarcity of Rats and the Black Death: An Ecological History." *Journal of Interdisciplinary History* 16 (1986): 455–470.

Deane, Phyllis. *The First Industrial Revolution*. Cambridge, England: Cambridge University Press, 1965.

Deane, Phyllis, and W. A. Coale. *British Economic Growth*. Cambridge, England: Cambridge University Press, 1962.

D'Elvert, Christian. "Zur Geschichte der Juden in Mähren und der österreichischen Schlesien." *Schriften der historisch-statistischen Secktion der k. k. mährischen Gesellschaft zur Beförderung des Ackerbaues, der Natur- und Landeskunde*. Vol. 30. Brünn: Winiker, 1895.

Desplat, Christian. "The Climate of Eighteenth-Century Béarn." *French History* 1 (1987): 27–48.

De Vries, Jan. *European Urbanization, 1500–1800*. Cambridge, MA: Harvard University Press, 1984.

————. "Measuring the Impact of Climate on History: The Search for Appropriate Methodologies." In Robert I. Rotberg and Theodore K. Rabb, eds., *Climate and History: Studies in Interdisciplinary History*, pp. 19–50. Princeton: Princeton University Press, 1981.

Deyon, Pierre and Franklin F. Mendels. "Proto-industrialization: Theory and Reality." *Eighth International Conference on Economic History*, Budapest: Akadémiai Kiadó, 1982.

Dickson, P.G.M. *Finance and Government under Maria Theresia, 1740–1780*. Oxford: Clarendon Press, 1987.

Dixit, A. K. *The Theory of Equilibrium Growth*. London: Oxford University Press, 1976.

Dowler, Elizabeth A., and Young Ok Seo. "Assessment of Energy Intake: Estimates of Food Supply v Measurement of Food Consumption." *Food Policy* 10 (1985): 278–288.

Driver, Edwin, and Aloo Driver. "Social Class and Height and Weight in Metropolitan Madras." *Social Biology* 30 (1983): 189–204.

Duby, Georges. "Medieval Agriculture, 900–1500." In Carlo Cipolla, ed., *The Fontana Economic History of Europe*. Vol. 1, *The Middle Ages*, pp. 175–220. London: William Collins and Sons, 1972.

Ducros, A., and P. Pasquet. "Evolution de l'âge d'apparition des premières règles (ménarche) en France." *Biométrie Humaine* 13 (1978): 35–43.

Duffey, Christopher. *The Army of Maria Theresa*. London: David and Charles, 1977.

Dufour, Jean-Marie. "Methods for Specification Errors Analysis with Macroeconomic Applications." Unpublished Ph.D. dissertation, Department of Economics, University of Chicago, 1979.

Dupâquier, Jacques. *La population rurale du Bassin Parisien à l'époque de Louis XIV*. Paris: Éditions de l'École des hautes études en sciences sociales, 1979.

Durand, John D. "Historical Estimates of World Population: An Evaluation." *Population and Development Review* 3 (1977): 253–296.

———. "The Modern Expansion of World Population." In Thomas R. Detwyler, ed., *Man's Impact on Environment*, pp. 36–49. New York: McGraw-Hill, 1971. Reprinted from *Proceedings of the American Philosophical Society* 111 (1967): 136–145.

Dyer, Ch. "Changes in Nutrition and Standard of Living in England, 1200–1500." In Robert W. Fogel, ed., *Long-Term Changes in Nutrition and the Standard of Living*, pp. 35–44. Berne: 9th Congress of the International Economic History Association, 1986.

Eckhart, Ferenc. *A bécsi udvar gazdasági politikája Magyarországon Mária Terézia korában*. Budapest: Budavári Tudományos Társaság, 1922.

Eckstein, Zvi, T. Paul Schultz, and Kenneth I. Wolpin. "Short-Run Fluctuations in Fertility and Mortality in Pre-Industrial Sweden." *European Economic Review* 26 (1984): 295–317.

Eddy, John A. "Climate and the Role of the Sun." In Robert I. Rotberg and Theodore K. Rabb, eds., *Climate and History: Studies in Interdisciplinary History*, pp. 145–167. Princeton: Princeton University Press, 1981.

Engels, Friedrich. *The Condition of the Working Class in England*. Translated by W. O. Henderson and W. H. Chaloner. New York: Oxford University Press, 1958.

Engels, Friedrich, *The Condition of the Working Class in England*. Stanford: Stanford University Press, 1968.

Engerman, Stanley L. "The Height of U.S. Slaves." *Local Population Studies* 16 (1976): 45–50.

Eveleth, Phyllis B., and James M. Tanner. *Worldwide Variation in Human Growth*. Cambridge, England: Cambridge University Press, 1976.

Falkner, Frank, and James M. Tanner, eds. *Human Growth: A Comprehensive Treatise*. 2d ed. New York and London: Plenum Press, 1986.

Faragó, Tamás. "Paraszti Háztartás—és Munkaszervezet—Típusok Magyarországon A 18. Század Közepén. Pilis-Buda környéki birtokos paraszti háztartások 1745–1770 között." *Történeti Statisztikai Füzetek* 7 (1985): 1–187.

Feder, Harvey H. "Essentials of Steroid Structure, Nomenclature, Reactions, Biosynthesis, and Measurements." In Norman T. Adler, ed., *Neuroendocrinology of Reproduction, Physiology and Behavior*, pp. 19–64. New York and London: Plenum Press, 1981.

Feigelman, Theodor, Rose E. Frisch, Maureen MacBurney, Isaac Schiff, and Douglas Wilmore. "Sexual Maturation in Third and Fourth Decades, after Nutritional Rehabilitation by Enteral Feeding." *Journal of Pediatrics* 111 (1987): 620–623.

Flinn, Michael W. "English Workers' Living Standards during the Industrial Revolution: A Comment." *Economic History Review* 37 (1984): 88–92.

Flinn, Michael W. *The European Demographic System, 1500–1820.* Baltimore: The Johns Hopkins University Press, 1981.

Floud, Roderick. "The Heights of Europeans since 1750: A New Source for European Economic History." National Bureau of Economic Research, Working Paper No. 1318, 1984.

———. "Inference from the Heights of Volunteer Soldiers and Sailors." Unpublished manuscript, Department of History, University of London, 1983.

———. "Measuring the Transformation of the European Economies: Income, Health, and Welfare." Unpublished manuscript, Department of History, University of London, 1984.

———. "Two Cultures? British and American Heights in the Nineteenth Century." Unpublished manuscript, Department of History, University of London, 1985.

———. "Wirtschaftliche und soziale Einflüsse auf die Körpergrössen von Europäern seit 1750." *Jahrbuch für Wirtschaftsgeschichte* (1985): 93–118.

Floud, Roderick, and Donald McCloskey, eds. *The Economic History of Britain since 1700. Vol. 1: 1700–1860.* Cambridge, England: Cambridge University Press, 1981.

Floud, Roderick, and Kenneth Wachter. "Poverty and Physical Stature: Evidence on the Standard of Living of London Boys, 1770–1870." *Social Science History* 6 (1982): 422–452.

Floud, Roderick, Kenneth Wachter, and Annabel Gregory. "The Heights of the British since 1700." Unpublished manuscript, Department of History, University of London, 1987.

———. "The Physical State of the British Working Class, 1860–1914: Evidence from Army Recruits." National Bureau of Economic Research, Working Paper No. 1661, 1985.

Fogel, Robert W. "Biomedical Approaches to the Estimation and Interpretation of Secular Trends in Equity, Morbidity, Mortality, and Labor Productivity in Europe, 1750–1980." Unpublished manuscript, Graduate School of Business Administration, University of Chicago, 1987.

———. "Nutrition and the Decline in Mortality since 1700: Some Preliminary Findings." In Stanley L. Engerman and Robert Gallman, eds., *Long-Term Factors in American Economic Growth.* National Bureau of Economic Research, Studies in Income and Wealth. Vol. 51, pp. 439–555. Chicago: The University of Chicago Press, 1987.

———. "Physical Growth as a Measure of the Economic Well-Being of Populations: The Eighteenth and Nineteenth Centuries." In Frank Falkner and James M. Tanner, eds., *Human Growth: a Comprehensive Treatise.* 2d ed. Vol. 3, pp. 263–282. New York and London: Plenum Press, 1986.

———. *Railroads and American Economic Growth: Essays in Econometric History.* Baltimore: The Johns Hopkins University Press, 1964.

Fogel, Robert W., Stanley L. Engerman, Roderick Floud, Gerald Friedman, Robert A. Margo, Kenneth Sokoloff, Richard H. Steckel, T. James Trussell, Georgia Villaflor, and Kenneth W. Wachter. "Secular Changes in American and British Stature and Nutrition." *Journal of Interdisciplinary History* 14 (1983): 445–481.

Fogel, Robert W., Stanley L. Engerman, and James Trussell. "Exploring the Uses of Data on Height: The Analysis of Long-Term Trends in Nutrition, Labor Welfare, and Labor Productivity." *Social Science History* 6 (1982): 401–421.

Fogel, Robert W., Stanley L. Engerman, James Trussell, Roderick Floud, Clayne L. Pope, and Larry T. Wimmer. "The Economics of Mortality in North America, 1650–1910: A Description of a Research Project." *Historical Methods* 11 (1978): 75–108.

Freudenberger, Herman. "An Industrial Momentum Achieved in the Habsburg Monarchy." *Journal of European Economic History* 12 (1983): 339–350.

———. "Industrialization in Bohemia and Moravia in the Eighteenth Century." *Journal of Central European Affairs* 19 (1960): 347–356.

———. "Progressive Bohemian and Moravian Aristocrats." In Stanley B. Winters and Joseph Held, eds., *Intellectual and Social Developments in the Habsburg Empire from Maria Theresia to World War I: Essays Dedicated to Robert A. Kann*, pp. 115–130. Boulder, CO: East European Quarterly, distributed by Columbia University Press, 1975.

———. "State Intervention as an Obstacle to Economic Growth in the Habsburg Monarchy." *Journal of Economic History* 27 (1967): 493–509.

———. *The Waldstein Woolen Mill: Noble Entrepreneurship in Eighteenth-Century Bohemia*. Boston: Baker Library, Harvard School of Business Administration, 1963.

———. "The Woolen-Goods Industry of the Habsburg Monarchy in the Eighteenth Century." *Journal of Economic History* 20 (1960): 383–406.

Freudenberger, Herman, and Gaylord Cummins. "Health, Work, and Leisure before the Industrial Revolution." *Explorations in Economic History* 13 (1976): 1–12.

Friedman, Gerald C. "The Heights of Slaves in Trinidad." *Social Science History* 6 (1982): 482–515.

Frisch, Rose E. "Body Fat, Menarche, Fitness and Fertility." *Human Reproduction* 2 (1987): 521–533.

———. "Demographic Implications of the Biological Determinants of Female Fecundity." *Social Biology* 22 (1975): 17–22.

———. "Fatness, Menarche and Fertility." In Sharon Golub, ed., *Menarche: The Transition from Girl to Woman*, pp. 5–20. Lexington, MA: Heath and Co., 1983.

———. "Nutrition, Fatness and Fertility: The Effect of Food Intake on Reproductive Ability." In W. Henry Mosley, ed., *Nutrition and Human Reproduction*, pp. 91–122. New York and London: Plenum Press, 1978.

———. "Population, Food Intake and Fertility." *Science* 199 (1978): 22–30.

———. "Population, Nutrition and Fecundity." In Jacques Dupâquier, ed., *Malthus Past and Present*. London: Academic Press, 1983.

———. "Reply to James Trussell." *Science* 200 (June 1978): 1509–1513.

Furnass, S. Bryan. "Comment." In S. V. Boyden, ed., *The Impact of Civilisation on the Biology of Man*. Toronto: University of Toronto Press, 1970.

Gallman, Robert. "The Pace and Pattern of American Economic Growth." In Lance Davis, Richard Easterlin, and William Parker, eds., *American Economic Growth: An Economist's History of the United States*, pp. 15–60. New York: Harper and Row, 1972.

Galloway, Patrick R. "Annual Variations in Deaths by Age, Deaths by Cause, Prices, and Weather in London, 1670 to 1830." *Population Studies* 39 (1985): 487–505.

———. "Long-Term Fluctuations in Climate and Population in the Preindustrial Era." *Population and Development Review* 12 (1986): 1–24.

Garraty, John A. *Unemployment in History*. New York: Harper and Row, 1978.

Gerschenkron, Alexander. "The Discipline and I." *Journal of Economic History* 27 (1967): 443–459.

———. *Economic Backwardness in Historical Perspective: A Book of Essays*. Cambridge, MA: Harvard University Press, 1962.

———. *An Economic Spurt That Failed*. Princeton: Princeton University Press, 1977.

———. *Europe in the Russian Mirror: Four Lectures in Economic History*. London: Cambridge University Press, 1970.

Gilboy, Elizabeth. "Demand as a Factor in the Industrial Revolution." In R. M. Hartwell, ed., *The Causes of the Industrial Revolution in England*, pp. 121–138. London: Methuen, 1967.

Goehlert, Vincenz. "Die Ergebnisse der in Österreich in vorigen Jahrhundert ausgeführten Volkszählungen im Vergleiche mit jenen der neueren Zeit." *Sitzungsberichte der philos.-histor. Klasse der k. Akademie der Wissenschaften*, Vienna, 1854.

Goldsmith, Raymond. "The Economic Growth of Tsarist Russia, 1860–1913." *Economic Development and Cultural Change* 9 (1961): 441–476.

Goldstone, Jack. "The Demographic Revolution in England: A Reexamination." *Population Studies* 40 (1986): 5–33.

———. "State Breakdown in the English Revolution: A New Synthesis." *American Journal of Sociology* 92 (1982): 257–322.

Gómez Mendoza, Antonio, and Vincente Pérez Moreda. "Estatura y nivel de vida en la Espana del primer tercio del siglo XX." *Moneda y Credito* 174 (1985): 29–64.

Good, David F. *The Economic Rise of the Habsburg Empire, 1750–1914*. Berkeley: University of California Press, 1984.

Grab, Alexander. "The Politics of Subsistence: The Liberalization of Grain Commerce in Austrian Lombardy under Enlightened Despotism." *Journal of Modern History* 57 (1985): 185–210.

Greene, Lawrence, and Francis Johnston, eds. *Social and Biological Predictors of Nutritional Status, Physical Growth, and Neurological Development*. New York: Academic Press, 1980.

Gregory, Paul. *Russian National Income, 1885–1913*. New York: Cambridge University Press, 1982.

Grossman, Gregory. "The Industrialisation of Russia and the Soviet Union." In Carlo Cipolla, ed., *The Fontana Economic History of Europe*. Vol. 4, *The Emergence of Industrial Societies*, pp. 486–531. London: William Collins and Sons, 1973.

Grossmann, Henryk. "Die Anfänge und geschichtliche Entwicklung der amtlichen Statistik in Österreich." *Statistische Monatschrift* (1916): 331–423.

Grünberg, Karl. *Die Bauernbefreiung und die Auflösung des gutsherrlich-bauerlichen Verhältnisses in Böhmen, Mähren und Schlesien*. Vols. 1 and 2. Leipzig: Duncker und Humblot, 1893–1894.

———. *Franz Anton von Blanc, Ein Sozialpolitiker der theresianisch-josefinischen Zeit*. Munich: Duncker, 1921.

———. "Die Grundeigenthumsfähigkeit in den böhmischen Ländern vor 1848." *Schmollers Jahrbuch für Gesetzgebung, Verwaltung, und Volkswirtschaft* 21. Reprinted in Karl Grünberg, *Studien zur österreichischen Agrargeschichte*. pp. 101–177. Leipzig: Duncker und Humblot, 1901.

Grünwald, Joseph. *Drey Abhandlungen über die physikalische Beschaffenheit einiger Distrikte und Gegenden von Böhmen*. Prague and Dresden: Böhmische Gesellschaft der Wissenschaften, 1786.

Gullickson, Gay L. "Agriculture and Cottage Industry: Redefining the Causes of Proto-industrialization." *Journal of Economic History* 43 (1983): 831–850.

Gürtler, Alfred. *Die Volkszählungen Maria Theresias und Josef II, 1753–1790*. Innsbruck: Wagner, 1909.

Gutmann, Myron P. *Toward the Modern Economy: Early Industry in Europe, 1500–1800*. New York: Alfred A. Knopf, 1988.

Habakkuk, H. J. "English Population in the Eighteenth Century." *Economic History Review*, 2d ser., 6 (1953): 117–133.

Hajnal, John. "European Marriage Patterns in Perspective." In David V. Glass and David E. C. Eversley, eds., *Population in History: Essays in Historical Demography*. London: E. Arnold, 1965.

Hamilton, Gary, and F. H. Bronson. "Food Restriction and Reproductive Development in Wild House Mice." *Biology of Reproduction* 32 (1985): 773–778.

Hammer, C. U., H. B. Clausen, and W. Dansgaard. "Greenland Ice Sheet Evidence of Post-Glacial Volcanism and Its Climatic Impact." *Nature* (Nov. 20, 1980): 230–235, as cited by Mary Kilbourne Matossian, "Volcanic Activity and Disease in Europe, 1550–1900," unpublished manuscript, Department of History, University of Maryland, 1986.

Hammond, J. L. "The Industrial Revolution and Discontent." *Economic History Review*, 1st ser., 2 (1930): 215–228.

Hanley, Susan. "A High Standard of Living in Nineteenth-Century Japan: Fact or Fantasy?" *Journal of Economic History* 43 (1983): 183–192.

———. "Population Trends and Economic Development in Tokugawa Japan." Unpublished Ph.D. dissertation, Yale University, 1971.

Hansen, Stefan, Knut Larsson, Sven Carlsson, and Patrick Sourander. "The Development of Sexual Behavior in the Rat: Role of Preadult Nutrition and Environmental Conditions." *Developmental Psychobiology* 11 (1978): 51–61.

Harley, C. Knick. "British Industrialization before 1841: Evidence of Slower Growth during the Industrial Revolution." *Journal of Economic History* 42 (1982): 267–289.

Hartmann, Waltraud. "Beobachtungen zur Akzeleration des Längenwachstums in der zweiten Hälfte des 18. Jahrhunderts." Unpublished Ph.D. dissertation, Goethe University, Frankfurt, 1970.

Hartwell, R. M. "The Rising Standard of Living in England, 1800–1850." *Economic History Review*, 2d ser., 13 (1961): 397–416.

Hartwell, R. M., and Stanley Engerman. "Models of Immiseration: The Theoretical Basis of Pessimism." In Arthur J. Taylor, ed., *The Standard of Living in Britain in the Industrial Revolution*, pp. 189–213. London: Methuen, 1975.

Haselsteiner, Horst. *Joseph II und die Komitate Ungarns*. Vienna: Böhlaus, 1983.

Heckscher, E. F. "Swedish Population Trends before the Industrial Revolution." *Economic History Review*, 2d ser., 2 (1950): 266–277.

Helczmanovski, Heimold. "Austria-Hungary." In W. R. Lee, ed., *European Demography and Economic Growth*, pp. 27–78. New York: St. Martin's Press, 1979.

Herlihy, David J. "Attitudes Toward the Environment in Medieval Society." In Lester J. Bilsky, ed., *Historical Ecology: Essays on Environment and Social Change*, pp. 100–116. Port Washington, NY: Kennikat Press, 1980.

———. "The Economy of Traditional Europe." *Journal of Economic History* 31 (1971): 153–164.

———. *Medieval and Renaissance Pistoia: The Social History of an Italian Town, 1200–1430*. New Haven: Yale University Press, 1967.

Hicks, John R. *Value and Capital: An Inquiry into Some Fundamental Principles of Economic Theory*. 2d ed. Oxford: Clarendon Press, 1939.

Hildebrand, Bruno. *Die Nationalökonomie der Gegenwart und Zukunft*. Jena: G. Fischer, 1922.

Himmelfarb, Gertrude. *The Idea of Poverty*. New York: Knopf, 1983.

Hobsbawm, E. J., and R. M. Hartwell. "The Standard of Living during the Industrial Revolution: A Discussion." *Economic History Review*, 2d ser., 16 (1963–64): 119–146.

Hoffmann, Alfred. *Wirtschaftsgeschichte des Landes Oberösterreich*. Salzburg: Otto Müller, 1952.

Hoffmann, Walther. *Das Wachstum der deutschen Wirtschaft seit der Mitte des 19. Jahrhunderts*. Berlin: Springer, 1965.

Hohenberg, Paul M., and Lynn Hollen Lees. *The Making of Urban Europe, 1000–1950*. Cambridge, MA: Harvard University Press, 1985.

Hollingsworth, Thomas H. "Demographic Change and the Availability of Resources: The Main Stages in Development and Decline." In *International Population Conference, Florence 1985*, vol. 4. Liège, Belgium: International Union for the Scientific Study of Population, 1985.

————. "The Demography of the British Peerage." Supplement to *Population Studies* 18 (1964–65): 1–108.

————. "An Introduction to Population Crises." In Hubert Charbonneau and André Larose, eds., *The Great Mortalities: Methodological Studies of Demographic Crises in the Past*, pp. 17–20. Liège, Belgium: Ordina Editions, 1980.

Holmes, George. *Meat Situation in the United States*. United States Department of Agriculture, Report no. 109. Washington, DC: 1916.

Hopkins, M. K. "The Age of Roman Girls at Marriage." *Population Studies* 18 (1965): 9–27.

Horváth, Mihály. *Horváth Mihály Kisebb Történelmi Munkái*. Pest: Ráth Mór, 1868.

Hoskins, W. G. "Harvest Fluctuations and English Economic History, 1480–1619." In W. E. Minchinton, ed., *Essays in Agrarian History*, vol. 1, pp. 93–116. The British Agricultural Society. Newton Abbot, England: David and Charks, 1968.

————. "Harvest Fluctuations and English Economic History, 1620–1759." *Agricultural History Review* 16 (1968): 15–31.

Hübler, Franz. *Militär-ökonomie-system der k. k. österreichischen Armee*. Vienna: J. Geistinger'schen Buchhandlung, 1820.

Hufton, Olwen H. *The Poor of Eighteenth Century France, 1750–1789*. Oxford: Clarendon Press, 1974.

————. "Social Conflict and the Grain Supply in Eighteenth-Century France." *Journal of Interdisciplinary History* 14 (1983): 303–331.

Imhof, Arthur E. "Unsere Lebensuhr- Phasenverschiebungen im Verlaufe der Neuzeit." In Peter Borscheid and Hans J. Teuteberg, eds., *Ehe, Liebe, Tod. Zum Wandel der Familie, der Geschlechts- und Generationsbeziehungen in der Neuzeit*, pp. 170–198. Münster: F. Coppenrath, 1983.

Ippolito, Richard. "The Effect of the 'Agricultural Depression' on Industrial Demand in England: 1730–1750." *Economica* 42 (1975): 298–312.

Jackson, R. V. "Growth and Deceleration in English Agriculture, 1660–1790." *Economic History Review*, 2d ser., 38 (1985): 333–352.

John, A. H. "Agricultural Productivity and Economic Growth in England, 1700–1760." *Journal of Economic History* 25 (1965): 19–34.

Jones, Alice Hanson. *Wealth of a Nation to Be: The American Colonies on the Eve of the Revolution*. New York: Columbia University Press, 1980.

Jones, Eric L. "Agriculture and Economic Growth in England, 1660–1750: Agricultural Change." *Journal of Economic History* 25 (1965): 1–18.

————. *The European Miracle: Environments, Economies, and Geopolitics in the History of Europe and Asia*. Cambridge, England: Cambridge University Press, 1981.

————, ed. *Agriculture and Economic Growth in England*. London: Methuen, 1967.

Jordan, Thomas Edward. *Victorian Childhood: Themes and Variations*. Albany, NY: State University of New York Press, 1987.

Kahan, Arcadius. *The Plow, the Hammer, and the Knout: An Economic History of Eighteenth-Century Russia.* Chicago: The University of Chicago Press, 1985.

Keess, Stephen Ritter von, and W.C.W. Blumenbach. *Systematische Darstellung der neuesten Fortschritte in den Gewerben und Manufacturen und des gegenwärtigen Zustandes derselben.* Vols. 1 and 2, Vienna: Gerold, 1829–1830.

Kellogg, Vernon Vymon. *Military Selection and Race Deterioration: A Preliminary Report and Discussion.* Oxford: Clarendon Press, 1916.

Keys, Ancel, *et al. The Biology of Human Starvation.* Minneapolis: The University of Minnesota Press, 1950.

Kindleberger, Charles P. "Germany's Overtaking of England, 1806–1914." *Weltwirtschaftliches Archiv* 3 (1975): 253–281, 477–504.

Király, Béla K. *Hungary in the Late Eighteenth Century: The Decline of Enlightened Despotism.* New York: Columbia University Press, 1969.

Kiss, István. "Der Agrarcharakter des Ungarischen Exports vom 15. bis 18. Jahrhundert." *Jahrbücher für Wirtschaftsgeschichte* (1978): 147–169.

Klíma, Arnošt. "Mercantilism in the Habsburg Monarchy—with Special Reference to the Bohemian Lands." *Historica* 11 (1965): 95–119.

———. "Die Textilmanufaktur in Böhmen des 18. Jahrhunderts." *Historica* 15 (1967): 123–181.

Komlos, John. "The Age at Menarche in Vienna: The Relationship between Nutrition and Fertility." *Historical Methods* 22 (1989). Forthcoming.

———. "Economic Growth under the Romanovs and the Bolsheviks." *Rivista di storia economica,* 2d ser., 2 (1985): 194–201.

———. "The End of the Old Regime in Rural Austria." *Journal of European Economic History* 14 (1985): 515–520.

———. "Financial Innovation and the Demand for Money in Austria-Hungary, 1867–1913," *Journal of European Economic History* 16 (1987): 587–606.

———. *The Habsburg Monarchy as a Customs Union: Economic Development in Austria-Hungary in the Nineteenth Century.* Princeton: Princeton University Press, 1983.

———. "Height and Social Status in Germany in the Eighteenth Century." *Journal of Interdisciplinary History* (1990). Forthcoming.

———. "The Height and Weight of West Point Cadets: Dietary Change in Antebellum America." *Journal of Economic History* 47 (1987): 897–927.

———. "Institutional Change under Pressure: Enlightened Government Policy in the Eighteenth Century Habsburg Monarchy." *Journal of European Economic History* 15 (1986): 427–482.

———. "Patterns of Children's Growth in East-Central Europe in the Eighteenth Century." *Annals of Human Biology* 13 (1986): 33–48.

———. "Poverty and Industrialization at the End of the 'Phase-Transition' in the Czech Crown Lands." *Journal of Economic History* 43 (1983): 129–135.

———. "Stature and Nutrition in the Habsburg Monarchy: The Standard of Living and Economic Development in the Eighteenth Century." *American Historical Review* 90 (1985): 1149–1161.

Kováts, Zoltán. "A XVIII Századi Népességfejlödés Kérdéséhez." *Agrártörténelmi Szemle* 77 (1969): 218–225.

Krogh, Knud J. *Viking Greenland*. Copenhagen: The National Museum, 1967.

Krogman, Wilton Marion. *Child Growth*. Ann Arbor: University of Michigan Press, 1972.

Kunitz, Stephen J. "Speculations on the European Mortality Decline." *Economic History Review* 36 (1983): 349–364.

Kuznets, Simon S. *Modern Economic Growth: Rate, Structure, and Spread*. New Haven: Yale University Press, 1966.

———. "Population Change and Aggregate Output." In *Demographic and Economic Change in Developed Countries: A Conference of the Universities–National Bureau of Economic Research*. Princeton: Princeton University Press, 1960.

———. *Six Lectures on Economic Growth*. New York: Free Press, 1959.

Lamb, H. H. *The Changing Climate*. London: Methuen, 1966.

Landes, David S. *The Unbound Prometheus: Technological Change and Industrial Development in Western Europe from 1750 to the Present*. Cambridge, England: Cambridge University Press, 1969.

Landsberg, Helmut. "Past Climates from Unexploited Written Sources." In Robert I. Rotberg and Theodore K. Rabb, eds., *Climate and History: Studies in Interdisciplinary History*, pp. 51–62. Princeton: Princeton University Press, 1981.

Laslett, Peter. "Age at Menarche in Europe since the Eighteenth Century." *Journal of Interdisciplinary History* 2 (1971): 221–236.

Latin American Regional Reports, Brazil. February 12, 1987.

Layard, P.R.G., and A. A. Walters. *Microeconomic Theory*. New York: McGraw-Hill, 1975.

Lee, Ronald Demos. *Econometric Studies of Topics in Demographic History*. New York: Arno Press, 1978.

———. "Malthus and Boserup: A Dynamic Synthesis." In David Coleman and Roger Schofield, eds., *The State of Population Theory: Forward from Malthus*. Oxford: Basil Blackwell, 1986.

———. "Population Homeostasis and English Demographic History." *Journal of Interdisciplinary History* 15 (1985): 635–660.

Leibenstein, Harvey. *A Theory of Economic-Demographic Development*. Princeton: Princeton University Press, 1954.

Leitnertreu, Th. Leitner von. *Geschichte der Wiener Neustädter Militärakademie*. Hermannstadt: n.p., 1852.

Leridon, Henri, and Jane Menken, eds. *Natural Fertility Patterns and Determinants of Natural Fertility: Proceedings of a Seminar on Natural Fertility*. Liège, Belgium: 1979.

Le Roy Ladurie, Emmanuel. "L'aménorrhee de famine (XVIIᵉ–XXᵉ siècles)." *Annales E.S.C.* 24 (1969): 1589–1601.

———. *Le territoire de l'historien*. Paris: Gallimard, 1973.

Le Roy Ladurie, Emmanuel. *The Territory of the Historian*. Chicago: The University of Chicago Press, 1979.

———. *Times of Feast, Times of Famine: A History of Climate since the Year 1000*. Garden City, NY: Doubleday, 1971.

Le Roy Ladurie, E., and N. Bernageau. "Étude sur un Contingent Militaire (1868). Mobilité géographique, délinquance et stature, mises en rapport avec d'autres aspects de la situation des conscrits." *Annales de démographie historique* (1971): 311–337.

Le Roy Ladurie, E., N. Bernageau, and Y. Pasquet. "Le conscrit et l'ordinateur. Perspectives de recherches sur les archives militaires du XIXᵉ siècle français." *Studi Storici* 10 (1969): 260–308.

Le Roy Ladurie, Emmanuel, and Joseph Goy. *Tithe and Agrarian History from the Fourteenth to the Nineteenth Centuries: An Essay in Comparative History*. Translated by Susan Burke. Cambridge, England: Cambridge University Press, 1982.

Lewis, W. Arthur. "Economic Development with Unlimited Supplies of Labour." *Manchester School of Economic and Social Studies* 22 (1954): 139–191.

Liebel, Helen P. "Count Karl von Zinzendorf and the Liberal Revolt against Joseph II's Economic Reforms, 1783–1790." In Hans-Ulrich Wehler, ed., *Sozialgeschichte Heute. Festschrift für Hans Rosenberg zum 70. Geburtstag*, pp. 69–85. Göttingen: Vandenhoeck und Ruprecht, 1974.

———. "Free Trade and Protectionism under Maria Theresa and Joseph II." *Canadian Journal of History* 14 (1979): 355–373.

Liechtenstern, Joseph. *Allgemeine Uebersicht des Herzogthums Steiermark*. Vienna: n.p., 1799.

Lindert, Peter. "English Living Standards, Population Growth, and Wrigley-Schofield." *Explorations in Economic History* 20 (1983): 131–155.

———. "English Population, Wages, and Prices: 1541–1913." *Journal of Interdisciplinary History* 15 (1985): 609–634.

Lindert, Peter, and Jeffrey Williamson. "English Workers' Living Standards during the Industrial Revolution: A New Look." *Economic History Review*, 2d ser., 36 (1983): 1–25.

———. "Reinterpreting Britain's Social Tables, 1688–1913." *Explorations in Economic History* 20 (1983): 94–109.

Livi-Bacci, Massimo. "Fertility, Nutrition, and Pellagra: Italy during the Vital Revolution." *Journal of Interdisciplinary History* 16 (1986): 431–454.

———. "The Nutrition-Mortality Link in Past Times: A Comment." *Journal of Interdisciplinary History* 14 (1983): 293–298.

Lom, Frantisek. "Die Arbeitsproduktivität in der Geschichte der Tschechoslowakischen Landwirtschaft." *Zeitschrift für Agrargeschichte und Agrarsoziologie* 19 (1971): 1–25.

McEvedy, Colin, and Richard Jones. *Atlas of World Population History*. New York: Penguin Books, 1978.

McFall, Robert J. *The World's Meat*. New York: Appleton and Co., 1927.

McGill, William J. "In Search of the Unicorn: Maria Theresa and the Religion of State." *Historian* 42 (1980): 304–319.

McKeown, Thomas. "Food, Infection, and Population." *Journal of Interdisciplinary History* 14 (1983): 227–247.

———. *The Modern Rise of Population.* New York: Academic Press, 1976.

McKeown, Thomas, and R. G. Record. "Reasons for the Decline in Mortality in England and Wales during the Nineteenth Century." *Population Studies* 16 (1962): 94–122.

McMahon, Sarah. "Provisions Laid Up for the Family: Toward a History of Diet in New England, 1650–1850." *Historical Methods* 14 (1981): 4–21.

McNeill, William H. *Plagues and Peoples.* Garden City, NY: Anchor Press, 1976.

Main, Gloria L., and Jackson T. Main. "Economic Growth and the Standard of Living in Southern New England, 1640–1774." *Journal of Economic History* 48 (1988): 27–46.

Malthus, Thomas R. *An Essay on the Principle of Population.* 1798. Reprint. New York: Norton, 1976.

Manley, Gordon. "Central England Temperatures: Monthly Means 1659 to 1973." *Quarterly Journal of the Royal Meteorological Society* 100 (1974): 389–405.

Manniche, E. "Age at Menarche: Nicolai Edvard Ravn's Data on 3385 Women in Mid-19th Century Denmark." *Annals of Human Biology* 10 (1983): 79–82.

Marczali, Henrik. *Világtörténelem-Magyar Történelem.* Budapest: Gondolat, 1982.

Margo, Robert, and Richard H. Steckel. "The Height of American Slaves: New Evidence on Slave Nutrition and Health." *Social Science History* 6 (1982): 516–538.

———. "Heights of Native Born Northern Whites during the Antebellum Period." *Journal of Economic History* 43 (1983): 167–174.

Martinez Carrion, José Miguel. "Estatura, Nutricion y Nivel de Vida en Murcia, 1860–1930." *Revista de Historia Económica* 4 (1986): 67–99.

Martorell, Reynaldo. "Genetics, Environment, and Growth: Issues in the Assessment of Nutritional Status." In Antonio Velazques and Hector Bourges, eds., *Genetic Factors in Nutrition.* New York: Academic Press, 1984.

Martorell, Reynaldo, C. Yarborough, R. G. Klein, and A. Leichtig. "Malnutrition, Body Size, and Skeletal Maturation: Interrelationships and Implications for Catch-Up Growth." *Human Biology* 51 (1979): 371–389.

Massachusetts. *Seventh Annual Report of the Bureau of Statistics and Labor.* Public Document no. 15, 1886, part 3.

Mathias, Peter. *The First Industrial Nation: An Economic History of Britain, 1700–1914.* New York: Charles Scribner's Sons, 1969.

———. "Preface." In R. Max Hartwell, ed., *The Causes of the Industrial Revolution in England.* London and New York: Methuen, 1967.

Matis, Herbert. "Die Rolle der Landwirtschaft im Merkantilsystem-Produktionsstruktur und gesellschaftliche Verhältnisse im Agrarbereich." In Herbert Matis, ed., *Von der Glückseligkeit des Staates: Staat, Wirtschaft und Gesellschaft in Österreich im Zeitalter des aufgeklaärten Absolutismus*, pp. 269–294. Berlin: Duncker und Humblot, 1981.

Matossian, Mary Kilbourne. "Climate, Crops, and Natural Increase in Rural Russia, 1861–1913." *Slavic Review* 45 (1986): 457–469.

———. "Death in London, 1750–1909." *Journal of Interdisciplinary History* 16 (1985): 183–197.

———. "Mold Poisoning and Population Growth in England and France, 1750–1850." *Journal of Economic History* 44 (1984): 669–686.

Mayer, Franz. "Die volkswirtschaftliche Zustände Böhmens um den Jahren 1770." *Mittheilungen des Vereins für Geschichte der Deutschen in Böhmen* (1876): 125–149.

Mellor, John, and Bruce Johnston. "The World Food Equation: Interrelations Among Development, Employment, and Food Consumption." *Journal of Economic Literature* 22 (1984): 531–574.

Mendels, Franklin F. *Industrialization and Population Pressure in Eighteenth-Century Flanders*. New York: Arno Press, 1981.

———. "Proto-Industrialization: The First Phase of the Industrialization Process." *Journal of Economic History* 32 (1972): 241–261.

Menendez-Patterson, Angeles, Serafina Fernández, Jose Florez-Lozano, and Bernardo Marin. "Effect of Early Pre- and Postnatal Acquired Malnutrition on Development and Sexual Behavior in the Rat." *Pharmacology, Biochemistry and Behavior* 17 (1982): 654–664.

Menken, Jane, James Trussell, and Susan Cotts Watkins. "The Nutrition Fertility Link: An Evaluation of the Evidence." *Journal of Interdisciplinary History* 11 (1981): 425–441.

Mercer, A. J. "Relative Trends in Mortality from Related Respiratory and Airborne Infectious Diseases." *Population Studies* (1986): 129–145.

Mérei, Gyula. "A Magyar Királyság Külkereskedelmi Piaci Viszonyai 1790–1848 Között." *Századok* 115 (1981): 463–521.

Metcalf, M. G., D. S. Skidmore, G. F. Lowry, and J. A. Mackenzie. "Incidence of Ovulation in the Years after the Menarche." *Journal of Endocrinology* 97 (1983): 213–219.

Meuvret, Jean. "Les crises de subsistances et la démographie de la France d'Ancien Régime." *Population* 4 (1946): 643–650.

Mikoletzky, Hans Leo. *Österreich, das grosse 18. Jahrhundert: von Leopold I bis Leopold II*. Vienna: Österreichischer Bundesverlag, 1967.

Milward, Alan S., and S. B. Saul. *The Economic Development of Continental Europe, 1780–1870*. London: George Allen and Unwin, 1973.

Mingay, G. E. "The Agricultural Depression, 1730–1760." *Economic History Review*, 2d ser., 8 (1955): 323–338.

Mironov, Boris Nikolaevich. "In Search of Hidden Information: Some Issues in the Socio-Economic History of Russia in the Eighteenth and Nineteenth Centuries." *Social Science History* 9 (1985): 339–359.

Mitchell, Brian R. *European Historical Statistics, 1750–1970*. New York: Columbia University Press, 1975.

Mitchell, Brian R., and Phyllis Deane. *Abstract of British Historical Statistics.* Cambridge, England: Cambridge University Press, 1971.

Mokyr, Joel. "Demand vs. Supply in the Industrial Revolution." *Journal of Economic History* 37 (1977): 981–1008.

———. *Industrialization in the Low Countries, 1795–1850.* New Haven: Yale University Press, 1976.

———. "Is There Still Life in the Pessimist Case? Consumption during the Industrial Revolution, 1790–1850." *Journal of Economic History* 48 (1988): 69–92.

———. "Three Centuries of Population Change." *Economic Development and Cultural Change* 32 (1983): 183–192.

———. *Why Ireland Starved: A Quantitative and Analytical History of the Irish Economy, 1800–1850.* London: George Allen and Unwin, 1983.

———, ed. *The Economics of the Industrial Revolution.* Totowa, NJ: Rowman and Allanheld, 1985.

Mokyr, Joel, and Cormac O Gráda. "Poor and Getting Poorer? Living Standards in Ireland before the Famine." *Economic History Review*, 2d ser., 41 (1988): 209–235.

Moller, Herbert. "Voice Change in Human Biological Development." *Journal of Interdisciplinary History* 16 (1985): 239–253.

Morell, Mats. "Eli F. Heckscher, the 'Food Budgets' and Swedish Food Consumption from the 16th to the 19th Century." *Scandinavian Economic History Review* 35 (1987): 67–107.

Mosk, Carl. "Nutrition and Fertility: A Review Essay." *Historical Methods* 14 (1981): 43–46.

Moustgaard, Johannes. "Nutritive Influence upon Reproduction." *Journal of Reproductive Medicine* 8 (1972): 1–12.

National Research Council. *Nutrient Requirements of Laboratory Animals*, No. 10, 3d ed. Washington, DC: 1978.

Nef, John U. "Consequences of an Early Energy Crisis." *Scientific American* 237 (November 1977): 140–151.

———. "The Progress of Technology and the Growth of Large Scale Industry in Great Britain, 1540–1640" *Economic History Review*, 1st ser., 5 (1934): 3–24.

Nemeskéri, János, Attila Juhász, and Balázs Szabady. "Az 1973. évi sorköteles fiatalok testi fejlettsége." *Demográfia* 20 (1977): 208–281.

———. *A 18 Éves Sorköteles Fiatalok Fejlettsége Biologiai, Egészségi Állapota.* A Központi Statisztikai Hivatal Népességtudományi Kutató Intézetének és a Magyar Tudományos Akadémia Demográfiai Bizottságának Közleményei, no. 53, 1983.

Nobel, E. "Anthropometrische Untersuchungen an Jugendlichen in Wien." *Zeitschrift für Kinderheilkunde* 36 (1924): 13–16.

North, Douglass C. "A Note on Professor Rostow's 'Take-off' into Self-Sustained Economic Growth." *Manchester School of Economic and Social Studies* 26 (1958): 68–75.

North, Douglass C. *Structure and Change in Economic History*. New York: Norton, 1981.

North, Douglass C., and Robert P. Thomas. *The Rise of the Western World: A New Economic History*. Cambridge, England: Cambridge University Press, 1973.

O'Brien, Patrick, and Caglar Keyder. *Economic Growth in Britain and France, 1780–1914*. London: George Allen and Unwin, 1978.

Olney, Martha L. "Fertility and the Standard of Living in Early Modern England: In Consideration of Wrigley and Schofield." *Journal of Economic History* 43 (1983): 71–77.

Olson, Mancur. *The Rise and Decline of Nations: Economic Growth, Stagflation and Social Rigidities*. New Haven: Yale University Press, 1982.

Otruba, Gustav. *Österreichische Fabriksprivilegien vom 16. bis ins 18. Jahrhundert und ausgewählte verwandte Quellen zur Frühgeschichte der Industrializierung*. Vienna: Böhlau, 1981.

———. "Österreichs Industrie und Arbeiterschaft im Übergang von der Manufaktur zur Fabrikaturepoche (1790–1848)." *Österreich in Geschichte und Literatur* 15 (1971): 569–604.

Overton, Mark. "Estimating Crop Yields from Probate Inventories: An Example from East Anglia, 1585–1735." *Journal of Economic History* 39 (1979): 363–378.

Pelto, Gretel, and Pertti Pelto. "Diet and Delocalization: Dietary Changes since 1750." *Journal of Interdisciplinary History* 14 (1983): 507–528.

Pelzel, Franz Martin. *Geschichte der Böhmen*. Prague: Johann Adam Hagen, 1774.

Perez-Moreda, Vicente, and David S. Reher. "Demographic Mechanisms and Long-Term Swings in Population in Europe, 1200–1850." In *International Population Conference, Florence 1985*. Liège, Belgium: International Union for the Scientific Study of Population, 1985.

Petrán, Josef. "Der Höhepunkt der Bewegungen der untertänigen Bauern in Böhmen." *Acta Universitatis Carolinae. Philosophica et Historica* 3 (1969): 107–140.

Pirenne, Henri. *Medieval Cities: Their Origins and the Revival of Trade*. Translated by Frank Halsey. Princeton: Princeton University Press, 1925; paperback ed. 1969.

Pirquet, C. "Eine einfache Tafel zur Bestimmung von Wachstum und Ernährungszustand bei Kindern." *Zeitschrift für Kinderheilkunde* 6 (1913): 255.

Poos, L. R. "The Rural Population of Essex in the Later Middle Ages." *Economic History Review*, 2d ser., 38 (1985): 515–530.

Post, John. "Climatic Variability and the European Mortality Wave of the Early 1740's." *Journal of Interdisciplinary History* 15 (1984): 1–30.

Postan, Michael M. *The Medieval Economy and Society: An Economic History of Britain in the Middle Ages*. London: Weidenfeld and Nicolson, 1972.

Přibram, Alfred. *Materialien zur Geschichte der Preise und Löhne in Österreich*. Vienna: Ueberreuters, 1938.

Přibram, Karl. *Geschichte der österreichischen Gewerbepolitik von 1740 bis 1860. Aufgrund der Akten.* Leipzig: Duncker und Humblot, 1907.

Pryor, Frederic L., and Stephen B. Maurer. "On Induced Economic Change in Precapitalist Societies." *Journal of Development Economics* 10 (1982): 325–353.

Purš, Jaroslav. "Struktur und Dynamik der industriellen Entwicklung in Böhmen im letzten Viertel des 18. Jahrhunderts." *Jahrbuch für Wirtschaftsgeschichte* (1965): 160–196.

Ranis, Gustav, and John C. H. Fei. "A Theory of Economic Development." *American Economic Review* 51 (1961): 533–565.

Rechkron, Rechberger von. *Das Bildungswesen im Österreichischen Heere.* Vienna: n.p., 1878.

Reynolds, Lloyd. "The Spread of Economic Growth to the Third World: 1850–1980." *Journal of Economic Literature* 21 (1983): 941–980.

Rhees, Reuben W., and Donovan E. Fleming. "Effect of Malnutrition, Maternal Stress, or ACTH Injections during Pregnancy on Sexual Behavior of Male Offspring." *Physiology and Behavior* 27 (1981): 879–882.

Richardson, Benjamin Ward. *The Health of Nations: A Review of the Works of Edwin Chadwick, with a Biographical Dissertation.* London: Longmans, Green and Co., 1887.

Riggs, Paul. "The Standard of Living in Britain's Celtic Fringe, c. 1800–1850: Evidence from Glaswegian Prisoners." Unpublished manuscript, Department of History, University of Pittsburgh, 1988.

Riley, James C. *The Eighteenth-Century Campaign to Avoid Disease.* London: The Macmillan Press Ltd., 1987.

———. "Insects and the European Mortality Decline." *American Historical Review* 91 (1986): 833–858.

———. *International Government Finance and the Amsterdam Capital Market, 1740–1815.* Cambridge, England: Cambridge University Press, 1980.

———. *The Seven Years War and the Old Regime in France: The Economic and Financial Toll.* Princeton: Princeton University Press, 1986.

Robinson, Warren, and Wayne Schutjer. "Agricultural Development and Demographic Change: A Generalization of the Boserup Model." *Economic Development and Cultural Change* 32 (1984): 355–366.

Roehl, Richard. "French Industrialization: A Reconsideration." *Explorations in Economic History* 12 (1976): 230–281.

Roelle, Joseph-René. *Operations des Changes des Principales Places de l'Europe.* Lyon: Librairies Associes, 1775.

Rostow, Walt W. *How It All Began: Origins of the Modern Economy.* London: Methuen, 1975.

———. *Politics and the Stages of Growth.* Cambridge, England: Cambridge University Press, 1971.

———. *The Stages of Economic Growth: A Non-Communist Manifesto.* Cambridge, England: Cambridge University Press, 1960; 2d ed., 1971.

Rostow, Walt W. "The Take-off into Self-Sustained Economic Growth." *Economic Journal* 66 (1956): 25–48.

———, ed., *The Economics of Take-Off into Sustained Growth*. London: Macmillan, 1963.

Rothenberg, Gunther E. "The Austrian Army in the Age of Metternich." *Journal of Modern History* 40 (1968): 155–165.

———. *Die österreichische Militärgrenze in Kroatien, 1522 bis 1881*. Vienna: Herold, 1970.

Rozdolski, Roman. *Die Grosse Steur- und Agrarreform Josefs II. Ein Kapitel zur österreichischen Wirtschaftsgeschichte*. Warsaw: Panstwowe Wydawnictwo Naukowe, 1961.

Rule, John. *The Labouring Classes in Early Industrial England, 1750–1850*. London and New York: Longman, 1986.

Ruwet, Joseph. *Soldats des régiments nationaux au XVIIIᵉ siècle*. Brussels: Palais des Académies, 1962.

Salz, Arthur. *Geschichte der Böhmischen Industrie in der Neuzeit*. Munich and Leipzig: Duncker und Humblot, 1913.

Sandberg, Lars G., and Richard H. Steckel. "Heights and Economic History: The Swedish Case." *Annals of Human Biology* 14 (1987): 101–110.

———. "Overpopulation and Malnutrition Rediscovered: Hard Times in 19th Century Sweden." *Explorations in Economic History* 25 (1988): 1–19.

———. "Soldier, Soldier, What Made You Grow So Tall? A Study of Height, Health, and Nutrition in Sweden, 1720–1881." *Economy and History* 23 (1980): 91–105.

Sandgruber, Roman. *Die Anfänge der Konsumgesellschaft: Konsumgüterverbrauch, Lebensstandard und Alltagskultur in Österreich im 18. und 19. Jahrhundert*. Vienna: Verlag für Geschichte und Politik, 1982.

———. *Österreichische Agrarstatistik 1750–1918*. Vienna: Verlag für Geschichte und Politik, 1978.

Schacht, Robert M. "Estimating Past Population Trends." *Annual Review of Anthropology* 10 (1981): 119–140.

Schimmer, G. A. "Die Bewegung der Bevölkerung in Wien seit dem Jahre 1710." *Statistische Monatschrift* 1 (1875): 119–133.

Schmid, Ferdinand. *Das Heeresrecht der österreichischen-ungarischen Monarchie*. Vienna: F. Tempsky, 1903.

Schnabel, G. N. *Statistische Darstellung von Böhmen*. Prague: n.p., 1826.

Schofield, Roger S. "The Impact of Scarcity and Plenty on Population Change in England, 1541–1871." *Journal of Interdisciplinary History* 14 (1983): 265–291.

Schreyer, Joseph. *Fabriken und Manufakturenstand in Böhmen*. Frankfurt and Leipzig: n.p., 1799.

———. *Kommerz, Fabriken und Manufakturen des Königreichs Böhmen, theils, wie sie schon sind, theils, wie sie es werden könnten*. Prague and Leipzig: Schönfeldisch Meiznerischen Buchhandllung, 1790.

Schumpeter, Joseph. *The Theory of Economic Development*. Cambridge, MA: Harvard University Press, 1934.

Schwarz, L. D. "The Standard of Living in the Long Run: London, 1700–1860." *Economic History Review*, 2d ser., 38 (1985): 24–41.

Schwicker, Henrik J. "Magyarország s a Bajor Öröködési Háboru." *Századok* 12 (1878): 487–509.

Scrimshaw, Nevin. "The Value of Contemporary Food and Nutrition Studies for Historians." *Journal of Interdisciplinary History* 14 (1983): 529–534.

Sen, Amartya. *Poverty and Famines: An Essay on Entitlement and Deprivation*. Oxford: Clarendon Press, 1981.

Sen, Gautham. *The Military Origins of Industrialization and International Trade Rivalry*. London: Frances Pinter Publishers, 1984.

Shammas, Carole. "The Eighteenth-Century English Diet and Economic Change." *Explorations in Economic History* 21 (1984): 254–269.

Shattuck, Lemuel. *Report of the Sanitary Commission of Massachusetts*. 1850. Reprint. Cambridge, MA: Harvard University Press, 1948.

Shay, Ted. "The Level of Living in Japan, 1885–1938: New Evidence." Unpublished manuscript, Department of Economics, Harvard University, 1986.

Shorter, Edward. "L'âge des premières règles en France, 1750–1950." *Annales E.S.C.* 36 (1981): 495–511.

Silberberg, Eugen. "Nutrition and the Demand for Tastes." *Journal of Political Economy* 93 (1985): 881–900.

Simon, Julian L. *The Economics of Population Growth*. Princeton: Princeton University Press, 1977.

———. "Population Growth May Be Good for LDC's in the Long Run: A Richer Simulation Model." *Economic Development and Cultural Change* 24 (1976): 309–337.

———. "The Present Value of Population Growth in the Western World." *Population Studies* 37 (1983): 5–21.

———. *Theory of Population and Economic Growth*. Oxford: Basil Blackwell, 1986.

———. *The Ultimate Resource*. Princeton: Princeton University Press, 1981.

Simon, Julian L., and Gunter Steinmann. "The Economic Implications of Learning-by-Doing for Population Size and Growth." *European Economic Review* 26 (1984): 167–185.

Slicher van Bath, B. H. *The Agrarian History of Western Europe, A.D. 500–1850*. Translated by Olive Ordish. London: Edward Arnold, 1963.

Slokar, Johann. *Geschichte der österreichischen Industrie und ihrer Förderung unter Kaiser Franz I*. Vienna: F. Tempsky, 1914.

Slonaker, James Rollin, and Thomas Card. "The Effect of the Restricted Diet on the Number of Litters and Young Born." *American Journal of Physiology* 54 (1923): 167–180.

Smout, T. Christopher. *A Century of the Scottish People, 1830–1950*. London: Collins, 1986.

Sokoloff, Kenneth. "The Height of Americans in Three Centuries: Some Economic and Demographic Implications." National Bureau of Economic Research Working Paper No. 1384, 1984.

Sokoloff, Kenneth, and Georgia C. Villaflor. "The Early Achievement of Modern Stature in America." *Social Science History* 6 (1982): 453–481.

Solow, Robert. "Technical Change and the Aggregate Production Function." *Review of Economics and Statistics* 39 (1957): 312–320.

Sonnenfels, Joseph von. *Grundsätze der Polizey, Handlung, und Finanz.* Vienna: Joseph Edlen von Kurzbeck, 1787.

———. *Politische Abhandlungen.* Vienna: n.p., 1777.

Stark, Werner. "Die Abhängigkeitsverhältnisse der gutsherrlichen Bauern Böhmens im 17. und 18. Jahrhundert." *Jahrbücher für Nationalökonomie und Statistik* 164 (1952): 348–374.

Steckel, Richard H. "Birth Weights and Infant Mortality among American Slaves." *Explorations in Economic History* 23 (1986): 173–198.

———. "Height and Per Capita Income." *Historical Methods* 16 (1983): 1–7.

———. "A Peculiar Population: The Nutrition, Health and Mortality of American Slaves from Childhood to Maturity." *Journal of Economic History* 46 (1986): 721–742.

———. "Slave Height Profiles from Coastwise Manifests." *Explorations in Economic History* 16 (1979): 363–380.

Steegman, A. Theodore, Jr. "18th Century British Military Stature: Growth Cessation, Selective Recruiting, Secular Trends, Nutrition at Birth, Cold and Occupation." *Human Biology* 57 (1985): 77–95.

Steegmann, A. Theodore, Jr., and Haseley, P. A. "Stature Variation in the British American Colonies: French and Indian War Records, 1755–1763." *American Journal of Physical Anthropology* 75 (1988): 413–421.

Steinmann, Gunter. "A Model of the History of Demographic-Economic Growth." In Gunter Steinmann, ed., *Economic Consequences of Population Change in Industrialized Countries. Proceedings of the Conference on Population Economics Held at the University of Paderborn, West Germany, June 1–June 3, 1983. Studies in Contemporary Economics*, vol. 8, pp. 29–49. Berlin: Springer-Verlag, 1984.

Stern, Walter. "The Bread Crisis in Britain, 1795–96." *Economica* 31 (1964): 168–187.

Stoch, M. B., and D. M. Smythe. "Fifteen-Year Developmental Study on Effects of Severe Undernutrition during Infancy on Subsequent Physical Growth and Intellectual Functioning." *Archives of Disease in Childhood* 51 (1976): 327–336.

Stokes, Houston. "The B34S Data Analysis Program: A Short Write-up." Working Paper Series, Report FY 77–1, revised 14 July, 1981, College of Business Administration, University of Illinois at Chicago Circle.

Stone, Richard. "Some Seventeenth Century Econometrics: Consumers' Behaviour." Unpublished manuscript, Département d'Économétrie, Université de Genève, Switzerland, 1987.

Stracker, Oskar. "Körpermasse der Kinder und Jugendlichen im Jahre 1962." *Österreichische Ärztezeitung* 18 (1963): 1–24.

Tanner, James M. *Education and Physical Growth*. New York: International Universities Press, 1961.

———. *Foetus into Man: Physical Growth from Conception to Maturity*. Cambridge, MA: Harvard University Press, 1978.

———. "Growth as a Target-Seeking Function: Catch-up and Catch-down Growth in Man." In Frank Falkner and James M. Tanner, eds., *Human Growth: A Comprehensive Treatise*. 2d ed, Vol. 1, pp. 167–179. New York and London: Plenum Press, 1986.

———. *A History of the Study of Human Growth*. Cambridge, England: Cambridge University Press, 1981.

———. "Trend towards Earlier Menarche in London, Oslo, Copenhagen, The Netherlands, and Hungary." *Nature* (London) 243 (1973): 95–96.

Taylor, Arthur J., ed. *The Standard of Living in Britain in the Industrial Revolution*. London: Methuen, 1975.

Taylor, Carl E. "Synergy among Mass Infections, Famines, and Poverty." *Journal of Interdisciplinary History* 14 (1983): 483–501.

Teuteberg, Hans J., and Günter Wiegelmann. *Der Wandel der Nahrungsgewohnheiten unter dem Einfluss der Industrialisierung*. Göttingen: Vandenhoeck und Ruprecht, 1972.

Thirring, Gusztáv. *Az 1804. évi Népösszeirás*. Budapest: Hornyánszky Viktor, 1936.

Thirsk, Joan. "The Horticultural Revolution: A Cautionary Note on Prices." *Journal of Interdisciplinary History* 14 (1983): 299–302.

Thirsk, Joan, and J. P. Cooper. *Seventeenth-Century Economic Documents*. Oxford: Clarendon Press, 1972.

Thomas, Brinley. "Escaping from Constraints: The Industrial Revolution in a Malthusian Context." *Journal of Interdisciplinary History* 15 (1985): 729–753.

Trussell, James. "Menarche and Fatness: Reexamination of the Critical Body Composition Hypothesis." *Science* 200 (June 1978): 1506–1509.

Trussell, James, and Kenneth W. Wachter. "Estimating the Covariates of Historical Heights." National Bureau of Economic Research, Working Paper No. 1455, 1984.

Tunzelmann, G. N. von. "The Standard of Living Debate and Optimal Economic Growth." In Joel Mokyr, ed., *The Economics of the Industrial Revolution*. Totowa, NJ: Rowman and Allanheld, 1985.

———. "Trends in Real Wages, 1750–1850, Revisited." *Economic History Review*, 2d ser., 32 (1979): 33–49.

Udry, J. Richard, and R. L. Cliquet. "A Cross-Cultural Examination of the Relationship between Ages at Menarche, Marriage, and First Birth." *Demography* 19 (1982): 53–63.

Ugarte, Alois Graf von, Joseph Freiherr von der Mark, and Franz Graf v. Woyna. *Über das Conscriptions- und Recrutierungs-System*. Vienna: n.p., 1804.

Uhlig, Otto. *Die Schwabenkinder aus Tirol und Vorarlberg*. Innsbruck: Universitätsverlag Wagner, 1978.

United States Department of Commerce. *Historical Statistics of the United States: Colonial Times to 1970*. 2 vols. Washington, DC: U.S. Bureau of the Census, 1975.

United States Department of Health, Education and Welfare. "Weight and Height of Adults 18–74 Years of Age: United States 1971–74." DHEW Publications No. (PHS) 79–1659 and No. (PHS) 79–1656.

Utterström, Gustaf. "Climatic Fluctuations and Population Problems in Early Modern History." *Scandinavian Economic History Review* 3 (1955): 3–47.

———. "Some Population Problems in Pre-industrial Sweden." *Scandinavian Economic History Review* 2 (1954): 103–165.

Villermé, L. R. "Mémoire sur la taille de l'homme en France." *Annales d'hygiène publique* 1 (1829): 551–559.

———. "De la stature et du poids de l'homme." *Annales d'Hygiene Publique et de Médecine Légale* 10 (1833): 27–35.

Wachter, Kenneth W. "Graphical Estimation of Military Heights." *Historical Methods* 14 (1981): 279–303.

Wachter, Kenneth W., and James Trussell. "Estimating Historical Heights." *Journal of the American Statistical Association* 77 (1982): 279–293.

Wangermann, Ernst. *From Joseph II to the Jacobin Trials: Government Policy and Public Opinion in the Habsburg Dominions in the Period of the French Revolution*. London: Oxford University Press, 1959.

Ward, W. Peter. "Weight at Birth in Vienna, Austria, 1865–1930." *Annals of Human Biology* 14 (1987): 495–506.

Ward, W. Peter, and Patricia C. Ward. "Infant Birth Weight and Nutrition in Industrializing Montreal." *American Historical Review* 89 (1984): 324–345.

Watkins, Susan Cotts, and Etienne van de Walle. "Nutrition, Mortality, and Population Size: Malthus's Court of Last Resort." *Journal of Interdisciplinary History* 14 (1983): 205–226.

Weinbrenner, Joseph. *Patriotische Gedanken und Vorschläge über den gehemmten Ausfuhr Handel*. Vienna: n.p., 1781.

Weinzierl-Fischer, Erika. "Die Bekämpfung der Hungernot in Böhmen, 1770–72." *Mitteilungen der österreichischen Staatsarchiv* 7 (1954): 478–514.

Williams, Martha Weidner. "Infant Nutrition and Economic Growth in Western Europe from the Middle Ages to the Modern Period." Unpublished Ph.D. dissertation, Department of Economics, Northwestern University, 1988.

Williamson, Jeffrey G. *Did British Capitalism Breed Inequality?* Boston: Allen and Unwin, 1985.

———. "Urban Disamenities, Dark Satanic Mills, and the British Standard of Living Debate." *Journal of Economic History* 44 (1981): 75–84.

———. "Was the Industrial Revolution Worth It? Disamenities and Death in 19th Century British Towns." *Explorations in Economic History* 19 (1982): 221–245.

———. "Why Was British Growth So Slow during the Industrial Revolution?" *Journal of Economic History* 44 (1984): 687–712.

World Health Organization. *Energy and Protein Requirements. Report of a Joint FAO/WHO/UNO Expert Consultation*. Geneva: World Health Organization, 1985.

Wrede, Major Alphons Freiherr von. *Geschichte der k. und k. Wehrmacht*. Vienna: C. W. Seidel, 1898.

Wrigley, E. Anthony. "Urban Growth and Agricultural Change: England and the Continent in the Early Modern Period." *Journal of Interdisciplinary History* 15 (1985): 683–728.

Wrigley, E. Anthony, and Roger S. Schofield. "English Population History from Family Reconstitution: Summary Results, 1600–1799." *Population Studies* 37 (1983): 157–184.

———. *The Population History of England, 1541–1871: A Reconstruction*. Cambridge, MA: Harvard University Press, 1981.

Wurm, Helmut. "The Fluctuations of Average Stature in the Course of German History and the Influence of the Protein Content of the Diet." *Journal of Human Evolution* 13 (1984): 331–334.

Wyshak, G., and Rose E. Frisch. "Evidence for a Secular Trend in Age of Menarche." *New England Journal of Medicine* 306 (1982): 1033–1035.

Zafir, Mihály. "Az 1881. évi Népélelmezési Statisztika mai Szemmel." *Statisztikai Szemle* 61 (1983): 1017–1034.

INDEX

Abramowitz, Moses, 289
Africa, disease environment in, 217–18.
  See also capital: human, in Africa
agricultural production, 13; in Bohemia,
  149, 168; and exclusion of Hungary
  and Galicia from industrialization drive,
  128 n 38; government measures to increase, 155 n 177; labor productivity in
  Denmark, 73; in England, 191–92,
  192 n 13, 197; in Styria, 71 n 50; in
  Sweden, 46 n 89. *See also* institutional
  change
America. *See* heights: in United States;
  population, urban: in America
Annales school of historians, 167
aristocracy: as administrators of laws, 149,
  149 n 146, 150–51; heights of, 95; income reduced, 159; opposition to reform, 122; peasants' obligations to,
  152–53, 155 n 180; and poor relief,
  150; prohibited from buying peasant
  land, 156; promote industrialization,
  129–31, 154; rental income, 111, 153,
  155; rights of, 151; threatened by reform, 160–61. *See also* nobility
army, Habsburg: age of eligibility, 236;
  and beggars, 227; conscription law,
  53 n 113; exemptions, 226–29; French
  in, 76, 93, 234–35; recruiting system
  of, 225–39; recruiting in Austrian
  Netherlands, 233; recruiting in Germany, 74; size of, 74; social composition of, 54, 226
Artzrouni, Marc, 17, 277
Austria and Habsburg Monarchy. *See under* industrialization; institutional

change; Lower Austria; meat consumption
"Austrian" model. *See* industrial revolution: "Austrian" model of

Bairoch, Paul: and estimate of industrial
  production, 168 n 3; and relationship
  between demographic and industrial
  revolutions, 205 n 67
Bidschow County. *See* Bohemia
biological standard of living. *See* standard
  of living
birth weight. *See* weight at birth
Black Death (bubonic plague) of 1340s,
  284; as a Malthusian crisis, 212–13
Blanc, Franz Anton von (Austrian reformer), 125 n 19, 127
Blum, Jerome, 149 n 146, 152 n 165
Body-Mass Index. *See under* nutrition
Bohemia: famine in, 71, 122 n 8, 123,
  157 n 191; GNP, 168 n 3; industrialization in, 11, 178, 180–81; Reichenberg,
  13; underemployment in, 225 n 3. *See
  also* agricultural production: in Bohemia; grain; industrial labor force;
  Malthusian crisis; population growth;
  population, urban
Boserup, Ester, 1, 121
Boserupian effect, 16. *See also* population
  growth: beneficial effects of
Bosnia-Herzegovina. *See* heights
Brno (Brünn), Moravia, 144 n 119, 146.
  See also industrialization
bureaucracy, Habsburg, size of, 122,
  122 n 9

calorie. *See* nutrition

319

Cameralism, 123
Cameron, Rondo, 15, 209, 216
capital: accumulation of, 4, 216–18, 289–
90; capital/labor ratio, 219; defined,
281; depreciation, 281 n 7; human,
217–18, 281; human, in Africa, 218;
and institutions, 217; and property
rights, 281
Carlschule (Stuttgart), 86 n 85
"catch-up" growth, 27
child labor. *See* female labor and child labor
cities. *See* urban areas
Cobb-Douglas production function, 280
commercialization. *See* market integration
conscription. *See* army, Habsburg
cotton textiles. *See* industry
credit of Habsburg Monarchy, 131 n 51
crisis. *See* epidemics; famine; Malthusian
crisis; peasants
Crouzet, François, 177
customs union, Habsburg, 137 n 82

David, Paul, and production function
during industrial revolution, 289
demographic crisis. *See* Malthusian crisis
demographic revolution: in England,
196–97; and age structure, 195; and
baby boom of 1730s, 141, 205; dating
of, 188–90; and harvests, 192; and nutrition, 191–95, 197; origin of, 141;
and weather, 192, 195. *See also* population growth
De Vries, Jan, 208 n 1
disease: adjustment to, 217–18; in Africa,
217; environment, 61–62, 70; measles,
217; and medical technology, 42 n 72;
and nutritional status, 34, 38–41,
194 n 25, 212; in sixteenth century,
217; and urbanization, 212–13. *See also*
epidemics
domestic industry. *See* France: domestic
industry in

economic crisis in Habsburg Monarchy,
141
economic development. *See under* Galicia;
Hungary
economic growth: cyclical nature of, 15,
15 n 45; during Napoleonic Wars, 170;

persistence of, 14; sustained, 221; in
United States, 5 n 10, 8 n 24. *See also*
modern economic growth
emigration, discouraged, 146 n 125
England: age structure, 65; class differences, 95; emigration from, 191 n 7;
enclosure of commons, 121; famine in,
16–17; food consumption in, 62; infanticide in, 191 n 7; livestock production in, 191–92; marriage market in,
196; malnourishment in, 201; mortality
in, 44 n 79; output per capita, 168 n 3;
population growth in, 177; poverty in,
178; service sector of, 168 n 4; seventeenth-century crisis in, 215; weather in
eighteenth century, 95, 191–92. *See also*
under agricultural production; demographic revolution; food prices;
heights; industrial revolution; Malthusian crisis; meat consumption; population, urban
Enlightenment: and antireligious sentiment, 143; and government policy, 125
entrepreneurs: Christian, 136 n 81; role
in industrial revolution, 171
epidemics, 219; cordon sanitaire,
126 n 26; and shipping, 212–13;
spread of, 213; urban, 284
exports. *See under* Galicia; Hungary; Ireland

factories, 83 n 83; inspectors, 122 n 10;
privileged, 144–45; relief granted,
171–72; sale restrictions, 138; tariff
protection, 137
family: formation, 199; structure, 74
famine: and cannibalism, 212; in Bengal,
216 n 33. *See also* Bohemia; England;
France
female labor and child labor: in Habsburg
Monarchy, 141, 145, 171; nutritional
status, 115 n 155; promoted and opposed, 134 n 66
fertility, human: and nutrition, 34–38,
34 n 30, 194–95, 195 n 32; marital,
196. *See also* menarche, age at
Floud, Roderick, 52 n 110
Fogel, Robert W., 5 n 10, 16, 25–26, 40–
41
food: expenditures, 24, 43 n 73; imports,